THE CHURCH THE CHURCHES

AND

THE MYSTERIES

OR REVELATION AND CORRUPTION

BY

G. H. PEMBER, M.A.

"To obey is better than sacrifice."
"This is the love of God, that we keep His commandments."
"In vain do they worship Me, teaching for doctrines the commandments of men."

FLEMING H. REVELL COMPANY
NEW YORK CHICAGO TORONTO
1901

PREFACE

AT a time when momentous changes are taking place in the Ecclesiastical world, and our National Church is not merely commencing, but has almost accomplished, a retrograde movement from Bible light to Mediæval darkness, it behoves sincere and thoughtful believers to consider the situation. What could have made the present religious tendencies possible in the twentieth century, in our own country, and after all the sad experiences of the past? For surely we might have hoped that the English Church, after having recovered so much truth at the time of the Reformation, would, from that epoch, have continued to draw nearer and nearer to the Apostolic ideal of the first century.

This, however, has been by no means the case: on the contrary, her course has ever been fitful and unsteady ; and she has, at last, deliberately reversed her steps, and set her face determinedly toward the veiled Paganism of priests and sacraments—even as the five-and-twenty men seen by Ezekiel had turned their backs upon the Temple of the Lord, in order that they might worship the sun toward the East.[1]

[1] Ezek. viii. 16.

The causes of this portentous change are, doubtless, many. Among them we might mention the enmity of the carnal mind against God, which prompts men to instinctive disobedience ; the mighty power with which Satan holds sway over human minds, and casts obstacles, absolutely insurmountable to mere human efforts, in the way of the servants of God ; the fact that a National Church, with honours and emoluments to bestow, must inevitably number among her clergy many who, though upright and sincere according to the world's standard, are not actuated solely by the love of Him Who died for sinners, and, therefore, cannot enjoy the guidance of His Spirit ; and so on.

But it is to another cause of decadence that we would now invite attention—a cause which affects, more or less, every church and sect. We mean the fact, that each succeeding generation of men is found to depend too much, if not altogether, upon ancient custom, vague tradition, the laws of some church, or its own idea of what is right, and so does not continually refer for motives of belief and action to the written and unchanging Word of God. And yet it is for obedience to this latter, that men are responsible to Him, and by it they must be judged before His Throne, even as He has said ;—

"He that rejecteth Me, and receiveth not My sayings, hath one that judgeth him : the Word that I spake, the same shall judge him in the Last Day." [1]

[1] John xii. 48.

Now, the consequence of this sin to those who are guilty of it is twofold. For, in the first place, not being acquainted with the Word of God and the promises commandments and predictions contained therein, they have no means of becoming conformed to His mind; while they are, also, depriving themselves of the most powerful incentive and aid to holiness. And, secondly, for the same reason, they fail to remove the old leaven of Paganism and human methods from their creed and worship, and so leave it to work, from time to time, with disastrous issues.

It is hoped that the present volume may afford some help to those who are conscious that they have fallen into such errors as we have described, but are, nevertheless, honestly desirous of following out and realizing the Lord's words :—

"He that hath My commandments, and keepeth them,

He it is that loveth Me :

And he that loveth me shall be loved of My Father,

And I will love him,

And will manifest Myself unto him." [1]

It is, then, His commandments that must be learnt from His Own Word and scrupulously observed, if we love Him. From all other pretended authorities we must stand aloof: it was to guard us from these, and from every admixture of guile and evil, that He

[1] John xiv. 21.

preserved for us a <u>written revelation</u>, which all may read and understand.

We have, therefore, essayed, in the following pages, to search that revelation anew, with diligence and prayer. Beginning with an investigation of the meaning and Scriptural use of the word *ecclesia*, usually rendered " Church," we have endeavoured to point out the practical bearings of that meaning and use. This is followed by an attempt to discover what conditions and behaviour the Scriptures require of those who would be members of the now invisible Church, which shall hereafter constitute the Body of Christ and the Heavenly Kingdom : to what laws, ordinances, and church-government, they ought to be subject ; and with what gifts they should be endowed. And, in the first part of this inquiry, we have striven to show the clear distinction drawn by the New Testament between the gift of God which must be accepted as such, and the prize of our upward calling for which we must earnestly contend.

Lastly, since many laws ordinances and Ecclesiastical Hierarchies, which pass for those of Christ, are found to be very different from, and even antagonistic to, the teaching of Himself and His Apostles in the written Word, an effort has been made to unveil the source of the influence by which so marvellous a corruption was effected.

But this book, although complete in itself, is designed, also, as an introduction to the third volume in the series of which it forms a part, that is, to *The Great Prophecies of the Centuries concerning the Church*. For it seemed necessary to set forth what appeared to us to be the Scriptural idea of the Church, before we proceeded to consider the Divine forecast of its course upon earth.

To avoid confusion, it may be well to say that we do not use the word " Catholic " in its generally accepted meaning. It is not found in Scripture; but was adopted, in a technical sense, by those Ecclesiastical Christians who, taking their model from the Pagan Mysteries, believed in salvation by priests and sacraments. And with them it was used to indicate the orthodox—that is, the orthodox from their own point of view—as distinguished from heretics. We, therefore, resign the word to those to whom it of right belongs; and regard it as a designation of Hierarchical as opposed to Evangelical and Apostolical Christians, of those who profess to recognize two authorities, the Church and the Bible, as contrasted with believers who will receive nothing as Divine Truth, unless it can be proved, and that in an intelligible and straightforward manner, from Holy Writ.

CONTENTS

THE CHURCH AND ITS MEMBERS

BAPTISM

xi

THE GIFTS OF MINISTRY

DIVERS GIFTS OF THE SPIRIT: THEIR CONNECTION WITH THE BODY: AND RULES FOR THEIR USE

"BECAUSE OF THE ANGELS"

OR

THE JUDICIAL COURTS OF HEAVEN

THE MYSTERIES AND CATHOLICISM

APPENDIX

THE CHURCH AND ITS MEMBERS

I

THE CHURCH AND THE CHURCHES

IN our former volume, which deals with Israel and the Gentiles, we endeavour to show that the revealed purpose of God in regard to this world— or, in other words, the general scheme of prophecy— is dependent upon the Four Epochs of Israelitish history. It is with the third only of these epochs, the period of the Great Exile, that we are now concerned.

During its course, which commenced spiritually with the rejection of the Lord Jesus, but historically with the dispersions by Titus and Hadrian, and which seems now to be nearing its end, Israel is alienated from God, and no longer holds the official position of His people upon earth. But the two high prerogatives attached to that position, the sovereignty and the priesthood, have not been abolished. For the former, of which the nation was deprived long before its dispersion, passed in succession to the Four Gentile World-powers, and is now in the hands of the Kings of Christendom, who represent the broken parts of the Fourth Empire—parts soon to be reunited. Meanwhile, the priesthood, changed in its character in accord with the changed circumstances, is vested in the body called the Church, which is the subject

3

of this volume, and every real member of which is a priest unto God.

Hence all such Hebrew predictions as relate to the progress and glory of the Israelitish nation, or even to God's special dealings with it, are for the present suspended : only the fearful threats of exile and suffering are now in process of fulfilment, as, indeed, they have been for more than eighteen centuries.

On the other hand, those prophecies which refer to the Gentiles and the Church span the whole of the wide chasm between the two Advents. And, since we have already examined the Divine utterances respecting the former, we must now turn our attention to what is said of the Church.

It will, however, be well first to inquire into the meaning and use of the Greek word *ecclesia*, which we usually render by "church"; and also, if we can, to discover what manner of persons are recognised by the Most High as members of the body so called, and what are the laws and ordinances to which they are subject.

Now, the *ecclesia* of the Greeks was the assembly, in a free city, of those who, being possessed of the full rights of citizenship, were summoned from the population for the transaction of public affairs.[1] No

---

[1] Originally the word seems to have meant "the calling out," or "summoning," of the citizens to an assembly by the herald or crier : then it was transferred to the assembly itself. In the Septuagint, it is often used as an equivalent for the Hebrew קָהָל "congregation." Hence in one passage of the New Testament (Acts vii. 38) it retains its old application, and refers to the Israelites in the wilderness.

In Matt. xvi. 18, however, the Lord uses it of a society not in existence when He spoke, but which He was about to form— "Upon this rock I will build My Church." And so, His Apostles

stranger, nor slave, nor any one who had been convicted of crime, could be admitted into its honoured
circle.

Hence the peculiar appropriateness of the term when
applied to the Church, whose members are now being
called by God out of the masses of mankind, in order
that they may rule the world in the coming age. For
all who are appointed to this dignity must be citizens
of the Heavenly City:[1] no alien can stand among
them. The slaves of sin and of Satan may not
sit in their councils.

" Neither fornicators, nor idolaters, nor adulterers,
nor effeminate, nor abusers of themselves with men,
nor thieves, nor covetous, nor drunkards, nor re-
vilers, nor extortioners, shall inherit the Kingdom
of God."[2]

So much, then, for the meaning of the Greek word
which the Lord Himself selected as the designation
of His Church. But a knowledge of the manner in
which it is used in Scripture is, also, of the last
importance; since by it an ominous secret, a hidden
pathway of apostasy from God, is revealed to us.
For, in the teaching of the New Testament, the term
"church" is found only in two senses.

First, the Church, absolutely, is the great Assembly
which is now being summoned by God out of every
tribe and tongue and people and nation, the complete
and heavenly body which the Lord will shortly present
to Himself as a glorious Church, not having spot or

recognised the term as appropriated for the assembly which He
claimed as peculiarly His own, and which was incorporated on the
memorable Day of Pentecost.

[1] Phil. iii. 20, R.V.

[2] 1 Cor. vi. 9, 10. We shall presently show that the Heavenly
Kingdom is but another name for the glorified Church.

wrinkle or any such thing; but holy and without blemish.[1]

And, secondly, every local assembly of believers is also called a church,[2] perhaps because it ought to be a miniature of the whole Church. Hence we read of "the church which was at Jerusalem,"[3] "the church of the Thessalonians,"[4] "the church in thy house,"[5] and so on.

In exact accordance with these examples, whenever the assemblies of a district, province, or country, were to be mentioned collectively, the plural was always used.[6] So we have, "the churches of Galatia,"[7] "the churches of Macedonia,"[8] and "the churches of Judæa."[9] And the same rule applies when all the assemblies existing at one time in the world are to be included; so that we find the expressions, "all the churches of the saints,"[10] and "the churches of God."[11]

[1] For this meaning see Matt. xvi. 18; 1 Cor. xii. 28; Eph. 1. 22, iii. 10, 21, v. 23, 24, 25, 27, 29, 32; Col. i. 18, 24; 1 Tim. iii. 15; Heb. xii. 23.

[2] See Matt. xviii. 17; Acts ii. 47, v. 11, viii. 1, 3, xi. 22, 26, xii. 1, 5, xiii. 1, xiv. 23, 27, xv. 3, 4, 22, xviii. 22, xx. 17, 28; Rom. xvi. 1, 5, 23 — Gaius probably gave up his house for church-meetings; 1 Cor. i. 2, iv. 17, vi. 4, x. 32, xi. 18, 22, xiv. 4, 5, 12, 19, 23, 28, 35, xv. 9—i.e., the church at Jerusalem (comp. Acts viii. 1, 3); 2 Cor. i. 1; Gal. i. 13; Phil. iii. 6, iv. 15; Col. iv. 15, 16; 1 Thess. i. 1; 2 Thess i. 1; 1 Tim. iii. 5, v. 16; Philem. 2; James v. 14; 3 John 6, 9, 10; Rev. ii. 1, 8, 12, 18, iii. 1, 7, 14.

[3] Acts viii. 1.

[4] 1 Thess. i. 1.

[5] Philem. 2.

[6] See Acts ix. 31, xv. 41, xvi. 5; Rom. xvi. 4, 16; 1 Cor. vii. 17, xi. 16, xiv. 33, 34, xvi. 1, 19; 2 Cor. viii. 1, 18, 19, 23, 24, xi. 8, 28, xii. 13; Gal. i. 2, 22; 1 Thess. ii. 14; 2 Thess. i. 4; Rev. i. 4, 11, 20, ii. 7, 11, 17, 23, 29, iii. 6, 13, 22, xxii. 16. From these passages it is evident that the Lord Jesus never contemplated any hierarchical unity of all Christian believers during the present age—not even in one province or country, much less in Christendom or the world.

[7] 1 Cor. xvi. 1.

[8] 2 Cor. viii. 1.

[9] Gal. i. 22.

[10] 1 Cor. xiv. 33.

[11] 1 Cor. xi. 16.

It thus appears, that the use of the term "the Church" to designate in the aggregate all the assemblies of a particular sect, of a kingdom or country, of Christendom, or of the world, is absolutely unscriptural. "According to all that I show thee, the pattern of the Tabernacle, and the pattern of all the furniture thereof, even so shall ye make it,"[1] was the commandment given by God to Moses. Nor can there ever be a departure from Divine instructions without a speedy sequel of disorder and apostasy.

In the case before us, by speaking of the "churches," in the plural, whenever more than one local assembly was intended, the Lord has manifestly signified that every several assembly, consisting of all the believers of any one place or district, should be independent and self-governed—a microcosm of the Church which is His Body. Had this intimation been respected, no room would have been found for sects, for national and international Churches, or for any such idea as the Union, or Reunion, of Christendom. And, when error appeared in any particular assembly, its members would have had the power of instantly ejecting the false teachers, just as the local churches were wont to do in the earliest days of Christianity.[2] There could have been no interference from other infected churches; nor would there have been a bishop of the diocese, insisting upon his own will, and forcing strange ornaments rites and doctrines upon unwilling or half-willing congregations.

Who can look back upon the history of the past without detecting the many disasters that are due to this single divergence from the Divine pattern!

[1] Exod. xxv. 9. [2] Rev ii. 2.

II

PREDESTINATION

HAVING thus investigated the meaning of the term "church," and the correct use of the word according to the New Testament, we must now inquire what manner of persons will be ultimately found in the glorified assembly. For it is, of course, a gross mistake to suppose that the aggregate of the visible churches upon earth—made up, as they are, of all who choose to profess belief in the Lord Jesus, however careless their behaviour or corrupt their creed—will hereafter form the glorified Church above : this fact few will venture to deny. But we must go still further ; for, as we shall presently show, not all even of those who truly believe, and are saved through faith, will necessarily be incorporated in the Church, which is Christ's Body.

Hence it becomes a matter of the last importance to discover what qualifications are required for so great an honour. If, then, we turn to the Bible, we shall find them divided into two classes : for one of them is such that it can be absolutely known only to God; while the others, which depend upon the first, are, also, more or less open and manifest to men.

As regards the first, then, no one can be a member of Christ's Body unless he was predestinated thereto by God before the foundation of the world. This truth is unmistakably affirmed in the well-known words of Paul ;—

" Blessed be the God and Father of our Lord Jesus Christ, Who blessed us with every spiritual blessing in the supercelestial[1] places in Christ; even as He chose us out for Himself[2] in Him before the foundation of the world, that we should be holy and without blemish before Him in love; having predestinated us unto adoption as sons, through Jesus Christ, unto Himself, according to the good pleasure of His will, to the praise of the glory of His grace, which He freely bestowed on us in the Beloved."[3]

Here Paul invites the Ephesians to join with himself in blessing God as the One Who blessed us with every spiritual blessing in the supercelestial places in Christ. And, in the Greek, the aorist tense indicates that His blessing was bestowed at some definite point of time in the past, that is, when He raised Christ "from the dead, and made Him to sit at His right hand in the supercelestial places."[4] For in that same moment the Father also "put all things in subjection under His feet, and gave Him to be Head over all things to the Church, which is His Body."[5]

Now, when we are told that God gave Him to be Head over all things to the Church, we are, so far, merely informed that He became its governmental Head, or King. But, when it is added that the Church is His Body, much more is indicated; for it then

---

[1] ἐν τοῖς ἐπουρανίοις, "in the places upon the heavens," or "above" them; that is, apparently, above the created heavens of this earth. For the expression seems to include the Second Heaven (cp. 2 Cor. xii. 2), into which evil spirits still have access (Eph. vi. 12; Job i. 6, ii. 1; 1 Kings xxii. 19-22), though they are, probably, not able to penetrate into the Third. Compare the expression in Ps. viii. 1;—"O Lord, our Lord, how excellent is Thy Name in all the earth! Who hast set Thy glory above the heavens."

[2] Such is the meaning of ἐξελέξατο: it is strange that the R. V. has not fully expressed it.

[3] Eph. i. 3-6.   [4] Eph. i. 20.   [5] Eph. i. 22.

appears, that He is not as an earthly ruler, having no further connection with His subjects than to enforce their obedience, but is One Who directs them by means of a vital union, of a life-power which, flowing from Himself, pervades them, and transmits both the perception of His will and the instinctive desire and capability of carrying it out.

And so, when Christ, the Head, was exalted with every blessing to the supercelestial places, far above the toil and anguish which He had voluntarily undergone below, it was as the Representative and Forerunner of the members that He rose. And hence they, too, must soon pass into the same glory, and experience to the full the blessings of their Head, from Whom even now vitalising currents are ever being communicated to them, while they are yet tarrying in the weary land. Thus the blessings bestowed upon the Head were at the same moment secured to the meanest of His members.

But why does God thus favour some men above all others, so as even to make them members of the Christ, His Son? Because He chose them for this honour, in Christ, before the foundation of the world; because, in short, they are His elect.

If, then, this be so, surely another and very serious question arises. Upon what ground did the Great God make such a selection from the human race? Was His choice arbitrary, and without reference to anything save His own absolute will?

Had this been the case, His action would have been perfectly just; for a Creator has an indisputable right to dispose as He wills of the creatures which He has called into being. Here no human rule of justice could apply, since there is no relation among men which bears the slightest resemblance to that of a Creator to the created.

But the Bible, while it carefully reserves for the Creator the right of arbitrary choice, never asserts that He exercises such a right. On the contrary, it affirms that His election is based upon His foreknowledge, as we may learn from the Epistle to the Romans ;—

"For whom He foreknew, He also predestinated to be conformed to the image of His Son, that He might be the Firstborn among many brethren : and whom He predestinated, them He also called : and whom He called, them He also justified : and whom He justified, them He also glorified." [1]

Similarly, Peter describes those to whom he is writing as "elect according to the foreknowledge of God." [2]

Now, this fact of the foreknowledge of God must, of course, be remembered and applied when we are dealing with such passages as the well-known words respecting Esau and Jacob ;—

"For the children being not yet born, neither having done anything good or bad, that the purpose of God according to election might stand, not of works, but of Him that calleth, it was said unto her, The elder shall serve the younger. Even as it is written, Jacob I loved, but Esau I hated." [3]

Here, then, in accordance with the previously quoted text,[4] we must understand God's preference to be based upon His foreknowledge of the characters of Jacob and Esau. He perceived that the former, however inferior in some respects to his brother, would ultimately yield to the Divine discipline, and suffer himself to be

[1] Rom. viii. 29, 30.
[2] 1 Peter i. 2. Comp. Rom. xi. 2.
[3] Rom. ix. 11-13.
[4] Rom. viii. 29.

moulded by it. Esau, on the other hand, would not do so; and, therefore, could not be delivered from all sin and evil, as his brother was.

It thus appears, that, when God confines a spirit within its human body, He has already, by His infallible foresight, perceived whether it will yield to His discipline, and so be restored to obedience, or not; and if He has seen that it will do so, He has also predestinated it to be conformed to the image of His Son. In due season His predestination is sealed by an effectual call; and when, in response to the call, the man believes in the Lord Jesus Christ, his gracious Creator at once justifies him from all his sins, and, as soon as the process of salvation is completed, exalts him to glory.

But how great should be the feelings of awe excited in our mind by the disclosure, that the elect of God were chosen before the foundation of the world! What possible connection could the faithful of to-day have had with a period so far remote? How did God then know them individually, and so thoroughly, too, that He was enabled to make His choice?

Revelation offers no answer to this question: its solution lies among the secret things that belong unto the Lord our God. Hereafter He may reveal it, and then will all the enigmas and difficulties that group around the conditions of our present life be dispelled in a moment, and the great truth, that in all things God is love, shine forth gloriously, as the sun in a cloudless sky.

For, even in the case of those who will not be softened by the gift of the Beloved Son, God, to the last, remains true to His own words ;—

" As I live . . . I have no pleasure in the death

of the wicked ; but that the wicked turn from his way, and live." [1]

Therefore, He does not predestinate to destruction, though He may set the self-doomed upon the high places of the earth, and so give him further opportunity of learning the Divine power and forbearance ; until, at length, ruin descends upon persistent obstinacy, and flashes forth another warning against the folly of contending with God.

This was exemplified in the case of Pharaoh, whom God, as Paul tells us, willed to harden. [2] But the story cannot be understood, unless we carefully examine its details in the Book of Exodus. There we shall find the statement, that, on six consecutive occasions, Pharaoh hardened,[3] his heart, or, that his heart was hardened.[4] And it is only *after* these many provocations that we meet with the terrible words ;—

"And the Lord hardened the heart of Pharaoh." [5]

Thus, as in other recorded instances, God bore with Pharaoh, and suffered His Holy Spirit to strive with him, until his obstinate rebellion had exhausted even Divine patience. Then the oft-rejected Spirit ceased to strive, and the forsaken king was delivered into the hands of the Wicked One.

---

[1] Ezek. xxxiii. 11. [2] Rom. ix. 17, 18.
[3] Or, "made heavy."
[4] The inaccuracy of the A.V. has concealed this fact; but the English reader will be able to discover it in the more correct renderings of the R.V. See Exod. vii. 13, 22, viii. 15, 19, 32, and ix. 7.
[5] Exod. ix. 12. The third clause of this verse, "as the Lord had spoken unto Moses," connects it with Exod. vii. 3, and reminds us that God had foreseen and predicted what would ultimately take place: that is, that Pharaoh would continue to harden his heart, until, at last, God would complete the awful process by withdrawing His Holy Spirit, and so leaving the obdurate rebel to perish in his sins.

In no case, then, does God arbitrarily predestinate men to destruction : the fault lies in the lost themselves ; for His Spirit is ever ready to assist them to repentance, until they have crossed the boundary of His forbearance. To a careless reader, indeed, and one who does not compare spiritual things with spiritual, certain passages might seem to be opposed to this view. But, if they really were so, they would contradict others which affirm, that God does not desire the death of sinners. These apparently contradictory verses must, therefore, be capable of some different explanation.

Let us, then, take, as an instance, the passage in the ninth chapter of the Epistle to the Romans, which, regarded superficially, is, perhaps, the most difficult of all. Paul has just inferred from the history of Pharaoh, that whom God wills He hardens. And a supposed objector, who has not troubled to examine the history, and, consequently, has failed to observe the critical point at which God willed to harden the proud king, exclaims ;—Then "why doth He still find fault ? For who withstandeth His will?"

Now, the spirit that prompts this question is manifest : the man does not propound it because he desires a reasonable answer, but only to express his own opposition to the ways of God. Therefore Paul offers no explanation, but merely admonishes the arrogant objector, that it is the duty of mortals to yield to Divine decrees, whether they can understand them or not. "Nay but, O man, who art thou that repliest against God ? " " Why dost thou strive with Him ? For He giveth not account of any of His matters." Thou wouldest not refuse to the meanest artificer the right to dispose as he pleases of the work of his own hands, and wilt thou refuse the same to the great Creator and Lord of all? May He not, if He so wills, bear long with vessels of wrath that have been prepared for destruction,[1] in order to show forth His wrath and make known His power?

Such is the only kind of answer which murmurers against God will ever obtain from Him. It is not to rebels that He reveals His secret things ; and hence the words under our consideration merely indicate His stern refusal to concede to His creatures any right of questioning His purposes or actions. But to humble faith, as we have already seen, He will, at least partially, raise the curtain of His mystery even in the present age.

One further remark in connection with the subject of this chapter may, perhaps, be useful. The fact

[1] Rom. ix. 22. It should be observed, that, in the original, the perfect passive participle is here used; but we are not told by whom the vessels of wrath had been " fitted for destruction." In the next verse, however, it is said of the vessels of mercy—"which He (God) afore made ready for glory." This difference is significant, and evidently implies that God does not predestinate men to perdition. For such a doom they fit themselves, as we may learn from this same Epistle ;—" Or despisest thou the riches of His goodness and forbearance and longsuffering, not knowing that the goodness of God leadeth thee to repentance? but after thy hardness and impenitent heart treasurest up for thyself wrath in the day of wrath and revelation of the righteous judgment of God? (Rom ii. 4, 5).

With Rom. ix. 22 and 23, we may compare Matt. xxv. 34 and 41. For, in v. 34, the Lord says to the sheep ;—" Come, ye blessed of My Father, inherit the Kingdom prepared *for you* from the foundation of the world"; while, in v. 41, He dismisses the goats with the words ;—" Depart from Me, ye cursed, into the eternal fire which is prepared *for the Devil and his angels.*" Thus we see that the Lord has been careful to make ready abodes of joy for the saved, but has prepared no special place of punishment for unsaved men, who, consequently, have to be cast into the fire prepared for Satan and his angels. This again, emphasises the fact, that God has not foredoomed any man to perdition.

that God can foresee what use each spirit will make
of its earth-life before He encloses it in the body, and
yet can avoid influencing for evil the many spirits that
are being lost, seems to our finite minds incomprehensible, nay impossible.

Nevertheless, the fact is beyond dispute. For—to
cite a single instance—how, unless He could foresee
the course of every earth-life, could He have predicted,
some seven hundred years before the event, that certain
spirits, whom He would by that time have placed upon
the earth, would dare to subject His own Beloved Son
to shame and spitting?[1] And if He had intended
to impel them to so appalling a crime, how could He
have declared that He desires not the death of a
sinner?

Thus the Divine predestination is guided by the
Divine foreknowledge; nor does it interfere with the
freewill of man.   But, truly, when our thoughts are
directed towards God, we have need to remember that
we are finite beings striving to contemplate the Infinite,
and must be careful lest we regard Him merely as a
magnificently endowed man ; for the impossible is unknown to Him. In such a quest, then, humility, awe,
and faith, are the qualities which become us; for to
the humble alone He giveth grace and revelation. But
these qualities alas! seem to be disappearing from
among men; for we are already entering upon the
days of the final apostasy.

[1] Isa. l. 6.

III

PREDESTINATION AND WORKS

IN the foregoing chapter we have seen, that no one can become a member of the Church, which is Christ's Body, unless he was so predestinated by God before the foundation of the world; and that this seal is invisible to men and known to God Alone. But there are also other seals which are not hidden from human ken, and which, indeed, must be openly exhibited in every member of Christ before he can be recognised, either by his fellows or by his own conscience, as one bearing the mark of the Lord.

To speak briefly, these visible seals are as the fruits of a tree which prove it to be good : they are the outward conduct of the man as the result of the Spirit's work within him, the walk, more or less worthy of his vocation, which shows that he is following after the Lord Who bought him.

Sometimes in Scripture the invisible and the visible seals are mentioned together, so that we can perceive their connection. Thus, in regard to salvation, the Lord Himself first says ;—

"And this is the will of Him That sent Me, that of all that which He hath given Me I should lose nothing, but should raise it up at the Last Day." [1]

Then, having thus described God's side of the matter, He continues in the next verse as follows ;—

"For this is the will of My Father, that every one that beholdeth the Son, and believeth on Him, should have everlasting life ; and I will raise him up at the Last Day." [2]

[1] John vi. 39.   [2] John vi. 40.

Here the Father gives to the Son those whom His foreknowledge has appointed to life ; and the chosen are revealed to themselves and to others as, one by one, they are led to believe on the Lord Jesus, and to know that He will raise them up on the Last Day.

So, in the second Epistle to Timothy, we read ;—

" Howbeit the firm foundation of God standeth, having this seal, The Lord knoweth them that are His : and, Let every one that nameth the Name of the Lord depart from unrighteousness." [1]

Here, again, the first seal is known only to the Lord ; while the second refers, not, as in the previous instance, to the simple faith of the elect person, but to the fruits of that faith as manifested in his careful walk and avoidance of sin—to the conduct, in short, for which, since his Lord has perfectly fulfilled the law in his stead, he can receive a reward.

Yet once more, in the eighth chapter of the Epistle to the Romans, Paul says ;—

" And we know that to them that love God all things work together for good, even to them that are the called according to His purpose." [2]

The arrangement of this passage is different from that of the other two, in that the visible seal is mentioned first. But those who manifest by their lives that they love God, and are His devoted servants in Christ Jesus, cannot but rank high among His saints : they discover in themselves so much of the nature of their Head that we need not hesitate to recognise them as His members. And so, Paul goes on to tell us, that a grace so wondrous has been bestowed upon them because they are the called according to God's purpose. Foreseeing that they would respond to His touch, He

[1] 2 Tim. ii. 19.   [2] Rom. viii. 28.

had predestinated them before the foundation of the world. At the right moment He called them, set before them their sins more in number than the hairs of their head, and then showed them that all that was against them should be blotted out for ever by the Blood of Jesus Christ that was shed for them. Forgiven so much, and moved by His Holy Spirit, what could they do but love much?

These three instructive examples exhibit to us the connection between the invisible and visible seals. Where the first is, the others must follow in due course: if any one be predestinated to be conformed to the image of God's dear Son, the signs of a Christ-like disposition will presently begin to be developed in him. And these last are visible to mortal eyes, or can be detected by human perception: indeed, they afford the only proof by which we can know that we have become the children of God.

Hence they are often set forth in the Scriptures as though they were the actual means by which we gain the great prize as distinguished from the gift of everlasting life; and the outward and practical means they undoubtedly are. But other passages make it clear that behind such symptoms are the energies of the indwelling Spirit, Who joins us to the Lord as one spirit, and so makes holy thoughts and deeds possible to us.

So, then, the disposition and the conduct that win the prize are really as much gifts of grace as everlasting life itself; for, although we must both will and run, it is, nevertheless, not of him that willeth, nor of him that runneth, but of God That showeth mercy.

And the prize, as we hope presently to demonstrate, is the First Resurrection—that path by which alone we can attain to membership with Christ and a place in the Heavenly Kingdom. For the Body of Christ must be completed, and the Kingdom established, at the time of the Second Advent; so that those who are not raised to life until the General Resurrection can have no part or lot in them.

To sum up, then, what has been said in this and the preceding chapter, predestination is the secret stamp of God set upon those in whom His fore-knowledge discerns the capability of becoming His children. In no way does it interfere with man's freewill, but merely indicates the prescience of God as to the possible right tendency of that freewill, and His fixed purpose to render it every needful direction and assistance. Our attention, therefore, must be concentrated, not upon speculative searchings into predestination, but upon prayer and sanctified effort to develop in ourselves, and in others, such signs as will testify that the invisible mark of God is indeed upon us, that we are verily sealed by His Holy Spirit unto the day of redemption.

IV

REDEMPTION BY THE BLOOD. A KINGDOM AND PRIESTS

THE first characteristic of the members of Christ's Body is one which they have in common with all the saved, and which is put forward by Paul when he speaks of the believers in Ephesus as "the Church of God, which He purchased with His Own Blood."[1] For all those who are elected to have part in the General

[1] Acts xx. 28.

Assembly and Church of the Firstborn attribute their salvation and their glory to Him Who His Own Self bare our sins in His Own Body on the tree, and Who, though He appeared upon earth in human form, was both the Son of God and Himself God.

This they are represented as doing in the grand ascription of praise contained in the first chapter of the Apocalypse, where also they add some important particulars. "Unto Him That loveth us," is their triumphant cry, "and loosed us from our sins by His Blood ; and He made us to be a Kingdom, to be priests unto His God and Father—to Him be the glory and the dominion for ever and ever. Amen."[1]

Here the redemption by the Blood is first mentioned, and then the Lord is said to have made His redeemed people "to be a Kingdom, to be priests unto His God and Father." We must, therefore, try to discover what is involved in these words, not forgetting to notice, that, while the word "Kingdom" is in the singular number, "priests" follows in the plural.

The reason for this difference is obvious. Believers can act as priests individually ; but it is only after the whole Church has been gathered in that her members can be formed into the Kingdom. They must reign collectively, since every single member has a post foreordained for him in the Divine purpose, the vacancy of which would render the governmental body incomplete.

And, indeed, it is in the appearing of the Kingdom that the unity of the Church will be first displayed to angels and to men ;—

"When Christ, Who is our life, shall be manifested, then shall ye also with Him be manifested in glory."[2]

[1] Rev. i. 5, 6.　　　[2] Col. iii. 4.

It is to this great event that our Lord refers when He says ;—

" That they may all be one ; even as Thou, Father, art in Me, and I in Thee, that they also may be in Us: that the world may believe that Thou didst send Me.

" And the glory which Thou hast given Me I have given unto them, that they may be one, even as We are One ;

" I in them, and Thou in Me, that they may be perfected into one ; that the world may know that Thou didst send Me, and lovedst them even as Thou lovedst Me." [1]

Many are striving to reduce this glorious prayer to a prophecy of the miserable uniformity in apostasy which they are hoping to bring about under the name of the Reunion of Christendom.   But a moment's passionless consideration will show that such words have no place in the present order of things.   For how can the Lord and His people be manifested to the world as One, when some of those people are in Paradise, some upon earth, and some, possibly, not yet born ?   No : the full numbers of the Church must be made up, and her every member gathered in, before her oneness in the Lord can be revealed.

Moreover, the Lord intimates that the effect of the visible unity of Himself and His Church will be, that the world will believe on Him.   We are, however, assured in many Scriptures, that such a change in the feelings of men can never take place in the present age ; but that they will continue to grow more determined and unanimous in their rejection of the Saviour, until He appears in flaming fire, and establishes

[1] John xvii. 21-3.

His Kingdom. Then, but not till then, as we learn from Isaiah ;—

"The earth shall be full of the knowledge of the Lord, as the waters cover the sea." [1]

But it is at the time of His appearing that He will share His glory with His own. For, to quote again a verse we have just used :

"When Christ, Who is our life, shall be manifested, then shall ye also with Him be manifested in glory." [2]

With this fact in our mind, that the Church cannot reign until all her members have been gathered in, we can understand the vigorous irony by which Paul strove to break up the complacency of the Corinthians ;—

"Already ye are filled, already ye became rich, ye reigned without us : yea, and I would that ye did reign, that we also might be reigning with you." [3]

It is easy to grasp the situation expressed in these words. While the Apostle was labouring and suffering for the Gospel, the Corinthians were living in ease, were acting as if the time of toil and pain had already passed, and the Kingdom were really established. I would, Paul says, that it were even as you seem to suppose ; for then we Apostles, also, should be reigning with you. For he knew well that one part of the Church could never begin to reign without the other.

But the priestly functions of the Church can be

---

[1] Isa. xi. 1-9. The reader will carefully notice, that the spread of the knowledge of the Lord is attributed directly to His actual reign in righteousness.

[2] Col. iii. 4.

[3] 1 Cor. iv. 8.

discharged by her members individually, because each of them is a priest unto God. Hence, also, these functions can be exercised, to some extent at least, in the present age. What they are here below, may be inferred from the duties of the Israelitish priesthood, if only those things be changed which have to be changed in such applications. For, in the first place, there is no priestly *caste* in churches, as there was in Israel : all their members are priests. And, accordingly, Peter addresses the sojourners of the dispersion, of whom he presently particularises slaves wives and husbands, as " a holy priesthood, to offer up spiritual sacrifices, acceptable to God through Christ Jesus," [1] and as " an elect race, a royal priesthood." [2]

So, too, in the verse which we are considering, the whole Church, men and women alike, claim, in reference to the next age, to have been made a Kingdom and priests by the Lord.[3] In another place, again, we are told, that all those who have part in the First Resurrection " shall be priests of God and of Christ, and shall reign with Him a thousand years." [4] Hence we find that the First Resurrection is the great prize for which Paul was striving,[5] since it is the only means by which we can attain to the celestial priesthood and the heavenly Kingdom.

Thus, even in the present age, all the members of the Church that are upon earth stand in the same relation to the world as the Levitical priests did to the other tribes. But, in the next age, the whole Church will, probably, take the place of that heavenly priesthood which furnished a pattern for the Levitical ;

[1] 1 Peter ii. 5.
[2] 1 Peter ii. 9.
[3] Rev. i. 6, v. 10.
[4] Rev. xx. 6.
[5] Phil. iii. 11, 14.

while the Israelitish nation, no longer deputing the single Tribe of Levi to represent them, will be unto God a Kingdom of Priests[1] upon the earth.

But, to return to our immediate subject, what were the duties of the Levitical priests in the times of the Law? We will mention but two things which were specially important: they had to offer sacrifices for themselves and for others, and. they were to hold themselves in readiness to advise, exhort, or instruct, the people. "For," as Malachi has it;—

"The priest's lips should keep knowledge, and men should seek the law at his mouth: for he is the messenger of the Lord of Hosts."[2]

Since, however, the One and Only Sacrifice for sin has now been offered, members of the Church cannot present typical offerings as the Aaronic priests did. Nevertheless, in their intercessions before the Throne of God, they must plead the awful and never-to-be-repeated Sacrifice of the Lord Jesus, whether their prayers be on behalf of themselves, or of their brethren in Christ, or of the outside world.

Moreover, it is incumbent upon them to communicate to others whatsoever knowledge they may have received of the Lord; to strengthen, stablish, settle, and instruct, those that are within the fold of Christ; and to give a reason for the hope that is in them to those that are without,[3] while they act as ambassadors for Christ in beseeching them to be reconciled to God.[4]

And he who is engaged in such services, because the desire of his heart is to do the will of God, may have confidence that he is a full member of the earthly priesthood, and a probationer of the heavenly.

[1] Exod. xix. 6.
[2] Mal. ii. 7.
[3] I Peter iii. 15.
[4] 2 Cor. v. 20.

V

THE FIRST RESURRECTION

JOHN v. 24—29.

THUS the Heavenly Kingdom and the Heavenly Priesthood are reserved for those only who have part in the First Resurrection. We must, then, endeavour to ascertain what that Resurrection is, and when it will take place. And, to this end, we shall find no Scripture more helpful than the memorable discourse of the Lord in the fifth chapter of the Gospel of John.

The Pharisees, it will be remembered, were accusing Him of breaking the Law, because He had not only healed an impotent man on the Sabbath day, but had actually directed him to carry away his bed forthwith. And His reply to the first part of the charge was, that His Father was working up to that very moment, and, therefore, that He also worked.

Now, the assertion that the Father was working on the very day on which He rested from creation, and which He blessed and hallowed, has perplexed many. But a solution of the difficulty may be found in what, on another occasion, the Lord Himself says respecting the Sabbath.

In the twelfth chapter of the Gospel of Matthew, He shows that the disciples did no wrong in plucking ears of corn, and rubbing out the grain to appease their hunger, on the Sabbath; because this was a work of necessity; and, again, that He Himself did not violate the Law by healing a man on the hallowed day; because that was a work of mercy. "For," He adds, "the Sabbath was made for man, and not man for the Sabbath." In other words, God instituted the day of rest for the benefit of man ; and so, if at any time its obligations should, through temporary circumstances, be adverse to man's real interests, they might be waived for the nonce, lest the institution should defeat its own purpose.

Upon this principle, we can readily understand, that, as soon as the fall had occurred, God's Seventh Day's rest was broken. Once more He took up His work, and began the new creation, which will occupy as many thousand years as His previous work did days, and be succeeded by the glorious Millennial rest, the Sabbath-keeping that remains for His people as well as for Himself.

Hence in repairing the consequences of the fall on the Sabbath day, the Son was acting in concert with His Father ; and all those who love Him must do likewise. For the entrance of lawlessness and misery into the world has rendered it necessary to defer the rest, until a reign of righteousness can again be established.

Perhaps, one might summarise the Lord's teaching on this subject as follows ;—Man should still cease from his own work on the Sabbath—except in cases of necessity, or of showing mercy—but he is required to give up the rest for the present, in order that he may do God's work, that is, everything that helps forward the new creation.

The Lord's answer made the Jews still more eager to slay Him ; for now, they said, He had not merely broken the Sabbath, but had also claimed God as His Father, thus making Himself equal with God. And by this last charge they showed how fully they had comprehended His intimation, that He was literally the Son of God, and, therefore, of the same nature as His Father.

This truth He assumes in His further reply. As being of one nature and one will with the Father, He can do nothing save that which He sees the Father doing. And the Father loves Him, and shows Him all that He Himself does, wakening His ear morning by morning to hear as they that are taught.[1] But soon the Father would show Him greater works than any which He had hitherto done—works of resurrection and judgment. For the Son, also, had the power of quickening, or bestowing everlasting life, upon those who were dead through trespasses and sins ; and, moreover, was entrusted with all judgment to decide who should be quickened and who should not. For it was the purpose of the Almighty God, that all men should honour the Son, even as they honoured the Father.

Such is the argument up to the twenty-fourth verse, in which the Lord proceeds to explain what He means by the power of quickening and of judgment, and reveals the three mighty acts by which He will manifest His possession of that power to the universe. This paragraph is most important : we must, therefore, examine it verse by verse.

" Verily, verily, I say unto you, He that heareth My word, and believeth Him That sent Me, hath eternal life, and cometh not into judgment, but hath passed out of death into life."

With His most solemn formula the Lord introduces this wondrous and gracious revelation, that, at the very moment when we receive His word, and believe the testimony which His Father has given concerning Him, we have crossed the boundary which separates death from life—aye, and have done so before the

[1] Isa. l. 4.

awful Judgment-throne is set up between them. In that instant, by the word of His power, by that mighty working whereby He is able even to subject all things unto Himself, a germ of immortality has passed into our being, which—like all the gifts and callings of God—when once given, can never be withdrawn.[1] For we have been transferred into the covenant of grace, whereby He Who knew no sin was made sin for us,[2] so that we are now reckoned by God as having died on the cross in Him, and, therefore, as having in Him expiated to the full all our sins. Thenceforth it may be said of us ;—" Ye died, and your life is hid with Christ in God,"[3] safe for ever.

Yes, that life is now worth preserving ; for the object of God in suffering the sinless Christ to become sin for us was, that we might be made the righteousness of God in Him.[2] And He " was made unto us wisdom from God, and righteousness, and sanctification, and redemption."[4] Such being the case, how could we ever perish ? How could God sanction so great a waste as the destruction of those whom He has created anew in Christ Jesus, and made perfect in Him ! Nay, how could He abandon those of whom we read in the most astounding verse in the Bible ;—" I in them, and Thou in Me, that they may be perfected into one ; that the world may know that Thou didst send Me, *and lovedst them even as Thou lovedst Me.*"[5]

True, then, were the words of the Lord when He said ;—" Whosoever liveth and believeth on Me shall never die."[6] And true, also, the words of His Apostle ;— " And this is the record, that God gave unto us eternal life, and this life is in His Son. He that hath the Son

[1] Rom. xi. 29.   [3] Col. iii. 3.   [5] John xvii. 23.
[2] 2 Cor. v. 21.   [4] 1 Cor. i. 30.   [6] John xi. 26.

hath the life: he that hath not the Son of God hath not the life." [1]

The first, then, of the three mighty acts is a resurrection of the spirit, or the spiritual resurrection, which involves everlasting life, and is identical with the new birth, or the new creation in Christ Jesus. It is an absolute and undeserved gift from God, and can only be obtained as such.

But we must carefully notice, that it is said to be conferred upon those who hear and believe His *word*,[2] whether directly from His Own lips, as in the transitional period of His ministry upon earth, or from the inspired record of the New Testament, in which He has been speaking to all men until now. In the twenty-fifth verse, He proceeds as follows:—

" Verily, verily, I say unto you, An hour cometh, and now is, when the dead shall hear the voice of the Son of God, and they that hear shall live. For as the Father hath life in Himself, even so gave He to the Son also to have life in Himself; and He gave Him authority to execute judgment, because He is a Son of man."

With equal solemnity the Lord predicts His second great act of power. And, in this case, He gives a note of time—" An hour cometh, and now is." But John, who records this discourse, uses elsewhere the Greek original for " hour " in the sense of " dispensation " or " age "; [3] and such seems to be the meaning of the word in the passage before us, the present dispensation being evidently signified by the coming hour.

Again, a dispensation may be said to be coming, and yet, in a sense, even already present, during the transitional period between the preceding age and

---

[1] I John v. 11, 12.   [2] τὸν λόγον μου.   [3] I John ii. 18.

itself. And such an interval between Israelitish and Christian time is clearly marked out for us by the Lord's own words ;—

"The Law and the Prophets were until John: from that time the Gospel of the Kingdom of God is preached, and every man entereth violently into it."[1]

Thus the transition-period began with the preaching of John the Baptist, and continued until that Day of Pentecost on which the new dispensation was fully established by the descent of the Holy Spirit. Hence we may see why Peter, in unfolding the Gospel to Cornelius, describes it as—

"That saying . . . which was published throughout all Judæa, beginning from Galilee, after the baptism which John preached."[2]

That we have here given the true interpretation of the phrase " coming and now is " may, apparently, be proved by a reference to our Lord's discourse with the woman of Samaria, to whom He first says, "Woman, believe Me, the hour cometh, when neither in this mountain, nor in Jerusalem, shall ye worship the Father."[3] Then, in other words, He repeats His declaration ;—" But the hour cometh, and now is, when the true worshippers shall worship the Father in spirit and truth."[4] Now, no one will deny that both of these declarations point to the present age, and the note of time in the latter is expressed in precisely the same terms as in the verse before us.

The event, therefore, to which the Lord alluded must take place within the period of the Christian dispensation, which was then coming, and, indeed, since the

[1] Luke xvi. 16.
[2] Acts x. 37.
[3] John iv. 21.
[4] John iv. 23.

transition to it had commenced, might have been said to be already present.

But what is the event itself? " The dead shall hear the voice of the Son of God, and they that hear shall live." Now, in this sentence, the expression " the dead " must be taken literally of the physically dead. For we have no qualifying clause to intimate that the spiritually dead, the dead by reason of trespasses and sins, are meant.

Nor is there anything in the context to suggest such a sense to us, as there is in the oft-quoted, but by no means parallel, passage in which the Lord says ;—" Let the dead bury their dead." [1]

And, lastly, it is said that the dead will hear the personal *voice* [2] of the Son of God, not His recorded *word* [3] as in the twenty-fourth verse. This voice is evidently His bidding, or word of command ; [4] and those of the dead who hear it shall immediately live. Just as at the tomb in Bethany, He will again cry, with a far louder voice, Come forth ! and many a Lazarus will respond to the word of Almighty power.

But there is here a division among the dead : it is only they who have heard that will live—a plain intimation that some of the dead will not hear, and, therefore, will not live ; and that the Lord is speaking of a select, and not of the general, resurrection.

Now, that the New Testament recognises two resurrections in the future, scarcely needs proof—though proof in abundance may be culled from the following pages by those who require it. Consequently, we find in the Greek original two different expressions, which

---

[1] Matt. viii. 22.   [2] τῆς φωνῆς.   [3] τοῦ λόγου.
[4] κέλευσμα: I Thess. iv. 16. The rendering of the A. V. and R. V., " with a shout," is not very intelligent.

are carefully distinguished for us in the Revised Version,
but not in the less accurate rendering of the Authorised.
These are, " the resurrection *from* the dead," and "the
resurrection *of* the dead "—the latter obviously pointing
to the general resurrection of all that are at the time
in their graves ; while the former indicates the coming
forth of one or more persons from the innumerable
multitude of the dead, and is hence applied, exclusively,
either to the resurrection of the Lord or to that of the
Church of the Firstborn.

Since, then, the verse which we are considering
speaks of some only of the dead as hearing and living,
it must refer to the resurrection of those who are
to form the Church, which is also called the First
Resurrection.

In the next two verses, the Lord shows that He is
fully able to bring about the resurrection of the body
as well as that of the spirit, since the Father has conferred His Own power of quickening whom He will
upon the Son. And so, in the twenty-fifth verse, the
voice that will summon the dead is called " the voice
of the Son of God."

But the Lord is not merely a life-giving Agent Who
restores the dead : He also possesses authority to
decide who is worthy to attain to the First Resurrection.
And this authority is given to Him, because He is a [1]
Son of Man : for men must be judged by one of themselves, and the Lord Jesus is the Only Sinless Man.
To Him, therefore, appertains the right of judging
the whole human race. And to this fact Paul, in

[1] The A.V. and R.V. should not have inserted the definite article.
The Lord has power to raise the dead, because He is the Son of
God—there is but One Begotten Son of God : He has authority to
exercise judgment over men, because they must be judged by a
peer, and He is a Son of Man, One belonging to their own race.

3

declaring the true God to the Athenians, alludes in the words ;—

"He hath appointed a day, in the which He will judge the world in righteousness by a Man Whom He hath ordained."[1]

In the twenty-ninth verse, the Lord foretells the last of His three great acts of power, the general and final resurrection, elsewhere called the Last Day ;—

"Marvel not at this ; for an hour cometh, in which all that are in the tombs shall hear His voice, and shall come forth ; they that have done good, unto a resurrection of life, and they that have done ill, unto a resurrection of judgment."

Here He repeats the formula, "An hour cometh," but does not add, "and now is." For the resurrection *of* the dead takes place at the close of the Millennium, or age to come,[2] and not in the present dispensation.

Then, not merely some of the dead, as in the twenty-fifth verse, but all that are at the time in the tombs, shall hear the *voice* of the Son of God—"the *voice*," as in the twenty-fifth verse, not "the *word*," as in the twenty-fourth—and shall come forth, though to very diverse fates. For some when they hear shall live, as in the twenty-fifth verse, and shall not come into judgment,[3] because they believed the Word of the Lord when they were upon earth. But the evil-doers, who would not work the work of God by believing on Him Whom He sent,[4] will come forth to judgment.

We may find a description of this awful scene in the twentieth chapter of the Apocalypse, where John sees the Great White Throne, and the dead, the great and

---

[1] Acts xvii. 31.
[2] Rev. xx. 7-15.
[3] John v. 24.
[4] John vi 29.

the small, standing before it. "And if any one," he tells us, "was not found written in the Book of Life, he was cast into the Lake of Fire"[1]—a form of expression which would never have been used, unless the Apostle had intended us to understand that some were written therein. Hence, in the Apocalypse, as well as in his Gospel, he testifies that the Last Day will witness the resurrection of many that are saved, and of all the lost.

Thus the revelation which we have been considering resolves into an announcement, that all power in regard to the resurrection and judgment of the human race had been given into the hands of the Lord by His Father; and that He would exercise that power in three distinct ways.

I. By the spiritual resurrection of all who are willing to believe on Him. This act, which we sometimes call conversion, confers everlasting life as a gift of God that can never be recalled. But it does not decide when the saved believer will enter upon the full fruition of life, namely, by receiving a glorious and immortal body in place of that which sin has made subject to death.

II. By the First Resurrection; when, as we shall presently see, those only, whose love and conduct after conversion have caused Him to deem them worthy, will come forth from the dead, to form the complete Church, and to act as members of the Heavenly Kingdom.

III. By the final resurrection of all the remaining dead; when those who have been saved, but did not attain to the First Resurrection, will be raised to life: and those who have rejected the Saviour will come forth for judgment. This resurrection does not take place until the close of the Millennial reign, that is, until at least a thousand years after the First Resurrection.

[1] Rev. xx. 15.

VI

The Prize, which is the First Resurrection

PHIL. iii. 10–14

SEEING, then, that the whole Church is to be manifested in glory with Christ, when He appears to bring the present age to a close, and to establish His Kingdom,[1] it follows that all her members must have part in the First Resurrection. Therefore, if we can discover what qualifications are required of those who would win that prize, we shall know, also, the conditions of membership in the Church which is the Lord's Body.

And, perhaps, the passage which supplies the simplest information on this point is the third chapter of the Epistle to the Philippians, in which Paul has explained the course adopted by himself in order that he might attain to what he calls "the select resurrection out from among the dead."[2]

In the beginning of the chapter, he warns the Philippians to beware of the Judaizers, whom he stigmatises as mere mutilators[3] of the flesh; "for we," he urges, "are the circumcision, who worship by the Spirit of God, and glory in Christ Jesus, and have no confidence in the flesh." It was not, however, because he was unable to boast of the flesh, after the manner of the Judaizers, that he thus spoke. Far from it: for none of them could claim more advantages in

---

[1] Col. iii. 4.

[2] This is a literal rendering, for Paul does not use the simple word ἀνάστασις, but ἐξανάστασις, that is, "resurrection out from" (among the dead); and he repeats the preposition ἐκ before νεκρῶν.

[3] Called in our versions "the concision."

that way than had fallen to his lot. He had been duly circumcised on the eighth day. He was of the genuine stock of Israel, and no descendant of engrafted proselytes. He was of the Tribe of Benjamin, which had never forsaken its God and its King, as the Ten Tribes had done; but had remained faithful to the Temple and the royal line of David. Moreover, he was a Hebrew, and no Hellenist: he spoke the Hebrew tongue, and practised the Hebrew customs. And he was descended from Hebrew ancestors: no foreign element, no strange women, had been introduced into his family.

As regards religious standing in his nation, he was a Pharisee; and, if that was not enough, he had been a persecutor of the Church, as every orthodox Pharisee must be. Nor could any blame be cast in his teeth so far as the outward requirements of the Law were concerned.

Such qualifications as these, coupled with his natural abilities and fervour, might have placed him at the head of Judaism; but what was his own view of them? He had caught a glimpse of something far better, and now summed up all these advantages under the one head of loss. Nay, he counted as loss all things whatsoever that held him back from the knowledge of Christ Jesus, his Lord; for Whose sake he did, indeed, literally forfeit all things at his conversion, and still, after a calm survey of his position, reckoned them as mere refuse, if he could but gain Christ, could but be found in Him on the Great Day, not having a righteousness of his own, such as was supposed to come from the outward observance of the Law, but that which is through faith in Christ, the righteousness which is of God by faith.

Such is the first part of the knowledge of Christ, that which brings salvation, and of which we read ;— " By the knowledge of Himself shall My righteous Servant justify many ; and He shall bear their iniquities.[1] But Paul had no intention of stopping at salvation : he wished to draw ever nearer to Him "in Whom are all the treasures of wisdom and knowledge hidden ;"[2] to gain the great prize of standing before Him in the happy days of the age to come.   And this desire he expresses in words which we must carefully examine.

" In order that I may know Him, and the power of His resurrection, and the fellowship of His sufferings, becoming conformed unto His death ; if by any means I may attain unto the select resurrection from the dead."[3]

In these verses, we may learn what should be the aspiration of every one who has believed unto salvation.

Paul had given up all things that he might win Christ, and be saved from sin and death by His Blood and righteousness.   And, that purpose having been accomplished, he would make it a stepping-stone to something more.   For now, as one of the sons whom God was bringing to glory, he would go on to know the Leader of his salvation, not merely as a Saviour, but intimately, and experimentally. Only in this way could his sanctification be completed : only by a continual contemplation of the glory of the Father, as mirrored in the Lord Jesus, could he be changed from glory to glory into the same image.

It has, however, seemed strange to some, that, when he entered into particulars, he should have desired to know the power of Christ's resurrection

[1] Isa. liii. 11.   [2] Col. ii. 3.   [3] Phil. iii. 10, 11.

before he had experienced the fellowship of His sufferings, or become conformed to His death. But no man can endure—much less desire—the fellowship of the sufferings, until he has first been strengthened by the power which proceeds from faith in his Lord's resurrection. He must be assured in his mind, that that wondrous event was the seal of his own justification, the proof that Christ, although He submitted to every human condition, has been a spotless sacrifice on his behalf, and so has burst the bonds of death, because, as a sinless man, He could not be holden of them. He must have perfect confidence, that, in the purpose of God which cannot be broken, he himself was as certainly raised from death and lifted into the heavenly places, when his Lord arose, as if he had been actually and corporeally exalted at the same moment.

So, then, knowing that he was raised together with Christ, he can now seek those things that are above, where Christ is seated at the right hand of God: he can set his mind on the things that are above, and turn away from the things that are upon the earth, For to these last he knows that he died in Christ, and that his life is now hid with Christ in God. Therefore, he exults in the full assurance, that, when Christ, Who is his life, shall be manifested, then shall he also with Him be manifested in glory.

He that with the eyes of faith has beheld this ineffable vision, this hope that cannot be disappointed, has seen a great light, and, filled with the Spirit of God, will be drawn on, rejoicing, over mountain and plain, through thorns and marshes, until he gains the place from which the celestial beams shone forth upon him. For, when he has entered upon this phase, he has become dead to the world, even as his Lord was : the pain of suffering is rendered tolerable by the love of Christ : the darkness from below is penetrated by the rays of glory from above, and, like Paul, he can rejoice even in tribulation.

But what was the goal towards which Paul was thus directing his efforts ?   " If by any means," he continues, " I may attain to the select resurrection out from among the dead."   In other words, his aim was to be numbered with those blessed and holy ones who shall have part in the First Resurrection.[1]   But we must note, that he had, at the time, no certain assurance that he would compass the desire of his heart.   His diffidence is shown in the expression, "if by any means," and contrasts strongly with his perfect confidence in regard to his salvation by faith.   For, in the latter case, nothing was required of him, save to receive the gift of God which is without repentance.   But the First Resurrection is a reward for obedience rendered after the acceptance of salvation, and Paul knew not the standard which God had fixed in His Own purpose.

Just before his death, however, it was graciously revealed to him that he was one of the approved.[2]   And, accordingly, in his latest Epistle, he triumphantly exclaims ;—" I have fought the good fight, I have finished the course, I have kept the faith : henceforth there is laid up for me the crown of righteousness, which the Lord, the Righteous Judge, shall give to me at that day, and not only to me, but to all them that have loved His appearing." [3]

[1] Rev. xx. 6.

[2] Comp. 1 Cor. ix. 27 ;—" Lest by any means, after that I have preached to others, I myself should be disproved."

[3] 2 Tim. iv. 7, 8.   Comp. Heb. iii. 14 ;—" For we are become partakers with "—or, " companions of "—" Christ, if we hold fast the beginning of our confidence firm unto the end."

But, at the time when he was writing to the Philippians, he could not speak with such confidence; and was anxious that they should understand his position, probably because he perceived among them some tendency to abuse the Gospel of grace, the perhaps half-unconscious admission of a feeling, that, since Christ had done all for them and given them His righteousness, it did not so much matter what their own conduct might be.

This is an error which develops in many ways, and is most common and disastrous in our own times. And it was, doubtless, to check its silent workings among the Philippians that Paul continued so earnestly and affectionately to press the point;—

"Not that I did at once attain,[1] or have been already made perfect; but I am pressing on, if so be that I may lay hold of that for which I was laid hold of by Christ. Brethren, I count not myself to have laid hold; but one thing I do, forgetting the things that are behind, and stretching out after the things that are before, I press on toward the goal for the prize of God's upward calling in Christ Jesus."

Here Paul again urges the fact, that, devoted as he was to his Master, he had as yet no absolute certainty of attaining to the First Resurrection. For, as he taught the Colossians, that question depended upon his own conduct, whether he could continue in the faith, grounded and steadfast, and without being moved away from the hope of the Gospel.[2] For, otherwise,

---

[1] ἔλαβον is an aorist, and not a perfect tense: it must, therefore, refer to a particular time, that is, to the time of Paul's conversion. Similarly, two other aorists in this passage, ἐξημιώθην (I suffered the loss of) in v. 8, and κατελήμφθην (I was laid hold of) in v. 12, point to the same crisis in the life of the Apostle.

[2] Col. i. 22, 23.

though most assuredly saved by grace, he would be disproved for the heavenly prize.

What, then, was his purpose in the face of this uncertainty? Would he seek some Cabbalistic means of discovering the exact standard of merit required by God, and so set himself to attain to it? No: the Holy Spirit had shown him the folly of Rabbinical speculations and niceties: he would neither calculate nor conjecture; but, by the help of God, his prayers, his efforts, the whole business of his life, should be directed to one object, if so be that he might lay hold of that for which he had been laid hold of by Christ. And the glow of hope must have flashed brightly as he wrote the last words; for it was in order that he might attain to the First Resurrection and the Kingdom that the Lord Jesus had laid hold of him for conversion on the road to Damascus. It was, therefore, His wish that Paul should attain, and nothing could prevent the accomplishment of that wish, unless the Apostle himself should refuse to follow the leadings of his Lord, and so quench His Spirit. But that, by His grace, Paul would not do.

Once more, with affectionate vehemence, he repeats, that he does not count himself to have yet laid hold; but that there is one thing upon which he is firmly resolved. He will not waste time by dwelling upon the past; for, whatever sins or services it may have recorded, these cannot now be either recalled or improved. And so, stretching forth after the glorious possibilities of the future, and pressing on in the direction of his goal, he will earnestly strive for the prize of the heavenly calling in Christ Jesus.

The upward, or heavenward, calling is, of course, contrasted with the earthly calling of Israel. And its introduction here is sufficiently startling for those who have been taught that simple belief in Christ will win heaven for them, and membership in the Lord's Body. For Paul unmistakably affirms, that these high privileges are a prize and not a gift, and are accessible only by the gate of the First Resurrection—a gate through which, after all his sacrifices and labours and sufferings for Christ, he was not yet absolutely sure that he would be permitted to pass.

VII

THE KINGDOM AND EVERLASTING LIFE

HERE it will be well to investigate another point. We have already seen, that the members of Christ are to be formed into a Kingdom, and to live and reign with Him. Accordingly, in writing to the Colossians, Paul, after mentioning Aristarchus, Mark, and Justus, says ;— " These only are my fellow-workers unto the Kingdom of God, men that have been a comfort unto me." [1] In another Epistle, he speaks of the hope that the Thessalonians would " be counted worthy of the Kingdom of God," for which, also, they were suffering. [2] The Kingdom, then, was the reward to which these early Christians aspired.

It is, however, important to see that we have a clear conception of the Kingdom. For Daniel, also, speaks of a Kingdom which the God of Heaven will set up upon the earth, and which will destroy all others, and will stand for ever. [3] This is, undoubtedly, the Millennial Kingdom of Israel : is it, then, identical with that for which we are bidden to hope ?

[1] Col. iv. 11.   [2] 2 Thess. i. 5.   [3] Dan. ii. 44.

Apparently not : yet the two are parts of one great whole. The relations between them may be inferred from a passage of Isaiah, wherein the prophet declares, that the Lord will punish two governing bodies— "the Host of the High Ones on high, and the Kings of the Earth upon the earth."[1] Now, the former of these are, doubtless, Satan and his angels, the present spiritual rulers of the earth ; while the latter are the kings of Christendom. Hence we may infer, that God's present arrangements for this world comprise two governing bodies, a spiritual or heavenly, and a human or earthly. And, since both of these bodies have failed to rule in righteousness, both will be deposed by the Lord Jesus, Who, together with His Church, will then take the place of the former, and will establish the Twelve Tribes of Israel in the room of the latter.

These governments will form the great Kingdom of God, which will thus consist of two spheres, the heavenly and the earthly, the last mentioned being the Millennial Kingdom of Israel, while the other is identical with the glorified Church. And hence it is that Paul cries out with exultant faith ;—" The Lord will deliver me from every evil work, and will save me unto His Heavenly Kingdom."[2]

The glorified Church, then, which is Christ's Body, and the Heavenly Kingdom of God, are merely different expressions for the same assembly. Since, therefore, the whole Church must be revealed in glory at the Lord's appearing, at which time also the Kingdom will be set up, it is clear that no one can become a member of the Heavenly Kingdom, unless he has part in the First Resurrection.

And since, again, as we have already proved from

[1] Isa. xxiv. 21.   [2] 2 Tim. iv, 18.

the words of Paul to the Philippians, the attainment of the First Resurrection does not follow as a necessary result from simple faith in Christ, but must be won, in the strength of the Lord, by self-denial and faithfulness after conversion—since this is so, it appears that membership in Christ's Body and a place in the Heavenly Kingdom are a reward for works done after conversion, being, indeed, "the things which God has prepared for them that love Him." [1]

This conclusion will be found, not merely to be in accord with all other Scriptures, but also to throw much light upon certain obscure passages. And, if we run through the New Testament, we shall find, that, while simple faith and eternal life are linked together, the Kingdom is invariably connected, directly or indirectly, with the fruits of faith, with love, work, and conduct.

As an instance of the first of these cases, we may quote the following words of the Lord ;—

"And this is the will of Him That sent Me, that, of all that which He hath given Me, I should lose nothing, but should raise it up at the Last Day.

"For this is the will of My Father, that every one that contemplateth the Son, and believeth on Him, should have eternal life ; and I will raise him up at the Last Day." [2]

Now, the first of these verses, as we have already seen, is explained by the second. Those who are given to the Lord come to Him, because His Father draws them ; and so contemplate Him, and believe on Him. To all such, eternal life is assured by the very definite promise that follows: they can never be judged for their lives, because they have already passed from death

[1] 1 Cor. ii. 9, 10.　　　　[2] John vi. 39, 40.

unto life ; and, consequently, the Lord will raise them up on the Last Day.

But which is the Last Day ? It is, of course, the day of the General Resurrection, and of the Great White Throne. All doubt as to the correctness of this interpretation may be speedily removed by a reference to the solemn words of the Lord ;—

"He that rejecteth Me, and receiveth not My sayings, hath one that judgeth him : the Word that I spake, the same shall judge him in the Last Day." [1]

Here it is certain that the reference is to the judgment of the Great White Throne ; for no despiser of the Lord Jesus will have part in the First Resurrection.

Hence, to those who believe on Him, but go no further, the Lord does, indeed, give eternal life ; but the fruition of it will not begin until the Last Day, until the thousand years of the Millennial reign are ended. Such persons will not, therefore, be permitted to enter the Kingdom of the Heavens.

And so, whenever mere believing is in question, without any reference to what should follow it, we shall find it connected with eternal life, but not with the Kingdom. The Kingdom, on the other hand, as we remarked above, is always set before us, either directly or indirectly, as the reward of the conduct or works of the saved.

For the poor in spirit, and those who have endured persecution for righteousness' sake, will inherit it.[2] Unless our righteousness shall exceed the righteousness of the Scribes and Pharisees, we cannot enter into it.[3] A mere assertion that Jesus is our Lord will not

[1] John xii. 48.   [2] Matt. v. 3, 10.   [3] Matt. v. 20.

procure admission for us :[1] the forceful take it by force.[2] No one who looks back is fit for it :[3] except a man be born again, he cannot even see it :[4] and except he be born of water and the Spirit, he cannot enter into it.[5] We can reach it only by passing through much tribulation :[6] the condition is, that, if we endure with Him, we shall also reign with Him.[7]

Very significant, too, is the reason which the Lord gives for His promise to the disciples on the eve of His death ;—

"Ye are they which have continued with Me in My temptations ; and I appoint unto you a Kingdom, even as My Father appointed unto Me."[8]

Because they had willingly shared in the trials of their Master, therefore the Kingdom was theirs.

Similarly, Peter, after enumerating the qualities that must be and abound in believers, adds ;—

"For if ye do these things, ye shall never stumble. For thus shall be richly supplied unto you the entrance into the eternal Kingdom of our Lord and Saviour Jesus Christ."[9]

Since, then, the Kingdom is the reward of works done after conversion, we are not surprised to find that only the worthy can obtain it. So, as Paul tells the Thessalonians, God, by exposing them to persecution, had given them an opportunity of exercising faith and patience, in order that they might "be counted worthy of the Kingdom of God," for which they were suffering.[10] Nor must we omit to notice, that the Lord Himself speaks of those "that have been

---

[1] Matt. vii. 21.   [5] John iii. 5.   [8] Luke xxii. 28, 29.
[2] Matt. xi. 12.   [6] Acts xiv. 22.   [9] 2 Peter i. 10, 11.
[3] Luke ix. 62.   [7] 2 Tim. ii. 12.   [10] 2 Thess. i. 4, 5
[4] John iii. 3.

accounted worthy to obtain that age and the resurrection from [1] the dead." [2] For, since "that age" is coupled with the resurrection from the dead, or the First Resurrection, it is clear that the former must be the Millennial Age, during which those who have part in the First Resurrection will reign with Christ, while the rest of the dead will not be raised until the Last Day. [3]

By this utterance, the Lord not only declares that the worthy alone will enter into the Kingdom, but also gives us the clue to another of His sayings, which will be more fully examined by-and-by. In explaining to Peter what those shall have who have left all to follow Himself, He says, that they "shall receive an hundredfold, and shall inherit eternal life." [4] Here, then, it is to be observed, that the reward is placed before eternal life. And this points again to the fact, that the reward will be given during the thousand years which precede the Last Day. The same lesson seems also to be taught in the parable of the "Labourers in the Vineyard," of which we shall have more to say elsewhere.

Seeing, then, that the saved are involved in some uncertainty in regard to their reward—though they are sure of their salvation—the Scriptures, as we might reasonably expect, do not fail to warn them of the danger to which they are exposed. We have already seen that transgressors of various kinds—that is, of course, transgressors after conversion—such as those whose righteousness does not exceed that of the Scribes and Pharisees, or those who have not been born of water and the Spirit, cannot enter into the Kingdom. So,

---

[1] See pp. 32, 33.
[2] Luke xx. 35.
[3] Rev. xx. 4, 5.
[4] Matt. xix. 29.

again, when our Lord declares that the poor in spirit, and those who have passed through persecution for righteousness' sake, will be admitted, He manifestly implies that the high-minded, and the cowardly who avoid persecution at the cost of faith, will be rigorously excluded. And there are many other passages from which similar inferences may be drawn.

But there are also warnings of another type. For instance, Paul, after reminding the Colossians that the Lord had reconciled them by His death, in order that He might present them " holy, and without blemish, and unreprovable, before Him," adds the very significant words, " if, at least, ye continue in the faith, grounded and steadfast, and be not moved away from the hope of the Gospel which ye heard."[1] Are we, then, to regard the " if " as meaningless? Or does it furnish us with a fearful comment on the case of those who did run well, but do so no longer; or of those whose love grows gradually colder as their years increase? We cannot doubt that it does; and are not, therefore, surprised when the same Apostle exhorts us, in reference to obedience, to work out our own salvation with fear and trembling.[2] Nor is he singular in giving such advice; for Peter also forcibly urges the same thing, when he says;—

" And if ye call on Him as Father, Who without respect of persons judgeth according to each man's work, pass the time of your sojourning in fear."[3]

Have such searching passages as these received the attention which they certainly demand from all believers? Alas! no: they are almost entirely disregarded. And so, we see the nominal churches filled with Laodicean complacency and self-satisfaction, while

---

[1] Col. i. 21–23.   [2] Phil. ii. 12.   [3] 1 Peter i. 17.

we know not where to find the man that is poor and of a contrite spirit, and that trembleth at God's word.[1] But there are many similar notes of warning in the New Testament, and two of them, at least, are so striking and instructive that they may claim each a chapter for itself.

VIII

THE CONFLICT AND THE CROWN

1 COR. ix. 24—x. 11

IN the First Epistle to the Corinthians, Paul is addressing believers who deemed themselves already full and rich, and acted as if they were even now reigning, and had left the time of toil and trial behind them. Nay, they had among them men who frequented the festivals of idolaters ; were giving the reins to their lusts, instead of cleansing themselves from every filthiness of flesh and spirit ; were going to law with each other before Heathen magistrates; and, apparently, would deny themselves in nothing for Christ's sake.

To this sin-bespattered church the Apostle describes his own life of self-denial, and his habit of yielding to others in all indifferent matters, so that he might, at least, save some. He then exhorts the Corinthians to similar conduct, likening the Christian's struggle against indolence, self-indulgence, and every other kind of sin, to the conflicts for victory at the Isthmian Games, which were celebrated every two years in the vicinity of Corinth.

" Know ye not that they which run in a race run

[1] Isa. lxvi. 2.

all, but one receiveth the prize? Even so run, that ye may attain. And every man that striveth in the Games is temperate in all things. Now they do it to receive a corruptible crown, but we an incorruptible. I, therefore, so run, as not uncertainly; so fight I, as not beating the air: but I buffet my body, and bring it into bondage: lest by any means, after that I have preached to others, I myself should be disproved."[1]

Now, in this passage, it is abundantly evident that Paul is not dealing with the gift of God, but with something that must be won by effort, that is, with the prize that is set before those who are already saved.

Every Corinthian would be acquainted with the rules and customs of the Isthmian Games. He would know that only freeborn Greeks could enter the lists, and that all foreigners and slaves were rigorously excluded. Hence he would readily learn, that only those whom the truth in Christ Jesus and the second birth had made free could take part in conflicts for the prize to which Paul was pointing; and that none of the subjects of other lords than Christ, none of the many slaves of sin, might be permitted to run on the spiritual course. The prize, which in the Isthmian Games was a crown, would appropriately indicate that Kingdom of God of which Paul had often spoken in the earlier portion of the Epistle.

Readily, too, would Corinthians be able to see the application of the words;—"Even so run, in order that ye may attain." For they knew well that the athlete, when he was starting for the race, would fix his eye upon the goal, and merge every other thought and care in the struggle to reach it. So must it be with the Christian runner: he must have the glory of the King

[1] 1 Cor. ix. 24-27.

and the Kingdom ever before his eyes, and his one great effort must be to reach it.

In the twenty-fifth verse, Paul turns to another feature of the Games, the fact that those who would take part in them were compelled to pass through a long and severe course of training. During the ten months immediately preceding the day of the contest they were subjected to a continual round of exercises, and were expected to practise the strictest self-control, and to abstain from every kind of food, or other gratification, which might tend to impair their strength or shorten their breath.

Similarly, the believer, if he would obtain the prize, must deny himself, and take up his cross daily, and follow his Master. The delicacies of this world, its self-indulgences, its pastimes however refined, its honours, or even its intellectual pleasures, would render him totally unfit to run the race that is set before him. Like the athlete, he must turn away even from those things which in themselves are lawful and innocent, if they be not expedient for his great purpose.

And he must remember, that, while the athlete endures the discipline and severities of his training for a corruptible crown—that is, for the garland of pine-leaves which was the meed of victory at the Isthmian Games—the believer is called to do so for an incorruptible crown, which in the next age will distinguish him as one of those who are living and reigning with Christ.

Such is the Apostle's advice; but he is careful to follow in his own case the precepts which he gives to others. For he, too, is subject to the same conditions as the Corinthians and all other believers; and, therefore, runs "not as uncertainly," that is, not as one who does not see the goal clearly, and so cannot run in the straight direction to it.

Or, if he may compare himself to a boxer in the Games, his blows do not miss their aim as if he were beating the air, but smite his adversary with crippling force. And this adversary is his own body, in which he strikes down every craving for indulgence, mortifying its deeds by the power of the Spirit, and driving it away from its life after the flesh.

For, if he fails to do this, he knows well that he will be disproved and rejected by the Lord at His Coming; and that neither his salvation by the Blood of the Lamb, nor the fact that he has preached to others, will avail to secure his entrance into the Heavenly Kingdom.

Thus Paul has plainly distinguished between salvation and the reward, and shown, that, although a man may have been saved by grace, so that he will be raised to eternal life on the Last Day, it has yet to be determined whether he will obtain the reward of the Millennial Age. He now points out, that this way of God with man is not new, but is in perfect analogy with His treatment of Israel in the days of old ;—

"For I would not, brethren, have you ignorant, how that our fathers were all under the cloud, and all passed through the sea; and were all baptized unto Moses in the cloud and in the sea; and did all eat the same spiritual food; and did all drink the same spiritual drink: for they drank of a spiritual Rock That followed them, and the Rock was the Christ. Howbeit with most of them God was not well pleased: for they were overthrown in the wilderness."[1]

[1] 1 Cor. x. 1-5.

After the Israelites had been brought out of Egypt, their circumstances might have been likened to those of a runner who had already started for the goal.

They were on the march to the Promised Land, the occupation of which ought to have been to them as the Millennial glory. But, like runners who miss the prize through their want of self-denial and endurance, all the male adults who left Egypt, save two only, had failed to reach the land, and had perished in the wilderness.

The " for " of the first verse, which is undoubtedly the true reading, connects the following paragraph closely with the last verse of the ninth chapter. The danger of disproval was real ; for, in spite of all their privileges, the Israelites who came out of Egypt never obtained the Kingdom prepared for them.

Of course, in saying that he did not wish the Corinthians and the Jews that were among them to be ignorant of the history to which he alludes, Paul does not mean to imply that they were unacquainted with the facts, but that they did not understand the all-important bearing of the events upon themselves.

It is to be observed, also, that he says nothing of the deliverance of Israel from death by the blood of the lamb sprinkled upon the side-posts and lintel of their houses, which answers to conversion and salvation ; for he is writing to believers, who have passed that stage, with the view of teaching them what they must do after conversion. Accordingly, he begins with a mention of that event in the history of Israel which corresponds to Christian baptism, to receive which is the first duty of every convert.

The expression, " our fathers," used in addressing a church of mingled Jews and Gentiles, intimates that the Church, in her official position as God's witness upon earth, springs from the Jews, consisting, as it does mainly, of branches of wild olive grafted upon the Jewish stock.[1] Hence the fathers of the Jews may be regarded as also the fathers of the churches. And so, Paul in this passage becomes all things to all men, in order to blend them into one in Christ. Towards the end of the ninth chapter, he becomes a Gentile to the Gentiles, and evolves lessons for them from their own Isthmian Games. In the first verse of the tenth chapter, he comprehends both Jews and Gentiles in the one word, " brethren," and gives the Gentiles a share in the Jewish fathers. And, finally, he turns to the Jewish Scriptures, and proceeds to teach the whole church from them.

In the expression, "all our fathers," we may detect a reference to the preceding words, " Know ye not that they which run in a race run all, but one receiveth the prize." For all those fathers left Egypt, and started for the goal, yet only two out of the great multitude, Joshua and Caleb, possessed the Kingdom. An awful warning for us, and a confirmation of the Lord's saying —" Many are called, but few chosen."

Yet again, all these fathers went through an experience answering to baptism. They passed between the watery walls of the Red Sea and underneath the cloud ; and so, being completely immersed in cloud and sea, they were buried with Moses by baptism, and emerged with him on the other shore. And, just as the believer is separated by baptism from his former life, so they, by passing through the Red Sea, made its returning waters an insurmountable barrier between themselves and the land of bondage, so that the Egyptians, whom they had seen that day, they saw no more for ever.

[1] Rom. xi. 17, 18.

But not only were the fathers baptized into their own covenant: they were also sustained by supernatural food. In the journey from Egypt to Canaan they had to pass through a wilderness, in which they must have perished from hunger, had not God sent them angels' food from heaven; or died of thirst, unless He had, on two occasions, caused water to issue for them from a dry rock. And these supplies of manna and water correspond to the bread and wine of the Lord's Supper, which are figures of the Lord's broken Body and Blood, of the spiritual food whereby we are kept in spiritual life as we pass on, through the wilderness of this world, to our own Promised Land of Rest.

Here, however, there is an apparent difficulty. For what meaning can we give to the word " spiritual " in its application to the manna and the water, each of which gifts was, without doubt, material in itself? The difficulty will be obviated if we take the adjective in the sense of " created by the Spirit's power," " supernatural." This will be very near to its usual meaning; for is not a similar creative power indicated by the expression " born of the Spirit ": [1] or by the verse, " If any man be in Christ Jesus, there is a new creation." [2]

Indeed, the creative energy of the Spirit seems to be mentioned at the very beginning of the Bible: for, in the second verse of Genesis, it is said, that " the Spirit of God moved," or, rather, " brooded," " upon the face of the waters." Also in the thirty-sixth Psalm;—

" By the Word of the Lord were the heavens made,
And all the host of them by the Spirit of His
      mouth."

[1] John iii. 8.   [2] 2 Cor. v. 17.

A further illustration may be obtained from the fourth chapter of the Epistle to the Galatians, in which Ishmael and Isaac are contrasted as the son "born after the flesh" and the son "born after the Spirit"—the birth of the former having occurred in the ordinary course of nature, while that of the latter was brought about by the power of the Divine Spirit, in circumstances which rendered nature impotent.

But Paul's explanation of the miraculous nature of the water presents another difficulty. He says, that the water was spiritual, because it came from a spiritual Rock Which followed the Israelites in their journeyings, and Which was the Christ, or the Messiah. It is, therefore, clear that he is not alluding to the material rock from which the water gushed; for that was not spiritual. Nor could we for a moment accept the Rabbinical fable, that the rock rolled after the Israelites whithersoever they went, or allow that Paul would have argued from so grotesque a story. To us it seems evident, that the two epithets "spiritual" and "following," together with the absence of the definite article, point to something quite different.

In the account of the miracle at Rephidim, the Lord says to Moses;—

> "I will stand before thee there upon the rock in Horeb; and thou shalt smite the rock, and there shall come water out of it." [1]

It is, probably, to this Presence upon the rock that Paul alludes; and we must remember, that it was the Second Person of the Trinity, the Christ or the Messiah Himself, Who dealt with Israel in the wilderness. For it was not the mere rock of stone, from which the water actually gushed, that supplied the wants of Israel;

[1] Exod. xvii. 6.

but He That, all unperceived, stood upon it, causing it by His spiritual power to satisfy the needs of His people, and able, also, to accompany them as an Omnipotent Protector and Helper whithersoever they might go.

And it seems probable, that this truth was declared to the Israelites by Moses, and that we may thus account for the fact, that, in after time, "the Rock" became a frequent appellation of Jehovah. In the Song of Moses, we find the following instances ;— "The Rock, His work is perfect:" "And lightly esteemed the Rock of his salvation:" "Of the Rock That begat thee thou art unmindful:" "Except their Rock had sold them, and the Lord had delivered them up:" "For their rock is not as our Rock." [1]

Such, then, were the privileges of the fathers, all of whom were blessed with these seals of God's favour. Yet with the most of them He was not well pleased: unlike His Beloved Son, they were disobedient, and so fell in the wilderness. They had been brought through the Red Sea with a mighty hand and with an outstretched arm ; they had been fed with supernatural food, and supplied with supernatural water ; and yet, with only two exceptions, they perished by the way, and never possessed the Good Land. Not even Moses himself, nor Aaron the High Priest, was suffered to pass the streams of Jordan : the punishment of disobedience was inflicted inexorably and impartially.

Let us, however, be careful that we take a true view of the case. The fathers who died in the wilderness were not, on that account, necessarily "lost," in our sense of the term. With the exception of those who were destroyed in the act of rebellion, time for repent-

[1] Deut. xxxii. 4, 15, 18, 30, 31.

ance was usually accorded to them, and pardon for sin might be obtained ; but not the restoration of their hope : they could not now taste the milk and honey of Palestine, or be set over the kings of the earth : they had lost the Land, and the sovereignty of the world.

"These things," the Apostle adds, with a reference to the judgments implied in the word "overthrown," "became figures of us, to the intent that we should not lust after evil things, as they also lusted." That is, the Lord caused these things to be recorded, in order that believers of this age might know what manner of treatment to expect, if they should provoke Him as Israel had done. For, in that case, they, too, should lose the Kingdom proposed to them.

Paul then mentions four of the evil things of Israel, four special sins, the commission of which was soon followed by the appalling cry—"There is wrath gone out from the Lord !" These sins were idolatry, fornication, tempting God, and murmuring against Him.[1]

The first of them is illustrated by the sin of the golden calf. The people themselves would not have called this idolatry ; for they intended the creature to represent the Creator, the Lord God That brought them out of the land of Egypt ! But of what avail was their intention ? Only a few days had passed by since the awful voice of God, pealing from the summit of the burning and quivering mountain, had commanded that no image of any form " that is in heaven above, or that is in the earth beneath, or that is in the water under the earth," should be made for worship. And the Word of God, and not our own ideas and opinions, is the law by which we must be judged.

[1] See I Cor. x. 7-10.

Moreover, the utter folly and profanity of the Israelites, in representing the Almighty Jehovah under the similitude of an ox that eateth grass, showed clearly enough from what source their inspiration had come; while, as usually happens in such cases, the manner of worship, also, was Pagan. In the presence of their golden calf, "the people sat down to eat and to drink, and rose up to play." Now, the expression "to play" refers to the lascivious dances which were customary at Pagan festivals, and were deliberately intended to rouse the passions, and to stimulate the demon-worshippers, already inflamed with food and wine, to the abominable acts which were to follow.

Israel, then, would quickly have gone on to the second sin, also, had not God interfered, and sent down Moses as a swift avenger. Soon three thousand dead bodies were defiling the camp, and the whole congregation was crouching in terror of instant destruction.

The warning, however, produced but a temporary effect. Some while afterwards, men of Israel dared to present themselves at the idol-feasts of the Midianites, and ate and drank and played with the daughters of the Heathen. This time the Lord did not interpose until the second sin had been perpetrated. Then the dread pestilence was sent forth from Him, and the camp was filled with the cries of the smitten and the moans of the dying. Three-and-twenty thousand persons perished in one day; nor did the fierce anger of the Lord cease, until the offending chiefs of the people had been hanged up before Him, in the face of the sun.

The third sin, the tempting of God, is that to which Satan vainly urged the Lord Jesus, when he bade Him cast Himself down from the pediment of the Temple, and expect the angels of God to convey Him in safety to the court below. It is, as Godet puts it, to demand, that, if God be God, "He will manifest His power, either by delivering us from a danger, to which we have rashly exposed ourselves ; or by extricating us from a difficulty, which we have wilfully created while reckoning upon His aid ; or by pardoning a sin, for which we had beforehand discounted His grace."

This is one of the worst of sins, and many a time did the Israelites commit it in the wilderness, until, at last, God swore in His wrath that they should not enter into His rest. The particular instance to which Paul here alludes occurred towards the close of their wanderings, just after the second miraculous production of water, which took place at Kadesh. They were near to the borders of Canaan, but the king of Edom had refused to allow them a passage through his land. In consequence of this hostile attitude, they were compelled to march round the frontiers of his realm, and the soul of the people was discouraged because of the way.

Forgetful, as usual, of all the great things which the Lord had done for them, and even of their recent deliverance at Kadesh, they began to tempt when they should have entreated, and actually dared to speak against God, and against His servant Moses, with the sullen cry ;—

"Wherefore have ye brought us up out of Egypt to die in the wilderness ? For there is no bread, and there is no water ; and our soul loatheth this light bread."[1]

Then it was once again necessary that judgment should take the place of mercy : fiery serpents swarmed into the camp, and much people of Israel died.

[1] Num. xxi. 5.

Lastly, murmuring is a sin to which the Israelites were ever prone, and from which nothing seemed able to deter them. Here Paul, probably, alludes to what happened after Korah and his company had been consumed by fire from the Lord, and Dathan and Abiram, together with all their families, had been engulfed in the earth. For the people, though abjectly cowed at the moment, had recovered themselves by the morrow, and began to murmur against Moses for having "killed the people of the Lord." But, in the midst of their blasphemies, they were appalled by the sudden appearance of the Glory. In a moment the Destroyer was upon them, he who had slain the firstborn of Egypt ; and, before Aaron could prepare his censer to stand between the dead and the living, fourteen thousand and seven hundred of the people had perished.[1]

But what have these ancient events to do with us ? They were recorded for our admonition, in this last of the ages before the coming of the King.[2] For believers, also, are prone to the same sins as Israel ; and God is not changed, but still visits such transgressions with severe penalties, even as He did in the days of old. Disobedient Israelites lost the Promised Land ; and believers of this age, who follow in their steps, will come short of the First Resurrection and the Kingdom.

And, if we turn to the specified sins, is not idolatry, in its most undisguised form, reappearing among ourselves, even in this enlightened country ? What mean those shops filled with images—crosses, crucifixes, Madonnas, and saints ? Why is the interior of our churches so utterly changed from the simplicity of fifty or sixty years ago ? What has that altar and wafer-throne to do with the worship of the Lord Jesus

[1] Num. xvi. 41–50.   [2] I Cor. x. 11.

as commanded in the New Testament, the only Divine authority in the world on such matters? Is it urged that the wafer represents the Presence of the Lord Jesus, and that He is adored through it? So said the Israelites of the calf: but the Apostle calls them idolaters, and God smote many among them for their sin, and threatened the whole congregation with death.

The Israelites, moreover, had not only worshipped their idol: they had also commenced the ordinary Pagan dances. And, as is well known, some of the dances indulged in by modern society are lineal descendants of those ancient and lascivious performances. Nor would it be difficult to find men who could readily explain the connection between such amusements and fornication. Yet many believers sanction them by their presence, if they do not actually take part in them. How can such persons expect even to see the Kingdom of the Heavens!

And, besides all this, the Christian law extends to our words and thoughts; so that anything which leads our mind from God is reckoned by Him as idolatry, whether it be covetousness or some other of the countless forms of worldliness.

But, as soon as any kind of idolatry has turned us from God, we are close upon the confines of the second sin, and know not into what abyss of abominations we may fall. For men who do not like to retain Him in their knowledge are given up to a reprobate mind, to do those things which are not fitting, and even to unnatural feelings, as Paul has shown in the first chapter of his Epistle to the Romans. And, as the Lord Himself explains, even where no crime is actually perpetrated, if we cherish an unclean thought in our hearts, God regards us as adulterers, fornicators, or abominable, according as the case may be.

As regards the third sin, is it not a matter of frequent experience to hear "Christians" expressing wonder, sometimes one might almost say annoyance, or even exasperation, because God does not immediately hear their spasmodic prayers, and work deliverance for them from some trouble into which they never ought to have fallen? And, perhaps, these complainers may be persons who rarely if ever pray—but, at best, only *say prayers* in a perfunctory manner—unless they are in bitter distress, or are eagerly lusting after something earthly. Nay, it is by no means uncommon to find believers deliberately walking into temptation, or, for their own convenience or worldly benefit, taking a step which they know to be contrary to God's will, and stifling conscience with the sentiment, that one can be kept in any circumstances. All such conduct is a direct tempting of God.

The fourth sin is, alas! only too prevalent among believers of our time. How many murmurings and words of discontent may be heard on all sides of us! And are there none within us? Yet, from whomsoever they may proceed, such expressions reveal a terrible fact, namely, that those who give utterance to them are seeking their own glory at the expense of their Lord's. For Him they are representing, more or less, as unjust or even cruel, and themselves as undeserving sufferers. Moreover, such complaints disclose another secret, that the murmurers have no adequate consciousness of their own sin: for, otherwise, they had not dared to complain of any circumstances in which they could have been placed; nor would they have lacked meekness to take the lowest room. But if they do not realise the fathomless depths of their own iniquity, then Christ cannot be precious to them : they know nothing of that overwhelming sense of His love which makes every service that can be rendered to Him sweet, whether it be the highest or the lowest, whether it be done in conditions of honour or of dishonour, of pleasure or of pain.

If, then, we desire entrance into the Kingdom of the Heavens, we must put away from us the four great sins, idolatry, fornication, the tempting of God, and all murmuring against Him ; and that, not only in their grosser manifestations, but also in their most spiritual and insinuating forms.

IX

THE REST THAT REMAINETH FOR THE HOUSEHOLD OF GOD

HEB. iii. and iv.

THERE is yet another among the many passages on this momentous subject which we must not pass by— that which is contained in the third and fourth chapters of the Epistle to the Hebrews. To discuss it verse by verse, as we would fain do, would occupy more space than our limits will afford. We must, therefore, ask the reader to study the two chapters carefully, in the Revised Version, before he peruses our explanatory sketch of their contents.

The Epistle was written to Hebrews who believed in the Old Testament ; it was, therefore, necessary to prove to them, that Christ as the Son of God is greater than all other celestial messengers. Now, the Israelitish dispensation was ordained through angels by the hand

5

of a mediator, that is, of Moses. Hence the Lord Jesus had to be exhibited as far above both the angels and Moses.

Accordingly, His superiority to angels is demonstrated in the first chapter; while, in the second, there is an answer to the very natural question, Why, then, was He made lower than the angels?

But the answer involves a revelation of the Lord Jesus as sent of God to be the Leader and High Priest of His people. And to this Paul refers when, in the third chapter, he proceeds to show that the Lord is also greater than Moses, the human lawgiver. For he calls upon the Hebrews as holy brethren in Christ, and partakers, no longer of the earthly, but of the heavenly calling, to fix their attention upon the perfect fidelity of this Envoy from God and High Priest, this wondrous Being Who united in Himself the functions of Moses and Aaron.

They are to notice, that He is faithful to Him That appointed Him; even as Moses was in all God's House,[1] that is, among the people through whom God was then acting upon the world: for these are His House upon earth. And they must carefully consider this, in order to perceive why the Lord Jesus has been thought worthy of far more honour than Moses. For, while His faithfulness was perfect like that of the Lawgiver, His authority was greater, inasmuch as He was the Founder of the House over which Moses presided simply as an exalted member of it. For every house is founded by some one; but it is God That has founded all things, and Christ, as His Son, stands in the same relation to them as His Father

---

[1] Or, "household." οἶκος is often used in this sense, as in Acts xvi. 31.

does. Thus Moses was faithful in all God's House as a servant, to bear witness to the things which should afterwards be spoken; but Christ is over the whole House as a Son, wielding all the authority of His Father.

Now, the House, or Household, itself is, doubtless, the institution of God upon the earth, the aggregate body of those through whom He acts, from time to time, upon mankind. And in the days of Moses this body was formed out of the Twelve Tribes of Israel, which are destined to rule over the earth in the coming age. But now it is composed of true believers in the Lord Jesus, whose calling is to be with Him in the supercelestial places.

Of the relation between these two classes, Paul gives us a clear idea when he represents Israel as an olive-tree, the branches of which were broken off in order that those of a wild olive might be engrafted upon it.[1] In this latter condition, the tree corresponds to the churches upon earth in the present age, deriving all their life, as they do, from a Hebrew stock. "For," even to us, "salvation is from the Jews":[2] the Lord Himself and His Apostles were Hebrews, and all the Scriptures were given through the medium of the same people. But, as Paul hints, the wild branches will, in their turn, be broken off, and the natural branches restored.[3] Soon the Lord will have gathered to Himself all the true members that constitute His House, the now invisible Church, from among the churches below; and then He will reject what is left, spuing the Laodicean assemblies out of His mouth, and resuming His dealings with the Twelve Tribes, which, from that time, will be once more the House of God upon earth.

[1] Rom. xi. 17, 18.　　[2] John iv. 22.　　[3] Rom. xi. 19–24.

Perhaps the plainest definition of the House of God, as it is at present, is that which is given by Paul after he has told the Corinthians that they are God's building ; "[1] —

"Know ye not that ye are a Temple of God, and that the Spirit of God dwelleth in you? If any man defile the Temple of God, him shall God destroy ; for the Temple of God is holy, which Temple ye are."[2]

And again ;—

"For we are a Temple of the Living God : even as God said, I will dwell in them, and walk in them ; and I will be their God, and they shall be My people."[3]

But there is an important passage in the First Epistle to Timothy, in which the House of God is identified with the Church, and another of its features, which is, of course, but a consequence of the indwelling of God, is set forth ;—

"These things write I unto thee . . . that thou mayest know how men ought to behave themselves in the House of God, which is the Church of the Living God, a pillar and ground of the truth. And confessedly great is the Mystery of Godliness, He Who was manifested in flesh, justified in spirit, seen of angels, preached among nations, believed on in the world, received up in glory."[4]

Here, then, the House of God, in the present age, is identified with the Church of the Living God. And the epithet "living" points to the difference between the true and only God and Apollo, Diana, the Madonna, the saints, and any other idols, pictures, or fetiches ; even as Paul says to the Thessalonians ;—

[1] 1 Cor. iii. 9.
[2] 1 Cor. iii. 16, 17.
[3] 2 Cor. vi. 16.
[4] 1 Tim. iii. 14–16.

"Ye turned unto God from idols, to serve the Living and True God, and to wait for His Son from the heavens." [1]

The House, or Church, is said to be "a pillar and ground," or "foundation," of the truth. Now the pillar of a structure supports its roof; while the base, or foundation, sustains the pillar. Thus, since the Church is said to be both pillar and foundation, we must understand her to be represented as the sole upholder of truth upon the earth.

But here many have found a difficulty; for, as they have justly remarked, the Truth needs no support, but, on the contrary, must sustain the Church, and is, in fact, the Lord Jesus Himself. This is indisputable, but we must distinguish between the absolute Truth and truth as revealed and acknowledged in the world. It is the latter which is here meant; and that does require the Church as an agency upon earth to preserve and to propagate it, even as the Lord Jesus declared to her earliest members,

"Ye shall be my witnesses;" [2]

and so gave them this very commission.

We must, however, be careful not to fall into the pit digged for us by certain zealous ecclesiastics. The passage is concerned exclusively with the real and invisible Church, not with any human hierarchy. There is here no monopoly granted to some visible society, no infallibility conferred upon any organized community which chooses to call itself the Church of Christ. On the contrary, in this passage we are provided with a sure test, whereby, as with the touch of Ithuriel's spear, we may compel any pretending body to reveal its true shape, and its real origin. For only if a community

[1] I Thess. i. 9, 10.   [2] Acts i. 8.

supports, exclusively and jealously, the truth that comes directly from the Word of God, can it be what the Bible means by a church of Christ.

Any society, then, which would be regarded as such, must not base its claims upon Apostolical Succession, even if there were such a thing, or upon a display of holy living according to popular conceptions, or upon an apparent power of "doing good." For all these things Satan causes his own people both to teach and to do, whenever it suits his purpose to transform himself into an angel of light. Simple Scriptural doctrine and Apostolical teaching are the only reliable credentials for a church of Christ; and even these will not suffice, unless the life and conduct of its members correspond to their doctrine, and they walk in love.

Let us, therefore, not be deceived, but always apply the test which God has given; and apply it, not only to corporate bodies, but also to ourselves as individuals; that we may know whether we are members of the real and, at present, invisible Church, or whether we are still to be reckoned among mere professors and hypocrites whose hope shall perish.

Having thus set forth the real Church as the up-holder of the truth in the world, the Apostle introduces the great Mystery of Godliness, evidently with the view of suggesting that the latter is the all-important centre of the truth which it is the Church's duty to preserve and proclaim. No one, he intimates, to whom the Mystery has been communicated, can possibly doubt its greatness. And he refers to it again in the ninth verse of this chapter, where he says, that a deacon must hold " the Mystery of the Faith in a pure conscience."

It is called the Mystery of Godliness, because its

apprehension is the root of all godliness, and the power whereby we are drawn nearer to God, and led to follow after that holiness without which no man can see Him. Consequently, in the latter days, the departure from faith in it is that which will bring about the apostasy described in the opening verses of the fourth chapter.

The Mystery, as we are presently shown, is the Lord Jesus Himself—His manifestation in flesh, His work for us, and His return, by the path of resurrection, to glory. It is through the effect of these wondrous truths, wrought in us by the Holy Spirit, that our sanctification is carried on ; so that God may presently bring us whither our Saviour Christ has gone before.

But we have allowed ourselves to be drawn into a digression, and must return to our subject. Since the Jews are now rejected, the members of the true Church, who are from time to time upon the earth, form the House during the present age ; but a solemn warning follows. We really belong to this body only " if we hold fast our confidence and ground of rejoicing in the hope firm unto the end." [1] It is impossible to ignore this clause. Our membership does not simply depend upon the fact that we have believed but is conditioned upon the retention of our confidence and ground of rejoicing to the end. For these blessings, if our faith be real, were given to us when we believed, according to the glowing words of Paul ;—

"Therefore, being justified by faith, we have peace with God through our Lord Jesus Christ, through Whom also we have had our access by faith into this grace wherein we stand, and rejoice in hope of the glory of God." [2]

[1] Heb. iii. 6.   [2] Rom. v. 1, 2.

Here the verb "rejoice" is the root of the substantive rendered "ground of rejoicing" in the verse which we are considering.

But may we entertain a reasonable hope that the fulfilment of this condition is possible? Not if we are minded to walk in our own wisdom and strength ; but, if we rest our confidence upon that grace, or favour, of God to which the Lord Jesus has given us access, then we certainly may rejoice in hope. For what is there that can hinder the accomplishment of our desire, when He has said,

"Lo, I am with you alway, even unto the end of the age" ; [1]

when He has promised,

"My grace is sufficient for thee ; for My strength is made perfect in weakness" ; [2]

when His Apostle comforts us with the words,

"Faithful is He that calleth you, Who will also do it?" [3]

And what is the hope that we must hold fast to the end? It can only be the "one hope" of the heavenly calling,[4] "the hope of glory," [5] "the hope of the glory of God," [6] "the blessed hope and appearing of the glory of our great God and Saviour Jesus Christ," [7] "Who shall fashion anew the body of our humiliation, that it may be conformed to the Body of His Glory." [8]

Unless this hope be found in us, fresh and vigorous, when the Lord calls us, we shall not be counted worthy to stand with the Church of the Firstborn, and shall lose the reward of the Kingdom. For this, and this alone, can testify that we are prepared for glory, because

---

[1] Matt. xxviii. 20.   [4] Eph. iv. 4.   [7] Titus ii. 13.
[2] 2 Cor. xii. 9.   [5] Col. i. 27.   [8] Phil. iii. 21.
[3] 1 Thess. v. 24.   [6] Rom. v. 2.

it proves, that we have learnt the lesson of sublunary life, have detected the vanity of all that is earthly, and have no hope or expectation, save in the Lord our Creator and Redeemer.

In the next verse, Paul begins to illustrate, from God's dealings with Israel, the danger of losing his reward to which the believer is exposed.

" Wherefore, even as the Holy Ghost saith,
To-day, if ye shall hear His voice,
Harden not your hearts as in the Provocation,
As in the day of Temptation in the wilderness,
Wherewith your fathers tempted Me by proving Me,
And saw My works forty years.
Wherefore, I was displeased with this generation,
And said, They do alway err in their hearts :
But they did not know My ways ;
As I sware in My wrath,
They shall not enter into My rest." [1]

To understand these words from the Ninety-fifth Psalm, it will, first, be necessary to enquire into their historical allusions.

Now, in the Hebrew original of the passage, instead of the expressions " in the Provocation," and " in the day of Temptation," we find " at Meribah," and " in the day of Massah." The change was made by the Septuagint translators, from whom Paul quotes, and who, doubtless, intended to give the meaning of the Hebrew names in the words " Provocation " and " Temptation." For it will be remembered that Kadesh and Rephidim were significantly changed to Meribah and Massah, respectively ; because it was in these two places that the Israelites, when distressed for water, strove with and tempted the Lord, daring to insult Him

[1] Psa. xcv. 7-11.

with their murmurings, as if He were unable to supply their needs.

The first mentioned of the two provocations took place in the fortieth year of their wanderings ;[1] but it was no result of hope deferred ; for the other instance happened in the first year after their departure from Egypt.[2] Thus the identical results of these two trials of faith by means of water-famines, one at the beginning and the other at the end of their sojourn in the wilderness, prove that the same obdurate unbelief was found in them throughout the whole period.

And, probably, it was to set forth this fact that Moses, when pronouncing his farewell blessings upon the Tribes, said in regard to Levi ;—

"Thy Thummim and Thy Urim are with Thy godly one,

Whom Thou didst prove at Massah,[3]

With whom Thou didst strive at the waters of Meribah."

But the special sin of the Israelites, which caused the Lord to swear in His wrath that they should not enter into His rest, was their murmuring and disobedience after they had heard the evil report of ten of the spies. For the whole congregation believed it, and began to speak against the Lord, declaring that He had brought them to the borders of Canaan to destroy them, and to deliver their wives and children as a prey into the hands of the Canaanites. They refused to go up and possess the Land, and even proposed to elect a captain who should lead them back to Egypt.[4]

What wonder that God was wroth with these ungrateful and insolent sinners ! Had it not been for

[1] Num. xx. 1-13.
[2] Exod. xvii. 1-7.
[3] Deut. xxxiii. 8.
[4] Num. xiv. 1-4.

the intercession of Moses, He would have destroyed them in a moment; but, yielding to the entreaties of His faithful servant, He said ;—

"I have pardoned, according to thy word. But as truly as I live, and as all the earth shall be filled with the glory of the Lord, because all those men which have seen My Glory, and My signs, which I wrought in Egypt and in the wilderness, yet have tempted Me these ten times, and have not hearkened unto My voice; surely they shall not see the Land which I sware unto their fathers, neither shall any of them that despised Me see it."[1]

Only, Joshua and Caleb were exempted from this sentence ; and, after the Lord had pronounced it, He commanded ;—

"To-morrow turn ye, and get you into the wilderness by the way to the Red Sea."[2]

As we have already remarked, many of those who fell in the wilderness may have availed themselves of the time graciously given for repentance, and so have obtained mercy and hope in resurrection. But, from the moment in which God uttered their doom, they had lost, irrecoverably for that age, the Land and the sovereignty over the world which had been promised to them ; for such was the prize of their calling, the rest which God had prepared for them, even as the Heavenly Kingdom is our hope.

We can now see what the Spirit in David[3] intended to convey by the Ninety-fifth Psalm. It is a solemn warning to the Israelites of David's time to learn

[1] Num. xiv. 20-23.
[2] Num. xiv. 25.
[3] That David was the writer of the Ninety-fifth Psalm, we learn from Heb. iv. 7.

wisdom from the punishment of their fathers in the wilderness. "To-day, if ye shall hear His voice," if He should chance to speak to you to-day, beware, and do not let your hearts become hardened in disobedience, as they did. Nine times they tempted Him, and nine times He suffered His anger to pass by; but they sinned the tenth time, and the end of His forbearance had come. The inexorable word was uttered : there was now no fair land of rest for them : they must get them back into the wilderness to die.

This direful event happened in the second year after they had come out of Egypt. And, in the fortieth year, the men of the younger generation, also, were found tempting the Lord in Kadesh, at the waters of Meribah. They, too, were stiffnecked and rebellious, like their fathers. And so, they caused the Lord to say of their whole race, that they were a people who erred in their hearts, and understood not His ways, even as He had judged them to be, when, thirty-eight years earlier, He had sworn that their fathers should not enter into His rest. He would not again forbid them to go up and possess the Land, but they should find no rest there. And so, twice again, or ever they had set foot within the borders of Canaan, He signified by the mouth of Moses, that He would be compelled to cast them out of their good Land, and to scatter them among all nations for many long centuries, before He could settle them permanently in Millennial rest.

In the burning words that follow, Paul applies the teaching of the Ninety-fifth Psalm to the Hebrew Christians of his own times, and through them to all believers of the present age.

"Take heed, brethren, lest haply there shall be in any one of you an evil heart of unbelief, in falling away from the Living God: but exhort one another day by day, so long as it is called to-day; lest any one of you be hardened by the deceitfulness of sin. For we have become fellows[1] of Christ, if we hold fast the beginning of our confidence firm unto the end; while it is being said,

To-day, if ye shall hear His voice,

Harden not your hearts, as in the provocation."

Now, it must be carefully noticed, that in these verses Paul is addressing "brethren" in Christ, all of whom had obtained salvation, because they had believed in the Lord Jesus. It is to the saved that he says;—See to it, lest there should be in any one of you an evil heart of unbelief, in falling away from the Living God, lest any one of you should be hardened by the deceitfulness of sin. To such falls, then, the saved are liable; and, if we cease to watch and pray, the spirits of evil will sometimes bring them about almost imperceptibly. An unbelieving heart will often lead a man in its own way without causing him any anxious care. But he is on a down-gradient, and That from Which he is gliding so smoothly is the Living God, the only Source of life and light.

Sin may, however, for a while, be difficult even to detect: it is, perhaps, no more than a waning of the first love, a little carelessness in duty, a somewhat declining zeal in prayer: nevertheless, it ceaselessly carries on the process of heart-hardening, and will soon grow worse and worse, yet without causing uneasiness to its victim, who is becoming correspondingly callous.

[1] Not "partakers of," but "companions of." The word is the same as that which is used in chap. i. 9;—"Therefore God, Thy God, hath anointed Thee with the oil of gladness above Thy fellows."

As a precaution against such depths of Satan, Paul urges that believers should exhort one another daily so long as their probation lasts, that they who fear the Lord should speak often one to another. But by how many ordinary believers is this command obeyed ?

What result will follow if his admonition be neglected, Paul signifies in a very striking though indirect manner. He reminds us that we have become fellows, or companions, of Christ on a condition, that is to say, " if we hold the beginning of our confidence firm unto the end." But, if our love waxes cold, and unbelief commences its work of ruin, the close connection with our Lord will be severed, the unfruitful branch will be removed from the Heavenly Vine. We cannot, indeed, be deprived of eternal life, because that is the gift of God in His Son ; but we shall not enjoy it until the Last Day, and shall lose the honour and glory of being the Lord's companions and assessors during His coming reign. Very strongly has Paul set forth the condition of the promise in another passage, where he says ;—

" And if children, then heirs ; heirs of God, and joint heirs with Christ ; if so be that we suffer with Him, that we may be also glorified with Him."[1]

In the remaining verses of the third chapter, the absolutely essential condition of obedience is pressed home by further reference to the case of the Israelites.

" For who, when they had heard, did provoke ? Nay, did not all they that came out of Egypt by Moses ? "

There were, indeed, two exceptions ; but this number is so insignificant, as compared with the whole

[1] Rom. viii. 17.

remainder of the people, that Paul does not here stop to notice it. Only two of the fathers escaped, and all the others fell! How fearful a lesson for those who think, that, if they sin with a multitude, their transgressions may pass unnoticed.

"And with whom was He displeased forty years? Was it not with them that sinned, whose carcases fell in the wilderness? And to whom sware He that they should not enter into His rest, but to them that were disobedient?[1] And we see, that they were not able to enter in because of unbelief."[2]

Here we may observe, that sin in those who have believed is punished by God with the greatest severity; for it is the sin of treason and rebellion. It was the disobedience of Israel which caused Him to swear that they should not enter into His rest. And disobedience sprang from, and was nourished by, lack of confidence in His power—an irrational unbelief, contrary to all the experiences of the people before whose eyes He had shown so many and great signs of His might, an unbelief based, not upon conviction, but upon wilfulness of disposition and alienated desires.

Again, however, Paul reminds us, that this sad history is recorded as a warning to ourselves, because God's dealings with us are precisely analogous to His treatment of Israel;—

"Let us fear, therefore, lest haply, a promise being left of entering into His rest, any one of you should seem to have come short of it. For, indeed, we have had good tidings preached to us, even as also they; but the word of the report did not

---

[1] The A.V. has, "to them that believed not." This is a gross mistake.

[2] "Because of faithlessness," would, perhaps, be better.

profit them, because it was not incorporated by faith in them that heard."[1]

Here, as so often, believers are expected to fear. Many think, that, when they have once received life from the Lord Jesus, all that is necessary has been done. But, we repeat yet again, they are entirely mistaken: they have come only to the beginning, not to the end, of the struggle. Up to the time of conversion, all was done for them: but, by accepting the gift of God, they have entered the lists for the race and the battle, and have, in very truth, need of His grace to enable them to overcome.

No promise of entering into God's rest is left in express terms; but Paul presently shows us how we may infer it. And our great business is to take care that none of us should seem to have come short of it.

There is much delicacy in the use of the verb "should seem," which, probably, conveys a hint, that we have no power to pronounce judgment upon another: that must be left for the Righteous Judge. Nevertheless, if any man should have manifestly lost the desire for spiritual things, or should begin to walk carelessly before his God, there would be grave reason for anxiety on the part of his fellows.

We might, however, prefer the rendering "should think that he has come short of it." The meaning would then be, Lest any of you, in reviewing his life, and in noting how often the carelessness that springs from want of faith has led him into sin, should lose the power of the promise, become demoralised, and so fall into despondency.

For every promise of God, if received in faith,

[1] Heb. iv. 1, 2.

brings with itself a strength for the recipient, sufficient to sustain him until the time of its fulfilment. But, if faith wanes, the promise also begins to fade from our view: its certainty is gone, and the power which God bestowed with it is broken. The faithless one becomes spiritually nerveless, and his hope is obscured by the dark-gathering clouds of doubt.

To be living in godly fear is, therefore, the only safe condition for us: we must take heed lest we fall, even when we think that we stand, and ceaselessly pray, that the Great Saviour, according to His promise, will never leave us nor forsake us.

"For, indeed, we have had good tidings preached to us, even as also they: but the word of the report did not profit them, because it was not incorporated by faith in them that heard."

Our case, then, is exactly analogous to that of the Israelites: a heavenly rest has been offered to us, just as the Land of Canaan was to them. But, when the twelve spies returned and delivered their report, it is said of the people ;—

"Yea, they despised the pleasant land :
They believed not His word ;
But murmured in their tents,
And hearkened not unto the voice of the Lord.
Therefore, He sware unto them,
That He would overthrow them in the wilderness :
And that He would overthrow their seed among the nations,
And scatter them in the lands." [1]

They were not cheered and encouraged by the description of the pleasant land, because they did not believe that God was able to give it into their hands.

[1] Psa. cvi. 24–27.

6

Thus the word of the report did not profit them, since there was no faith in them to make the promise effectual.

For, as Hedinger puts it, faith is here represented as that which unites and combines together the Divine Word and those that hear it ; in some such way as the chyle in the human system serves to combine the nourishing particles of the food with the sustaining principle of natural life, the blood.

"For we which have believed are entering into the rest ; even as He hath said,

As I sware in My wrath

They shall not enter into My rest :

although the works were finished from the foundation of the world.

For He hath said somewhere of the Seventh Day on this wise, And God rested on the Seventh Day from all His works.

And in this place again,

They shall not enter into My rest.

Seeing, therefore, it remaineth that some should enter thereinto, and they to whom the good tidings were before preached failed to enter in because of disobedience,

He again defineth a certain day, saying in David, after so long a time, To-day, as it hath been before said,

To-day, if ye shall hear His voice,

Harden not your hearts.

For if Joshua had given them rest, He would not have spoken afterward of another day.

There remaineth, therefore, a Sabbath-rest for the people of God."

If, then, we have attained to faith, the immediate consequence of the promise to us is, that we are even now entering into the rest; for we have actually commenced the journey that leads to it, even as Israel reached Canaan by the passage through the wilderness. We have been delivered from death, in the spiritual Egypt, by the Blood of the Lamb: we have subsequently manifested our obedience by causing ourselves to be baptized into Christ's death, just as the Israelites were all baptized into Moses in the cloud and in the sea; and now we are crossing the desert that lies between us and the rest, and every day's march is bringing us nearer to the desired home.

The first clause of the third verse should not be rendered, " We who have believed do enter into rest," but "are entering into the rest." And, as the context plainly indicates, the reference could not be, as some have suggested, to any rest for our souls which we may find in the present life; but is that of which God spoke when, in the time of Moses, He said ;—

" As I sware in My wrath,
They shall not enter into My rest."

And yet, so far as He was concerned, the works had been finished from the foundation of the world: He had even then made all things good.   And, in the second chapter of Genesis, we are told, that " He rested on the Seventh Day from all His work which He had made."   Thus He had both prepared the rest, and had Himself actually entered into it.

But His purpose was, that His people should share it with Him; and that purpose was delayed by the Fall.   Moreover, the ruin of the First Creation caused Him to resume His work, in order that He might undertake the Second.

And so it was, that, until the times of Moses, no one had been found ready to enter into the rest.

Then a special invitation was given to the sons of Israel, who were brought out of the Land of Bondage by a mighty hand and by a stretched-out arm. But, of these, the first generation failed to attain to it : nor could Joshua procure it for their children.

Since, then, it remained that some must enter into it—for, although the purposes of God may be delayed, they cannot be frustrated ; and since those who were first invited did not enter in, because of disobedience on their part, the invitation was renewed by the Spirit of God in the days of David ; but was not even then accepted. For the awful admonition remained un-heeded,

"To-day, if ye shall hear His voice,
Harden not your heart."

Men were still carnal, self-willed, and estranged from God, and were quite unable to respond to an impulse, or direction, of the Spirit whenever it might come to them.

And now the offer is made to us, a fact which proves that the rest, or, as it is now called, the Sabbath-keeping—for at this point the word is significantly changed—still remains for the people of God, that is, is still in the future.

For, although God's earlier work was finished in the Six Days, yet the goodness and perfection of creation were not at that time final, but were speedily marred by the Fall. Thus it was that God commenced a new creation, by which those who were subjected to it should attain to the destined and final end of their being, to a condition in which they should be fitted to enter into His eternal rest.

Now, it should be noticed, that, in the ninth verse, the substitution of the word "Sabbath-keeping" for "rest" is evidently intended to connect the latter with the Six Working Days of the New Creation. For "the rest" is the Millennium, or period of one thousand years, in which God will reward His faithful servants.

And, since we know the duration of "the rest," or Sabbath-keeping, we seem able, also, to determine the length of the Six Working Days of the New Creation, each of which must, it would appear, be of the same length as the period of Sabbath-keeping, that is to say, one thousand years. And it was, probably, for the purpose of making this Divine proportion clear to us that Peter was inspired to say ;—

"But, beloved, be not ignorant of this one thing, that one day is with the Lord as a thousand years, and a thousand years as one day."[1]

It is, therefore, not unlikely that the frequent introduction, or suggestion, of the word "day" in the passage before us[2] refers to the Days of the New Creation, each of them a thousand years in length. In this case, the day in which God spoke to Israel in the wilderness would be the Third Day of the New Creation, since it was in the world's third millennium. Similarly, the time of David would be in the Fourth Day: the Church-period, during which the rest is being offered to us, would comprise the Fifth and Sixth: and the Sabbath-keeping, or rest, would be the Seventh. And the same clue may, perhaps, enable us to interpret the difficult passage with which the sixth chapter of Hosea begins.

[1] 2 Peter iii. 8.
[2] We find, "To-day if ye shall hear"; "he would not have spoken afterward of another day"; and "a Sabbath-keeping," or Sabbath day.

Now, if this exposition be correct, the Sabbath-keeping will begin after the end of the six thousandth year from the Fall; and such a calculation is, apparently, the only one revealed to us which throws light upon the appointed length of the present age. Practically, however, it does not afford us any more definite information than we can deduce from a study of the signs of the end, as described by our Lord and His Apostles. For, since human chronology has become hopelessly confused, we can only arrive at an approximate conclusion as to the year of the world in which we are now living.

"For he that has entered into his rest, hath himself also rested from his works, as God did from His." [1]

The promised rest, then, is to be truly Sabbatical; for none can enter into it, save those who have ceased from their works, even as God did from His works on the Seventh Day. Now, in regard to this verse, we must not forget that the whole passage before us is concerned, not with mere salvation, which is assumed throughout, but with the reward for works done after salvation—with the prize, and not with the gift. In other words, we are here dealing with matters that pertain to sanctification, and not to justification.

The work, then, of the man who has been already saved is that to which Paul refers when he says;—

"Work out your own salvation with fear and trembling; for it is God That worketh in you both to will and to work, for His good pleasure." [2]

Here it is taken for granted that salvation has been obtained through faith in the Lord Jesus; it is the man's own, and he must work from it. He has been

[1] Heb. iv. 10.   [2] Phil. ii. 12, 13.

laid hold of by Christ—to use Paul's words in another place—and he must now strive to lay hold of that for which Christ laid hold of him at his conversion, that is, to attain to the First Resurrection.[1]

And the first work to this end which Paul points out to the Philippians, who were in like circumstances, is as follows ;—

" Do all things without murmurings and disputings ; that ye may be blameless and harmless, children of God without blemish in the midst of a crooked and perverse generation, among whom ye are seen as lights in the world, holding forth the Word of life." [2]

Is this the manner of our conversation ? Are we thus meek and gentle, doing quietly what love and duty dictate, and finding fault neither with God nor man ? Do we make it our chief business to teach others the Word of God, first by our lives and then by our words ; so that we are, to some extent at least, answering to our Lord's description of His disciples ;—

" Ye are the light of the world " ?

Unless we are thus living and walking, our sanctification cannot be progressing. And yet, if it be not completed by the hour of death, or the moment when all the members of the Lord's Body that are still left upon earth hear the summons, Come up hither ! we shall lose the Millennial glories ; and, while others are living and reigning with Christ for a thousand years, we shall have to remain disembodied, and in the place of the dead.

Is it not worth some inconvenience to avert such a loss ? Is it not worth a struggle, worth many labours

[1] Phil. iii. 12 ; see p. 42.   [2] Phil. ii. 14–16.

and pains, and much endurance of neglect and the slight of the world, if we may so become priests of God and of Christ and reign with Him? Can we not watch with our Lord one hour; that we may be with Him on that glorious Day, when He shall see of the travail of His soul, and rejoice—He, Who once, for our sakes, "was despised and rejected of men; a Man of sorrows, and acquainted with grief"?

Happy will the believer be who shall be approved of Him on that Day: with rejoicing will he stand before the King. For his sanctification will have been accomplished: the toil, the mourning, the pain, every kind of suffering, the ordeal of death, all the discipline that was found necessary to perfect the New Creation in him, will be as a forgotten dream, and sweet and eternal peace will have come at last!

"Let us, therefore, give diligence to enter into that rest, that no man fall after the same example of disobedience.

"For the Word of God is living, and active, and sharper than any two-edged sword, and piercing even to the dividing of soul and spirit, of both joints and marrow, and quick to discern the thoughts and intents of the heart.

"And there is no creature that is not manifest in His sight: but all things are naked and laid open before the eyes of Him with Whom we have to do."

Some such thoughts as we have just expressed make the Apostle once more urge believers to labour, to use all zeal, that they may enter into such a rest. For, if they lapse into carelessness and disobedience, and so grieve the Holy Spirit of God, the prize will suddenly be removed from their sight, and their fate will resemble that of the Israelites who were commanded to get them back into the wilderness, and who never saw the pleasant land.

For if we do come short of God's standard, there is no escape from justice. His Word, whereby we must be tried and jndged, is a living Word, even as its Author is a Living God. Instinct with His life, it is an active witness, ever presenting new aspects of truth to us just as they are needed ; so that we are without excuse.

Moreover, it is all-piercing, penetrating dividing and dissecting our whole being more sharply than any two-edged sword : nay, it reaches even to the separating of soul and spirit, as well as of the joints and marrow ; that is, of both our immaterial and our material parts ; and so exposes even our deepest and most hidden motives, and passes judgment upon the inmost thoughts and feelings of our hearts. For nothing can be concealed from Him Whose Word it is ; but all things are naked and laid open before the eyes of Him to Whom we must render account.

To some these words may, perhaps, seem little more than vague sentiment. But they are not to be so regarded : we shall find them a stern and inexorable truth when we stand before the Judgment-seat of Christ ; or, if not there, at least when we cower in the resplendent brightness of the Great White Throne. We may avoid the probing of the Word now, if we are sufficiently foolish to do so ; but, in the coming hour of judgment, we must submit to it.

Let us briefly consider but one instance of its piercing and dissecting power. In the twelfth chapter of Matthew's Gospel, the Lord thus sums up a terrible discourse ;—

" And I say unto you, that every idle word that

men shall speak, they shall give account thereof in the Day of Judgment.

" For by thy words thou shalt be justified, and by thy words thou shalt be condemned."[1]

Do we feel disposed to exclaim against such a revelation ; to cry, How can I check and control every chance thought that comes to my lips ? But the Word of God, which can penetrate and dissect our whole being, affirms that we are able so to do, and that the utterance of our mouth affords a logical ground upon which we can be judged. If, then, our opinion be different, we had better change it as soon as may be. There can be no greater madness than to spring wildly against the knowledge or the decree of the Almighty.

And, indeed, if we quietly examine the passage, and see how the Lord leads up to its awful conclusion, we shall scarcely feel able to offer an objection. For this is what He says ;—

" Either make the tree good, and its fruit good ; or make the tree corrupt, and its fruit corrupt : for the tree is known by its fruit.

" Ye offspring of vipers, how can ye, being evil, speak good things ? for out of the abundance of the heart the mouth speaketh.

" The good man out of his good treasure bringeth forth good things : and the evil man out of his evil treasure bringeth forth evil things."[2]

Yes : however we may strive to blind ourselves to the fact, words are the true index of the heart ; and that is the principle upon which God's judgment proceeds. If the words be haughty or vain, it is because the heart is haughty or vain: if they be frivolous, it is frivolous: if they be harsh, it is cruel :

[1] Matt. xii. 36, 37.   [2] Matt. xii. 33–35.

if they be hypocritical, it is hypocritical : if they be rebellious and blasphemous, it, also, is rebellious and blasphemous : if they be humble God-fearing and full of grace, it, too, is humble God-fearing and full of grace. A terrible secret to know, but one which may be made as salutary as it is terrible. For the Bible is not only the inexorable Law of God's future Judgment : it is also given to us in the present life, that we may profit withal. And the passage which we have been considering is a specimen of its value. For, if we use the searching verses aright, they will show us how to judge ourselves, by taking heed to our words, and tracing them to what in God's sight is their true source, that is, to our own hearts, which are, naturally, deceitful above all things and desperately wicked. And, if we can judge ourselves, and act upon the judgment, we shall not be judged of the Lord.

But who is sufficient for these things? Who does not feel overwhelmed as he thinks of the condition of his heart, even so far as it is revealed by his words ; who is not inclined to doubt the possibility, that such a one as he can hold fast the confidence and the rejoicing of the hope firm unto the end ? Yet, whenever the Word of God wounds, it is also ready to heal : and, in the very next verse, the Great High Priest is set before us—He Who, after putting away sin by the sacrifice of Himself, has now gone into the Presence of God, there to appear for us.

Very tenderly we are reminded, that He is no stern, cold, unsympathetic, and lofty Being, incapable of fellow-feeling with our weaknesses. Nay, He has Himself lived in the flesh, and was tempted in all points like as we are, though He did not for an instant yield to temptation.

He will take our sins upon Himself: He will wash them away with His Own Blood, and will intercede effectually for us with His Father. And in Him we may have boldness to approach even to the Throne of Grace, where, for His sake, we may obtain mercy, and find grace to help us in every time of need.

So closes this searching and memorable appeal. The Lord grant that it may be effectual in our case, and in that of many others upon whom it is our duty to press it. Everlasting Life is, indeed, the inalienable gift of God: but, if its bestowal be not followed by obedience on our part, the result will be fearful loss. The crown of the Kingdom will fall from our heads: we shall have no boldness for the Judgment-seat of Christ, but shall shrink with shame from before Him at His coming.

X

Summary and Conclusion

WE have by no means exhausted the revelations that bear upon the subject before us: but can only commend the remainder of them to the attention of the interested reader. For the evidence which has been already adduced is amply sufficient to convince him, if he be willing to learn, of the Scriptural distinction between the gift and the prize, and of the necessity of striving for the latter.

According to Divine revelation, as we have plainly seen, eternal life is the free gift of God, through Jesus Christ our Lord: but those who receive it unconditionally, and go no further, cannot claim the full enjoyment of it until the Last Day, the time of the General

Resurrection. If, however, they can, also, win the prize, they shall then be thought worthy to attain to the First Resurrection, which involves membership in Christ's Body, and a participation with Him in His glorious Millennial reign.

And we have found, that, as soon as the gift has been accepted, we become eligible for the prize, which is straightway set before us; and we are invited, in the strength of the Lord, to range ourselves in the course for the race, and to put on the whole armour of God, that we may begin the good fight.

Very strangely, however, the distinction, on which we have been endeavouring to fix attention, is seldom pondered, or even known, by the great masses of professing Christians. On the contrary, they are accustomed to rest on a vague and general idea, that, if, as they say, they believe in Christ, they must, from that very fact, become members of His Body, and, presently, partners with Him upon His throne. For they regard these transcendent privileges as included in the gift of eternal life; forgetting, that, although all things are possible to him that believeth,[1] they are not immediately certain; for only to him that overcometh is the definite promise given, that he shall inherit all things.[2]

But, if any one demur to their soothing and comfortable but sloth-inducing creed, they straightway cry out, that he is denying the grace of God.

Very different, however, as we have seen in the preceding chapters, is the language of the Bible. For, while it tells us that the gift of God is eternal life,[3] it, at the same time, insists that we must run the race, and contend for the mastery, if we would win the crown;[4]

[1] Mark ix. 23.
[2] Rev. xxi. 7.
[3] Rom. vi. 23.
[4] I Cor. ix. 24–27.

that we must finish the work which we came here to do, if we would enter into God's Millennial Sabbath-rest;[1] that we can be heirs of God and joint-heirs with Christ, only "if so be that we suffer[2] with Him, that we may be also glorified with Him";[3] that it is to the overcomer alone that Christ will give to sit with Him upon His throne:[4] that we must endure[5] with Him now, if we would reign with Him hereafter;[6] that we cannot be members of His House and companions of Himself, unless we hold fast the beginning of our confidence firm unto the end;[7] that we have no right to expect the crown of righteousness, unless, when death is drawing near, we can say with Paul;—

"I have fought the good fight; I have finished the course: I have kept the faith."[8]

Alas, then, for the vain imagination of many who suppose, that, as soon as they have believed—or have persuaded themselves that they believe—and have obtained their standing in Christ, they are in virtual possession of all the glorious possibilities that are set before us! They should rather be grasping the solemn truth, that they have only just reached the field of battle, are only now entering the lists for the race; and that the agonising struggles and vicissitudes of the conflict are all before them.

With such foolishly optimistic views, it is not strange that they neglect the admonition to pass the time of their sojourning in fear;[9] that they ignore the warning, "Many are called, but few chosen";[10] and, that they are not rendered anxious even by the thought, that those

---

[1] Heb. iv. 9, 10.
[2] συμπάσχομεν.
[3] Rom. viii. 17.
[4] Rev. iii. 21.
[5] ὑπομένομεν.
[6] 2 Tim. ii. 12.
[7] Heb. iii. 6, 14.
[8] 2 Tim. iv. 7.
[9] 1 Peter i. 17.
[10] Matt. xxii. 14.

only who are accounted worthy shall escape the things that are coming to pass, and shall obtain that age and the resurrection from the dead.[1]

But the consequences of this grave mistake are serious and far reaching. To it we must attribute, in a large degree, the apathy of Christendom, the general indifference to the Mysteries of God, the worldliness, the overpowering desire for amusement and self-pleasing even in what is supposed to be worship, the lack of love and of effort in the service of the Lord, and the dismal absence of spirituality, all of which are now such conspicuous characteristics of the churches.

If our hope of the Lord's speedy return be well-founded, we can scarcely expect that the great bodies of professing Christians will be raised from their present low estate: apostasy, coupled with Laodicean complacency, is likely to grow worse and worse, until the end comes. Yet none the less must we strive in ceaseless prayer, that we may be enabled to act as the salt of the earth and the light of the world ; that we may be permitted, in some slight degree, at least, to check the corruption and dissipate the spiritual ignorance around us. And this we shall most effectually do, if the Spirit of the Lord be with us, by bringing forth His Divine teachings fresh from the Scriptures, and by endeavouring to set once more in the front those instructions and commands which, for many centuries, have been ignored and consigned to oblivion, because of their inconvenience to nominal Christians.

We have had much Gospel-preaching in the last half-century ; but although it has been blessed to very many individuals, yet its general and permanent effect can scarcely be called satisfactory. And the main

[1] Luke xxi. 36 and xx. 35.

reason of this seems to be, that so little real teaching
is available for those who have received the Gospel.
For, if sheep be not fed, they will die, even though they
still remain within the precincts of the fold.

We must, then, pray the Lord of the Harvest to
send us more teachers who may follow in the wake
of the evangelists—students who have no opinions of
their own or of their sect to defend; and are, therefore,
able to receive with simplicity, and without reserve,
whatever the Scriptures contain, and to expound it
in plain terms to others.

BAPTISM

XI

THE ONE SOURCE OF ABSOLUTE TRUTH

THUS far we have endeavoured to ascertain what manner of persons we must be as regards walk and work, if, with the glorified Church, we would have part in the First Resurrection and the joys to which it leads. But another question naturally follows;—What, precisely, are we required to receive as doctrine, to practise, and to teach?

This is a most important point; for the Lord Himself has declared, that we worship Him in vain, if we teach for doctrines the commandments of men.[1] Where, then, are we to find the commandments of God?

In the Scriptures alone; for there is absolutely no other Divine revelation accessible to us, which can unfold the mysteries of our being and the purposes of God, and which can tell us how we may be saved from sin and death, and in what way we may please God during our brief sojourn upon earth.

There are some, however, who would have us turn to nature as a revelation; and we may, indeed, discover the Eternal Power and Godhead of the Most High in the visible works of His hands; but nothing more.[2] His transcendent love, and an interpretation of the enigmas of life, are not to be found there, though for

---

[1] Matt. xv. 9.   [2] Rom. i. 20.

a time we may be inclined to think otherwise. If our creed be based upon the material world as we see it with our bodily eyes, we have, indeed, built our house upon the sand, and can reckon upon its shelter only during the uninterrupted calm of summer. We hold our faith just as we might gaze with glowing heart upon a peaceful and enchanting landscape, fairer than dreams could picture it, with its wooded hills, its fruitful plains, its streams of glittering silver, and its restful-seeming abodes.

But a closer investigation may reveal that its inhabitants are vile as its own distant aspect is beautiful. A long drought may cast the shadow of death upon its refreshing hues. The cyclone may whirl through it, tearing up its trees, unroofing its houses, and flooding its pleasant meadows with destruction. The earthquake, heralded by its subterranean trumpet of doom, may cause the firm ground to rock like the waves of the sea, and, in a few seconds, involve the works both of nature and of human toil in wild ruin, revelling in the slaughter of man and beast.

Do we not need some revelation, besides the things that are seen, to explain such appalling possibilities? Otherwise, how can we reconcile them with the sentiment that God is love, a sentiment without which every rational being must sink into despair? For of what avail are all his efforts, and what hope of the future can he possibly cherish, if the Almighty First Cause be against him!

But it may be objected, that, in the illustrations given above, we have presented only extreme and uncommon cases. Not so: they are of sufficiently frequent occurrence. Moreover, we might have drawn the same lesson from the lives of many individual

men, marred and desolated as they frequently are by
disease, by accident, by disappointment, by loss, or
by bereavement. And how often, too, are they cut
short by the sudden interposition of the Angel of
Death, as he sweeps away for ever the vision which,
just before, had seemed to be satisfying all desire.

No: nature, viewed as a whole, can teach us
nothing but that there is an Almighty First Cause,
and that the world which He has made, though it
may bewitch us for a season, is ultimately found to
teem rather with evil than good; while all its most
delicate pleasures and choicest delights reveal themselves to us, at last, as the handmaids of corruption
and death.

And when men, who have no other revelation than
nature, begin, spite of themselves, to be in some measure
conscious of the truth, how does it affect them? It
paralyses them into indifferentism and torpidity, relieved
only by cynicism; or else it urges them to eat and
drink, since they must die to-morrow; and spurs them
on to a maddening and reckless pursuit of whatever
pleasure they may happen to descry. So far, then,
for the supposed revelation in nature.

There are, however, many in these days who tell us
that we may find the commandments of God in the
decrees of what they call "the Catholic Church," the
term Church being used, not, in its Scriptural sense,
for the whole body of believers, but for a priestly
hierarchy—an organization which can find no warrant
even for its bare existence in the New Testament. For
the hierarchy is an absolutely Pagan institution, as the
Lord Himself points out, when He declares that its
members, although they say that they are Jews, that
is, that they are constituted after the Hebrew model,

are not really so, but are the Synagogue of Satan.[1] And, if we follow their directions, we shall learn to worship Isis under the name of Mary, and to receive the round wafer of Mithras instead of the bread which represents the broken Body of our Lord and Saviour. Hence the greatest living investigator of early Christianity has said ;—

> "The claim of the Church, that her dogmas are simply the exposition of the Christian revelation, because deduced from the Holy Scriptures, is not confirmed by historical investigation. On the contrary, it becomes clear that dogmatic Christianity, in its conception and in its construction, was the work of the Hellenic spirit upon the Gospel soil."[2]

What may be required to prove this statement, which is, however, now very generally admitted, we hope to supply further on. It will then be clear, that we cannot approach so corrupt a fountain as "the Catholic Church" with any hope of finding pure water. We are, therefore, thrown upon the Word of God as the only reliable exponent of His will ; and, consequently, as the sole rule of faith to all those who love Him.

Here, then, we find a great test, whereby a man may discover whether it be really God that he loves or some other object. For, if it be God, he will suffer nothing to turn him from the simple and obvious meaning of God's Word, and will believe the whole of it, receiving all its plain statements in their most literal acceptation, however impossible they may seem to those who have no God-consciousness, and being careful to follow its commands with exactitude and precision.

[1] Rev. ii. 9, iii. 9.
[2] Harnack's "Outlines of the History of Dogma," p. 5.

But, if, on the other hand, his heart be fixed ﹏﹍ some human organization to which he has attached himself, or upon some set of opinions which he has adopted ; then, while still, it may be, loudly professing that the Bible is his authority, he will ignore, so far as possible, those parts of it which do not suit his purpose ; or, if he be troubled with scruples, will endeavour so to manipulate the text as to make it mean what he wishes. This latter object is usually effected by means of mystic or symbolical explanations, which have often deprived men of the message of God, and sometimes even turned it into suggestions of the Evil One.

Those, then, who would aspire to the Kingdom must set aside all mysticism, by means of which Satan may insert his own teachings into the very Bible itself ; and must interpret nothing symbolically, save what is manifestly symbol, lest they should be robbed of some truth specially needful to their case. Nor must they be deceived by the presentation of isolated texts, which is frequently misleading, but be ever ready with their "It is written again."

If these rules be observed, those who study the Scriptures, not in the pride of intellect, but with ceaseless prayer for guidance from on high, will soon discover and hold fast the great truths which God has vouchsafed to us, and which are designed to restore our spiritual sight, and to lead us to our lost fealty, and to peace and union with Himself. They will believe in the Almighty Creative and All-ruling Trinity, Which is One God. They will acknowledge, that man has fallen from righteousness—hopelessly, so far as himself is concerned—and become subject to sin, and, therefore, to death. They will rejoice, because the Second Person of the Trinity, the Word, was made flesh, and dwelt among us, that He might put away sin by the sacrifice of Himself, and might through death destroy him that hath the power of death. They will exult in His resurrection and ascension, and in that He has now entered into the heavens, there to appear in the Presence of God for us.[1] They will gladly confess, that He is made unto them wisdom from God, and righteousness, and sanctification, and redemption;[2] that there is no other name given under heaven whereby men can be saved;[3] that whosoever cometh unto Him, He will in no wise cast out;[4] and that He is able also to save to the uttermost them that draw near unto God through Him, seeing He ever liveth to make intercession for them.[5] They believe that He is able to keep them from falling; and they look for Him to appear a second time, apart from sin, for their salvation.[7]

These, and whatever other doctrines revelations and commands are to be found in the New Testament, must be believed, acted upon, and openly confessed, by all true children of the Kingdom. Nor must another side of the question be passed by. Nothing that concerns the Blessed Trinity, or the Divine purposes and our relation to them, must be taught as doctrine, unless it be manifestly drawn from the Scriptures. No traditions or speculations are permissible, no curious peering into matters which God has not seen fit to reveal. For "the secret things belong unto the Lord our God: but the things that are revealed belong unto us and to our children for ever, that we may do all the words of this law."[8]

God Himself has selected and given to us the things

---

[1] Heb. ix. 24.   [4] John vi. 37.   [7] Heb. ix. 28.
[2] 1 Cor. i. 30.   [5] Heb. vii. 25.   [8] Deut. xxix. 29.
[3] Acts iv. 12.   [6] Jude 24.

that we are to know, and His object in so doing is, not to fill us with the knowledge that puffeth up, but so to equip us that we may both understand and keep the laws which He has laid down for this time of discipline and probation. Further knowledge He will give us by-and-by; when, after having put off this mortality, we shall be able to receive it without that inrush of vanity which seems almost invariably to accompany any acquisition of wisdom or power in the present life.

Some of the revelations which are much neglected we have already discussed in a former volume: others will come before us a little later. But we must now dwell for a while upon three subjects, most important to be understood, before we investigate the prophecies which are concerned with the history of the Church upon earth. These are Baptism, the Lord's Supper, and Church-government.

XII

The Two Ordinances

BAPTISM and the Lord's Supper are, then, the only ordinances appointed for the members of the Church in this age. In the preceding dispensation, ritual had been largely used; but the result was failure. For it was found that men almost invariably forgot the deep significance of the ordained rites, instead of being reminded of it by what they did, thinking that, if they diligently performed the outward act, they had fulfilled all righteousness; and so, they changed what God had enjoined for instruction, and the calling forth of thanksgiving and praise, into mere ordinances of superstition. Hence, in the new epoch, the sacrifices, the solemn feasts, and the elaborate ceremonies, of Hebrew times were altogether withdrawn, and but two rites, of a very simple nature, imposed upon Christian believers. Nor were these set forth so persistently and so continually as the Hebrew ordinances. No Book of the New Testament is wholly devoted to Baptism and the Lord's Supper, as that of Leviticus is to the Aaronic ritual. Of the twenty-one Epistles addressed exclusively to members of the churches, one only, the First to the Corinthians, devotes parts of two chapters to the Lord's Supper; while the others do not even introduce the subject. In the same twenty-one Epistles, less than a dozen passages contain a reference to Baptism. Thus the section of the Scriptures which is addressed exclusively to the churches has very little, indeed, to say of these two outward ordinances, and in this respect presents a great contrast to the generality of mediæval and of modern Anglican teaching. Nevertheless, it does not permit them to be neglected; for both of them were ordered by the lips of the Lord.

The inference is, that, while we must be careful to obey our Lord's commands to the very letter, He did not intend the outward ordinances to be perpetually in our minds; but only that which they were designed to teach.

XIII

THE MEANING OF THE WORD BAPTISM

TURNING now more particularly to Baptism, we will first inquire into the exact meaning of the term. Now $\beta \alpha \pi \tau i \zeta \epsilon \iota \nu$, "to baptize," and $\beta \acute{\alpha} \pi \tau \iota \sigma \mu \alpha$, "Baptism," have their root in the verb $\beta \acute{\alpha} \pi \tau \epsilon \iota \nu$, "to dip," which is especially used of tempering red-hot steel, of dyeing cloth, or of drawing water by dipping a bucket into a well. In each of these cases, it will be noticed that complete submersion is required for the due performance of the act. And precisely the same idea is found in βαπτίζειν, which also means "to dip under water," to sink ships, and to draw wine from bowls by dipping cups into it. Since, then, this is the word which was appropriated for Christian Baptism, it is sufficiently clear, that the latter was an immersion, and not a sprinkling. And we shall presently find, that this conclusion is corroborated by the Scriptural explanation of the rite.

XIV

THE BAPTISM OF JOHN

THE first baptism of which we hear in the New Testament is that of John, the Lord's forerunner. It was totally distinct from the rite which was commanded by the risen Lord: so much so, indeed, that all who had received it were, nevertheless, afterwards baptized upon the Name of Jesus. This we may learn from the case of those disciples of John whom Paul found at Ephesus.[1]

In the second Gospel, John is said to have preached "a baptism of repentance for a remission of sins;"[2] that is, a baptism indicative of repentance with a view to the remission of sins. It involved a confession of the need to be cleansed from sin and transgressions; but it did not actually effect the cleansing, any more than the bathings and washings of the Law rendered a man actually pure before God. Nevertheless, God

---

[1] Acts xix. 1-7. [2] Mark i. 4.

would have the latter done, both as an expression of the need and to typify the real cleansing which should be ultimately provided for those who obeyed Him. Thus the baptism of John, not only indicated repentance, but also looked forward to an actual remission of sins, for which God was then preparing the means. And in what way this remission should be obtained John expounded; for when the Pharisees demanded why he dared to baptize, seeing he was neither the Messiah nor one of those whom they expected as His forerunners, he in effect replied;—" I do, indeed, baptize, and that with good reason: for in the midst of you there stands One Whom ye know not, the Messiah, no longer the Coming One, but He Who has come. He is the Lamb of God That taketh away the sin of the world, and it is to prepare men to receive Him that I am sent forth baptizing [1] with the baptism of repentance."

Such, then, was John's baptism ; but what actual benefit did it confer upon those who submitted to it? That benefit which always follows obedience—the power to obey again, and so to be placed securely upon the highway of salvation. This we may see in the seventh chapter of Luke, where we read ;—" And all the people, when they had heard, and the publicans, justified God, having been baptized with the baptism of John. But the Pharisees and the lawyers rejected for themselves the counsel of God, not having been baptized of him." [2]

[1] John i. 25–31.
[2] Luke vii. 29, 30.   Compare Alford's note ;—" It has been imagined that these words are a continuation of our Lord's discourse; but surely they would thus be most unnatural. They are evidently a parenthetical insertion of the Evangelist, expressive, not of what had taken place at John's baptism, but of the present

This passage is very significant, and a solemn warning to us. It shows that the Pharisees, having rejected the first command of God, to submit to the baptism of repentance, were unable to obey the second, that they should believe in the Lord Jesus Christ unto eternal life. But the common people, because they had been obedient in the matter of John's baptism, received power to believe in the words of the Lord Jesus, and so to become children of God.

It is a fearful thing to neglect either of the two rites which the Saviour has distinctly commanded as part of the testimony of His people. But what will be done to the men who have dared to add other rites to His, and so to usurp His place, Who Alone is Master and Lord? Or to those who have perverted His simple directions into elaborate and magical ceremonies, reft of the meaning which He had given them, and, therefore, while powerful, it may be, to affect the intellect and the emotions, bringing no grace to the spirit within?

XV

THE COMMISSION OF THE LORD

WHEN we read that the Lord, also, caused His disciples to baptize in the days of John the Baptist, we must, of course, understand that He was then co-operating with the latter, and baptizing with the baptism of repentance. But He did not long continue to do so. His baptisms are mentioned for the last time in the fourth chapter

effect of our Lord's discourse on the then assembled multitude. Their whole diction and form is historical, not belonging to discourse. Besides, if ἀκούσας were meant to signify 'when they heard him' (John), then βαπτισθέντες should be βαπτιζόμενοι."

of the Fourth Gospel; for, when He uttered the discourse which is recorded in the fifth, it is evident that John the Baptist had passed from the scene, his mission having ended in failure. Thenceforth the Lord no longer commanded baptisms, until after His death and resurrection; for the Jews had now rejected Him, and the order of things was being changed.

But, just before His ascension, He gave a commission to His disciples—not merely to the Eleven—which demands our earnest heed. A summary, or, perhaps, a fragment, of it is found in each of the synoptic Gospels; and, so far as these passages are concerned with our subject, we quote and comment upon them below.

MATT. xxviii. 18–20.	MARK xvi. 15–18.	LUKE xxiv. 46–48.
"All authority was given[1] unto Me in heaven and upon earth. Go ye, therefore, and make disciples of all the nations, baptizing them into the Name of the Father and of the Son and of the Holy Spirit, teaching them to observe all things whatsoever I commanded you; and, lo, I am with you all the days, until the consummation of the age."	"Go ye into all the world, and preach the Gospel to the whole creation. He that has believed, and has been baptized, shall be saved: but he that has disbelieved shall be condemned. And these signs shall follow them that have believed. In My Name shall they cast out demons: they shall speak with new tongues: they shall take up serpents, and, if they drink any deadly thing, it shall not hurt them: they shall lay hands upon the sick, and they shall recover."	"And He said unto them, Thus it has been written, that the Christ should suffer, and rise again from the dead the third day; and that repentance and remission of sins should be preached upon His Name unto all the nations, beginning from Jerusalem. And ye are witnesses of these things."

---

[1] ἐδόθη.

Turning, then, first to the passage from Matthew, we find the Lord claiming, that supreme authority was vested in Himself from the moment of His resurrection ; and, upon that ground, He commands His disciples to go forth to all the nations. He has, therefore, ceased to confine His gracious dealings to Jews, and has inaugurated a new order of things, in which He will choose out a peculiar people for Himself, no longer from one nation only, but from all. He is about to pour out His Spirit upon all flesh.[1] His followers are, therefore, to make disciples in every country.

How they were to effect this, their Lord, as we learn from the parallel passages in Mark and Luke, explained to them : they were to go forth in all directions, and, wherever they came, to preach repentance, and to announce the love and mercy of God and His free salvation in Christ Jesus. And, as often as the Lord opened the heart of any one so that he received the Gospel, they were to baptize him, and then to teach him, without reservation, all things whatsoever the Lord had commanded them, to declare unto him the whole counsel of God.

Thus the order was to be ;—First, repentance and conversion ; secondly, baptism ; and, thirdly, teaching. And this was the order adopted by the Apostles from the very first preaching of the Gospel, when Peter cried [2] ;—

" Repent and be baptized, every one of you, upon the Name [3] of Jesus Christ for the remission of your sins ; and ye shall receive the gift of the Holy Ghost."

---

[1] Joel ii. 28 ; Acts ii. 16, 17.   [2] Acts ii. 38.
[3] ἐπὶ τῷ ὀνόματι. An expression which is not found elsewhere in

Here the directions of the Commission were strictly carried out. Repentance and remission of sins were preached in the Name of the Lord, those who accepted the message were baptized, and baptism was followed by the gift of the Spirit Who enabled the converts to understand even the deep things of God.

The same order may be observed throughout the " Acts," if we except the case of Cornelius and his friends, who were not only converted, but also received the gift of the Spirit, before they were baptized. The reason of this deviation from the ordinary rule is, however, obvious. The Jewish companions of Peter still retained their prejudices, and thought that a Gentile might not be baptized, unless he had been previously circumcised. Therefore, the Lord graciously helped their infirmities, and dispelled their illusion, by at once bestowing upon the Roman converts that power which was usually given after baptism.[1]

There are, however, some who, to support an unscriptural practice, would persuade us that to "make disciples, baptizing and teaching them," means to make them such by baptizing and teaching them. In other words, that the baptism and the teaching make the disciples. Had this been intended, we should have expected past instead of present participles. And in that case, too, the practice of the Apostles, who would baptize only after a clear confession of Christ, would have been contrary to their Master's Commission.

But it was not so : and if the proof given above is insufficient, the Lord's own procedure, at least,

reference to baptism. It means "upon the ground of the Name of Jesus Christ": that is, their belief and trust in the Lord Jesus as their Saviour was to be the ground or reason of their baptism.

[1] Acts x. 44-8.

will be decisive. For, in the first verse of the fourth chapter of John's Gospel, we are told that He "made and baptized"[1] more disciples than John the Baptist.

His way, then, was first to make disciples, and afterwards to baptize them. And if any man has found a more excellent way than this, whatever else may be said of him, he is not a follower of the Lord Jesus.

It is thus manifest, that none but those who are sufficiently intelligent to understand, that Christ died to procure remission of sins for them upon their repentance, can be baptized in accordance with the Lord's Commission. And, consequently, infant baptism is altogether excluded by it.

Our Lord goes on to say, that converts are to be baptized "into the Name of the Father, and of the Son, and of the Holy Spirit." But the English Version translates "in the Name," and this has become the normal liturgical formula. It is, however, a palpable mistake founded upon the inaccurate rendering of the Vulgate; and we should read "baptizing them into the Name"—the Greek εἰς 'into,' or 'unto,' being the preposition which invariably, in the New Testament, precedes the person or thing with which one is to be incorporated by baptism. The solitary instance in the tenth chapter of "Acts," which is sometimes dragged out as an exception to this rule, is irrelevant. For a glance at the context will show, that the words, "in the Name of Jesus Christ," are to be connected with the principal verb of the sentence—"He commanded them, in the Name of Jesus Christ, to be baptized;" that is, he commanded them on the authority of the Lord Jesus, as opposed to those who might have forbidden the baptism.[2] The order of the

---

[1] Literally, "makes and baptizes." [2] Acts x. 48.

words in the best MSS. favours this meaning, and we may compare with it the words of Peter to the impotent man, "In the Name of Jesus Christ of Nazareth, rise up and walk." [1]

But, while the preposition εἰς is invariably used of that to which one is to be united by baptism, the element in which the immersion takes place is frequently preceded by ἐν, 'in,'—as "in water," "in the Holy Spirit," and "in fire."

The Lord directs that converts should be baptized "into the Name" of the Blessed Trinity. Now, in the spiritual world, names are not given for the mere sake of distinction, but also to express the real nature of the person or thing named. Hence "the Name," here as in some other passages, signifies the very meaning and essence of the Subject, so far, at least, as it has been revealed. So, in the hundred and thirty-eighth Psalm, the Israelites, when, at length, they see the "word," that is, the promises, fulfilled, are represented as crying out, "Thou hast magnified Thy word above all Thy Name": that is, This glorious fulfilment surpasses all other revelations and manifestations, all that we had ever previously known of Thee.

Similarly, to be baptized into the Name of the Father, and of the Son, and of the Holy Spirit, is to become incorporated, as it were, by baptism with what that Name expresses, with all that has been revealed respecting the Blessed Trinity; to be put into the place of responsibility and obedience which naturally results from a knowledge of what They are; to accept the merciful the loving and the glorious salvation which They have prepared, and the precious promises which They have given.

[1] Acts iii. 6.

Nay, the incorporation leads us on far beyond even this, though it is only with bated breath, with palpitating heart, and with downcast eyes, that we can think of anything so transcendent, if, at least, we realize that of which we think. For has not the Lord Jesus Himself said ;—"That they all may be one, as Thou Father art in Me, and I in Thee, that they also may be one in Us. . . . I in them, and Thou in Me, that they may be perfected into one ; that the world may know that Thou didst send Me, and lovedst them even as Thou lovedst Me"?[1]

It is thus clear, that those only who can in some degree understand these wondrous things, and who receive them with the warmth of a humbled and grateful heart, are fit subjects for baptism. Woe, then, to those who taught the churches to break up the order of the Almighty by sprinkling unconscious infants, and persuading them in after-life that they had obeyed the command in regard to this awful and testing ordinance. Woe to those who, without a particle of warrant from Scripture, were the first to introduce sponsors, falsely teaching that they can promise and vow for the same unconscious infants, whereas

> "None of them can by any means redeem his
>   brother,
> Nor give to God a ransom for him."[2]

It will, perhaps, be well to make one more remark in regard to the Lord's charge as given by Matthew. Immediately after the command to make disciples, and then to baptize and teach them, comes the gracious promise, "And, lo, I am with you all the days, even until the consummation of the age." By this it is plainly intimated, that the three previously mentioned

[1] John xvii. 21, 23.   [2] Psa. xlix. 7.

things are to be done throughout the dispensation, even to its close. Hence those who, like the "Friends," would persuade us, that baptism was only for Apostolic times, are shown to be grievously mistaken.

In turning to the parallel passage in Mark, we are met by the assertion, that the last twelve verses of that Gospel are spurious. We do not think so. Like some other passages, they contain statements and opinions which could never be admitted or realized by the corrupted churches, and were, consequently, found to be inconvenient. This sufficiently accounts for the fact, that they have been omitted in some manuscripts, and tampered with in others. But there is abundant testimony in their favour, and their genuineness was never denied until the very end of the last century. We cannot, of course, enter into the subject here ; but those who are troubled with doubts might, possibly, find them removed by a perusal of Dean Burgon's monograph on the verses in question.

The corroboration in the fifteenth and sixteenth verses of what has been said above is decisive. For the command to preach the Gospel to all the world is followed by the declaration, that he who has believed and has been baptized shall be saved, but that he who has disbelieved shall be condemned. Here it is distinctly stated, that belief must precede baptism. But, in speaking of condemnation, these verses assign it only to unbelief, and not also to lack of baptism ; because, until the churches had become corrupt, so monstrous an act as the baptism of one who either did not, or could not, profess intelligent belief in the Lord Jesus, was unknown and unthought of.

The report of the Commission in the third Gospel contains no mention of baptism, but only of the command that the disciples should preach to all the nations, beginning from Jerusalem ; to which is added a promise of power from on high. With this the account in the " Acts "[1] is in substantial agreement. As to the cause of the omission by Luke of the command to baptize, we may remark, that the Lord has preserved for us four reports of the Commission, and that, in this case as in others, He has communicated different portions, or aspects, of the discourse in each account, according to the requirements of the context ; by which plan these fragments, or different views, are more clearly and certainly impressed upon our minds than if they had been given together in one long report. Hence, probably, the reason, or rather a reason, why we have four Gospels instead of one : the human mind cannot at once receive and comprehend every aspect of the transcendent events connected with, or sayings uttered by, the Lord Jesus.

At the same time we may add, that the preaching of the word, that is, the acting as witnesses for Christ, is commanded in each of the four reports ; for, of course, in Matthew's Gospel, it is included in the order to make disciples. And, although the promise of the Spirit is not actually mentioned by Matthew or Mark, yet the former tells us of the Lord's pledge to be always with His disciples, which would be fulfilled by His Spirit ; while Mark specifies some of the gifts of power which are, also, bestowed by that One and the Selfsame Spirit.

[1] Acts i. 7, 8.

XVI

CIRCUMCISION AND BAPTISM

BEFORE we go on to inquire what the Acts and the Epistles teach respecting baptism, we will endeavour to remove a misconception which tarries in many minds. It is affirmed that circumcision and baptism are precisely similar rites, each of them being the gate of entrance into that body of which it is the visible seal ; and, therefore, that, since infants were circumcised, infants, also, should be baptized. Such a conclusion is, however, one of those plausible fallacies which may be exposed in a very few words.

Circumcision and baptism are precisely analogous rites ; but that very fact, when we understand its bearings, is the decisive proof that infants cannot be baptized. For the case stands as follows.

Abraham believed God, and his faith was reckoned to him for righteousness. Then, on account of that imputed righteousness, the promises were made not only to himself, but also to his seed,[1] to which he thus became the federal head and channel of all blessings. Consequently, every Israelite, from the fact that he was Abraham's seed, was born into the covenant, and became an heir of the promises from the moment of his birth. Hence he could reasonably as an infant receive the seal of that covenant of which he was a partaker as an infant.

But the case of those who belong to the present dispensation is different. Not Abraham, but the Lord Jesus is now the federal Head of the elect, through Whom Alone they can receive blessing. At what time,

[1] Gen. xv.

then, do they enter into His covenant? Not at the moment of the natural birth, but at that of the spiritual ; that is, at conversion. " Ye must be born again," [1] is His Own Word, which is echoed by His Apostle when he says ;—" Wherefore, if any man is in Christ, he is a new creation : the old things are passed away ; behold, they are become new." [2] Immediately, then, after his second birth, a man should be baptized as a spiritual infant ; for, as one who has just been born into Christ, he has a right to the promises of the covenant of grace, and, therefore, also to its visible seal. Thus the analogy between circumcision and baptism is perfect.

XVII

BAPTISM IN THE ACTS

IN the Acts of the Apostles, we learn how the Lord's disciples carried out His instructions ; and it is needless to say, that they admitted to Baptism only those who intelligently knew and believed in Him. Of the multitude that listened to Peter on the day of Pentecost, none but the three thousand who received his word were baptized. [3] The Samaritans were baptized after they had believed the preaching of Philip ; [4] and, in this case, men and women are specified, but not children. The eunuch recognised the Lamb of God Who taketh away the sin of the world, and went down into the water. [5] Paul acknowledged Jesus as Lord, and then obeyed His command. [6]

And so we might go on to the end of the book ; but it will suffice to mention two other cases, which

---

[1] John. iii. 7. [3] Acts ii. 41. [5] Acts viii. 36-8.
[2] 2 Cor. v. 17. [4] Acts viii. 12. [6] Acts ix. 17, 18.

are sometimes claimed in support of the unlawful practice of infant baptism.

The first is that of Lydia, who gave heed to the things that were spoken by Paul, and was baptized together with her household.[1]   It is suggested that there *may* have been infants in the household ; that, if so, they were probably baptized ; and hence, that we have here a precedent for infant baptism.   A vague and foolish argument, which sets in high relief the weakness of the cause for which it pleads.   For, had there been infants in the household, they would certainly have been excluded from a function which, as we have been previously instructed, demands faith, and, therefore, sufficient intelligence to form and hold an opinion.

Moreover, both in this and in the two similar passages, God has carefully guarded us from the error which He foreknew.   Here it is evident from the context that Lydia had no husband : for no husband appears, she herself invites the Apostles, and the house is called her house.   Nor is it likely that she was a widow : for, had she been so, she would, probably, have been designated as such, after the usual manner of the Bible. Certainly, then, no plea for infant baptism can be drawn from Lydia's household.

The second instance is that of the gaoler of Philippi, of whom it is said that he "was baptized, he and all his." [2]   But no infants were included in the latter phrase. For, in the previous verse,[3] we are told that Paul had spoken "the word of the Lord to him and to all that were in his house ; " while, in that which follows,[4] we are further informed, that the gaoler "rejoiced with all

---

[1] Acts xvi. 14, 15.   [3] V. 32.
[2] Acts xvi. 33.   [4] V. 34.

his household, because he had believed in God." Those, therefore, who were able to listen to the word of the Lord, and to rejoice that faith had been given to them to receive it, were no infants, but intelligent subjects for baptism.

There is mention, in the New Testament, of one other household in connection with baptism, which we will notice at once, though it does not occur in the "Acts." In the first chapter of the First Epistle to the Corinthians, Paul remarks that he baptized the household of Stephanas.[1] But, in the last chapter of the Epistle, he tells us of that same household, that they were the firstfruits of Achaia, which proves that they had been converted ; and then adds, that "they set themselves to minister unto the saints."[2] It is thus very evident that they were no infants, but of an age sufficiently mature for baptism.

XVIII

BAPTISM IN THE EPISTLES

IN the Epistle to the Romans, after a glorious exposition of the grace of God as manifested in justification by faith and the transfer of believers from the federal headship of Adam to that of Christ, Paul proceeds, in the sixth chapter, to urge, that the reception of this grace must necessarily be followed by holiness of life.[3] For he foresaw that God's free gift would be abused

[1] 1 Cor. i. 16.
[2] 1 Cor. xvi. 15.
[3] If the English reader would understand this passage—Rom. vi. 1-11—he must study it in the R.V. In the A.V., the sense is destroyed through inaccuracies in the rendering of the Greek tenses. Thus, in vv. 2 and 8, we find "are dead" and "be dead," where the reading should be "died"; and, in v. 6, "is crucified" instead of "was crucified."

by men of perverse mind, and so distorted as even to be made an excuse for sin. If Christ has really done all for us, they would say, our conduct can be of little importance: we may go our own way, and do our own pleasure.

Hence the Apostle himself proposed the question which he knew would be suggested to many minds;— "What shall we say then? Are we to persist in sin, that grace may abound?"[1] But he quickly gives the very decided answer;—"Away with the thought! We who died to sin, how shall we any longer live therein!"[2] What, then, is his exact meaning when he speaks of believers as having died to sin?

Now, we must again observe, that the Greek aorist tense, which is rendered by "we died," points to some single and definite act in the past. When, therefore, did we perform this definite act of dying? Undoubtedly, in our Lord and Saviour when He expired on the cross for our sins, although His precious work was not, of course, imputed to us as individuals until the moment when we believed on Him. "For that which He died, He died unto sin once for all;[3] but that which He liveth, He liveth unto God."[4] Sin had a claim upon Him, because in His own spotless Person He bore our sins; but He submitted Himself to death, and by that act the claim of sin was cancelled. Hence all those, too, who died in Him were legally released from the claims of sin; for "he that has died has been freed"—literally "justified"— "from sin."[5] Thus it was that Paul could say;—"Likewise reckon ye also yourselves to be dead, indeed, unto sin, but alive unto God in Christ Jesus."[6]

[1] Rom. vi. 1.
[2] Rom. vi. 2.
[3] ἐφάπαξ.
[4] Rom. vi. 10.
[5] Rom. vi. 7.
[6] Rom. vi. 11.

Such, then, is our legal position before God, unworthy sinners though we be. But, when we fully apprehend it, and are able to realise that it was purchased by the Life of the Sinless One freely offered for our sakes, that fact is, by the Spirit's power, made to work strongly and effectually for our actual deliverance from sin, creating, as it does, in us a burning desire for holiness. We feel, that, since the Lord of Love has died for our sins, we also must die unto sin, break with it completely and for ever. We can no longer by wilful transgression range ourselves with the murderers of the Lord Jesus. The Spirit, by Whose entrance we were enabled to believe, presses us to set our will against sin. We feel like a Bechuana convert, mentioned by Godet, who exclaimed, " The cross of Christ condemns me to be holy." The principle of, and the desire for, sinlessness and perfect holiness have been implanted in us by the Spirit of Christ, though it will not be until the close of the present life that the one will attain to full maturity or the other be fully satisfied.

But, lest any one should still doubt whether he really may reckon himself to be, in Christ, dead unto sin, the Apostle adds ;—" Or are ye ignorant, that as many of us as were baptized into Christ Jesus were baptized into His death ? We were, therefore, buried with Him by baptism-unto-death, that, like as Christ was raised from the dead by the glory of the Father, so we also might walk in newness of life."

Here we must carefully observe that baptism is not regarded as a figure of that death with Christ which must previously have taken place, namely, at the moment of conversion ; but of the burial which follows death, and is the proof of it. Do you not know, the Apostle asks, what you professed by your baptism ?

Every man who offers himself for that ordinance confesses, that he is dead to this world and to sin in Christ, and that he requires burial. When he goes down into, and is covered by, the waters of baptism, he, in a figure, shares the grave of the Lord Jesus; and, being thus made like to his Lord in death, he must become like Him also in resurrection, and must emerge from the waters to walk in newness of life, to reckon himself as alive unto God, and to strive in prayer for the power of the Spirit, that he may be ever approaching nearer in reality to that which he is reckoned to be in Christ.

So Paul taught the Romans; and his Epistle to the Colossians contains a very similar passage. For, when speaking to the latter of the necessity, and the marvellous privilege, of holding fast to Christ, he says;—" In Whom ye were also circumcised with a circumcision not made with hands, in the putting off of the body of the flesh, in the circumcision of Christ, having been buried with Him in baptism, wherein ye were also raised with Him, through faith in the effectual working of God, Who raised Him from the dead." [1]

To bring out the full meaning of this passage, we should quote at much greater length; but, since we may have to return to it later, these two verses will suffice for our present purpose.

Now, the construction of the sentence in the Greek is, " In Whom ye were also circumcised when ye were buried with Him in baptism "; that is, your baptism was the visible sign of the circumcision without hands, or the spiritual circumcision, which is communicated by the Lord Jesus Himself to those who believe on Him. And, while the circumcision of the former

[1] Col. ii. 11, 12.

dispensation was the putting off of a`small part only of the flesh, this is the laying aside of the whole body of it by our death unto sin in Him ; and so, as we found above, the asking for burial with Him by baptism is our public profession that the death has taken place. We do not, however, descend to remain in the grave from which He so quickly rose. For, if we enter the waters with a true heart, what was done so many centuries ago takes effect in our own particular case. We are raised together with Christ to newness of life, as we come out of the waters, through our faith in the effectual working of God in raising Him from the dead. For that act of the Father becomes to us the pledge that He will raise us up also—now to newness of life, and, at the First Resurrection, to full glory and immortality of spirit, soul, and body.

Again ; the First Epistle of Peter contains a passage [1] which calls for special attention. The Apostle has been exhorting those whom he is addressing to endurance and courage under suffering, even if the suffering be unjust ; and he presses home his appeal by the example of our Lord. For Christ, also, he urges, suffered for sins once, though only once, the Righteous One in the stead of the unrighteous, that He might bring us to God ; and His suffering went even as far as death. But, mark the result : at the moment when He was put to death in His flesh, He was made alive in His Spirit. His life ceased upon earth, but was immediately resumed in another sphere. And just as, when in the flesh, He had preached to men, so now in spirit He journeyed to Hades, and there preached to spirits, even to the imprisoned spirits of those who had been disobedient

[1] 1 Peter iii. 17–22.

during the hundred and twenty years of God's forbearance, while Noah was preparing an Ark for the salvation of his house. The few who entered that Ark—only eight persons out of the multitudes of the world—were saved by means of and through water; " which also, in a correspondingly typical manner, now saves us, even baptism—not the putting away of the filth of the flesh, but the inquiry of a good conscience toward God, through the resurrection of Jesus Christ, Who is on the right hand of God, having gone into heaven, angels and authorities and powers being made subject to Him." [1]

Here we have a further unfolding of the import of baptism, which is, we learn, a type corresponding to that of the waters of the Deluge.

When the impending catastrophe was foretold to Noah, he was moved by godly fear, and, under Divine guidance, prepared an Ark for the saving of his house. By the appointed time, he and his family had entered the vessel, and God had shut them in. Then the fountains of the great deep were broken up, and the windows of heaven were opened ; so that the flood spread over all things, and, rising ever higher and higher, destroyed every living creature that was upon the face of the ground. Nor would it have been less fatal to Noah and his family, had it not been for the Ark in which they were enclosed. For the strong-ribbed vessel, carefully pitched within and without with pitch, was upborne by the rushing waters of the deep, and, being covered on the top, was also protected from the descending rain. Hence, when every other living being was drowned, eight persons were borne safely over the ruined earth by the destroying element

[1] 1 Peter iii. 21, 22.

itself, and were presently landed in a new world, where the discordant sounds of violence and bloodshed were unheard, the seasons succeeded each other in due order, and all was peace and quietude.

Thus the waters of the Deluge and those of baptism are corresponding types : each of them represents the overwhelming floods of death, which is the wages of sin.

When the world had filled up the measure of its iniquity, the Deluge came, and engulfed in its destroying waters every living creature that was upon the earth, except those who were in the Ark—which signifies the righteousness of Christ—and who were borne safely through the ruin into a new world.

So he who feels that he has died in Christ Jesus for his trangressions and sins, enters the baptismal waters to be buried therein, in a figure, with his Lord. And being thus by his faith and obedience vitally connected with his Saviour in death, he shall also be united with Him in resurrection, and prefigures this by coming forth from the watery grave to newness of life.

But Peter warns us, that it is not the mere outward washing, the putting away of the filth of the flesh, that saves, but the craving of a good conscience toward God, the sincere confession before Him of humble belief in all that baptism expresses, and the grateful and joyful reception of His unspeakable gift. This is what really saves : the mere outward immersion in water and emersion from it save only in type.

Hence, although Simon Magus had been, to all outward appearance, baptized as truly as the rest of the multitude who afterwards received the gift of the Spirit ; yet, since he had not the desire of a good conscience toward God, the outward form brought him no salvation :

he was still, as he presently learnt from the lips of Peter, "in the gall of bitterness, and in the bond of iniquity." [1]

From this passage, then, it is abundantly evident, that only those who are of mature age can be baptized ; since it is the inquiry of a good conscience toward God which makes the rite effective. And the same lesson is taught by Paul in the words ;—

"But now that faith is come, we are no longer under a tutor. For ye are all sons of God, through faith in Christ Jesus. For as many of you as were baptized into Christ did put on Christ." [2]

Here "faith" stands in the place of "the inquiry of a good conscience toward God"; and, without the exercise of it, no one can be baptized into Christ.

We have already examined the reference to the baptism of Israel in the Red Sea ; [3] and need only add, that, both in this and in the other great corresponding type, the Deluge, two points are carefully preserved.

First, those who were finally delivered from the Egyptians by the passage through the Red Sea, had been previously saved from the destroying angel, by believing in God and obeying His command to sprinkle the blood of a lamb on the lintel and side posts of their doors. And those who were carried in safety through the destroying Flood, and into a new world, had entered into the Ark of their own free will, because they believed that what God had said He would surely perform. Similarly, no one can be fit for baptism, until he has intelligently set his seal to this, that "God is true," and has trusted in His salvation.

Again, there was the water underneath the Ark, while the descending rain enveloped it from above.

[1] Acts viii. 23.   [2] Gal. iii. 25–7.   [3] I Cor. x. 1, 2.

Similarly, the Israelites are said to have passed underneath the cloud and between the two walls formed by the waters of the Red Sea. Thus, in each case, complete immersion is set forth as the only possible figure of a passage through death and burial into a new life.

So far as memory serves us, we have now considered the principal passages in the Epistles which contain a reference to baptism, except one in the letter to the Ephesians. In the fourth chapter of that Epistle, Paul urges the necessity of preserving " the unity of the Spirit in the bond of peace." For the Church, that is, the invisible and real Church, is one Body animated by One Spirit, even the Holy Spirit of God ; while her members have but one hope of their calling.[1] Moreover, they have but " One Lord, one faith, one baptism, One God and Father of all, Who is over all, and through all, and in all."[2] Here, then, the Church herself is first described, and afterwards her path of salvation is marked out. She has One Lord, Who is the Way the Truth and the Life ; one faith, in His incarnation and appearing in the world to put away sin by the sacrifice of Himself ; one baptism, which is her public profession of faith in Him and oneness with Him in death and resurrection, and which is rendered valid by the desire of her good conscience toward the One God and Father of all.

There is one baptism, and that may not be avoided by those who would be children of the Kingdom ; but it must be a baptism, and not the mere sprinkling or dipping of an unconscious subject. And, consequently, those who have been put through so empty and useless a form in their infancy, or before they were

[1] Eph. iv. 4.   [2] Eph. iv. 5, 6.

real believers, are not anabaptists when they seek to obey God by desiring a real baptism: for they have not been previously baptized at all.

XIX

Baptism and the Kingdom

WE will conclude our investigation into the nature of Scriptural baptism by glancing at a passage in the third chapter of the Fourth Gospel, which seems to reveal a connection between baptism and the Kingdom. When Nicodemus came to the Lord, he, doubtless, expected to be told, that all Jews, and especially Pharisees and teachers in Israel, were sure of the Kingdom. But, before he had time to open his case, the Lord, knowing his thoughts, abruptly said;—"Verily, verily, I say unto thee, Except a man be born from above, he cannot see the Kingdom of God."[1]

Nicodemus, perceiving that a new birth was required, showed, perhaps, his bewilderment still more than his carnality by asking, Whether a man that was old could enter a second time into his mother's womb and be born? To which the Lord replied;—"Verily, verily, I say unto thee, Except a man be born of water and Spirit,[2] he cannot enter into the Kingdom of God."[3]

In His first words, then, the Lord speaks of the birth "from above," by which He evidently means what we call conversion, which occurs when the Father, through the Spirit, draws to the Son such as shall be saved. Those who thus come to Him for deliverance

---

[1] John iii. 3.
[2] Not "the Spirit": there is no article in the Greek.
[3] John iii. 5.

from sin, He will in no wise cast out : they will obtain everlasting life, and will see the Kingdom, *but not necessarily have part in it.*

In the fifth verse, however, the Lord mentions another element of a new birth, namely, " water "; and He places ' water' before ' Spirit.' Moreover, when this second element is introduced, a greater result is promised ; for to enter into the Kingdom is more than to see it.

We have, then, to explain the two terms, 'water' and 'Spirit'; and this can only be done by taking the striking circumstances of the time into consideration. For, in those days, all Judæa was excited by the ministry and baptism of John, which, doubtless, formed the main topic of conversation. Now John had foretold, that, when Jesus came, He would baptize with the Holy Ghost and with fire ;[1] while the Lord Himself had been recently baptized by John, and the Spirit had descended upon Him as He was coming up out of the water.[2] Hence the mention of ' water' and ' Spirit' would naturally suggest baptism to the mind of Nicodemus, and in its immersion and emersion he would readily discern a figure of death and new birth.

Now the Pharisees and lawyers had rejected the baptism of John. Our Lord's words are, therefore, a warning to Nicodemus, that he must break with his party, and submit to the ordinance of God ; for, otherwise, he could not receive the Spirit, and so believe on the Messiah, and enter into His Kingdom.

But, in the baptism which the Lord Himself afterwards instituted, the order is precisely the same ; for, on the day of Pentecost, Peter cried aloud ;—

[1] Matt. iii. 11.   [2] John i. 32–3; Matt. iii. 13–17.

" Repent and be baptized, every one of you, upon the Name of Jesus Christ, for remission of sins ; and ye shall receive the gift of the Holy Spirit." [1]

There is, however, a point which seems to require explanation. The water of baptism is here set forth as an indispensable factor in that new birth which, looking beyond mere salvation, has hope also of the Kingdom : indeed, the two terms 'water' and 'Spirit' are parallel, and, apparently, it is to bring out this fact that the article is omitted before Spirit ; so that it is not so much the Person of the Blessed Trinity That is indicated, but rather His influence, or power, regarded as an element. We should also notice, that in the original both terms are governed by one and the same preposition.[2]

Now the water, as we have already seen, represents burial as the proof of death : and, by going down into it, he who would be baptized thankfully confesses that he died to sin in Christ Jesus, and, in a Divinely commanded figure, seeks to share the grave of his Saviour, that God may fulfil His promise by raising him to newness of life, even as He raised up Christ Jesus from the dead. He has already confessed his sins and his faith in the Lord : his immersion is the last thing which God requires of him as an applicant for that new birth which looks forward to the Kingdom.

---

[1] Acts ii. 38.

[2] Many confuse this passage by explaining that "water" is used figuratively for the Word of God, by taking heed to which we can cleanse our ways. We would ask such persons how they propose to interpret the second word "Spirit." If they give it a literal sense and understand it to mean the Spirit of God, then they must take "water" also in a literal sense. For, when two words of the same clause are joined by a copulative and governed by the same preposition, it is impossible to take one of them in a literal and the other in a figurative signification.

Therefore, the moment that he enters into the baptismal waters, his part has been accomplished. He has repented and has been baptized : therefore, in Christ, he stands before God as one who is sinless, and to whom the Holy Spirit can now be given. Thus the water aids in the new birth, not through anything in itself, but because by entering it the repentant and believing sinner has finished what is required of him ; and it now only remains for the God Who cannot lie to fulfil His part, and bestow the gift of the Spirit.

But, still further, by submitting to baptism immediately after his conversion, the believer has publicly testified, that, by God's grace, he will henceforth walk in the path of obedience, that path which leads the saved to the Kingdom, to the great reward of the reign with Christ. Therefore, God responds to this act by bestowing the gift of the Spirit, by which alone a man can be endued with power to win the prize.

To understand this gift, we must remember that there are various operations of the Spirit. There is one which affects the world in the present age, and so convinces men of sin, of righteousness, and of judgment, that, although they are not converted, they feel to some extent a consciousness of God, and are not wholly unrestrained. This influence, as we shall subsequently see, will be withdrawn at the time of the end.

A second operation was illustrated when the Lord breathed upon His disciples, and said, " Receive ye the Holy Spirit." For, although the power then given unquestionably strengthened their faith, and inspired them to enact laws for the churches, yet it did not endue them with full power from on high, nor suffice for the carrying out of the Commission which He afterwards gave them, namely, to preach to all nations.

Therefore, they were bidden to retire into privacy in Jerusalem, until they should be baptized with the Holy Ghost. And, as soon as He had descended in power upon them, they were not said merely to have received Him, but to have been baptized in Him and filled with Him, and were at once enabled to enter upon their great work.

So the man that is " born from above "—a somewhat vague phrase, chosen, apparently, to distinguish this influence from that which should afterwards follow it— is led to Christ by the Spirit Which imparts to him the faith that saves. And if he goes on to obey the command, and by baptism in water to give his public testimony to his Lord, then he may receive the baptism of the Spirit ; and, not merely be saved, but also be endued with power to serve. And so, while he is already sure of eternal life, he will, also, if he continue faithful, gain the reward of those that serve, even the Kingdom of the Heavens.

Of course, any lack of love or impurity of motive in baptism, or any cowardice which keeps the baptized from confessing his act, will cause the gift of the Spirit to be withheld. Yet, provided that the ordinance was valid, that is, if it was the baptism of an intelligent person desiring by it to obey the Lord, we have no warrant for repeating it. If the promised result does not follow, our only resource is incessant prayer, that the hindering sin, known or unknown, may be overcome and pardoned, and the gift graciously vouchsafed.

We must not omit to notice, that, in the " Acts," whenever it is recorded that the Spirit came upon the baptized, the effects were immediately evident to the bystanders ; and that, unless the Spirit were grieved or quenched, the spiritual faculty, and the wisdom and power to work for God in the capacity indicated by the gifts, remained. And hence we are able to understand Paul's meaning when he divides believers into two classes, the carnal and the spiritual: the former have believed and have been baptized; but the latter have also received the crowning gift of the Spirit. Hence the carnal are saved, because they have believed on the Lord Jesus; but they cannot understand the deep things of God, which are communicated by His Spirit Alone. On the other hand, the spiritual, who being joined to the Lord are one spirit, can both understand, and are, or should be, endowed with various supernatural powers distributed to them by that One and the Self-same Spirit, according to His will. They are not only saved from the eternal wrath, but they have communion with God, and the work of sanctification is in full progress within them—that work which must be finished before the transformation of this body of humiliation into the likeness of Christ's Body of Glory can be effected, before the believer, now wholly sanctified in spirit soul and body, can be caught up into the Presence of his Lord.

Hence it is only the spiritual who will rejoice to hear the summons from His lips;—" Come up hither!"

It is only the spiritual who will enter into the Kingdom of the Heavens.

Reader, to which division of believers do you belong? Are you yet carnal, and walking much as other men? Are you vainly striving to make the best of both worlds, to serve God and Mammon? Do the lusts of the flesh—not the grossest of them, perhaps—still retain their hold upon you? Is your anger unbridled, and are you among the evil-speakers who bite and devour one another? Can you take pleasure in human art and intellectual pursuits, while you feel little or no

inclination to, or taste for, the deep things of God?
Can you rejoice continually in earthly objects of love,
and yet spend day after day with scarcely a thought
of Him Who His Own Self bare your sins in His Own
Body on the tree? Alas! the time is short, and He
is at hand! But another moment, and He may have
found you unready!

XX

Paganism and Infant Baptism

Thus the Scriptural teaching of baptism is simple and
consistent with the principles of this dispensation, which
require that every action of a believer should be done
intelligently, willingly, and with a view to the glory
of God. As soon as a man perceives his sinfulness,
mourns over it with godly sorrow, and thankfully
accepts God's way of salvation through Jesus Christ
our Lord, his sincerity is tested by the command to
be baptized. He must be publicly immersed, as a
sign to all men, that, by his union with the Lord in
death, his sins have been expiated, and that, as his
Lord rose from the dead, so he has been brought
into newness of life, and has entered upon the path
of obedience.

But, in course of time, this solemn and significant
ordinance of God was changed, by the already prepared
wiles of Satan, into the semblance of a magical rite,
into a mummery, not merely worthless, but seriously
marring the faith as delivered by the Apostles.

Forgetful of the words of Peter, that baptism is
valid only if there be in the baptized the desire of a
good conscience toward God, men soon began to regard
the virtue of the ordinance as consisting in the mere

immersion into water, provided this were done under the authority of priests of human appointment, and according to accepted forms. And this doctrine they learned, not from the Word of God, but, as in the case of nearly all the early corruptions of Christianity, from the Pagan Mysteries or Sacraments, in the religion of which purification by water was the first step. For in the Chaldean Mysteries, from which all the others seem to have been copied, the applicant for initiation was baptized; and it is said that the ceremony was carried out in a manner so thorough that he was not raised out of the water until he was half-drowned, and did not always survive.

Now, of course, none but adults could be admitted to the baptismal sacrament of initiation, since its object was to prepare the candidate for immediate instruction in the doctrines of the Mysteries. At the same time, according to Pagan theology, none but those who were so admitted could escape the gloom and torment of the realms of Pluto. This is the reason why Virgil, after narrating the descent of Æneas to the infernal regions, and his passage over the Acheron, goes on to say ;—

"Forthwith, on the very verge of the threshold, cries and a prodigious wailing were heard, the weeping spirits of babes whom, before they had tasted sweet life, the day of doom had torn from their Mothers' breasts, and plunged into premature death." [1]

These innocent babes were excluded from the Elysian fields, and consigned to the realms of sorrow, because they had not received priestly purification from the stains of their previous lives ; or, in short, because

[1] Virg. Æn. vi. 426-9.

they had died without the sacrament. Here, then, is
the source from which the unscriptural doctrine of the
sacraments sprang.

Now the Mysteries, as they spread over the world,
were often modified by the nations that adopted them,
though they always remained substantially the same.
And to certain peoples it seems to have occurred, that
something should be done for infants. Accordingly,
we find that our Anglo-Saxon ancestors, among others,
were wont to purify babes, and, as they imagined, to
cleanse them from sin, by water-baptism. Very interesting, too, is the fact, that, when Cortez entered the
country of the Mexicans, the Spanish priests, who first
mingled with the people, were astonished to find them
practising an elaborate rite of infant baptism, which
bore a strong resemblance to the Catholic ceremony.

Either, then, a feeling akin to that of some of the
Pagan nations must have moved the minds of certain
Christians, who had interpreted Christian baptism by
what they knew of the Pagan sacraments ; or, perhaps,
the churches when they began to imitate the Pagan
hierarchies, took infant baptism directly from them ;
and, by so doing, as well as by the novel introduction
of sponsors, altogether destroyed the Christian meaning
of the ordinance, and substituted the Pagan superstition.

A striking illustration of the connection of infant
baptism with Paganism may be found in the fact, that
the Catholic poet Dante, in his *Inferno*, places unbaptized persons in the very same position as Virgil's
uninitiated babes, that is to say, in the vestibule of Hell.
We subjoin Cary's translation of a portion of the
Fourth Canto ;—

> " Onward, this said, he moved ;
> And entering, led me with him, on the bounds

Of the first circle that surrounds the Abyss.
    Here, as mine ear could note, no plaint was heard,
Except of sighs, that made the eternal air
Tremble, not caused by tortures, but from grief
Felt by those multitudes, many and vast,
Of men, women, and infants. Then to me
The gentle guide ;—'Inquirest thou not what spirits
Are these which thou beholdest ? Ere thou pass
Further, I would thou know, that these of sin
Were blameless ; and if aught they merited,
It profits not, since baptism was not theirs,
The portal to thy faith.'"

XXI

INFANT BAPTISM UNKNOWN FOR MORE THAN TWO CENTURIES

IT is admitted, by all unbiassed scholars, that no traces of infant baptism are to be found in Christian writings, until the close of the second century. To this fact Suicer gives testimony as follows ;—

    " For the first two ages, no one received baptism who was not first instructed in the faith and doctrine of Christ, so as to be able to answer for himself that he believed, according to the words, ' He that believeth, and is baptized.' "

    But this assertion, as we shall endeavour to show, does not go far enough ; for no distinct mention of infant baptism occurs until the second half of the third century.

    Those who vainly strive to controvert this fact use two arguments.

    I. They point out, that, according to the earliest of the so-called Fathers, children are conceived and born in sin. That, by the expression of such an opinion, these same Fathers admitted, that infants need regeneration ; and so, since baptism is the only means of regeneration, must have baptized infants.

But not one of the Apostolic Fathers even mentions, much less recommends, infant baptism. It is clear, then, that they did not look for help in that direction ; for had they deemed that an infant's salvation depended upon its baptism, the matter would have been far too vital and urgent to be passed by in silence.

Probably, they had noticed those Scriptures which tell us, that the Lord Jesus was a propitiation not only for the sins of those who believe on Him, but also for the whole world ; and so, that His death must in some way affect every one who comes into the world. This it seems to do, because He took upon Himself the original sin of all men, and for a while, probably, bears their actual sins also ; "for the Lord hath made to light upon Him the iniquity of us all." But, when the testing time comes, God's plan of salvation is revealed to each individual, and, in some form or another, the question is put, What thinkest thou of Christ? If the response be, 1 thankfully receive Him as my Saviour, my Lord, and my God, that man's sins will remain for ever where God placed them ; he has everlasting life, and will not come into judgment. If, however, he spurns God's offer and rejects the Christ, then his sins must return upon himself, and he shall bear his iniquity.

But infants and children of tender age cannot have come to this test ; therefore, their sin or sins remain upon their Saviour, and He, in His love and mercy, is responsible for them. We do not, then, wonder that He said ;—"Suffer the little children to come unto Me, and forbid them not ; for of such is the

Kingdom of God."[1]   No longer does it seem strange
that He should threaten with appalling woe the man
that would make them stumble;[2] or that He should
speak of them as being guarded by angels who have
access at all times to the Presence of His Father[3]—
angels who will know whither to conduct their spirits,
should it please God to withdraw them from earth in
infancy.

We cannot penetrate His plans, which we shall
by and by find to have been conceived in the
supremest love; but it would almost seem as though
some spirits were so tender that it suffices to dip
them into the turbid waters of life but for a moment,
and immediately to draw them out again.   And, if
this be so, how wondrous a song of gratitude must
they pour forth unto God as they cast their first
backward glance upon the constraints and sufferings
from which they have been released !   But we know
not the certainty of such things, and may be well content to leave them in the hands of Him Who is love.

Moreover, those who adopt the argument which we
are considering have to encounter a still greater difficulty; for the Bible does not teach regeneration by
baptism, but by faith in Christ.   All that it affirms
in regard to baptism is, that it saves us typically,
because it is the outward symbol of what faith has
already affected—even as circumcision was to Abraham
the outward seal of the covenant which God had
previously made with him on the ground of his faith.

II. Pedo-baptists also affirm, that infant baptism
is positively mentioned by two Fathers, one of whom
flourished in the middle, and the other at the close,
of the second century.

[1] Mark x. 14.   [2] Matt. xviii. 6.   [3] Matt. xviii. 10.

This, if it were true, would be but little to rely upon ; for there would still be no New Testament proof, and no historical notice of the practice for more than a century after the Lord's death. But it is not true, as we may readily see, if we examine the only passages which are adduced in support of the assertion. These are but two in number, one of which, from Justin Martyr's First Apology,[1] runs thus ;—

"And many men and women, who were made disciples of Christ from their childhood, remain pure at the age of sixty or seventy years."

Of the way in which Pedo-baptists use this extract, we will give but one specimen. Bishop Harold Browne translates " in their infancy," instead of "from their childhood," and then remarks ;—

" How can infants be made disciples but by baptism ? And if these had been baptized in their infancy, it must have been during the lifetimes of the Apostle John, and of other Apostolic men."[2]

Thus the Bishop affects to have proved, not merely that infant baptism was a custom of the ancient churches, but, still further, that it was an Apostolical practice. Such a conclusion may, however, be very easily confuted.

But, first, it will be well to point out, that, even if his translation and his premises were correct, he would still be far from proving either that the Lord Jesus had commanded infant baptism or that the Apostles had sanctioned it. For there is not a single reference to such a practice in the New Testament, which, moreover, always insists upon belief as

[1] Chap. xv.
[2] Browne's *Exposition of the Thirty-nine Articles*, p. 674.

an absolute necessity before baptism. And almost any Epistle will show us that many things were taught and practised in the churches, even in Apostolic times, which were very decidedly antagonistic to the precepts and teachings of the Apostles themselves.

But, apart from all this, the Bishop had no right whatever to translate " in their infancy," instead of "from their childhood." For the Greek word signifies a 'child,' 'boy,' or 'youth,'[1] and not an 'infant.' And it is interesting to notice, that, when Paul said to Timothy, " From a babe thou hast known the Holy Scriptures, which are able to make thee wise unto salvation, through faith which is in Christ Jesus,"[2] the Apostle used a word descriptive of a more tender age[3] than that which we find in the extract from Justin.

As to the idea that a child or youth can only be made a disciple by baptism, the verse just quoted makes it clear that the Apostle Paul did not share the Bishop's opinion.

Moreover, we have already shown that the Lord's way of procedure was to make disciples first and to baptize them afterwards.[4]

Lastly, as we have already said, even if infant baptism could be detected in the Apostolic age, that would be no proof that the Apostles had sanctioned it. For their Epistles teem with references to heresies existing in the churches at the very time when they were writing.

The second passage is one in which Irenæus is confuting the doctrine, that Christ was baptized, and began to preach, at the age of thirty, in order by His

---

[1] παῖς.
[2] 2 Tim. iii. 15.
[3] βρέφος.
[4] John iv. 1. See pp. 112, 113.

previous thirty years of silence to signify the thirty silent Æons of the Gnostics. This absurd theory Irenæus rejects in the following words ;—

"The fact is, that, being thirty years old when He came to baptism, He then proceeded to Jerusalem at the full age of a teacher, so that He could be called Teacher with propriety by all men. For He did not wish to seem one thing while He was another, as they say who bring in an imaginary Christ :[1] but what He was, that He also seemed. Being, then, a Teacher, He had also a Teacher's age, not rejecting nor overpassing man, nor abrogating, in His own case, His own law for mankind ; but sanctifying every age by that semblance which it had to Himself. For He came to save all through Himself—all, I mean, who through him are born again unto God—infants, and little ones, and youths, and young men, and elders. On that account, He passed through every age, having become an infant for infants, to sanctify infants ; among little ones a little one, to sanctify those who are of that same age, being made to them, also, an example of piety righteousness and obedience ; among youths, becoming a pattern to youths, and sanctifying them for the Lord."[2]

Now Wall, Bingham, and other Pedo-baptists, eagerly seize upon this passage, and affirm that infants are here placed among the regenerate, and, therefore, must have been baptized. But the calmer judgment of Hagenbach, himself also a Pedo-baptist, will not sanction this biassed conclusion ;—

"The passage only expresses the beautiful idea that Jesus was Redeemer *in* every stage of life, and

[1] That is, the Docetæ.   [2] Iren. Adv. Hær. II. xxxix.

for every stage of life ; it does not, however, say that He redeemed children by the water of baptism, unless baptism be interpreted into the term *renasci.*"[1]

But the strongest possible reason against the opinion, that Irenæus was thinking of infant baptism, is to be found in the very argument which he is pressing. For he speaks of the Lord Jesus as sanctifying every period of life by passing through it Himself, and by giving an example to those that were old enough to consider it. And the *parvuli*, that is, the little ones or children, are represented as the youngest that are able to do this. But, although a pattern could not be set before unconscious infants, still the logic of the passage seems to require that all that should be done with infants was done in the case of the infant Christ. And yet it is recorded, that He was baptized, not as an infant, but when He was about thirty years old.[2]

If, then, Irenæus had believed in infant baptism, he would surely, since his argument compelled him to show that Christ was baptized at a mature age, have remarked, that, in this particular, the Lord's example was not to be followed.

But, although we cannot admit any reference to infant baptism in this passage, we notice one point of great interest as indicating the trend of thought at the time. While passing by infants as being without intelligence, Irenæus regards children—*parvuli*—as capable of following Christ's example. This view seems to have subsequently led to the baptizing of such children as were thought to be old enough to understand the rite. For, some twenty years later,

---

[1] The word which we have translated "born again." See Hagenbach's *History of Doctrines*, vol. i., p. 282.
[2] Luke iii. 22, 23.

we find Tertullian opposing that very practice. It appears to have been defended by our Lord's reception of children—children, not infants ; for they were old enough to come to Him—although He did not order that they should be baptized, but only that they should not be forbidden to come to Him. To this Tertullian responds ;—

" Let them come, then, while they are growing up, while they are learning, while they are being taught to what they are coming. Let them be made Christians [1] when they are able to know Christ. Why does the age of innocence hasten to the forgiveness of sins ? We are more cautious in worldly matters, seeing that we would commit Divine treasure to those to whom we do not commit earthly property. Let them first know how to ask for salvation, that you may seem to give to him that asketh." [2]

Upon this passage we will quote the comment of Neander, who was himself a Pedo-Baptist, lest our own should seem to be biassed ;—

" Tertullian evidently means, that children should be led to Christ by instruction in Christianity ; but that they should not receive baptism, until, after having been sufficiently instructed, they were led, from personal conviction and by their own free choice, to seek for it with sincere longing of the heart. . . . It would appear in fact, from the principles laid down by him [Tertullian], that he did not believe that *any efficacy whatever* resided in baptism, if it were unaccompanied by the conscious participation and individual faith of the person baptized ; nor could he see any danger accruing to the age of innocence from the postponement of the ordinance."

[1] That is, Let them be baptized.　　[2] Tert. De Bapt. xviii.

Passing now to the second quarter of the third century, we find three references to the baptism of children—*parvuli*[1] still, and not *infantes*—in the writings of Origen. These references are so similar that it will suffice to quote one of them only, which we will take from his remarks on the ninth verse of the fifth chapter of the Epistle to the Romans. He has been speaking of original sin, and proceeds thus ;—

"On this account, too, the church adopted a tradition received from the Apostles, and gave baptism even to children. For they to whom the secrets of the Christian Mysteries were committed knew that there was in every human being a real stain of sin, which must be washed away by water and Spirit."[2]

In regard to this passage, the argument that sin is washed away by baptism has been already proved to be unscriptural. Without shedding of blood, even the precious Blood of the Son of God, there can be no remission of sins.

The reference to Apostolical tradition is not worthy of much attention. Such tradition was often cited in support of false doctrine, and was as destructive of the truth of God as the tradition of the Pharisees had been before it. Of its probable origin we shall have something to say in the last section of this book :[3] for the present, we may be sure that God has caused all the Apostolical teachings that were intended for us to be recorded in the written Word. To commit Divine truth to the uncertainty and corruptions of human tradition has never been His wont.

---

[1] All three passages have come down to us only in the Latin version of Rufinus.

[2] The other passages are to be found in the Eighth Homily on Leviticus, and in the Fourteenth on Luke.   [3] See Chap. LXIX.

But from this passage it is clear, that even Origen, if the translation of his works by Rufinus may be trusted, did not permit the baptism of infants, but only of children—*parvuli*—who, since they came to the Lord when He was upon earth, were supposed to have some little idea, at least, of the meaning of the ordinance.

XXII

ANOTHER KIND OF GOSPEL

WE find, then, no distinct mention of infant baptism, either in the " Acts of the Apostles " or in any uninspired Christian writings, up to the middle of the third century. But immediately after that time there is evidence that the practice was in vogue among the churches of Northern Africa ; for in A.D. 253 Cyprian wrote his well known letter to Fidus, a bishop. From this document it appears, that, while infant baptism was practised in the district, there was some difference of opinion as to the exact time at which it should take place. Fidus desired to have a canon passed fixing the eighth day, as in the case of circumcision ; but sixty-six bishops, assembled in council at Carthage, thought otherwise, and Cyprian, as President, thus expressed their judgment ;—

" In this course which you deemed right to be taken, none of us agreed with you. On the contrary, we decided unanimously, that the mercy and grace of God are not to be refused to any one that has been born into the world. For, seeing that the Lord in His Own Gospel says, The Son of Man is come, not to destroy men's souls, but to save them ; therefore, so far as lies in us, if we can compass it, no soul

must be lost. . . . As to what you say, that the babe
is not clean to the touch in the first days after its
birth, and that each of us would shrink from kissing
such an object, even this, we think, ought not to be
any obstacle to the communication of heavenly grace ;
for it is written, 'To the pure all things are pure';
and none of us ought to shrink from that which God
has deigned to make. For, although the babe is still
fresh from its birth, yet ought no one to shrink from
kissing it at the imparting to it of grace, and at the
salutation of peace; since, in the kiss of an infant, every
one of us ought to be led by his religious feelings to
think of the very hands of God that have just completed their work, which in some sort we are kissing
in the newly framed and lately born man, when we
take in our arms that which God has made."

Thus, in the judgment of Cyprian and the African
bishops, the grace and mercy of God are given in
baptism, and that, too, in the baptism of an unconscious
babe. If baptism be withheld, the unbaptized is outside
the pale of salvation. Hence bishops must be diligent
to have infants baptized as soon as possible after birth,
lest they should die before the rite has been duly
performed, and so be eternally lost! For they are not
members of the Church until they have been baptized,
and "outside the pale of the Church there is no
salvation."

In such circumstances the decision was, of course,
inevitable, that the clergy must not shrink from imprint-
ing the customary baptismal kiss upon a newly born
babe. It would be difficult to find such doctrine as
this in the New Testament ; it belongs to that different
Gospel which Paul warned the Galatians not to receive,
even though he himself or an angel from heaven should

preach it ; that lying Gospel which teaches that men can be ceremonialized into eternal life.

The issues, then, were far too tremendous to admit of nice scruples. And those who had the unpleasant duty to perform might console themselves with two arguments —which, however, to us seem mutually destructive.

First, they might remember that to the pure all things are pure. And, secondly, they might regard the child as fresh from the hands of his Creator, and so consider, that, in kissing it, they were in some sort kissing the very hands that made it.

Such strange doctrine has, of course, no connection whatever with Christianity. It is the old sacramental teaching of the Mysteries, providing an abode for itself in the nominal Church, where it might continue in safety after the tottering edifice of avowed Paganism should have crashed to the ground. And by it the power of salvation was transferred from the Lord Jesus into the hands of bishops and priests. Infant baptism is now that which brings salvation—a dead rite performed upon the unconscious, and no longer a living faith in the only Name given under heaven whereby men can be saved.

Even the argument, that the new-born babe is fresh from the hands of God, is not merely unscriptural, but actively opposed to Bible doctrine. For the only man who ever came fresh from the hands of God was Adam, who is, therefore, called " the son of God ",[1] that is, in the sense that God was his Creator, the sole and immediate cause of his being. But all those that came afterwards were procreated by fallen Adam and his fallen descendants. Had they been directly created by God, they could have had no taint of

[1] Luke iii. 38.

original sin; but must have fallen by individual and wilful violation of commands which they understood, if they were to sink into Adam's condition. He who wishes to be misled in regard to the meaning of Scripture could scarcely find more promising guides than the so-called "Fathers."

In the latter part of the fifth century, Augustine took up the doctrine which Cyprian had confirmed. His line of argument is thus stated by Hagenbach.

"Every man is born in sin, and stands, therefore, in need of pardon. He obtains this by baptism, which cleanses children from original sin, and those who are baptized in later years, not merely from original sin, but also from their actual transgressions committed before baptism. Since baptism is the only and necessary condition of salvation, it follows that unbaptized children are condemned."[1]

Thus Augustine did not hesitate to push Cyprian's doctrine to its logical ultimate. According to this great theologian, children who are unbaptized cannot escape the flames of Hell. However, he did soften so far as to concede that they might be located in a milder spot than more hardened sinners. And in this he followed his Pagan teachers; for Virgil, also, is careful to place his wailing infants at the entrance to, and not in the midst of, the infernal regions, where they lament in company with those who have been condemned on false accusations and with suicides.

As a further specimen of the sort of teaching which was tolerated in Augustine's time, we may mention his explanation of the case of the dying thief, which seemed opposed to his theory of no salvation without baptism. He thought that the thief might have been baptized

[1] *History of Doctrines*, vol. ii p. 74

with blood instead of water; or, perhaps, from the water which flowed from the side of Jesus;[1] or, otherwise, we must assume that he had been baptized at some former time![2] Anything rather than that the Church should be deprived of its monopoly of bestowing eternal life by baptism.

As regards the suggestion, that the thief might have been baptized in his own blood, Augustine seems to be making a confused allusion to an idea of those days, that an unbaptized martyr was as though he had been baptized, because he had been bathed in his own blood. But it is slightly illogical to apply such a theory to the thief, who confessed that he was suffering justly for his crimes.

Another kind of baptism was also supposed to be valid, the baptism of tears. That, however, must have been a hard thing to compass; for Gregory of Nazianzus hints that it would be necessary to wet one's couch with tears every night, and, indeed, to shed so many that their sum total should be equal to the flood of the baptismal waters![3]

Alas for the great " Father " so renowned in Ecclesiastical history, whose name is so familiar to the ears of men! Well would it have been for him if he could have exchanged all his learning and eloquence for the precious secret contained in the verse ;—

> " Not the labours of my hands
> Can fulfil Thy law's demands;
> Could my zeal no respite know;
> Could my tears for ever flow;
> All for sin could not atone,
> Thou must save, and Thou alone."

[1] John xix. 34.
[2] Hagenbach's *History of Doctrines*, vol. ii. pp. 71-3.
[3] Orat. xxxix. 17, lx. 9.

XXIII

SACERDOTAL CEREMONIES

WE may appropriately close this subject with a few particulars of the very elaborate arrangements and ritual that were, more or less, connected with baptism from the third or fourth to the sixth or seventh centuries.

The nominal Church had at that time lapsed into a sort of secret society, and dealt with those who sought admission into it much as if they were candidates for initiation into the Pagan Mysteries. Any one who wished to become a " Christian " had to signify his desire to a Bishop Priest or Deacon, by whom he was solemnly designated as a Catechumen-elect, and signed with the sign of the cross. Shortly afterwards some little information was imparted to him respecting the Faith and the Law ; and if he assented to what he heard, he could then be numbered among the Catechumens.

" A Catechumen was made either in private or in public. If in public, he was signed with the sign of the Cross by the Presbyters, the Clergy, and by his godfathers and godmothers also, anciently on the forehead only, afterwards on the forehead and breast, especially among the Gauls ; and sometimes on his eyes, ears, nostrils, and breast ; in some places on the shoulders and mouth also. Then the Bishop laid his hands upon him ; prayers, as usual, accompanying the imposition of hands, that the Catechumens might be sanctified by the sign of the Cross, and by Prayer, and by the laying on of hands." [1]

[1] Pelliccia's *Polity of the Christian Church*, Translated by the Rev. J. C. Bellett, p. 3.

After this ceremony, he had to submit to a long period of probation—usually as much as two or three years—during which he passed through three grades or orders.

First, he was placed among the *Hearers*, who were allowed to enter the church, and to listen to the reading of the Scriptures and the discourse of the Bishop.

If his behaviour pleased the Bishop, he was in due course promoted to the ranks of the *Prostrators*[1] or *Kneelers*. These were so named, because at the end of the sermons they had to kneel down and receive imposition of hands from the ministers of the church, who, at the same time, prayed for them in a set form of words, to which the faithful gave assent by saying the Amen.

After he had passed a considerable time in these lower grades, he was, if he were still approved of the Bishop, raised to the highest, that of the *Candidates*,[2] and was baptized at the next opportunity, that is to say, on the next Easter Sunday or Pentecost. For those were the only days in the year on which baptisms were permitted in the West, although the Eastern Church allowed them also at the Feast of the Epiphany.

During their long probation, the Catechumens were supposed to be under instruction by means of catechizing or lectures, but what they could have been taught, beyond ordinary morals, is not very apparent ; since the main doctrines of Christianity appear to have been jealously reserved—just as, in the case of the

---

[1] *Substrati.*
[2] *Competentes*. By the Greeks these were called φωτιζόμενοι, or, those who are being illuminated, because they were taught the doctrine of the Trinity, and instructed in the Creed and the Lord's Prayer, just before their baptism. Hence baptism itself was called φωτισμός, that is "illumination."

Mysteries, the secret doctrines were never divulged to outsiders, and very few of them even to the initiates of the Lesser Mysteries. The following extract from Pelliccia gives some curious information on this point, which shows how far the nominal Church had drifted from the Apostolic directions, and to what an extent it had adopted Pagan customs.

"It is, however, to be borne in mind that 'Catechizing' was also the name sometimes given to the discourses delivered by the Bishop to the faithful concerning the more sacred mysteries of the faith; wherefore Cyril of Jerusalem forbids the faithful to repeat to the Catechumens what they had heard at the Catechizing; and when the teacher of the Catechumens gave them his instructions, he used to wrap up the more sacred mysteries of the faith in certain obscurities of language, lest, if they changed their minds and relapsed into Heathenism, they should disclose to the Heathen the most mysterious doctrine of Religion. And so, since 'Jesus had not committed Himself unto them' as yet [*i.e.*, according to S. Augustine's language, had not yet given Himself to them in the Sacrament of His Body and Blood], the Catechumens were kept in ignorance of the mysteries of Baptism, Confirmation, Holy Orders, and other Sacraments, which it was unlawful to administer [or to speak plainly of] in their presence. Only the Candidates for Baptism [*competentes*] were instructed in the mystery of the Trinity, and in the Creed and Lord's Prayer—which were imparted to them a few days before they were baptized. For this reason, even in that part of the public service at which Catechumens were present, the faithful used to recite the Creed and the Lord's Prayer *secreto*, in a very low voice : and hence also, even in our own day, in the public recitation of the offices at the canonical hours, we say the Creed and the Lord's Prayer secretly to ourselves." [1]

Of the ceremonies used for baptism the Pseudo-Dionysius has given a full account ; but his style is so turgid and cumbersome, and so difficult to render literally into good English, that we will avail ourselves of an abbreviated paraphrase by the present Bishop of Durham ;—

"The order of Baptism, then, is as follows. The sacred minister (Hierarch, that is, Bishop) proclaims to all the Gospel, that God Himself deigned to come to us through His love, and to make like to Himself whatever is united with Him. Hereupon whoever is enamoured of this Divine fellowship finds some Christian to take him to the minister, who receives them joyfully with a mental thanksgiving and bodily prostration to the source of all good. Then he summons all the sacred body to the holy place, and after chanting a Psalm with them, and saluting the holy Table, he goes forward and asks the candidate, What he desires ?

"According to the instruction of his sponsor, he asks to 'obtain by his mediation God and the things of God.' And, having promised to live according to the rules of Christian citizenship, he receives imposition of hands from the Bishop, who seals him, and charges the priests to enrol his name with the name of his sponsor. A prayer follows, in which the whole congregation join, and, afterwards, the deacons unfasten the sandals of the candidate, and unclothe him. He is then turned to the West, and,

[1] *Polity of the Christian Church*, p. 4.

with gestures of abhorrence, he thrice renounces Satan in a set form of words. Next he is led to the East, and instructed to declare thrice his allegiance to Christ, with eyes and hands upraised to heaven. A blessing and imposition of hands follow. Then the deacons complete the unrobing, and the priests bring the holy oil. The Bishop begins the unction by a triple cross, and leaving the priests to complete it, goes 'to the mother of adoption' (the font), and consecrates the water with prayers and three cross-formed affusions of the holy chrism, and bids the candidate be brought to him. His name is then called out with the name of his sponsor, and he is brought to the Bishop. Again the priests declare his name with a loud voice, and the Bishop thrice dips him, invoking at each immersion the three Persons of the Blessed Trinity. Then he is consigned to his sponsor, and, being reclothed in a white robe, is brought back to the Bishop, who seals him with the sacred chrism, and pronounces him capable of being admitted to the Eucharist." [1]

In this extract, the first thing that strikes us is a very serious deficiency in the Gospel preached by the Hierarch or Bishop. For his address contains not even so much as an allusion to the expiation of our sins by the Blood of the Lord Jesus; without which, what possibility can there be of union with God? Nevertheless, Dionysius apparently implies that the elaborate rite of Church-baptism will do all that is required.

In the original, the friend whom the candidate asks to become his sponsor is represented as being immediately seized with horror, and an overwhelming sense of his incompetence to undertake so great a responsibility.

[1] Westcott's *Religious Thought in the West*, pp. 169-70.

If this behaviour could be observed in every case, as the text seems to hint, it must have been affected—a mere conventional pantomime, very much in accord with what follows.

The idolatrous salutation of the " Table " must not be overlooked ; nor yet the fact, that the Bishop is asked to be a mediator between the candidate and God, in spite of the Scriptural declaration, that there is but One Mediator between God and man, that is, the Man Christ Jesus. [1]

Again, the baptism is permitted on the promise of the candidate to live according to the rules of Christian citizenship, not on the ground of his faith in the Lord Jesus.

Of the turning to the West and, subsequently, to the East, we will speak presently.

The gestures of renunciation, which, according to the original, are the beating of the candidate's upturned hands towards the West, and his blowing with scorn upon Satan, are a foolish piece of acting ; while his renunciation of the Devil and all his works, especially since, so far as Dionysius tells us, it is made in his own strength, is a vow uncalled for and impossible to be kept. No vows are required from followers of the Lord Jesus ; for by using such expressions they would only be assuming a power which they do not possess, and their failure to fulfil their promise would render them guilty of perjury before God, and, therefore, liable to His chastisements. If they see the necessity of performing an arduous duty, or of giving up the indulgence of an evil practice, it is not theirs to vow to the Lord that they will carry out either of these purposes ; but to entreat Him for such guidance and grace and strength

[1] 1 Tim. ii. 5.

as will be sufficient for the effort or the self-denial. For they know, that, while they can do all things if He be their Helper, yet, without Him, they can do nothing.

The anointing with oil is unscriptural, and has no connection with baptism; while the marking of three crosses upon the candidate removes the ceremony still further from anything that is Christian.

The dedication of the water, again, is unscriptural and worse than useless; since from many passages we find that the blessing of the priest was supposed to impart to it a magical virtue, without which the baptism was believed to be futile. The trine immersion, too, is a human fancy, which conceals the true meaning of the rite.

The final sealing of the baptized with "the most Divinely operating myrrh-oil,"[1] as the original has it, shows that the chrism, also, was supposed to have a magical power.

So completely, then, did Satan succeed in annulling the Lord's simple and significant rite of baptism. Nor was that the end of the mischief; for the candid reader cannot but feel, that the Church-baptism described above—as well as the wearisome and useless delay which preceded it—was not merely non-Christian, but positively anti-Christian. It is not enough to say, that its ceremonial acts had no affinity with the command of the Lord and the expositions of His Apostles: nay, they are set in the most direct opposition to the fundamental doctrines of the faith. And, through their introduction, the ordinance ceased to be expressive and commemorative of the believer's death burial and resurrection with Christ, and became a veritable Pagan Sacrament, supposed to bring about a union with God

---

[1] τῷ θεουργικωτάτῳ μύρῳ.

through the magic power of the priests, and by means of their enchanted water and oil.

And, although some of the ceremonial acts were subsequently omitted; nevertheless, the real meaning of baptism had been lost, and has never since been recovered by the Catholic Churches.

XXIV

The West and the East

WE have seen above, that, when the candidate for baptism was called upon to renounce the Devil, he was set with his face towards the West, that being the quarter assigned to the Power of Darkness. On this renunciation Pelliccia remarks ;—

"Although among the Latins in some Churches, down to the ninth century, the Bishop was satisfied with the Catechumen repeating the formula once ; yet, generally, from the fourth century, the renunciation was repeated twice, first, of the Devil and his works, second, of the world and its luxury—the same formula which is used in our day by the Church of Milan : and, at length, about the eighth century, that threefold renunciation which obtains among ourselves came into use. Until the Catechumens had concluded this ceremony of renunciation, they stood facing the West, and, when it was finished, they turned to the East ; and, among the Greeks, at each repetition of the words ' I renounce,' they stretched out their hands one after another, as if putting the Devil to flight." [1]

After the renunciation, then, they turned round to the East, as though the Spirit of God and the Godhead

[1] *Polity of the Christian Church*, p. 15.

Itself were to be found in that quarter. And the consequence of this foolish idea was, that the Christian churches began to be as carefully oriented as the Pagan temples had been before them, and that Christians turned to the East in worship, just as the Pagans did.

But they ought to have been well aware of three overpowering reasons, at least, against such a practice.

I. Their great Lord Himself had declared, in reference to the age which He was about to inaugurate, that God is Spirit, and that they who would worship Him must do so in spirit and in truth.[1] And this fact He had given as a reason why men should cease to regard Jerusalem and Mount Gerizim as vantage-grounds for prayer. For spirit is not concerned with locality; and, therefore, to those who are worshipping a Spirit in spirit, it is a matter of absolute indifference in whatever part of the earth they may find themselves, or whether they may chance to be facing the North, or the South, or the East, or the West.

II. In the former and less spiritual dispensation, when God did give directions as to locality, it was the West, and not the East, which He chose as the quarter to be honoured by the manifestation of His Presence, and toward which, consequently, His worshippers were to look.

For we read that the longer sides of the Tabernacle were to face the South and the North respectively, so that they extended from the West to the East.[2] And the West-end was to be completely shut in with boards, because the Holy of Holies was to be there.[3] But the East-end was the way of entrance into the Holy Place, and was only covered with curtains that could be raised by any one wishing to enter. The

[1] John iv. 21-4.　　[2] Exod. xxvi. 18-20.　　[3] Exod. xxvi. 22-5.

Ark of the Covenant, then, with its Mercy-seat and Cherubim over which the Glory of the Lord appeared, was set, by His express command, in the West, and thither, in the previous dispensation, His worshippers turned, and were thus distinguished from all the idolaters on the face of the earth.

Precisely the same arrangement was made in the Temple built by Solomon ; and this we may prove by a very significant passage of Ezekiel. For that prophet, in relating how he was caught up by the Spirit and conveyed to Jerusalem, in order that he might see the abominations which had provoked the Lord to doom both City and Sanctuary to destruction, thus describes the last and worst of them ;—

"And He brought me into the inner court of the Lord's House ; and, behold, at the door of the Temple of the Lord, between the porch and the altar, were about five and twenty men, with their backs toward the Temple of the Lord, and their faces toward the East ; and they worshipped the sun toward the East." [1]

These five and twenty men, whose number seems to indicate that they were the High Priest and the heads of the twenty-four courses or orders of priests,[2] when they looked toward the East were compelled to turn their backs upon the Temple of the Lord, which must, therefore, have been in the West.

Thus, in the Tabernacle and first Temple, the faces of the worshippers of Jehovah were directed toward the West. Nor was the way in which He prevented the godly Israelites from acquiring the habit of looking toward the East during their time of exile without significance. For, until their dispensation had come

---

[1] Ezek. viii. 15, 16.   [2] 1 Chron. xxiv. comp. Luke i. 5.

to a manifest end in the destruction of the City and Sanctuary by Titus, all the countries to which they were carried captive were in the East. Consequently, in looking toward Jerusalem, the exiles would have to turn more or less to the West, and would so continue to be plainly separated from the Heathen around them, since the latter invariably turned to the East. As an instance of this, a glance at the respective positions of Babylon and Jerusalem on the map will show, that Daniel's window, which looked toward Jerusalem, must have faced the South-West.[1]

Lastly, in the great Millennial Temple, when the calling of men will once more, so far as revelation has hitherto taught us, be earthly, and not heavenly as it is now, the Holy of Holies will still be found in the West. For, in the forty-seventh chapter of Ezekiel, we read ;—"The forefront of the House was toward the East."[2] And, of course, if the front or entrance to the House be on its Eastern side, then the Holy of Holies, being at the opposite end, must necessarily be toward the West.

Hence the reason why the Glory of God will return to the Temple by the way of the East[3] is obvious. It will move toward the great entrance-gate at the East-end, and so, passing over the threshold, will go through the House to the Holy of Holies at the West-end, and there abide. It will thus return by the same route as that by which Ezekiel saw it departing. For then it left the Holy of Holies in the West, passed through the Holy Place, stood upon the threshold at the East-end,[4] and went straight on by the East gate[5] to the Mount of Olives on the East side of the city.[6]

---

[1] Dan. vi. 10. [3] Ezek. xliii. 1–5. [5] Ezek. x. 19; xi. 1.
[2] Ezek. xlvii. 1. [4] Ezek. ix. 3; x. 4. [6] Ezek. xi. 23.

III. There is in the Old Testament a manifest hint, from which, especially if they had compared it with Heathen theology and practice, the Christians might have understood why it was that the Lord placed His Sanctuary in the West, and counted as rebels those who deliberately turned to worship toward the East. For, in the verse quoted above from the eighth chapter of Ezekiel, the five and twenty men were said to be doing so, in order that they might worship the sun.

Now the sun, or rather the sun-god, was the most universal object of worship among ancient nations, whether he was adored as Bel, Baal, Ra, Apollo, Mithras, or by any other of his countless names. He would, therefore, naturally have appeared to stand in the sharpest opposition to the God That made the heavens, and the earth and sea and fountains of waters. Of this all the early Christians must have been well aware, residing as they did in the midst of Pagans, and having themselves, in very many cases, been converted from Paganism. They knew, also, that the sun-worshippers were always accustomed to turn to the East, and should have noticed the many passages in the Old Testament against sun-worship; and especially the obvious fact, that it was in order to separate Israel to Himself from the world of idolaters, that God had revealed His awful Presence in the West, and commanded His earthly people to turn thither in prayer.

These three reasons, then ;—That God is Spirit, so that His worshippers have nothing to do with locality ; that, when, in a former dispensation, He did mention a locality, He chose the West as His quarter ; and that all Pagans were accustomed to turn to the East—the knowledge of these three facts, of which they most certainly were, or might have been, possessed, left the nominal Christians without excuse.

But alas! they were declining that separation from the world which the Word of God required, and were casting about how they might compromise and assimilate themselves, in some respects at least, to their Pagan fellow-citizens. And to effect this purpose, they adopted, among other things, the practice of turning to the East from the sun-worshippers: soon afterwards they began to call the Lord's day Sunday; and also transferred their celebration of His birth from April, the month in which it seems really to have taken place, to the twenty-fifth of December, a day devoted by the whole Pagan world to an annual festival, because, for astronomical reasons, it was believed to be the birthday of the sun-god. The reputed followers of Christ had turned away from Him, and, retracing their steps, had, as it were, recrossed the dividing waters, the great river Euphrates; since they were no longer willing to be reckoned as spiritual Hebrews, but were minded to get them back again into the land of Chaldean idolatry.

XXV

CONCLUDING REMARKS

WE need trace the corruption of baptism no further: we have followed it to the point at which a mere empty form takes the place of faith in the Lord Jesus, and of an open profession of that faith by simply passing under the waters, according to His command. An attempt had, indeed, been made to infuse life into the dead rite by attributing power to the sacerdotal ministry and the consecrated water, the effect of which was, that the Lord's ordinance was transformed into a Pagan sacrament. And this idea, in some shape or another, has descended to modern times. Belief in it was that which prompted Francis Xavier to be confident that he had made another Christian, whenever he could utter his set form of words, as he cast water on the face of a Heathen child. It was this doctrine which caused the enrolment of a society in London, in connection with the Established Church, a distinguished member of which reported, that the society had hunted up, and brought to the clergy for baptism, some hundred and fifty babes in the course of three months. And, again, it has suggested the arrangement, at certain metropolitan clergy-houses, whereby a priest is kept ready, every night, with a case by his side containing all requisites for a baptism, even to a bottle of water, in order that, if during the dark hours news should be brought of a dying infant, he may hasten without delay to perform his function, and—what? Save the babe from everlasting perdition, we suppose; and we may honour his zeal. But would that it were exercised according to knowledge!

Of late, however, many believers in the Lord Jesus have been impelled to obey His command, that baptism should follow conversion; and we cannot but place this fact among the ever multiplying signs of His speedy return. And that the more, since those who are being thus baptized do not seem necessarily to leave the churches to which they have previously belonged; for, in such circumstances, the movement cannot be said to indicate the mere extension of a particular sect, but must be the manifestation of a desire to walk more carefully in the paths of obedience. A people is being prepared for the Presence of the Lord; and how can they meet Him with joy, unless they have thrust all obstacles aside, and done that which He has so plainly commanded?

But there are some, on the other hand, who regard an outward rite, like baptism, as a thing of very slight importance. Let our hearts but be right with God, they say, and then it matters little whether or not we have been dipped in water. Such persons should remember, first, that it is impossible for any insignificant command to come from the Lord of Glory, nor is He accustomed to say that which He does not mean to enforce; and, secondly, that their hearts cannot be right with Him, if they are wilfully disobeying even the least of His commandments.

And if they hanker after a philosophic reason for the two rites which He *will* require of us: they can, in this case, have one. After we have been saved by the Blood of the Lord Jesus, there is but one purpose for which we remain in the world; that is, that we may learn obedience to the Great Creator and God of Love. For it is only by discipline of this kind that we can become sanctified and fitted for translation to a province of His boundless realms where sin and sorrow are unknown.

Now, roughly speaking, the inhabitants of earth may be divided into two classes—those who are disposed to formalism, and those whose tendency lies in the opposite direction, that of mysticism. In the previous dispensation, the services of God were largely made up of outward observances, though none of them was without its spiritual meaning. And the result was, that, when our Lord appeared upon earth, the religious leaders of Judæa were mere formalists: they had altogether lost sight of the inward teaching of

ceremonies and ordinances, and practically regarded
them as a species of magical rites, supposing that,
if they were careful and accurate in the external
performance of them, they had done all that was
required. There was not a spark of intelligent
spirituality in their services ; and, consequently, their
moral character remained unregenerate, carnal and
selfish as ever, nay, growing continually worse through
the added sin of hypocrisy. Moreover, many among
them, feeling an utter lack of power in their religion,
had seceded—one party organizing itself into a
doubting sect, that believed neither in resurrection
nor angel nor spirit ; while another formed a political
clique, which began to work out the aspiration of its
faith by means of worldly intrigues.

The dispensation of ceremonial observances had
failed, and the Lord proceeded to establish a different
order of things in its stead. In the new era, nothing
of the Mosaic ritual was retained : the worship was
to be entirely spiritual, and its every act performed
intelligently and in love. Yet, knowing that mysticism
must be checked as well as formalism, the Lord
appointed two, and but two, simple outward rites, in
order that, while formalists were being taught that
God as a Spirit could be worshipped only in spirit
and in truth, those, also, who were mystically inclined
might have an easy means of testing their obedience.
For they, too, would have to overcome their own
prejudices by submitting to baptism and by joining
in the Supper of the Lord, if He really was their Lord
in anything more than name ; while formalists must
know, that, unless they could worship God in a spirit
of love and devotion, and without any ritual or
sensuous aids, their faith was a mere sentiment,

lacking God-consciousness, and absolutely devoid of power.

One more remark seems to be needed. Why is it that the evangelists of our days do not immediately enjoin baptism on their converts? Did not the Same Lord, Who bade them go "and make disciples of all the nations," add, in the very same sentence, the command that they were also to baptize those same nations? Is one part of His charge to be kept, and not the other? Did He caution us to have the fear of man always before our eyes? And, when He sits upon His Judgment-seat, will He admit the excuse to be sufficient, if those who have preached the Gospel urge, that, since many people would certainly have been offended, had they persisted in carrying out the whole of His charge, they had deemed it best to ignore the objectionable part of it?

THE LORD'S SUPPER

XXVI

THE BREAD OF LIFE

John vi. 25–64.

THE second and only other rite appointed by the Lord Jesus for His followers in the present age is called "the Lord's Supper,"[1] or, "the Communion of the Blood and Body of the Christ."[2] Both of these names are given to it in Scripture, but no other: and it will be noticed, that they contain no allusions to either sacrifice or priest, suggesting nothing more than a commemorative meal. Had they been retained to the exclusion of all unscriptural designations, they would have preserved the nominal Churches from much error. For, as ecclesiastical history teaches, the introduction of other and unauthorised names has been usually connected with the bringing in of errors, which have finally severed every link between the ordinance as used by the vast majority of "Christians" and that which was originally instituted by the Lord.

Even the term "Eucharist," innocent as it seems, was probably framed to suggest the sacrifice of peace- or thank-offerings, and so to give a sacrificial character to the rite ; while the name ' Mass ' was taken, through the Latin *missa*, from the *mizd*, or round wafer, which was eaten in honour of Mithras the Sun-god, and

---

[1] I Cor. xi. 20.
[2] I Cor. x. 16, where Paul mentions the Blood before the Body.

which was substituted in the churches for the broken bread of the Lord's Supper. This change completely obliterated the reference to His broken Body, and turned His Supper into a Pagan festival. Moreover, it also destroyed the idea of the Communion, since the rite, thus transformed, could no longer yield the lesson which Paul had drawn from it ;—

" The loaf which we break, is it not a communion of the Body of the Christ ? seeing that we, who are many, are one loaf, one Body ; for we all partake of the one loaf." [1]

Now, if we would fully investigate the Scriptural meaning of the Lord's Supper, we must first examine His discourse in the sixth chapter of the Fourth Gospel ; where, without any reference to the rite itself, He opens to us, in wondrous words, the great truth of which the Commemorative Meal was afterwards appointed to be an emblem.

On the day before He delivered this discourse, He had, by His creative power, multiplied five barley cakes and two small fishes, so that they became sufficient to feed five thousand men, besides women and children, and afterwards to fill twelve baskets with the fragments that remained.

Excited by the miracle, the people would have hailed Him as the Royal Messiah ; nor was their purpose in any way distasteful to the equally eager disciples. But He sternly commanded the latter to retire to their ship, and pull for the opposite shore. Meanwhile, after He had dispersed the multitude, He departed into a mountain, and continued in prayer until the night was far spent. Then, in the fourth watch, He walked upon the sea to His disciples, who

[1] 1 Cor. x. 16, 17.

had been distressed by a storm, and were unable to make way against the wind and waves. Though terrified at first by His appearance amid the troubled waters, they soon recognized Him, and gladly received Him into the ship; and, at that moment, the vessel, which, with all their hard rowing, had only reached the middle of the lake, was found to be at the farther shore. With the coming of their Master all necessity for toil and distress had suddenly ceased, and they were safe in the desired haven—a wondrous figure of what shall happen to His labouring and afflicted people when He comes again.

On the next morning, the multitude, who knew that only one ship had been at the place where they were, and that the disciples had rowed away in it without their Master, began to look about for Him, but were unable to find Him. Then some vessels from Tiberias came by, and, getting on board, they went to the other side of the lake, and resumed their search. Soon they met with the Lord, either in the synagogue or on His way thither, and accosted Him enthusiastically with the question;—"Master, when[1] didst Thou come hither?"

But this question He did not answer. He would not tell them of His miraculous passage across the lake: such a sign was not for these sensuous people, who were seeking Him merely in the hope that He would continue to feed their bodies, and to satisfy their carnal desires. His reply was addressed to their in-

---

[1] "The idea suggested by '*when*,' as contrasted with the more natural *how*, is that of separation from Christ; as if the people had pleaded, 'We sought Thee long and anxiously on the other side. Could it be that even then Thou hadst left us?' If this turn be given to the words, the connection of the answer is obvious;—'It is not Me that ye seek, but My gifts.'"

most thoughts, not to what they had said. With His impressive, "Verily, verily," He pointed out, that they had not even noticed the sign in what they had seen Him do, but cared only for the material relief. As Lange puts it, "Instead of seeing in the bread the sign, they had in the sign perceived nothing but the bread." Food for the body was all that they craved: the motives of their quest were earthly and sensual; whereas what He had come to satisfy was the hunger after righteousness, the thirst for God, even for the Living God.

Thus they had wearied themselves in seeking earthly goods; but He counselled them not to labour for the food that perishes, but for that which would remain with them, and become the germ of immortality. The material bread which He had created on the previous day was already ceasing to sustain them, but He, the Son of Man, was able to offer them the Bread of Everlasting Life. And on this point they needed not to doubt; for, in the acts of power which He did, they might perceive the seal of God, the Father, marking Him as the long promised Deliverer.[1]

Here we should observe the introduction of the term "Son of Man," which seems to hint that Christ, Himself the Bread of Life, had been brought within the reach of human faith by means of His incarnation. We shall presently find a further development of this hint.

The multitude saw no difficulty in the Lord's answer; and, accepting the exhortation to labour in a literal and legal sense, asked;—"What must we do that we may work the works of God?"

---

[1] This He had already pointed out in John v. 36;—"But the witness which I have is greater than that of John; for the works which the Father hath given Me to accomplish, the very works that I do, bear witness of Me, that the Father hath sent Me."

"This is the work of God," the Lord replied, "that ye believe on Him Whom He sent." In these days many insist that justification by faith is a dogma peculiar to Paul, and they are accustomed to group it with kindred teachings under the name of Paulinism, wishing to suggest thereby, that the inspired writers of the New Testament do not teach the same things, but put forth diverse and even contradictory doctrines.

Here, however, such critics are confuted; for, in this short answer, the Lord has condensed all that Paul afterwards taught on the subject of justification.

In regard to the response of the Jews, it has seemed strange to many, that those who had so lately witnessed the miracle of the loaves and fishes, and had forthwith desired to salute the Wonder-worker as their King, should have again demanded a sign from Him. To this it would be sufficient to reply with Lücke;—"The carnal belief in miracles is insatiable: it craves miracle after miracle." But we may also remember, that the Lord had just been depreciating His recent act of power by pointing to greater things, to a better bread than that of the previous day, which He was prepared to give them. Thus he had excited in these Jews, who were always looking for signs, the hope of a surpassing miracle. Quite naturally, then, they rejoiced in the prospect, and were eager for what He had promised; but, of course, expected to realize it in the material, and not in the spiritual, sphere. And so, they replied;—

"What, then, doest Thou for a sign, that we may see, and believe Thee? What dost Thou work? Our fathers ate the manna in the wilderness; as it is written, 'He gave them bread out of heaven to eat.'"

They quite understood that He was presenting Himself as the Messiah, and would see His credentials. The sign from heaven of which the Pharisees spoke was in their thoughts ; and it was, probably, in reference to it that they reminded Him of the manna from heaven. They seem to have imagined that His promised bread would be some ambrosial and yet material food similarly brought down from above.

But gradually and gently He proceeded to unveil His meaning ;—

"Verily, verily, I say unto you, Not Moses has given[1] you the Bread out of heaven ; but My Father giveth you the true Bread out of heaven. For the Bread of God is That Which cometh down out of heaven, and giveth life unto the world."

By thus contrasting the true Bread with the manna, the Lord would prepare the minds of the Jews to learn that the former is not material, but spiritual. So, in what follows, there is, it would seem, an intentional ambiguity ; since we may render either "the Bread of God is That Which cometh down," or, "is He That cometh down." The sense is—That only deserves to be called the Bread of God Which comes down out of heaven, and has the power of imparting life to the world. But this last word must have considerably startled the Jews, who would naturally have supposed that the true Bread, like the manna, was to be reserved for Israel alone. Nevertheless, since they retained their idea of material bread, they could still believe themselves in harmony with what the Great Teacher was saying.

"Lord," they cried, "evermore give us this bread." If He would but continue to feed their bodies, He might lead, and would find them close behind Him. But let

___

[1] δέδωκεν.

the supply go on regularly, day after day, just as the manna appeared every morning. And, of course, the bread which was now promised would be infinitely superior to the manna. This time, at least, there would be no temptation to say, " Our soul loatheth this light bread."

Such, apparently, was the trend of their thoughts: they were still able to misinterpret His words, and to believe that He would satisfy their carnal desires. But His reply destroyed this hope, and completely changed their feeling towards Him ; for He said ;—

" I am the Bread of Life: he that cometh to Me shall not hunger, and he that believeth on Me shall never thirst.

" But I said unto you, that ye have seen Me, and yet believe not.

" All that which the Father giveth Me shall come unto Me ; and him that cometh to Me I will in no wise cast out.

" For I am come down from heaven, not to do· Mine own will, but the will of Him That sent Me.

" And this is the will of Him That sent Me, that of all that which He hath given Me I should lose nothing, but should raise it up at the Last Day.

" For this is the will of My Father, that every one that contemplateth the Son, and believeth on Him, should have eternal life ; and I will raise him up at the Last Day." [1]

By these words the Lord clearly signified that He was dealing with spiritual, and not with material, things The thirty-fifth verse is the great clue to all that follows ; and, had the Jews believed and given heed to it, they would have been troubled with no subsequent difficulty.

[1] John vi. 35–40.

Not anything to be obtained from Him, but He Himself is the Bread of Life, even as, in the discourse of the previous chapter, He had said ;—

" For, as the Father hath life in Himself, even so He gave to the Son, also, to have life in Himself."

But, if the Son be the Bread of Life, how can the figure be carried out ? In what way can He be said to be eaten by those who desire life ? As regards our own necessary action in the matter, He does not leave such a problem for our poor minds to solve ; but at once explains, that, whoever comes to Him for salvation shall hunger nevermore, evidently because, in the figure which is presently introduced, he, by so coming, eats the Flesh of the Son of Man ; while he that believes on Him shall have his thirst finally quenched, because, by his act of faith, he has drunk the Blood of the Son of Man. Only those who neglect so plain an unfolding of all its mystery at the beginning of the discourse will stumble over what is said at the end of it. The eating and drinking are altogether spiritual, and are accomplished by an act of faith. Our part in the matter is wholly comprised in the coming to the Lord and in the believing on Him : the rest—however literally and exactly analogous to the actual eating and drinking of material sustenance by the organs of the body—is His care. He will see that it is effectually performed by our spirit, though we may be quite unconscious of the act, as, indeed, we are of many spiritual things that are carried on within us.

Faith, however, was just exactly what these Jews had not. They had seen the sign, which was the Lord Himself : they had looked on while He was exercising over the loaves and fishes a creative power which none but God could exhibit, and yet they had not believed. Did He not tell them so, when they found Him in Capernaum? Did He not say that all their desire was for a fresh supply of loaves and fishes, and that, apart from these, they cared not for Him upon Whom they had gazed as He was in the act of creating them?

They believed not; and He would tell them why they failed to do so. It was because His Father had not given them to Him. For all that which the Father had given Him should, without fail, reach Him, and should not break down by the way, like the multitude that desired nothing beyond the loaves and fishes.

Thus the bare fact, that a man moves toward Christ, seeks Himself, and not merely the earthly benefits which He is able to bestow, shows that he has been given to the Son by the Father. Therefore, the Son can in no wise reject him, because it was to do the Father's will that He came down from heaven.

There is something remarkable in the neuter expression, "all that which"; for it indicates, that those whom the Lord will receive are regarded as one whole, as a perfect number that cannot be broken: they are the "elect according to the foreknowledge of God."

In the thirty-ninth verse, the Lord reveals the will of the Father, that, of all which the Father has given Him, He should lose nothing, but should raise it up on the Last Day. In the next verse, as we have already remarked, He gives another view of the same will, that every one who contemplates the Son, and believes on Him, has everlasting life, and will be raised by Him on the Last Day. Thus each of these verses expresses the same truth, the one in its Divine, the other in its human aspect. The Father, through His foreknowledge, has predestinated some men to life, and given them to the Son. And those who are thus given are drawn by the Father into a contemplation of the Son, with the result that they believe on Him, and are saved. The visible cause of their salvation is that they believe on the Son; but they could not have done so, unless the Father had empowered them, because He foresaw that their spirits would yield to His discipline.

The Last Day must end all, and, therefore, is that great Day of the Lord, " in which all that are in the tombs shall hear His voice, and shall come forth; they that have done good unto the resurrection of life, and they that have done evil unto the resurrection of judgment." [1] The final resurrection to life is mentioned four times in this chapter; for in it the full meaning and power of the Bread of Life will be realized. But, of course, the saved may be raised before that time, may attain to the First Resurrection: that, however, as we have already seen, is a matter depending on the service that springs from faith, and the Lord is here dealing only with faith itself.

He who contemplates the Son with the result of believing on Him is in direct antithesis to the multi-tude, who had seen Him, and yet did not believe. The two words 'contemplateth' and 'believeth' answer to 'cometh and believeth' in the thirty-fifth verse, as they do, also, to 'eateth the Flesh' and 'drinketh the Blood' in the fifty-third verse.

Such, then, was the Lord's explanation; and, as the Jews listened to it, their feelings toward Him underwent a rapid change. Carnal things were what they desired, not spiritual; and a murmur of discontent, breaking out on all sides, revealed their disappointment.

[1] See p. 46.

They no longer owned Him as Master and Lord; but endeavoured to find some matter for criticism or complaint in what He had said. How could this man have come down from heaven? they asked. Are not His father, Joseph, and His mother well known to us, and has He not grown up among us? Then, in the midst of their excitement, the Lord again addressed them with words that were as fuel to their anger;—

"Murmur not among yourselves. No man can come to Me, except the Father which sent Me draw him: and I will raise him up in the Last Day.

"It is written in the prophets, 'And they shall all be taught of God.' Every one that heareth from the Father, and hath learned, cometh unto Me.

"Not that any man hath seen the Father, save He Which is from God, He hath seen the Father.

"Verily, verily, I say unto you, he that believeth (on Me) hath eternal life.

"I am the Bread of Life.

"Your fathers did eat manna in the wilderness, and they died.

"This is the Bread Which cometh down out of heaven, that a man may eat thereof, and not die.

"I am the Living Bread Which came down out of heaven: if any man eat of this Bread, he shall live for ever: yea, and the Bread Which I will give is My Flesh, which I will give for the life of the world."[1]

Stay these useless murmurings, the Lord seems to say. Your condition is not difficult to explain. "No man can come unto Me, except the Father Which sent Me draw him: and I will raise him up on the Last Day." You have not been drawn by My Father:

[1] John vi. 43-51.

therefore, you cannot come to Me; and, therefore, I cannot raise you up on the Last Day.

" In the Prophets," he continues, " it is written, They shall all be taught of God." The allusion is to the portion of Scripture which the Jews called " The Prophets "; for they divided the Old Testament into three divisions—the Law, the Prophets, and the Hagiographa. The particular prophecy from which the Lord cites is the glorious prediction of the restoration of Israel in the fifty-fourth chapter of Isaiah. There it is said of the restored nation;—" And all thy children shall be taught of the Lord; and great shall be the peace of thy children."[1]

With the full meaning of this prophecy we should all be familiar. When the Twelve Tribes were led into Palestine, they had rashly promised, in their own strength, to do all that the Lord their God had commanded them:[2] but they altogether failed to keep this promise. Hence they were driven from their own land, and have since been sifted among all nations, even as corn is sifted in a sieve.[3] They might, indeed, have been restored at the time of, or immediately after, the First Advent. But the Ten Tribes were then dwelling far away in unbelief; while the Two, which the Lord found in Palestine, had by no means been taught of God; for they still retained their pride and self-confidence, and would not come to the Deliverer. Hence it was necessary that the nation as a whole, unbelieving and unblessed as it was, should again be thrust out for a disciplinary exile of many weary centuries; until, at length, the people should be humbled in spirit, and ready to listen to the words of Jehovah.

But among them were a few whose lowliness and

---

[1] Isa. liv. 13.   [2] Exod. xxiv. 3.   [3] Amos ix. 9.

earnest seeking after God rendered them capable of being taught by Him even at that time : these were drawn to the Lord Jesus, and, having received of Him power to become children of God, were made partakers of a heavenly calling. Such seems to be the meaning of the second part of the forty-fifth verse, which tells us, that every one who was in the habit of listening[1] to the Father, and had learnt of Him, understood what he ought to do, and came to the Christ. For God would not permit the little flock of the faithful to suffer for the sins of the whole nation.

As an example of habitual hearing, we may compare what our Lord says of the manner in which He Himself was taught of the Father, during His sojourn upon earth ;—

> "He wakeneth morning by morning, He wakeneth Mine ear to hear as those who are taught. The Lord God hath opened Mine ear ; and I was not rebellious, neither turned away backward."[2]

Here it is plainly intimated, that the unbroken communion of the Lord with His Father enabled Him, as each morning dawned, to receive directions for His conduct during the day : and could we but follow in His steps, and preserve our communion, we, too, might be similarly taught of God. But how often is that communion broken for the sad reason, that, when we have heard, we are not able to say as did the Lord, "And I was not rebellious, neither turned away backward." In the case of the Jews, it is manifestly implied,

---

[1] By our rendering of this passage, it will be seen that we prefer the reading which gives the present participle, ἀκούων : the change to the aorist ἀκούσας is, probably, due to an unintelligent attempt to match the tense of μαθών. Thus the full sense will be, Every one who hears as a habit, and has, consequently, learnt.

[2] Isa. l. 4, 5.

that the sin of habitual inattention to the voice of
God had preceded, and brought about, their condition of
hardened and hopeless unbelief; so that they came into
the Lord's presence, not as the taught of God, but as
the slaves of sin.[1]

And yet, though all teaching must come from the
Father, no man has at any time seen Him. If we be
in communion with Him, we may hear His voice as
He speaks to us through His Spirit and by His Word,
but we cannot behold His face. Only He has seen
Him Who is from Him, and Who stands in the relation
of Son to Him. Therefore, those who would draw near
to the Father must do so through the Son, even as the
Son Himself has said, " I am the Way, the Truth, and
the Life : no man cometh unto the Father but by Me."

Thus the Lord passes naturally to the solemn
declaration of the forty-seventh and four following
verses. Object as you may, He says in effect, the fact
remains, and I put it plainly before you. He that
believeth on Me hath eternal life ; for I Alone am
that Bread from heaven Which gives life to the world.
The manna had no power to confer this gift upon your
fathers ; for they ate of it, and died. But the Bread
of Which I speak comes down from heaven for the
purpose that a man may eat of It, and *not* die. I am that
Living Bread Which came down from heaven—living,
I say, because It is not merely life-giving, but living
in Itself; and that, indeed, is the reason why It can
give life.[2] The inanimate manna could not do so ; but
I, because I live, can bestow life upon others also.
If any man eat of this Bread, he shall live for ever :
and the Bread That I will give is My Flesh, Which I
will give for the life of the world.

[1] Comp. John viii. 34.   [2] John xiv. 19.

Now, in regard to the declaration, that he who eats of the Bread out of heaven shall not die, we must note, that, in the forty-seventh verse, the Lord distinctly promises freedom from the curse of death to those who believe in Him. So, too, in another place, He says, " Verily, verily, I say unto you, If a man keep My word, he shall never see death." [1] And, again, " Whosoever liveth and believeth on Me shall never die." [2]

We may, therefore, decide with confidence, that, so far as our own conscious action is concerned, to believe and to eat the Bread out of heaven, Which is the Flesh of the Lord, are expressions of identical meaning.

Finally, the Lord proceeds to reveal more specifically what the Bread is, namely, His Flesh Which He is about to give for the life of the world.

Now, since He plainly says, The Bread is My Flesh, it is clear that the word 'flesh' must be taken literally ; for He would never have explained one figure by another. That is a truth attested not only by common sense, but also by many similar sayings—as, for instance, " The enemy is the Devil," or, " The harvest is the end of the age."

In some way, then, He must here be speaking of His literal Flesh. And it is interesting to notice the progression of terms by which He has led up to it. First, He spoke of 'food' in general, taking His idea from the circumstances of the previous day : then, more definitely, of 'bread': now of 'flesh,' which He presently and finally separates into 'flesh' and 'blood.'

But since His 'Flesh' now stands for the previously mentioned 'bread' and 'food,' it follows that it is to be eaten.

[1] John viii. 51.   [2] John xi. 26.

And, again, flesh could be eaten only after the blood had been drained from it—a fact which would the more readily occur to the mind of a Jew, because of the Mosaic prohibition of blood as food.

Hence, the multitude should, at least, have perceived that the Lord's death was signified in what He had said.

Now, in the fourth verse of the chapter, we are told that the Feast of the Passover was near at hand : it must, therefore, have been much in the thoughts of the people. And, evidently, the Lord would have had them connect His words with the Paschal Lamb which they were about to eat ; so that they might recognize its great Antitype in Himself.

Could they have got so far, the idea of the Lamb might have reminded some few among them of the testimony of John the Baptist—"Behold the Lamb of God, That taketh away the sin of the world." [1]

And might there not also have been present one or two, at least, who had heard of the angel's predic- tion ;—" He shall save His people from their sins "? This is by no means unlikely ; for the Jews had recently affirmed their full knowledge of Joseph and Mary.

How great, then, might have been their opportunity to collect, both from the Old Testament and from the signs of the times, such evidences as would have made faith easy ! But they had neither diligently considered the Scriptures nor compared them with current events, although they were well aware that the time for the Messiah's appearing had come, and were, indeed, in their own way, looking for Him. Thus they failed to perceive the Hope of Israel in the midst of them, until, at length, the day of their visitation had gone by.

[1] John i. 29.

Perhaps, His last words—"Yea, and the Bread which I will give is My Flesh, Which I will give for the life of the world"—had startled and irritated them more than anything which they had hitherto heard; for, in connecting Himself with the Paschal Lamb whose blood had saved the lives of the Israelites, while its flesh had strengthened them for their wilderness-journey, He had declared that the Flesh of the Lamb of God would be given, not merely to Israelites, but for the life of the world.

After such a declaration, we do not wonder to find the Jews so excited that they could no longer restrain themselves, but broke out into loud contentions. "How can this man give us His flesh to eat?" was their angry cry; not that they desired an explanation, but only because they were bent on forcing the crudest possible meaning out of what He had said, in order that it might appear the more unreasonable. For, perceiving that He would offer them nothing but spiritual pearls, and caring only for carnal food, they were grievously disappointed: they trampled His gifts underfoot, and were ready to turn and rend Him. But, while they were freely expressing their exasperation and hatred, He once more addressed them;—

"Verily, verily, I say unto you, Except ye eat the Flesh of the Son of Man, and drink His Blood, ye have not life in yourselves.

"He that eateth My Flesh and drinketh My Blood hath eternal life; and I will raise him up at the Last Day.

"For My Flesh is meat indeed, and My Blood is drink indeed.

"He that eateth My Flesh and drinketh My Blood abideth in Me, and I in him.

" As the Living Father sent Me, and I live because
of the Father ; so he that eateth Me, he also shall
live because of Me.

" This is the Bread which came down out of
heaven : not as the fathers did eat, and died : he
that eateth this Bread shall live for ever."

The Lord had not previously spoken of His Flesh
as being eaten, though He had implied as much by
presenting it as the Bread of Life. Hence He accepts
the inference of His opponents, and insists upon its
truth. Moreover, He now mentions the Blood as well
as the Flesh ; and thus, in still plainer terms, suggests
the antitype of the Paschal Lamb. For, although the
blood was not drunk at the Passover, it was, nevertheless, of the very greatest importance, seeing that, when
sprinkled upon the lintel and doorposts, it had saved
the people from the Angel of Death. Hence, securing,
as it did, the passing by of the Avenger—even as
afterwards its appearance upon the horns of the altar
testified that a vicarious life had been offered—the
blood indicated the satisfaction of justice, and the
consequent blotting out of sin. On the other hand,
the flesh, as we have already seen, imparted life.

The Lord's first reply, then, to the Jews' question
as to how He could give them His Flesh to eat was,
By the separation of Flesh and Blood ; that is, by submission to death. For, if He was to stand in our stead,
He must take upon Himself our sins ; and, therefore,
must die the violent death which the Law assigns to
sinners, a death in which the body is broken and the
blood poured out.

But, before we attempt to explain the eating and
drinking of which the Lord spoke, we may notice, that
the suggestion of drinking blood must have been most

revolting to the Jew, who insisted upon the outward precepts of the Law, although he had little perception of their real meaning. For the use of blood for food is strictly forbidden in the seventeenth chapter of Leviticus : no animal flesh might be eaten until all the blood had been drained out of it. And the precepts in regard to this point are thus severely summed up ;—

"Whatsoever man there be of the House of Israel, or of the strangers that sojourn among them, that eateth any manner of blood ; I will set My face against that soul that eateth blood, and will cut him off from among his people."[1]

But why so terrible and inexorable a sentence? The reason is given in the next verse ;—

"For the soul"—that is, the animal life—"of the flesh is in the blood ; and I have given it to you upon the altar to make atonement for your souls ; for it is the blood that maketh atonement by reason of the soul.[2] Therefore, I said unto the Children of Israel, No soul of you shall eat blood, neither shall any stranger that sojourneth among you eat blood."

That is, the soul or life of every man is forfeited ; for the wages of sin is death, and all have sinned. Therefore, no Israelite might take back life to himself ; no, not even in a figure by drinking that blood which is the life. And, whenever a sacrifice was offered, the blood of the victim was placed upon the horns of the altar, or poured out at its base, to signify that the offerer presented himself as one guilty of death, and as having no means of escape, save through the blood of another slain in his stead.

[1] Lev. xvii. 10.
[2] That is, by reason of the soul, or animal life, which is in it.

But the blood of the slain beast merely typified that of the true Victim, and could in itself do nothing towards the salvation of the offerer.   For, the whole creation having become involved in sin, whatever blood is shed is, so far as the sufferer is concerned, but a due payment of his own forfeited life to God, and has, consequently, no power to take away the sins of other created beings.   And to emphasize this fact, that every life is God's by a just debt, no Israelite was allowed to eat the blood in which it lay.   Nevertheless, God permitted men to pour out the blood of certain beasts before Him, or to sprinkle it upon the altar, both as a token of their submission to His righteous decree, that death must follow sin, and also as a sign of hope for themselves.   For, although the blood of bulls and goats, even when they were offered daily, could never take away sin, yet He was about to provide Himself with a Lamb, to find a ransom which should deliver men from going down into the pit.   His Son should assume our nature, and, being absolutely sinless, should of His own free will lay down His life.

Then the Blood which flowed from His broken Body should be found to be unforfeited : God would not claim it, because it had never been polluted by sin ; and for the same reason, the Levitical law could have no application to it : man might drink it ; and so, at last, receive pardon and life eternal through our Lord Jesus Christ.

Again, as regards both His Flesh and His Blood, we must remember, that, although generally similar to our own, they were by no means entirely so, because, in His case, they were united to sinless holiness, and filled with Divine life ; for He was the Word become Flesh.

Yet again, He is here dealing with them in a peculiar way; for, according to His explanation in the sixty-third verse, He is regarding them as no tangible part of Himself, but as being spirit and as being life, which would seem to point to their spiritual essence and counterpart, of whose conditions and properties we can know nothing now, save what is revealed. We are reminded of the words;—

"The first man Adam became a living soul: the Last Adam became a Life-giving Spirit."[1]

We are now more prepared to face the all-important question, What precisely does the Lord mean by His declaration, that we must eat His Flesh and drink His Blood, if we would have eternal life? The circumstances, the fact that the words produced so much exasperation among the Jews, and that the Lord, nevertheless, solemnly repeated them a second and a third time, forbid us to think that He was speaking figuratively. Apparently, He must have been referring to a literal, though purely spiritual, act, which corresponds to eating and drinking in the material and visible world.[2]

Stier well defines it as "the fervent and eager reception into ourselves of the invisible spiritual-corporeal Flesh and Blood of Christ, which assuredly is an actual eating and drinking on the part of the essential man"—that is, of the spiritual inner man.

---

[1] 1 Cor. xv. 45.
[2] The idea of eating something in order that it may become incorporated with oneself, and influence one's thoughts and words, is not unknown to Scripture. We may instance the roll, filled with lamentations and mourning and woe, which Ezekiel was commanded to eat, and which is represented as thus supplying the substance and tone of his future utterances (Ezek. ii. 8—iii. 4). Similarly, John was bidden to eat the little prophetic roll; and, as soon as he had done so, the angel said;—"Thou must prophecy concerning many peoples and nations and tongues and kings" (Rev. x. 8–11.).

More than this we cannot say with our present very limited perceptions. But, from what precedes, we know that, if we come to the Lord and believe on Him,[1] or contemplate Him and believe on Him,[2] or simply believe on Him,[3] the process of eating and drinking must have taken place; for we have everlasting life. While, then, it would seem that the process is something beyond mere faith, it is, at the same time, something which we do so instinctively intuitively and certainly, if we have faith, that faith itself may be said to be the cause of eternal life. And harsh as the figure of eating and drinking may seem to us, we shall, probably, by-and-by discover, that it sets forth the truth in as plain and literal a way as our present language and comprehension will permit.

Unless, then, we receive this true food, we have not life in ourselves ;[4] but he who does receive it has eternal life, and, as a consequence, will be raised up on the Last Day. And herein will be fulfilled the Lord's own words ;—

"Verily, verily, I say unto you, Except a grain of wheat fall into the earth and die, it abideth by itself alone; but, if it die, it beareth much fruit."[5]

For, by His death and glorious resurrection, He is enabled to offer His spiritual-corporeal Flesh and Blood as food whereby His atonement and His life are communicated to those who, through grace, have believed on Him, and whom He can thus raise in

---

[1] John vi. 35.

[2] V. 40.

[3] V. 47.

[4] "The meaning of this saying, then, is ;—Unless by faith you appropriate My death (blood), and My life (flesh), you will die; because you will possess neither reconciliation with God nor life in Him."—Godet.

[5] John xii. 24.

immortal bodies, like to His Own Body, even as many grains of corn spring from the one which has died in the earth.

Well, then, may He say in the fifty-fifth verse, " For My Flesh is meat indeed, and My Blood is drink indeed;" seeing that they nourish and vitalise to so absolute a degree as to produce in those who receive them the capability of being raised to eternal life on the Last Day. But that which gives them their virtue is the fact, that, by appropriating them, the believer abides in Christ, and Christ in him: his spirit is completely interpenetrated by the Spirit of Christ: he is joined unto the Lord, and has, consequently, become one spirit [1] with Him.

But where Christ abides, thither He brings with Him that life which the Father has given Him to have in Himself. And as the Living Father sent forth Christ into the world, and was, therefore, pledged to supply Him with life; so that He lived while upon earth through the Father; even so, every one that eateth Christ—that is, believes on and trusts in Him— lives through Him. For He alone has access to the Only Source of life; and, drawing it from His Father, communicates it to all those that feed upon Him. They live through Him: they renounce all life strength and wisdom of their own, and live in His life, looking for the wisdom and knowledge which He imparts from His own inexhaustible treasures. With Paul they say ;—

" I live, yet no longer I, but Christ liveth in me: and the life which I now live in the flesh I live in faith, the faith which is in the Son of God, Who loved me and gave Himself up for me." [2]

[1] 1 Cor. vi. 17.   [2] Gal. ii. 20.

Through Him they are even now united to the Father ; because the streams of life from the Father reach them through Him ; and preparation is being made for the complete fulfilment of those words at present so awful and incomprehensible to us ;—

" I in them, and Thou in Me, that they may be perfected into one." [1]

Finally, in the fifty-eighth verse, the Lord summed up the whole discourse. This, He said, is the Bread Which came down from heaven—not such as that which you mentioned, of which your fathers ate, and died ; but Bread of which if a man eat, he shall live for ever.

At this point He seems to have left the synagogue, accompanied now only by His disciples ; for the lately enthusiastic crowd, offended with the strangeness of His discourse, and seeing that He had no intention of dispensing among them the good things of this life, had lost all desire of following Him.

Even the disciples were agitated ; and began to murmur among themselves, This is a hard saying : who can listen to Him ? And so, perceiving the thoughts of their hearts, He thus addressed them ;—

" Doth this cause you to stumble ?

" What, then, if ye should behold the Son of Man ascending where He was before ?

" It is the Spirit that quickeneth ; the flesh profiteth nothing : the words that I have spoken unto you are spirit, and are life.

But there are some of you that believe not."

That is, Does the thought of eating My flesh offend you ? To do so, in your way of understanding it, will seem still more impossible when you see Me ascending in My Body to the place from which I came—so

[1] John xvii. 23.

impossible that you may then, perhaps, have a better comprehension of My meaning. For the life-giving principle of which I speak is spirit, and not the mere flesh which can do nothing. It is My spiritual corporeality that I shall give as the Bread of Life. The words which I have just spoken unto you, " My Flesh " and " My Blood," mean spirit and life with which they are interpenetrated and instinct. Therefore, they cannot be eaten by the carnal man, but only by the mouth of the new man within, who, having been born of the Holy Spirit, can believe on Me. But there are some of you in whom the new man does not exist ; for they do not believe on Me.

Very quickly was the truth of these last words manifested ; for, from that time, many of His disciples turned away, and walked no more after Him. His fan was in His hand : He had commenced the winnowing of His floor ; and the winds of carnality and unbelief were rapidly separating the chaff from the wheat.

Such is the memorable discourse in which the Lord explains the communication of eternal life by Himself, so far as it can be explained to mortal men. We might, no doubt, offer conjectural solutions of the mystery which surrounds its obviously literal meaning. A search into such knowledge of spiritual things as is revealed, might bring to our notice the expression, " There was in their synagogue a man in an unclean spirit " ;[1] which seems to imply that the spirit formed a sort of film or mist in which the man breathed and walked ; and we might infer some similarity in the nature of all spirits, good or bad. We might urge, that this inference is supported by many things that are revealed concerning the Spirit of God ; as that He was to be poured out upon all

[1] Mark i. 23. See the Greek text.

flesh,[1] that men are said to be baptized, or immersed, in Him ;[2] while He is described as coming,[3] or falling,[4] upon them, and as being the Agent Who sheds the love of God abroad in our hearts.[5]   We might picture a spiritual body as a nucleus of spiritual flesh surrounded by a luminous halo, more or less brilliant, proceeding from the spirit within.   We might remember that Adam, though his body was psychic and not spiritual, was, nevertheless, enshrouded with rays of brightness given forth by his spirit, and forming at once his covering and his glory, until the fatal moment when he sinned, and stood dismayed as his raiment of light dimmed and was gone.

Or we might, with a more direct bearing upon our subject, point to the glorious light which flashed from the Body of our Lord on the Mount of Transfiguration ; so that His face was like the sun shining in his strength. And so, we might, finally, imagine the exceedingly transcendent and far-reaching halo which now surrounds His glorified Body, the spiritual and life-giving emanations from His Divine flesh, which, by some unknown law, we may, possibly, be absorbing, though we know it not, whenever our spirits draw near to Him in faith.

But, in such speculations, we might be very far from the truth : therefore, it is wiser to regard the exact way in which we draw life from Him as one of the secret things which belong unto the Lord our God.

For of conditions and actions in the spiritual world we are profoundly ignorant, and possess no organs whereby we may detect them.   So far as they are concerned, we resemble the guards of Herod who were

---

[1] Joel ii. 28.
[2] Matt. iii. 11 ; Mark i. 8, etc.
[3] Acts xix. 6.
[4] Acts x. 44 ; xi. 15.
[5] Rom. v. 5.

as dead men when the glory of the angel appeared in the prison, and were altogether unaware of it : who heard not the command to Peter to rise and come away, nor the clash of the chains as they fell from his hands upon the stones : who knew not when their prisoner was being led between them through the strong doors of the first and second ward, nor were awakened even by the opening of the great iron gate that led into the street. They were unconscious even of the action of spirit upon material things : how much further removed from mortal perceptions must be the action of spirit upon spirit !

Thankful, then, should we be that our part in the momentous transaction is so clearly and repeatedly marked out by the Lord. For, after all, the words of Augustine, " Believe, and thou hast eaten," contain the whole practical truth for us. Let us but believe, that God so loved the world as to give His Only Begotten Son for it ; let us fervently desire, as our sole means of pardon and eternal life, all that our Lord and Saviour has done for us, all that the offer of His Flesh and His Blood imply—then the mouth of faith will be opened wide, and it will remain with the God Who cannot lie to fill it with the food of life, according to His Own promise.

XXVII

THE LORD'S SUPPER

To many readers of the previous chapter it may, perhaps, seem that we have altogether ignored a most important part of the subject : for does not the wonderful discourse on the Bread of Life refer to the Lord's Supper ?

We will reply to this question by asking another. The Lord's Supper took the place of Israel's greatest Feast : had the deliverance of the Hebrews from the destroying angel, effected by means of the sprinkled blood, any reference to the Feast of the Passover? Certainly not, will be the ready answer : such an idea would be preposterous. It was the Feast that referred to the deliverance, not the deliverance to the Feast. For the Feast was simply a commemorative meal, intended to keep alive the remembrance of the great event, the gratitude with which it should have inspired all the generations of Israel, and the strong confidence in the Lord which should have been its permanent result.

Now, the case of the Lord's Supper is precisely similar. The sixth chapter of John contains no reference whatever to it ; since, indeed, it had not, at the time, been instituted. But that memorable discourse tells us of the way in which we may obtain pardon and life by eating the Flesh and drinking the Blood of the Son of Man. And, *if we have fulfilled its conditions*, then we are bidden not to neglect the Supper, which is, like the Feast of the Passover, a commemorative meal, an emblem, for ourselves and the world, of the awful Sacrifice which wrought our salvation, and a continual remembrance, until He come, of the dear Lord Whose Body was broken, and Whose Blood was shed, to deliver us from the sword of the Avenger.

Hence we find no promise of eternal life in connection with the Supper ; for only those who have already received the gift of God have a right to partake of the commemorative bread and wine.

But the extreme simplicity of the ordinance is best

seen in a synopsis of the four accounts of its institution which have been preserved for us, and which we subjoin in parallel columns ;—

MATT. xxvi. 26–29.	MARK xiv. 22–25.	LUKE xxii. 19, 20.	1 COR. xi. 23–25.
And as they were eating, Jesus took bread, and blessed, and brake it ; and He gave to the disciples, and said, Take, eat ; this is My Body.	And as they were eating, He took bread, and when He had blessed, He brake it, and gave to them, and said, Take ye : this is My Body.	And He took bread, and when He had given thanks, He brake it, and gave to them, saying, This is My Body which is being given for you : this do in remembrance of Me.	For I received of the Lord that which also I delivered unto you, how that the Lord Jesus in the night in which He was betrayed took bread ; and when He had given thanks, He brake it, and said, This is My Body which is for you : this do in remembrance of Me.
And He took a cup, and gave thanks, and gave it to them, saying, Drink ye all of it ; for this is My Blood of the Covenant, which is being shed for many unto remission of sins.	And He took a cup, and when He had given thanks, He gave to them : and they all drank of it.	And the cup in like manner after supper, saying, This cup is the New Covenant in My Blood, even that which is being poured out for you.	In like manner also the cup, after supper, saying, This cup is the New Covenant in My Blood : this do, as oft as ye drink it, in remembrance of Me.
But I say unto you, I will not drink henceforth of this fruit of the vine, until that day when I drink it new with you in My Father's Kingdom.	And He said unto them, This is My Blood of the Covenant, which is being shed for many. Verily I say unto you, I will no more drink of the fruit of the vine, until that day when I drink it new in the Kingdom of God.		

Of these four accounts, it will be well to remember that the one which is taken from the First Epistle to the Corinthians was given by the Lord Himself. For Paul, when he had been called of God, did not confer with flesh and blood ; nor went up to Jerusalem to be taught by those who were Apostles before him ; but was guided into the desert of Arabia, there to receive his commission and doctrine directly from the Lord.[1] Luke's account was evidently obtained from Paul ; Matthew's is that of an eye-witness ; while Mark's was, probably, received from Peter.

Now, nothing could be more simple than the scene thus laid before us, and the few words that were spoken. There is no suggestion of sacrifice, or of any kind of worship, save the giving of thanks. The Lord and His Apostles were reclining upon couches in an upper chamber, clad in the ordinary dress of their time ; for the incident took place at a meal, but at a significant meal, that is, at the Feast of the Passover. This feast was a supper to commemorate the great deliverance of the Israelites out of Egypt, their escape from the tenth plague through the blood of a lamb sprinkled upon their door-posts and lintels, and their march out of the Land of Bondage on the self-same night.

But their deliverance was but a type of one still greater, when the Lamb of God should, by His Blood, save His people, not from Egypt, but from their sins. And it was the last mentioned and greater work that was now on the eve of its accomplishment : therefore, the Lord, after keeping the Passover with His disciples, instituted, in place of the supper which commemorated the type, one which should commemorate the antitype.

The Passover was a feast for the Children of Israel, the nation which had been delivered from Egypt.

The Lord's Supper is a feast exclusively confined to those who have been already delivered from sin and

[1] Gal. i. 15-17.

death by the breaking of His Body and the shedding of His Blood.

There was no deliverance in the Passover ; but it brought to mind the wondrous mercy of God in sparing those who took refuge behind the blood, when all the firstborn of Egypt were slain.

Similarly, there is no deliverance in the Lord's Supper ; but it is commemorative of that mighty salvation which He effected by His death upon the cross, eighteen or nineteen hundred years ago.

At the Passover, it was customary to divide bread and send round cups of wine, amid the singing of Psalms.

And the Lord, availing Himself of this practice, appointed the breaking of bread and the distribution of wine as symbols of His death and the shedding of His Blood for our sakes.

Not after the disciples had fasted, but as they were eating, He took a loaf, or rather cake, of bread, and, when He had blessed it, He broke it, and distributed the fragments to them with the words, " Take, eat ; this is My Body, which is being given "—or " broken "—" for you : this do in remembrance of Me."

From the words, " Take, eat," we may infer that the Lord gave the bread, as afterwards the wine, to His disciples, but did not Himself partake of either ; for the bread represented His Own Body and the wine His Own Blood. Hence it is impossible for any one to assume the place of Christ at the Supper. A president may, indeed, be appointed for the sake of decency and order, as was the custom in Justin Martyr's time : he is, however, no head over the rest of his brethren, but must partake of the bread and wine even as they do.

As regards the clause, " This[1] is My body," we must remember, that, in Greek as in English, the verb " to be " is often used in the sense of " to signify," as in the Lord's words, " The field is the world." And that such is its meaning here is certain from the circumstances ; for the Lord Himself was present in bodily form, and was holding the loaf in His Own hand.

In Luke the words, " which is being given for you," are added, while, in some manuscripts, Paul's account reads, " is being broken for you." This reading is, probably, genuine ; for the expression, " My Body which is for you," is harsh, incomplete, and improbable. It will be noticed, that, in each case, the present participle is used, because the suffering of the Lord, which would result in His death, had already begun. In a sense, it had been going on during the whole of His earthly life ; but now the end had actually come. He was bidding His disciples farewell with the full knowledge that He would be taken from them that very night. And the traitor was reclining at the table, just on the point of departing to accomplish his foul purpose.

It was thus, with the appalling horrors of that night and the following day before Him, that He said to His disciples, for Whom He was willing to endure treachery, insult, maltreatment, a violent death, and even the withdrawal for a season of His Father's love ;— " Do this in remembrance of Me." How should our emotions affections and spirit be stirred by such an appeal : with what feelings of awe, remorse for the sins

[1] " τοῦτο, ' this,' which I now offer to you, this *bread*. The form of expression is important, not being οὗτος ὁ ἄρτος, or οὗτος ὁ οἶνος, but τοῦτο, in both cases, or τοῦτο τὸ ποτήριον, not the bread or wine itself, but the *thing* in each case ;—*precluding all idea of a substantial change*."—Alford.

that slew Him, gratitude, and boundless love, should we continually and diligently obey His command!

It was, then, by the affecting words of His Own mouth that the ordinance was declared to be a commemorative feast; and nothing more. No promise whatever of eternal life, or of resurrection on the Last Day, is connected with it; nor, indeed, could be. For no man may approach the Lord's table, unless he has already believed on Him, and so, whether consciously or unconsciously, has already eaten His Flesh and drunk His Blood, not in mere outward emblem, but in spiritual reality. And surely this was what He meant, when, before the Supper, He declared all His disciples, save the traitor, to be clean every whit.[1]

When the repast was finished, the Lord took the cup, and, after He had given thanks, passed it to His disciples with the words, as recorded by Matthew, "Drink ye all of it." This is a startling instance of those supernatural anticipations of future error which are found in the New Testament: for "all" is not added when He gives the bread, but only in the case of the wine. And thus it brands the Roman Hierarchy as a disobedient and false Church, in that, from the thirteenth century, she has formally deprived her laity of the cup. In Mark's account the "all" is omitted from our Lord's words, but we find an evident reminiscence of it in the clause, "And they all drank of it."[2]

[1] John xiii. 10, 11. The rendering of the A.V. in v. 2, "supper being ended," is incorrect: it should be "when supper was laid, or prepared"; for, in v. 12, Jesus again reclines, and, even in v. 26, the supper is still going on. Moreover, the washing of feet would naturally take place before it commenced, not in the middle of it. The R.V. adopts another reading, γινομένου, and translates "during supper."

[2] Mark xiv. 23.

" For this is the Blood of the Covenant," continued the Lord, " which is being shed for many unto remission of sins." The versions of Luke and Paul are different. " This cup is the New Covenant in My Blood," that is, ratified in My Blood ; but the meaning is substantially the same. The blood of a lamb, sprinkled upon the doorposts and lintels on the night of the Passover, was the blood of the covenant which preserved the Israelites from death. And, in this present day of grace, it is the Blood of the Lamb of God That blots out the sins of them that believe on Him ; for without shedding of blood there is no remission.

In Matthew's Gospel, and substantially in Mark's, the Lord adds ;—" But I say unto you, I will not drink henceforth of this fruit of the vine, until that day when I drink it new with you in My Father's Kingdom."

And so, He suddenly diverted the thoughts of His disciples from the sufferings to the glory, from the night of weeping to the joy that should come on the resurrection-morning. While He was speaking, the clouds were gathering thickly above them : their beloved Master was near to insult and death. And, after His departure, the only thing certain for them in the world was tribulation ; and often would they assemble to break the bread and to drink the cup in circumstances of sorrow, anxiety, or even of terror. But by-and-by the feast held in the uncertain times, and under the care-haunted roofs, of earth should be transferred to the Kingdom of the Father. There would the Lord once more sit down, and Himself drink the fruit of the vine, not merely with His Apostles, but with the whole glorified Church of the Firstborn : there, at length, would He see of the travail of His soul, and rejoice. Thus, in partaking of the Lord's

Supper, we are not to confine our meditations to His sufferings and death, but must, also, look forward with hope, and joy, and thanksgiving, to their final and transcendentally glorious result.   To all whom He will ransom and save, the bitter is first presented ; but the sweet must come in due time, and, when it does come, they will enjoy it for ever in the Presence of their Saviour and King.

In the Lord's account, these words given by Matthew are omitted, and in their place we find ;—" This do, as oft as ye drink it, in remembrance of Me."   That is, Whenever as members of the New Covenant you keep this feast, see that in drinking the cup you do it in remembrance of Me.   Thus, according to His Own authentic narrative, the Lord a second time impressed upon His disciples the importance of the cup, and the fact that the ordinance which He had instituted was commemorative, and not life-giving.

In the next verse, His words are still further developed by Paul, who explains ;—" For as often as ye eat this bread and drink the cup, ye proclaim the Lord's death till He come."   That is, The Lord's Supper is a solemn feast, by the keeping of which His people are both to remind themselves of His death, and to proclaim it to the world, until His return.

XXVIII

The Lord's Supper in the Epistles

I Cor. x. 16–22 ; xi. 17–34

SUCH, then, seems to be all that can be gathered from the four narratives of the Lord's Supper. And the New Testament has but little more to reveal in regard to the subject. As we have already remarked, there are twenty-one Epistles addressed to believers, and one only of them contains notices of this ordinance—a clear proof, that the great majority of professing Christians give it a prominence which the Lord never intended.

In two passages, then, only, both of which are contained in the First Epistle to the Corinthians, do we find direct allusion to the Lord's Supper.

The Corinthian Christians lived in the midst of abounding idolatry, with which almost every act of social life was intertwined. They would be frequently invited to sacrificial feasts by their Pagan relations and friends, and Paul presses upon them the duty of declining such invitations. This he does by an inference drawn from a very important law in connection with the unseen world.

Every religious act brings us into contact with the power, good or bad, towards which it is directed, and helps to establish the influence of that power over us. In regard to those who would seek the Lord, James has clearly enunciated this law in the words, " Draw nigh to God, and He will draw nigh to you." [1] Similarly the Psalmist says ;—

> " The Lord is nigh unto all them that call upon
> Him,
> To all that call upon Him in truth." [2]

On the other hand, those who adore the Powers of Darkness—whether directly, or through the false gods or idols which they have set up—are in the hands of the Evil One, and all who join with them must come under the same influence.

Upon this principle, Paul, in warning the Corinthians to flee from idolatry, reminds them, that, whenever they

[1] James iv. 8.   [2] Psa. cxlv. 18.

bless the cup and break the bread, they show forth and strengthen the communion existing between themselves and the Lord Jesus—a communion so real that it unites all those who have part in it into one Body, because each of them individually is joined to their One Lord. Similarly, in the preceding dispensation, those Israelites who partook of the sacrificial feasts were sharers at the altar of Jehovah, and were thus assured of reconciliation peace and communion with Him.[1]

But, at this point, Paul seems to assume an objection on the part of those to whom he was writing, as though their thoughts were running somewhat in this way;—What you have said is very true. We quite understand that the Mighty God of Abraham and the Father of our Lord Jesus Christ does, indeed, draw nigh to them that draw nigh to Him, and join them in communion with Himself. But what has that to do with idolatry? You surely do not mean to say, that what is true of God can also be applied to mere idols, or to fictitious gods like Zeus, Apollo, or Ceres?

No: replies Paul, I do not for a moment say that an idol is a real existence, or that it makes any difference to a piece of meat if it happens to have been offered to a nothing. But what I do say is this, that behind those idols and fictitious gods there are real existences, the demons of the air; and that those who offer to idols, and partake of the sacrificial feasts that follow the offerings, do actually offer to, and feast with, demons, and thus become ensnared by them, and subject to their influence.

Therefore, he concludes, I do not wish you to be

[1] 1 Cor. x. 14–18.

14

in communion with demons. You cannot drink the cup of the Lord and the cup of demons : you cannot partake of the table of the Lord and of the table of demons. And if you persist in attempting such folly, do you know what you are doing? You are provoking the jealousy of the Almighty, and will soon feel how fearful a thing it is to fall into the hands of the Living God.[1]

Thus, two points relating to the Lord's Supper may be learnt from this passage.

First, there is a real power in the blessing of the cup and the breaking of the bread : these acts, if we do them in simple faith, draw down upon us more richly the blessings which they are intended to signify, and bring us into closer communion with the Lord.

Secondly, in the seventeenth verse, Paul shows, that the communion of each believer with the Lord establishes a communion of all believers with one another. "Seeing that," he says, "there is one loaf, we, who are many, are one Body. For we all partake of the one loaf."[2] The bread, or loaf, has been blessed and broken, and so is no longer "common bread," as Justin Martyr has it, but represents the Body of Christ. Hence those who take and eat portions of it signify by their act, that, however numerous they may be, they are one Body in Christ. And this is literally true of all real believers, and will be manifested to the world when they appear in glory as the Body of Christ their Head.

The only remaining passage which deals with the Lord's Supper is contained in the eleventh chapter of the same Epistle.

Paul had been commending the Corinthians for their

[1] I Cor. x. 20–22.   [2] I Cor. x. 17.

general attention to his teaching;[1] but, after expounding to them the position of the Christian woman, he adds, that there was one thing for which he could not commend them, namely, that they came together in assembly, not for the better, but for the worse.

For, in the first place, he had heard, and could not altogether disbelieve the report, that the divisions among them, of which he had already spoken, were apparent whenever they met in full assembly to eat the Lord's Supper. This did not surprise him, since he was well aware that these divisions must become still more rigid, until they had hardened into permanent sects. For it was by such trials that God, Who in the beginning divided the light from the darkness, would separate off from His Own elect the shallow enthusiasts, the mere seekers after something new, the men who were actuated by nothing more than a partizan-feeling—all those, in fine, who were influenced by any motive other than the love of the Lord Jesus Christ. Paul had, however, already spoken of the divisions into which the Corinthians had fallen,[2] and would, therefore, add no more upon that subject.

But the mention of the charge suggests a few practical remarks. It is very seldom that all the believers, even of a single congregation, find themselves in perfect agreement as regards Biblical interpretations doctrines or opinions. But differences of such a kind, provided they do not affect the Divinity and full propitiation of the Lord Jesus, call for an exercise of loving forbearance, and must by no means be allowed to engender anger and strife, and so to lead to a schism in the church.

[1] 1 Cor. xi. 2.   [2] 1 Cor. i. 11, 12.

Those, then, who feel themselves at variance with others, simply because the latter do not see eye to eye with them in secondary matters, have no right to eat at the Lord's table. For how can we dare to bring discordant, and perhaps even malignant, hearts within sight of the bread and wine which represent Christ's Body that was broken, and His Blood that was shed, for the ultimate purpose that we might all be one in Him ?

Still less right to communicate have those who, because they cannot agree in all points with their fellows, withdraw themselves, and set up another table, from which they presume to exclude true believers in the Lord Jesus. For "these are they who make separations, soulish, not having spirit." [1] Unless they judge themselves before the time of their visitation is ended, the judgment of the Lord will fall upon them. And, meanwhile, the table around which they sit is their own table, not the Lord's.

For if any man be building on the one foundation, we may not exclude him from the Lord's table, even though he be at the time carrying on his work with wood hay and stubble. Nor have we ourselves a right to partake of the bread and wine, unless we feel ourselves to be in peace harmony and love with all those who love the Lord Jesus in sincerity, and are trusting in Him Alone for salvation. And there must be no

---

[1] Jude 19. The A.V. and the R.V. have altogether missed the meaning of this verse. Our translation is literal; but we have been compelled to coin the adjective "soulish," because we can find no other English equivalent for the Greek ψυχικοί. The men described are merely intellectual Christians. They are moved by fleshly feelings, and also by emotions and reasonings of the soul; but they have no spiritual perceptions : they may be good partizans, but know nothing of the spiritual union of all believers in Christ.

hypocrisy in this matter; for the Lord is at hand, "Who will both bring to light the hidden things of darkness, and make manifest the counsels of the hearts." Let us, then, remember, that we are not in peace harmony and love with another believer, unless we would rejoice to see him joining us at the table of the Lord.

But to return to the Apostle's reproof of the Corinthians. It appeared, that, when they met in full assembly, it was not to eat the Lord's Supper, but rather their own. For, in their eating, every rich man would take his own meal before his poorer neighbour, showing neither care nor consideration for the latter; so that, when it was the time for the solemn part of the Supper, one man was drunken, while another was hungry. What! could they not satisfy their appetites in their own houses? Or did they deliberately wish to show their contempt for the assembly of God, by putting to shame the needy members of the flock? Could he commend them in such a matter as this? No: he did not commend them.

In regard to this accusation, we must, first, remember, that for some time it was the custom of the churches to take the Lord's Supper in connection with an ordinary meal, of which all the members partook, and which was called an *agape*, or love-feast. Thus an effort was made to perpetuate the circumstances in which the Communion was instituted. Now, so long as the Gospel was confined to Palestine, the churches were guided in arranging the details of the Communion by Hebrew ideas; but, as soon as Christian assemblies appeared also in Gentile lands, the Pagan rites and customs began to exercise their baleful influence. Consequently, when the love-feast and the Communion were proposed to the Corinthians, they seem to have been struck with the similarity of the former to their own club-feasts.[1]

These club-feasts were carried on in two different ways. Sometimes every member brought his own supper, and in this case the meal, which appears to have been a sort of picnic, was called "supper from the basket," on account of the wicker basket in which each man carried his provision. Sometimes the members deputed one of their number to cater for all, and afterwards repaid him by contributions. This was called a "subscription supper." But, since the contributions would naturally be equal, and there were, doubtless, many poor and some slaves among the Corinthian Christians, they saw that it could not afford a suitable model for a love-feast.

Consequently, they seem to have fallen back upon the "supper from the basket," and decided that every one should bring his own portion. It is strange that the incongruity of such an arrangement for a communion-meal did not strike them, especially when they had experienced its results. For the rich brought sumptuous fare and strong wines ; while the poor could bring little or nothing. Nevertheless, the rich seem to have got into the habit of going on with their own supper, without care for their needy brethren, or, at best, of merely passing to them whatever fragments might be left after their own repast. And so, when the time came to break the bread and to bless the cup, some of those present were half stupefied with meat and wine, while others were craving for food.

[1] ἔρανοι. The word ἔρανος is, probably, connected with ἐράω, ἔραμαι ; and, therefore, had originally somewhat the same meaning as ἀγάπη, a love-feast.

In such an assembly there could be little discernment of the Lord's Body, either in the bread which represented it, or in its living members who were present and formed the church.

In the twenty-third verse, Paul adopts the most effective way of rebuking these irregularities and touching the conscience of those who were guilty of them, by solemnly quoting what the Lord Himself had revealed concerning that night in which He was betrayed. Upon this passage we have already commented as far as the twenty-sixth verse, in which the Apostle affirms, that, as often as we eat the bread and drink the cup, we proclaim the Lord's death, until He come ; so that the Supper connects the two Advents. And, as he goes on to say in the twenty-seventh verse, since the Saviour's death is thus proclaimed, he that eats and drinks unworthily is guilty of His Body and Blood—guilty, that is, of slighting Him by going through the form of commemoration without that reverence and love for Him, and that grief for, and hatred of, sin, which the thought of His sufferings and death should ever awaken. For the unworthy partaker is he who joins in the Supper as if he were personally indifferent to all that it signifies ; as if the awful death of the Son of God were not the expiation of his own sins, and his only means of salvation ; as if there were no communion of believers indicated in the sharing of the one loaf, and he did not recognize in his fellows the members of the Lord's Body. By so doing, he eats and drinks judgment for himself, because he does not discern or appreciate the Lord's Body and Blood as represented by the bread and wine.

The truth of this statement had been lately experienced by the Corinthians themselves ; for it was their sin in connection with the Lord's Supper that had caused many among them to become weaklings and invalids, and had even brought about the premature death of some. And Paul, after reminding them of the judgments with which they had been visited, makes the following comment, taking care, however, with his usual tenderness, to include himself among them ;—

"For if we had judged ourselves, we should not have been judged. But now that we are being judged, it is by the Lord that we are being chastened, that we may not be condemned with the world."[1]

This last sentence is important ; since it shows that the Lord still treats even those who eat and drink unworthily as children, provided that they have a right to be at the table because of their faith in Him. For, although He will certainly judge and chasten them, yet His object in so doing will be to preserve them from the condemnation of the unbelieving world. Even in cases which He punishes with the death of the body, there will be time to repent before the sentence takes effect ; so that physical death in such a case does not entail eternal death. Nevertheless, it cuts short the unworthy partaker's opportunity of serving his Lord, and leaves him without hope of the First Resurrection and the Kingdom.

Wherefore, Paul concludes, do not continue to incur these penalties: wait for one another when ye come together for your love-feasts and the Lord's Supper: do not eat greedily what you have, without caring for your poorer brethren : let them share with you, and let them eat at the same time as yourselves. And to avoid the disgraceful scenes which have already

[1] 1 Cor. xi. 31, 32.

brought judgment upon you, take care to satisfy your carnal appetites at home before you venture to approach the table of the Lord.

XXIX

PATRISTIC CORRUPTION

WE have now, so far as we are aware, examined every passage of Scripture which refers to the Lord's Supper. Nothing could be more plain than the account given of its origin, its object, and its significance. But, as Olshausen remarks, " the simple words of the institution have been forced to bear meanings the most various and contradictory."

The mischief seems to have arisen as follows. Christian converts from Paganism brought with them into the churches Pagan ideas and doctrines, and especially the teaching of the Mysteries. Hence, over-looking, or, perhaps, never having read or heard the Scriptural truth, that salvation must be received by faith before either baptism or the Lord's Supper can be administered, they were naturally prompted by their Pagan training to attribute salvation to these rites themselves. Thus the rites began to be regarded as magic ceremonies, whereby sins were supposed to be washed away, and the new birth bestowed, by a bath of duly consecrated water, accompanied by a prescribed form of words ; or pardon and life eternal were under-stood to be conveyed by the drinking of wine and the eating of bread, which a duly qualified and authorised priest had changed by his spells into either the spiritual or literal Blood and Body of Christ. Then, as soon as the Supper had been moulded into some kind of

Mystery, the Pagan initiates, who had feigned themselves Christians and entered the churches for the deliberate purpose of corrupting them, seized upon their opportunity, and so used it that in time the presbyters became sacrificing priests, the broken bread was exchanged for round wafers, and the Lord's institution was fashioned into the likeness of a Mithraic initiation.

But in what is, probably, the earliest uninspired Christian writing that has come down to us, *The Teaching of the Twelve Apostles*, usually known as the *Didache*, there is a complete Communion Service, in which we observe a corruption of a different kind from that which has already been noticed. This work is supposed to have been compiled between A.D. 80 and A.D. 100, and, possibly, appeared before the Apocalypse was written. There are no traces of Paganism in it, and that for an obvious reason, since it exhibits signs of a Jewish origin. Its three very brief prayers seem to be simple and spiritual ; yet there is a strange and unaccountable deficiency in them, a deficiency which becomes very portentous when we remember the occasion for which they were intended. They contain no explanation of, or even allusion to, the awful meaning of the broken bread and the poured-out wine : indeed, there is no mention whatever of either the Body or Blood of the Lord.

The ninth chapter of the Manual begins as follows ;—

" Now in the matter of the Eucharist, give thanks after this manner.

First for the cup ;—

' We give thanks to Thee, our Father, for the Holy Vine of David, Thy servant, which Thou didst make known to us through Jesus, Thy Servant. To Thee be the glory for the ages.'

And for the broken bread ;—

'We give thanks to Thee, our Father, for the life and knowledge which Thou didst make known to us through Jesus, Thy Servant. To Thee be the glory for the ages.'

'As this broken bread was scattered upon the mountains, and, when gathered together, became one ; so may Thy Church be gathered together from the ends of the earth into Thy Kingdom ; for Thine is the glory and the power through Jesus Christ for the ages.' "

Out of the fulness of the heart the mouth speaketh : it is, therefore, scarcely possible to believe that the writer, or writers, of these prayers understood the Lord's propitiation for our sins by means of His broken Body and shed Blood. Yet the idea of the last sentence is very beautiful, and appears to have been suggested by Paul's words ;—"Seeing that there is one loaf, we, who are many, are one Body ; for we all partake of the one loaf."[1] The distinction between the churches scattered and militant upon earth and the Heavenly Kingdom— which, as we have already shown,[2] is the glorified and completed Church above—is also worthy of notice.

Here a few words of direction, a sort of rubric, are inserted.

"But let no one eat or drink of your Eucharist, except those who have been baptized into the Name of the Lord ; for concerning this the Lord has said ; —'Give not that which is holy unto the dogs.' "

Then the service is continued.

" Now, after that ye are filled, give thanks in this manner ;—

'We give thanks to Thee, Holy Father, for Thy

[1] 1 Cor. x. 17. [2] See pp. 44-5.

holy Name, which Thou didst cause to tabernacle
in our hearts, and for the knowledge and faith and
immortality which Thou didst make known to us
through Jesus, Thy Servant.
To Thee be the glory for the ages.'

' Thou, Almighty Sovereign, didst make all things
for Thy Name's sake ; Thou didst give food and
drink to men for enjoyment, that they might render
thanks to Thee ; but to us Thou didst freely give
spiritual food and drink and eternal life through
Thy Servant.'

' Before all things we give thanks to Thee that
Thou art Mighty.
To Thee be the glory for the ages.'

' Remember, Lord, Thy Church, to deliver her
from every evil, and to perfect her in Thy love. And
gather from the four winds her that has been sanctified
for Thy Kingdom, which Thou didst prepare for her :
for Thine is the power and the glory for the ages.'

' Let grace appear, and let this world disappear !
Hosanna to the God of David ! '

' If any one is holy, let him come : if any one is
not holy, let him repent. Maranatha. Amen.' "

It is certainly remarkable that these prayers should
express neither consciousness of sin nor thanksgiving
for its expiation, although those who use them are
made to take the place of accepted worshippers. But
" the Fathers " almost invariably fail to give a clear
account of our redemption through the Blood of the
Lord Jesus. We have, indeed, reason to praise Him
that He has preserved His inspired Scriptures for us ;
for, unless He had done so, the great fundamental truth
of the faith would have been lost.

We must understand the words, " after that ye are

filled," to refer to the love-feast in close connection with which the Lord's Supper was at that time taken. In those early days there was no thought of fasting before the breaking of bread : the Pagan Mysteries had not yet destroyed the ordinance of the Lord.

For the second time, we find the distinction clearly marked between the scattered churches upon earth and the Heavenly Kingdom into which they shall be gathered. In that gloomy epoch, when the little flock lived in the midst of Pagan darkness, and in times of fear and trial and suffering, the contrast must have been often suggested to them.

In the words, " Let grace appear, and let this world disappear," there is certainly a reference to the Lord's return, which also forms the subject of the last chapter of this Manual.

The very unusual expression, " the God of David," testifies to the author's belief in the Divinity of our Lord. For, since he is speaking of the Second Advent, the reference must, it would seem, be to the Lord Jesus.

The final appeal cannot be an invitation to the Supper, because that is now over. It must, therefore, be regarded as a call to non-communicants and unbelievers to join the church. Hence it would appear, that the later practice of excluding all but communicants from the room before the Supper commenced was as yet unknown. This is a very important point.

Maranatha is usually derived from the two Aramaic words *Maran* ' our Lord ' and *atha* ' has come.' But if we accept this explanation, we must render, " Our Lord has come," with a reference to the First Advent —a sense which would by no means suit the only Scriptural passage in which the word occurs.[1] Hence

---

[1] 1 Cor. xvi. 22.

many translate, 'The Lord cometh!' but this is inaccurate. Probably, we should divide the word differently—*Marana*[1] the Lord, and *tha* the imperative of *atha*. In this case, "Come, Lord!" will be very like the prayer at the end of the Apocalypse, "Even so, come Lord Jesus!" Why an Aramaic formula should be used by a Greek-speaking people, we can only conjecture. It may have been a sort of watchword used in Jerusalem, and conveyed from thence to other churches.

The Manual concludes its chapters on the Lord's Supper with the rubric ;—

"But allow the prophets to give whatever thanks they will."

It seems, then, that in those days, and in that locality, the service was under the control of the congregation, that a form of words was ordinarily used ; but that, if prophets were present, they might offer extemporaneous prayers.

This indicated an ominous fall in the Spirit-power of the churches. In the First Epistle to the Corinthians, no form of prayer is suggested, and it is evident that their congregation contained many Spirit-inspired prophets and teachers ; for Paul says ;—

"What is it, then, brethren? When ye come together, each one hath a psalm, hath a teaching, hath a revelation, hath a tongue, hath an interpretation. Let all things be done to edifying. . . . For ye can all prophesy one by one, that all may learn, and all may be comforted."

But when the *Didache* was compiled, some thirty years later, prophets could no longer be depended upon, and a form of prayer was necessary. The churches

[1] The third '*a*' will in this case be the post-positive article.

were fast losing their supernatural power. About fifty years later, in the time of Justin Martyr, there is no mention of prophets, and the liberty of extemporaneous prayer is restricted to "the President." The power of the Spirit of God to choose His Own organs was deliberately curtailed. He could no longer speak to the churches through such members as were able to receive and deliver His messages. Soon it became the custom to have one fixed and permanent minister over each congregation. He was frequently altogether incapable of hearing the Spirit's voice; for often his motive was ambition, and he had obtained his eminence through influence intrigue or bribery. And so, whenever this was the case, his congregation sat in darkness: so far as public teaching was concerned, it could obtain neither light nor guidance from the Spirit of God. The churches of Christendom had fallen into the snare of Satan, and were doomed to the superstition, the profanity, the idolatry, and the crime, of the Middle Ages.

So far, then, as the *Didache* is concerned, we can trace no disposition to regard the Lord's Supper as anything more than a service of thanksgiving and prayer.

But in a passage ascribed to Ignatius, which, if genuine, must have been written about twenty years later, we find something very different;—

"Assemble yourselves together in common, every one of you severally, man by man, in grace, in one faith and one Jesus Christ, Who after the flesh was of David's race, Who is Son of Man and Son of God, to the end that you may obey the bishop and the presbytery without distraction of mind, breaking one bread, which is the medicine of immortality, and the antidote that we should not die, but live for ever in Jesus Christ." [1]

Here we have quite a new order of things. Obedience is claimed for a previously unknown functionary, called by a name which in the Greek churches was originally used for the Hebrew elder or presbyter, but who is now set over the presbyters. And a magic power is attributed to the bread of the Lord's Supper, as though in itself it could give eternal life.

In another place, the same writer says of certain heretics ;—" They abstain from Eucharist and prayer, because they do not allow that the Eucharist is the Flesh of our Saviour Jesus Christ, which Flesh suffered for our sins, and which the Father of His goodness raised up." [2]

This looks something like transubstantiation ; [3] but the genuineness of the Seven Epistles is not altogether assured.

In the Epistle to the Smyrnæans yet a third innovation appears ;—

" Let that be regarded as a valid Eucharist which is under the bishop, or one to whom he shall have entrusted it. . . . It is not lawful either to baptize or to hold a love-feast apart from the bishop." [4]

[1] Ignat. Ad Eph. xx.
[2] Ignat. Ad Smyrn vi.
[3] But here Ignatius may mean no more than that the bread and wine represent the Body and Blood of Christ, the reality of which the Docetæ denied. If this be so, the passage is illustrated by Tertullian's argument against Marcion, who also taught that Christ's Body was but a phantom ;—" Then, having taken the bread and distributed it to His disciples, He made it His Own Body by saying, ' This is My Body,' that is, a figure of My Body. A figure, however, there could not have been, unless there had first been a true Body. There cannot be a figure of an empty thing such as a phantom "—Tert. Adv. Marcion, iv. 40.
[4] Ignat. Ad Smyrn. viii.

It is almost needless to say, that this is a precept not found in the New Testament, nor in any Christian writings earlier than the Ignatian Epistles. We see in it, that what we may call a Christianity of a secondary order, that is to say, Ecclesiastical as opposed to Apostolical and Scriptural Christianity, was being rapidly developed. We must not, of course, exaggerate the situation: the bishops of Ignatius' times, as we shall presently see, were not like those of our days, but merely chief pastors of a single congregation. Yet the bread of the Lord's Supper is said to be the medicine of immortality, and the antidote of death ; while it could be validly administered only by the bishop or his authorised representative. Salvation was being transferred into the hands of the ministers, who, on their part, were beginning to assume mediatorial and priestly functions.

As yet, however, the movement was not universal ; for in the writings of Justin Martyr, about A.D. 150, we do not find any real advance in the direction of Sacramentalism. A single passage has, indeed, been cited as a proof that Justin regarded the bread and wine as undergoing a magical change ; but a comparison with what he has written elsewhere forbids such a conclusion. To explain the reason why none but Christian believers were allowed to partake of the Lord's Supper, he says ;—

"For not as common bread and common drink do we receive these ; but, in like manner as Jesus Christ our Saviour, having been made Flesh by the Word of God, had assumed both flesh and blood for our salvation, so also have we been taught that the food for which thanks have been given by a prayer of the form derived from Him, and from which, by

its transmutation, our flesh and blood are nourished,
is the Flesh and Blood of that Jesus Who was made
Flesh."[1]

That so confused a passage as this should have
been seized upon by the Roman, Lutheran, and Reformed
Churches, each of which claims it in support of its
own peculiar views, is not wonderful. To extract its
meaning, we must notice the evident correspondence
between the expressions " the Word of God," and " a
prayer of the form derived from Him," that is, from
Jesus Christ. And the sense seems to be, that, just
as the Word of God created the Flesh and Blood of
Jesus Christ, so, after the bread and wine, which by
transmutation become forthwith a part of our bodies,
have been blessed according to the form of words which
Christ used, they are His Flesh and Blood.

Now, since Justin speaks of the elements after the
blessing as being no longer *common* bread and *common*
drink, it is clear that he regards them as still being
bread and wine. Hence he cannot here intend to
teach Transubstantiation. But, at first sight, his words
might be plausibly interpreted as signifying Consub-
stantiation. There are, however, considerations which
preclude even this view. Were Justin present among
us, and able to explain, he might, perhaps, say ;—You
forget the difference between my times and your own.
When I was upon earth, none of those who surrounded
me had conceived such an idea as that the bread and
wine could be either changed into the material, or
commingled with the spiritual, Flesh and Blood of
Christ. When, therefore, I said that the elements
were His Flesh and Blood, I had no suspicion that
my words would be taken to mean any more than

[1] Apol. Prim. lxvi.

that they stood for, or signified, the same. Nor did I see more reason for guarding my words in this case than in some others. Had I spoken of Christ as the Vine, or the Door, or the Lamb, it would not have occurred to me to warn my hearers that He was not literally and actually a vine, a door, or a lamb. Why, then, should I think such a course necessary in regard to the cake of bread which He was actually holding in His Own hands when He said, " This is My Body " ; and immediately added, " This do in remembrance of Me " ? Moreover, if you found the words of this passage uncertain, because you were reading into them the thoughts of later times, why did you not compare other remarks of mine upon the same subject, in which the language is unmistakable, and interpret this passage from them ?

To carry out the suggestion in the last sentence, we cannot do better than turn to the seventieth chapter of the *Dialogue with Trypho*, where we read ;—

"It is evident, then, that in this prophecy [he speaks] of the bread which our Christ delivered to us to eat in remembrance of His assumption of a bodily form for the sake of those who believe on Him, for whom He also became subject to suffering ; and of the cup which He delivered to us to drink with thanksgiving in remembrance of His Blood."

This extract makes it sufficiently clear that Justin regarded the Lord's Supper simply as a commemorative meal, and had no idea of a corporeal Presence. And, although he, and other early Christians, sometimes called the ordinance a sacrifice, this was only because the prayers and thanksgivings connected with it were regarded as a sacrifice presented to God. So, in the hundred and seventeenth chapter of the *Dialogue*, he says ;—

"That, then, both prayers and thanksgivings made by the worthy are the only sacrifices that are perfect and well pleasing to God, I myself affirm. For these alone Christians received in charge to offer even in the commemoration effected by means of their food dry and liquid "—that is, of the bread and wine— "by which remembrance is made of the suffering which the Son of God has endured for them." [1]

This sufficiently indicates what Justin meant by calling the Lord's Supper a sacrifice ; and in the same chapter he interprets the "incense" and "pure offering," which, according to Malachi's prophecy, the Gentiles were to offer to the Lord,[2] as "prayers and giving of thanks." Irenæus, too, in commenting upon the same passage, remarks, "Now John, in the Apocalypse,[3] declares that the incense is the prayers of the saints." [4] Similarly, Athenagoras speaks of the lifting up of holy hands in adoration to the great Creator as being a 'bloodless sacrifice' and a 'reasonable service.' [5]

The form of the Communion in Justin's time was most simple, and is thus described by himself ;—

"When we have ended the prayers, we salute one another with a kiss. Then bread and a cup of water and mixed wine is brought to that one of the brethren who is presiding. And he, after receiving it, offers praise and glory to the Father of the Universe, through the Name of the Son and of the

---

[1] Justin. Dial. c. Tryph. cxvii.
[2] Mal. i. 11.
[3] Rev. v. 8.   But see chap. lv.
[4] Iren. Adv. Hær. iv. 17.   But neither Justin nor Irenæus rightly interpreted the passage of Malachi.   See chap. liv.
[5] Athenag. Suppl. pro Christ. xiii.

Holy Spirit, and renders thanks at some length, because we have been thought worthy to receive these gifts at His hands. And when he has finished the prayers and the thanksgiving, all the people who are present signify their assent by saying, Amen! Now, 'Amen,' in the Hebrew tongue, means, 'So be it.' And when the president has thus rendered thanks, and all the people have signified their assent, the officers, who among us are called deacons, give to each of those present to partake of the bread and wine and water for which thanks have been rendered, and carry away portions to the members who are not present." [1]

In the thanksgiving, it would seem that there was a double meaning—thanks to God for the gifts of creation, the bread and the wine by which the present life is sustained, and thanks for the Blood and Body of the Lord whereby sins are expiated and life-for-evermore bestowed.

The bread and the wine are characterised simply as that for which thanks have been rendered, and there is no hint of either sacrifice or corporeal Presence.

Up to about A.D. 150, then, the Lord's Supper, if we except the dubious words attributed to Ignatius, seems to have been regarded merely as a commemorative meal, and a giving of thanks. And, which is also important, although it was carried out as the Lord and His Apostles had directed, it is rarely mentioned by the Apostolic Fathers, just as we find it discussed only in one of the twenty-one Epistles of the New Testament.

Hence, if the Seven Epistles of Ignatius in their shorter form are genuine, we must understand that

[1] Apol. Prim. lxv.

writer to have by no means represented the opinion of
all the churches. But, notwithstanding Dr. Lightfoot's
defence of the short recension, we cannot but regard
both it and the longer form with suspicion, and are
inclined to accept only the three still briefer letters,
which are contained in each of three Syrian manuscripts,
and which, so far as direct evidence goes, are all that
were preserved by Ignatius' own church. And in these
three Epistles, as given in the Syrian manuscripts, the
passages which we have quoted above do not appear.

Yet, however this may be, it is certain that, after
Justin's death, a mysterious power began to be attributed
to the elements, so that the Supper was gradually
changed into a superstitious and magical ceremony.
Hence the bread and wine were administered to infants
immediately after baptism, and regularly from that time
—a custom which is still retained in the Greek Church.

It seems scarcely credible that such a man as
Augustine could have deliberately affirmed, that, unless
children were made to partake of the Lord's Supper,
they could not be saved. Nevertheless, he did so, and
founded his doctrine on the Lord's words, " Except
ye eat the Flesh of the Son of Man and drink His
Blood, ye have not life in yourselves," interpreted by
his own foolish notion, that the reference was to the
commemorative bread and wine of the Supper. This
is a terrible instance of the disastrous superstitions that
may result when an emblem is mistaken for the reality
which it represents. And we may see by it how far
the Pagan doctrine, that man must be initiated and
ceremonially consecrated into life, had already supplanted the Scriptural truth, that nothing, save the
entrance into us of the Spirit of Life in Christ Jesus,
can free us from the law of sin and death.

In the *Apostolical Constitutions*, written, or rather compiled, about the end of the third century, we notice two things which mark the progress that had been made in assimilating the Lord's Supper to the Pagan Mysteries or Sacraments.

The first is, that, after the ordinary service, and with the view of proceeding to the Supper, a deacon is to stand up and say ;—" Let none of the Catechumens, let none of the hearers, let none of the unbelievers, let none of the heterodox, stay here!"[1] Thus all but the Communicants were warned off from the room, as though some dread and secret rites were about to be celebrated. And, of course, the consequence of this change was, that Christian worshippers could no longer use the Supper as a means of proclaiming the Lord's death till He come. Forgetful of this duty, they had begun to imitate the Pagan, " Procul o, procul este profani, totoque absistite luco!"[2] by which the uninitiated were ordered away before the Mysteries commenced.

And, again, the very term, "initiated," which the Pagans used, is now transferred to Communicants. " Let no one eat of these things who is not initiated ; but only those who have been baptized into the death of the Lord."[3] So, too, Chrysostom ;—" For we need both counsel and prayer. For which reason we also, first giving you counsel, then offer prayers for you. And this the initiated know."[4]

These two facts are very significant of the gradual but sure process by which Paganism was being substituted for Christianity.

[1] Apost. Const. viii. 12.
[2] Virg. Æn. vi. 258-9.
[3] Apost. Const. vii. 25.
[4] Chrys. Hom. xi. on the First Epistle to the Thessalonians,

Tertullian regarded the Lord's Supper as symbolical; and so did the Alexandrian Fathers, Clement and Origen, though the former treated it as a mystic symbol. But we may note, that Tertullian is the earliest extant writer who introduces the term "sacrament," and applies it to baptism and the Lord's Supper.

Now, the plural of this word, *sacramenta*, seems to have been used as a Latin rendering for the Greek 'Mysteries'; so that both the word itself and all that it connotes are essentially Pagan, and have no place in pure Christianity. It is, therefore, to be regretted that many, who do not believe in the possibility of ceremonializing men into life, should, nevertheless, continue to use so antichristian a term as 'sacrament.' For the ordinances of the Lord are merely acknowledgments and commemorations of things that have been previously accomplished. And we are commanded to perform them openly, both to remind ourselves of the great things which the Lord has done for us, and, at the same time, to show them forth to the world, until He comes.

But, although it became customary, in the third century, to speak of the ordinances as Mysteries or Sacraments, we do not find the term *missa*, the Mass, in use until a much later period; for its earliest occurrence is in the works of Ambrose of Milan. This word is doubtless identical with the Persian *mizd*, which signified the round wafer eaten in honour of Mithras, the Sun-god. The Mithraic Mysteries, in connection with which this wafer was used, were established in Rome at the beginning of the second century, and seem to have had much to do with the corruption of Christianity.

But it is in the writings of Cyprian, the great

sacerdotalist, that we perceive the first decided change in the doctrine of the Supper. With him, it is no longer the people offering a sacrifice of thanksgiving, but the priest taking the place of Christ, and imitating —not, as yet, repeating—what Christ did, so that he offers in the church a true and full sacrifice to God the Father.

Augustine, on the other hand, declares in strong terms that our Lord's words, "This is My Body," must be regarded as merely figurative. Nevertheless, he exhibits the grossest superstition in the matter of the bread and wine, as he does, indeed, in that of relics ; and tells a story of a mother who, having a blind son, succeeded in procuring sight for him by plastering his eyes with the consecrated bread.

Jerome understands the Supper to be "a daily offering of unspotted sacrifices for the sins of the bishop and the people who present them " ; while Gregory the Great sees in the daily sacrifice of the Mass a repetition of the sacrificial death of Christ.

XXX

MEDIÆVAL CORRUPTION

OUR limits will not permit of further details ; but, on the whole, the Catholic Church inclined steadily towards Transubstantiation, until about A.D. 830. Then Paschasius Radbertus, a monk of Corbie, in his work entitled *De sanguine et corpore Domini*, affirmed, that the elements are merely a veil which conceals the Body of Christ from us, and that this Body is the same as that which was born of Mary. He quotes instances in which the inward *Veritas* was reported to have come

to outward manifestation ; that is to say, in which the
Body and Blood of Christ had appeared in place of the
bread and wine ; but thinks that this does not always
occur, because the Supper is a mystery for faith to
believe, not a miracle to convince unbelief: moreover,
that the mercy of God remembers the natural horror
which men feel at the sight of flesh and blood, and
would also withdraw all occasions for blasphemy on
the part of unbelievers.

Thus, at last, Transubstantiation was definitely and
clearly set forth.   But there were several able opponents
of the new doctrine, especially Ratramnus, also of
Corbie, Rabanus Maurus, Scotus Erigena, and Florus of
Lyons, all of whom were in favour of the spiritualizing
theory.   Nevertheless, the view of Radbertus was
presently accepted by a large majority in the Church,
and was especially grateful to the Hierarchy, because
it exalted the priestly order by investing it with the
power of turning bread into a god.

And so, by the middle of the eleventh century
Transubstantiation had become the prevalent doctrine ;
so much so, indeed, that Berengarius, who assailed
it, was condemned by several synods.   His friend
Lanfranc of Bec, afterwards Archbishop of Canterbury,
procured a judgment against him at the Synod of
Rome, in A.D. 1050.   Subsequently, Berengarius gained
the friendship of Hildebrand, who was at first somewhat
inclined to support him.   He was, however, again
condemned at the Synod of Rome, in A.D. 1059, and
was compelled by Cardinal Humbert to profess a belief
in a doctrine of the Real Presence which exceeded even
that of Radbertus.   But, as soon as he had made good
his escape to France, he abjured this profession, and
wrote a powerful book in vindication of his own views

and against Lanfranc. In A.D. 1073, Hildebrand became Pope, and at first endeavoured to screen Berengarius. Finding, however, that his advocacy of the unpopular side was likely to bring him into some danger, he commanded Berengarius to confess and abjure his error, which the latter, who does not seem to have been remarkable for strength of mind, brought himself to do. And then the controversy ended.

In 1215, the Fourth Lateran Council was summoned by Innocent III., and a part of its first chapter is thus summarized by Landon ;—

" It further declares, that there is but one universal Church, out of which there is no salvation ; that there is but one sacrifice, namely, that of the Mass ; that in it Jesus Christ Himself is both the Priest and the Victim ; that ' His Body and Blood, in the sacrament of the altar, are truly contained under the species of bread and wine ; the bread being, by the Divine Omnipotence, transubstantiated into His Body, and the wine into His Blood ; that, for completing the mysterious union between Christ and His Church, we may receive His human nature, as He was pleased to take ours.' That this sacrament can only be celebrated by a priest, lawfully ordained, in virtue of that ecclesiastical power granted by our Lord to His Apostles and their successors." [1]

Thus Transubstantiation was formally recognized as an article of faith by the Roman Church in A.D. 1215 ; and in A.D. 1551, at the thirteenth session of the Council of Trent, this decision was confirmed.

[1] " This is the first appearance of a synodical authorization of the doctrine of Transubstantiation ; and, indeed, considering that these constitutions were not the work of the Council, but of Innocentius alone, the doctrine can hardly be said to have had the sanction of this Council "—Landon's *Manual of Councils*, p. 295, note.

The results which followed were such as might have been expected. On pretence of fear lest a particle of the Lord's Body should be lost through the falling of a crumb, round wafers were substituted for the bread that was to be broken ; and, ostensibly for a similar reason, the cup was altogether withdrawn from the laity, so that the priests were now the only full and perfect partakers of the Communion. But the real meaning of these changes can only be discovered by a study of the Pagan Mysteries.

The difficulty, that our Lord had specially bidden *all* to drink of the cup, was overcome by the assertion that there were no laymen present at the institution of the ordinance, since all the Apostles were priests ; while the fact that the distinction between clergy and laity is a thing, not merely unknown, but positively opposed, to the teaching of the New Testament was tacitly ignored.

On the other hand, to quiet the laity, a new doctrine was introduced, that of concomitancy, which taught that Christ is contained entire in either of the elements ; so that those who eat of the bread really partake of both Body and Blood. Of course, this altogether destroyed the teaching of the Lord, which, by separating the Blood from the Body, indicated that death had taken place. Yet, if it were objected, that administration in but one kind was contrary to His command, the only reply to be obtained was, that the Church had a Divine right to arrange such matters as it thought fit. Apparently, this must have meant that the Church had a Divine right to contradict itself as well as the Lord Jesus ; for, at the end of the fifth century, one of the infallible Popes, Gelasius I., solemnly denounced the practice of communicating in one kind. "A division," he said, "of one and the same mystery cannot be made without great sacrilege." It has sorely exercised the ingenuity of Roman theologians to show that Gelasius did not mean what he said.[1]

Again, since the bread was understood to have been turned into a god, the logical inference was that it must be worshipped. Hence it became the custom to keep a consecrated host in a golden or silver casket, often richly jewelled, which was placed in a niche on the right side of the high altar. No one might touch this save the priest, and when he elevated it at the Mass, or when it was carried through the streets in solemn procession, or to the house of a sick person, all who were near were expected to fall on their knees in adoration.[2]

But, although the doctrine of Transubstantiation had been formally adopted by the Church of Rome, it was not received so universally as its promulgators could have wished. Evidently miracles were needed to stimulate the credulity of the people; and when miracles are felt to be a necessity, in the Church of Rome, it is not long before they are announced.

Accordingly, while Pope Urban IV. was residing at Orvieto, in A.D. 1263, he was one day startled by exciting news from the neighbouring town of Bolsena.

---

[1] This they have attempted to do in three different ways. (1) By affirming that Gelasius was only speaking of priests, and not of the laity; in which case, it is strange that he was not a little more explicit. (2) By explaining, that, since his words were addressed to Manichæans, they can be applied only to Manichæans. But the Pope was laying down a general principle, and has in no way limited it. (3) By denying the genuineness of the words, which, however, there is no room to doubt.

[2] This is the sinister origin of the practice of kneeling at the administration of the Lord's Supper in the Reformed Church of England.

A young Bohemian priest presented himself in much agitation, and stated, that, like most of his compatriots, he had been a sceptic in the matter of Transubstantiation. But, while celebrating Mass in the chapel at Bolsena, he had with his own eyes beheld blood flowing from the wafer, and also bubbling from the chalice, in such abundance that it spread over the pavement of the chapel.[1] Convinced by the sight of such a prodigy, he had been instantly converted to the new dogma, and had hastened to report the miracle to the Pope, and to ask absolution for his previous unbelief.

Urban immediately despatched the Bishop of Orvieto to Bolsena to fetch the signs of the miracle, that is to say, the blood-stained wafer and corporal ; and, when he heard that the procession was approaching, he went out and met it on the bridge of Rio Chiaro ; and there fell on his knees to adore the welcome prodigy—a scene which is graphically portrayed in one of the frescoes that cover the walls of the memorial cathedral.

The fame of the miracle was soon diffused throughout Europe, and, in that credulous age, greatly helped to popularize the new doctrine. Moreover, some seven-and-twenty years later, in order at once to commemorate it, and to provide a depository for its signs, a superb cathedral was founded at Orvieto ; and there, to this day, the blood-stained napkin is exhibited in the Chapel of the Santissimo Corporale.

But the Pope's efforts were not yet exhausted. This miracle seems to have recalled to his mind another marvel, which had been communicated to him some time before, when he was only an archdeacon.

---

[1] The late Rev. Mourant Brock relates, that the stains of the blood were still on exhibition, beneath a grating on the floor, when he visited Bolsena in 1879.

There was a certain nun of Liége, named Juliana, who, about fifteen years after the Fourth Lateran Council referred to above, had begun to fall into ecstasies, in which she saw a full moon with a small portion of it always darkened. Then it was revealed to her, that the moon was the glory of the Church, but that the dark spot upon it signified the want of a special festival in honour of the Lord's Body. So humble-minded, however, was the nun that for twenty years she concealed this revelation, because she did not deem herself worthy to publish it. But, at length, she disclosed it to a canon of Liége, and he, again, passed on the secret to the archdeacon who afterwards became Pope Urban IV. The result of the matter was, that, in obedience to the visions, a festival of the Lord's Body was ordained in the diocese of Liége in 1259.

And so, in 1264, Urban IV. determined to extend the festival over the whole of Christendom. This, however, could only be done by slow degrees; for, in spite of ecclesiastical censure, the teachings of Berengarius still maintained so wide an influence that Urban's bull encountered much opposition. And it was only by the energy of Clement V., in 1311, that the Feast of Corpus Christi began, at last, to be generally celebrated. Then it soon became one of the greatest of the Roman festivals.

XXXI

SUMMARY AND CONCLUSION

BEFORE quitting the subject of the Lord's Supper, we will briefly recapitulate our main argument.

In order to examine what the New Testament reveals concerning this second outward rite, we turned, first, to the sixth chapter of the Gospel of John. In it we observed the Lord's thrice-repeated declaration, that whosoever believes on Him has eternal life from the very fact of his faith, without any other requirement.[1]

A little further on in His discourse, He describes Himself as being the Living Bread, of which if a man eat, he shall live for ever.[2]

But He had previously called Himself the Bread of Life, and then explained His meaning by adding ;—

"He that cometh unto Me shall never hunger, and he that believeth on Me shall never thirst." [3]

Evidently, therefore, to believe on Him is equivalent to eating Him as the Bread of Life.

Again, in the fifty-third verse, He also says ;—

"And the Bread which I will give is My Flesh, which I will give for the life of the world."

The Bread and the Flesh are, therefore, the same ; and, consequently, if to believe on Him is equivalent to eating Him as the Bread, it is also equivalent to eating His Flesh.

Lastly, He says ;—

"Verily, verily, I say unto you, Except ye eat the Flesh of the Son of Man, and drink His Blood, ye have not life in yourselves. Whoso eateth My Flesh and drinketh My Blood hath eternal life ; and I will raise him up at the Last Day." [4]

Now, these final expressions, "My Flesh" and "My Blood," are merely a division and particularization of that which has preceded, namely "My Flesh": they must, therefore, be explained in the same way. The Lord Jesus represents Himself as the Living Bread, which sustains life, not merely for a season, like material

---

[1] Vv. 35, 40, 47.   [3] V. 35.
[2] V. 51.   [4] Vv. 53 and 54.

bread, but for ever. He then states, that this Bread is His Flesh, which, if eaten, will confer eternal life. And, lastly, by speaking of His Flesh and His Blood separately, He develops His teaching in two ways.

For, first, the separation of flesh and blood indicates death ; and He thus hints at the necessity of His Own death, if He is to give life to those who believe on Him.

And, secondly, the mention of blood—without the shedding of which there can be no remission,[1] and which makes atonement for sins by reason of the soul, or life, that is in it[2]—brings out the fact, that eternal life cannot be communicated to man, unless there be also found an expiation for his sins.

Thus the great practical lesson of the discourse amounts to this ;—That whosoever believes in the Lord Jesus, and in the truths revealed concerning His Flesh and His Blood, has eternal life, and shall be raised up at the Last Day. He has secured the gift of God, which can never be withdrawn ;[3] and, at the Resurrection of the Dead—unless, by also securing the prize, he shall have previously attained to the First Resurrection— his name will be found written in the Book of Life.[4]

But, while to believe on the Lord Jesus is equivalent to eating His Flesh and drinking His Blood, it is not necessarily identical with the latter. For, undoubtedly, spiritual actions are sometimes unconsciously involved in those of the body. And, as we have explained above, it is after the Lord's death and resurrection that we are bidden to feed upon Him, even as He Himself reminds His disciples, that His words do not refer to flesh, but to spirit.[5]

It is, then, His essential or spiritual-corporeal Body

[1] Heb. ix. 22. [3] Rom. xi. 29. [5] John vi. 63.
[2] Lev. xvii. 11. [4] Rev. xx. 12, 15.

16

that is proffered to us as the food of immortality. And it is possible, that, when we draw nigh to Him in faith, we do really, though unconsciously, absorb His essential Flesh and Blood,[1] by our very act of faith, in some such way as can be set before our present faculties only under the figure of eating and drinking.

Of that we may know more hereafter; but, for the present, our part is to believe; and, if an unconscious act of spiritual eating and drinking be, also, necessary, God will see that we fail not in its performance, provided that we have done that for which He made us responsible. For to all who really believe, eternal life is promised absolutely without further conditions.

Such is the Lord's exposition of His marvellous and, so far as our part is concerned, most simple way of salvation.

Some time after He had given it, on the eve of His death, in a private upper-chamber, and while reclining at table with His disciples in the manner of His country and time, He instituted a Memorial Supper; but, of course, those only are to partake of it who have something to remember, *who have already eaten His Flesh and drunk His Blood by believing on Him.* And they are to do so for these three reasons;—

I. For a remembrance of Himself, of His Body that was broken, and His Blood that was shed, for them.[2]

II. To testify to the world, until He comes again, that they believe in His propitiatory death for their own sins, and not for theirs only, but also for those of the whole world.[3]

---

[1] That is to say, those elements of the spiritual body which correspond to the flesh and blood of the soul-body—$\sigma\hat{\omega}\mu\alpha$ $\psi\upsilon\chi\iota\kappa\acute{o}\nu$, I Cor. xv. 44.

[2] Luke xxii. 19.　　　　[3] I Cor. xi. 26; I John ii. 2.

III. To remind themselves, as they all partake of the one broken loaf, that their individual communion with Him causes them all, though many, to be one in Him.[1]

And these are actually the only reasons which the Scriptures set before us for the Commemorative Meal: all the points upon which men dispute are nothing but human figments added to the Divine Words; or, perhaps, it would be better to say, human figments which altogether conceal the Divine Words.

No special promises whatever are given in connection with the Supper: eternal life and cleansing[2] are already the possession of those who have a right to partake of it: and, indeed, to do so is simply to comply with the dying request of our Lord, Who willed that His Own people should in such a manner remind themselves of what He had done for them in the past, and give thanks.

There can, however, be little doubt that His blessing and His peace will ever rest upon those obedient ones who eat and drink with gratitude and adoring love; while, at the same time, it is reasonable that His anger and heavy judgments should light upon any one who can thoughtlessly, or in conscious sin, taste the emblems of His sufferings and death, and thus despise the Blood of the Covenant.

So simple, so devoid of all mystery, is the Lord's Supper as instituted by Himself, and revealed in His

---

[1] 1 Cor. x. 16, 17.
[2] John xiii. 10. The washing of the disciples' feet took place, of course, before supper. We have already explained the mistake of the A.V., which, in John xiii. 2, reads "supper being ended," instead of "supper being laid." The R.V. adopts a different reading, and translates, "during supper"; but, "while supper was being laid," would have been better.

Word ; but, in this case, men have, indeed, "sought out many inventions." [1]

Their first tendency, as we have seen above, was to add to the purely symbolic Supper a mystic power, understood to reside in the symbols themselves. This power was thought to proceed from a spiritual Presence of the Lord's Body and Blood in the elements, which could only be induced by priestly consecration.

Finally, the elements, after consecration, were regarded as being His real and actual Body and Blood ; and were, consequently, adored ; while the Mass was declared to be a perpetual repetition of His sacrifice on the cross.

And, since none but " priests " could produce the magic change in the elements, the " priest," and not the Lord Himself, thenceforth became, to vulgar minds at least, the immediate bestower of salvation.

It is scarcely possible to conceive a greater transformation than this, a more complete perversion of the simple words and action of the Lord. And the terms also and outward forms of the institution were changed as entirely as its design and doctrine. " The morning celebration," says Plumptre, "takes the place of the evening.[2] New names—Eucharist, Sacrifice, Altar, Mass, Holy Mysteries—gather round it. New epithets and new ceremonies express the growing reverence of the people. The celebration at the high altar of a basilica in the fourth century differs so widely from the

---

[1] Eccles. vii. 29.

[2] To make such a change compulsory is an act of rebellion. The Lord Himself instituted the Supper in the evening of the day before His death: how, then, can Ritualistic bishops dare to say that it must take place only in the morning ! In so doing, they testify that they are not His followers, and condemn the obedience of His Apostle as recorded in Acts xx. 7.

circumstances of the original institution, that a careless eye would have found it hard to recognize their identity."

We should think it would, and that for a very simple reason, because there was even then no identity in the matter. The Lord's Supper had already become a patchwork of Paganism, in which, however, the original piece could still, perhaps, be detected. But soon it was altogether concealed beneath the magic ceremony of High Mass, which may be seen to-day conducted, at the glittering altar of a gorgeous temple, by some prince of the Church in brilliant array, and often assisted by musical experts whose talents are ordinarily devoted to the Opera or the Concert-hall.

May the Lord turn away our eyes from such vanities, and keep us to the simple institution which He commended to them that love Him, which has no concern with priests, or fastings, or consecrations, other than the heartfelt prayer of thanksgiving. With those who abide in Him may we share the bread broken from one loaf, and the wine that represents His Blood, not merely in commemoration of what He has done for all mankind, but also in full assurance of what He has done for ourselves as individuals.

Most appropriately did He institute His Supper in the night; for it is emphatically a feast of the night, to be partaken of by those who must meanwhile be having tribulation in the world, but who are watching for the morning. For, be their lot hard as it may, they remember the glorious words, "Till He come": they rejoice as so many predicted events pass by, and they recognize in them "the hind of the dawn," the ever-brightening rays which announce that the night is, indeed, far spent, and the day at hand : they exult in the thought, that He Who, of His great love, His Own Self bare their sins in His Own Body on the tree, may at any hour appear to deliver them for ever from all their afflictions, and to transfer their feast from the dark chambers of earth to the radiant banqueting-hall in His Father's House.

THE GIFTS OF MINISTRY

XXXII

THE GIFTS OF MINISTRY AND THEIR PURPOSE

EPH. iv. 11–16

WE will now proceed to investigate the provision made for the government and instruction of the churches, and to inquire into the Divine arrangements respecting their officers and teachers.

There are many who think, that such matters were left to the discretion of the churches themselves : this, however, is a very serious mistake. Full directions respecting all the functionaries that were sanctioned by God are given in the New Testament ; while a prophetic intimation of them may be found even in the Old. For, in the sixty-eighth Psalm, there is a prediction that God Himself would provide, and endow with spiritual gifts, guides and rulers for His children of the present Dispensation. In the eighteenth verse, we read as follows ;—

> "Thou hast ascended on high; Thou hast led captivity captive :
> Thou hast received gifts (to distribute)[1] among men,
> Yea, among the rebellious also, that the Lord God might dwell with them."

[1] By supplying the words, "to distribute," the meaning is assimilated to Paul's presentation of it—"and gave gifts unto men" (Eph. iv. 8). Or we might, perhaps more simply, understand

Now, as Paul tells us, the reference of these verses is to the ascension of the Lord, and to His reception of the gifts of the Spirit that He might give them to men. And the gifts are distributed even among the rebellious, in order, both by the salvation of those who can be saved and by the ripening for judgment of the wilfully disobedient,[1] to bring on the time when it shall be said ;—

" Behold, the Tabernacle of God is with men, and He shall dwell with them."[2]

For the end of all His dealings with our race is its reconciliation to Himself, that He may cause the New Jerusalem to descend from heaven, of which John says ;—

" And the City hath no need of the sun, neither of the moon, to shine upon it ; for the glory of God did lighten it, and the lamp thereof is the Lamb."[3]

What gifts these are, which are being used to forward so glorious a purpose, we may learn from the subjoined words ;—

" And He gave some to be Apostles, and some, prophets ; and some, evangelists ; and some, pastors and teachers ; with a view to the perfecting of the saints, for work of ministering, for a building up of the Body of Christ, till we all attain unto the unity of the faith and of the full knowledge of the

the Psalmist to be laying stress on the fact, that certain individuals among men were given by the Father to the Lord Jesus, to be endowed by Him with the Spirit ; while Paul brings out the other side of the matter, that these endowed ones were intended as gifts for men, that is, to be bestowed upon men for their benefit. Both the Old and the New Testament are inspired, and the latter, in quoting from the former, often expands, or reveals another side of, the meaning.

[1] 2 Cor. ii. 15, 16.   [2] Rev. xxi. 3.   [3] Rev. xxi. 23.

Son of God, unto a perfect man, unto the measure of the stature of the fulness of Christ ; that we may be no longer children, tossed to and fro and carried about with every wind of teaching, in the sleight of man, in a craftiness tending to the system of error ; but, while we walk according to the truth in love, may grow up in all things into Him, Which is the Head, even Christ ; from Whom all the Body, being fitly framed and knit together by means of every joint of the supply, according to energy in the measure of each several part, maketh the increase of the Body for the building up of itself in love." [1]

In this important passage we note ;—

First, that persons endowed with powers fitting them for the vocations mentioned above are to be regarded as gifts from the Lord Jesus to men.

Secondly, that, in his enumeration of these gifts, the Apostle makes no reference whatever to priests, or to a clerical caste.

And, thirdly, that the work of these Divinely appointed teachers and rulers is not the support of any great Hierarchy, or Establishment, or Church, in this present world. But the object for which they are to labour is "the perfecting of the saints," [2] individually and generally ; not merely of those who are to be found in any particular church or sect, but of "all that call upon the Name of our Lord Jesus Christ in every place, their Lord and ours." [3] With this object before them, they are to apply themselves to the work of ministration,

---

[1] Eph. iv. 11–16.

[2] There is little doubt that the correct interpretation of the prepositions in this verse is that which makes "the perfecting of the saints" (πρός) to be the final object in view, while the other clauses (εἰς) indicate the means to that end.

[3] 1 Cor. i. 2.

and to the building up of the Body of Christ, both by instructing, exhorting, and helping, those who are already among the saved, and by the conversion of those that are without.

And, in speaking of conversion, we mean conversion to faith and trust in the Lord Jesus, not persuasion to join some visible body, or to attend some particular place of worship. Similarly, by " those that are without," we would signify those who are without the unseen pale of the Lord's followers, not those who do not belong to some earthly community. For every visible Church on earth contains children of the Evil One as well as children of the Kingdom, and reckons among its members many who need conversion. And there are some to be found, unattached, indeed, to any special visible communion, but who, nevertheless, hold fast the Head, and love Him with all their heart.

Sects and divisions among believers are not recognized in Scripture : there never was, nor ever will be, a visible Church, which, taken as a whole could be described as a branch of the True Vine. An earthly organization, even if it be rendering service to the Lord, can at its best, be no more than a trellis-work useful for holding together and supporting some of His members.

Hence those who are specially endowed by Him, and sent forth as His gifts to men, could not confine their efforts to any particular sect, though the direction of the Spirit, or their office, may restrict them to a particular locality. Their ministration is to all the saints with whom they are brought into contact, and it must continue, potentially at least, until all the members of Christ's Body attain to the unity of the faith and of the full knowledge of the Son of God.

The desired unity, then, is not based upon uniformity

in ritual or modes of worship, nor maintained by obedience to a clerical caste ruled by bishops, archbishops, patriarchs, or popes—all dignitaries of man's creation : it depends solely on the firm possession of faith in, and right views of, the Lord Jesus, and that, not merely in His humiliation as the Son of Man, but, also, in His highest dignity as the Only Begotten Son of God.[1]

To His people unity can accrue only from implicit faith in Him as their Lord and Saviour, combined with that after-knowledge[2] of the mysteries of God which follows salvation. We have the same distinction between the fundamentals that save and the more profound truths tending to sanctification, that are afterwards revealed, in a passage, already considered, in which Paul expresses his desire to be saved by the righteousness which is through faith in Christ, in order that he may then go on to know Him.[3] And the Lord Himself bade His missionaries to make disciples of all the nations, baptizing them—which, as we have seen, would involve previous instruction in fundamentals—and then teaching them all things whatsoever He had commanded.[4]

Further, this unity must become so perfect that all the members may be merged into one full-grown personality, the Body of Christ. Individually and collectively they must have come to the stature-measure of the fulness of Christ, that is, to the maturity and completeness of what is meant by the mystic Christ—that personality of which the Lord Jesus is the Head

[1] Till we all attain unto the unity of the faith, and of the full knowledge of the Son of God.—Eph. iv. 13.
[2] The Greek word is ἐπίγνωσις, which means, not merely knowledge (γνῶσις), but 'after-,' 'additional,' or 'full knowledge.'
[3] Phil. iii. 9, 10.   [4] Matt. xxviii. 19, 20.

and His Church the Body. And, until this has been effected, the ministries mentioned above must continue, even until the whole Church has been gathered in, and every member so instructed and disciplined that he is fit to take the place appointed for him in the Body. When this shall be, who can tell? But the Lord will know, and will then utter His voice, and, in a moment, gather His members into His Presence.

One of the offices of these gifts of Christ to men, while He is working through them for the completion of the Body, is deemed worthy of special notice. The endowed are to labour for the promotion of our spiritual growth; so that we may pass from the condition of babes in Christ to a maturity of faith and a firm hold of the truths of God. Then we shall no longer be tossed and carried about, like rudderless ships at sea, in an evil atmosphere of deceit and craft, the currents within which are ever impelling us towards Satan's skilfully arranged system of error. But we shall be taught to walk according to truth and in love, so that, in all our thoughts purposes and aspirations, we may be daily growing up into the Head, even Christ, and may be ever becoming more completely incorporated into His Body, and more perfectly submissive to the control of His Spirit. For He is the Head, the only Source of life: from Him all the Body, while it is being fitly framed and knit together, draws its vitality by means of every joint that distributes the supply, according to energy in the measure of each several part, and so carries on its growth for the building up of itself in love.

In interpreting this wonderful figure, we must remember that the expression, "the Body of Christ," is never used of any single professing church, or of any aggregate of professing churches existing upon earth at one particular time. It can only mean the union in glory of all the members of Christ, gathered in during the centuries that elapse between the First and the Second Advent. Hence the present participles indicate that it is now going through the process of "being fitly framed and knit together."

"The supply" is, of course, the Spirit of Life in Christ Jesus, descending from Himself, as the Head, to the lowest member of the Body.

"The junctures" or "joints"—which in a human body are the points of union by means of which the vital fluid is conveyed to the different limbs and parts—probably represent those who have received special gifts of ministry directly from the Lord Jesus ; for the New Testament knows nothing of Ecclesiastical Hierarchies and Apostolical Successions. There is but one means by which the members of the Body can be knit together, that is, if each one of them holds fast the Head ; for from Him Alone the vital streams of power can be drawn, and the Body caused to increase with the increase that comes from no inferior creature, but from God Himself.

XXXIII

THE FOUR GREATER GIFTS

EPH. iv. 11.

SUCH, then, is the work set before those ministers whom Christ has endowed to be gifts to men. In the present passage they are described as Apostles, prophets, evangelists, and pastors and teachers.

The fact, that, in the original, "some" is not repeated before 'teachers,' shows that the same men were regarded as both pastors and teachers, these offices not being distinct.

Four gifts, then, are here mentioned, and we may readily divide them into two classes. For Apostles, prophets, and evangelists, have no appointment or sanction whatever from men, but receive, directly from the Lord, such gifts as cannot be denied, are sent forth to do whatever the Spirit may dictate, and may not be confined to any one place or district.

Of these, the first two are to minister in any of the churches, or in any part of the globe, according to their guidance ; but the work of the third is without the pale of the churches : his sphere is the field which is the world.

Pastors and teachers, on the other hand, are local officers, and are appointed for the rule and instruction of particular churches. Originally, in the primal churches, whose members would have had little or no experience, they were chosen by the Apostles ; because the latter were endowed with a power of discerning spirits, and so, were specially qualified to discover those in whom God had placed the gift of ministerial talent for tending and instructing the flock. But, subsequently, they were selected and appointed by the congregation over which they were to preside.

XXXIV

Apostles

THE very word Apostle, that is, 'one sent forth,' signifies an itinerant preacher, a missionary, one whose sphere of action may be in any part of the world. Accordingly, Paul, the only Apostle of whose work we have any detailed account, is found to be ever moving from one place to another ; or, if he does remain in the same city more than a year, the fact is mentioned as an unusual thing.

Now, the manner of his life is, doubtless, recorded for us as a sample of the work of his order ; so that the first characteristic of an Apostle is his commission to preach everywhere and to all men. Hence the absurdity of those Patristic traditions which represent John as bishop, in something like the modern sense of the term, of Ephesus, Peter of Rome, and so on. For a bishop or presbyter is a local officer, and were an Apostle to accept such a position, he would by the very act surrender his Apostleship.

A second characteristic of an Apostle is, that he must have seen the Lord Jesus after His resurrection, and so have been an eyewitness of that all-important event. This was manifestly understood by the Eleven, who, when they determined, apparently without any command from the Lord, to elect another in the place of Judas, were careful to choose their two candidates from those who had been with them all the time that the Lord Jesus went in and out among them ; because the new Apostle must be a witness with them of His resurrection.[1] Hence, in Paul's case, there was a miraculous interposition, and the risen Lord appeared to him, in order that he might be fully qualified for his Apostleship. And, in his first Epistle to the Corinthians, we find him appealing to this fact in the words ;——

"Am I not an Apostle ? Have I not seen Jesus our Lord ?"[2]

The signs of an Apostle he describes as being an effectual energy in preaching the Gospel, so that men

[1] Acts i. 21, 22.　　[2] I Cor. ix. I.

17

are converted and churches founded, and the exercise of a miraculous power. Hence, in the passage just cited, he goes on to say ;——

" Are not ye my work in the Lord ? If to others I am not an Apostle, yet at least I am to you : for the seal of mine Apostleship are ye in the Lord." [1]

Again, in another place, he says ;——

" Truly the signs of an Apostle were wrought among you in all patience, by signs and wonders and mighty works." [2]

But the Apostle not only possessed the gift of the evangelist in the effectual preaching of the Gospel, and that of the prophet in showing signs and wonders, in predicting the future, and, generally, in speaking under the immediate influence of the Spirit : he had yet another power, greater than either of these. For he was able to confer the gifts of the Spirit by the laying on of his hands, and to do so in such a manner that the gifts bestowed were instantly manifested to all men. None but Apostles have ever exercised this power. Others have, indeed, laid claim to it ; but the laying on of their hands has proved a dead rite ; for no such effects have followed it as those which were produced by the Apostles, especially in the case of converts who had just been baptized.

Hence the five characteristic signs of an Apostle seem to be ;—

(1) A commission to preach to all men, and to supervise and instruct churches, in any part of the earth, whithersoever he may be directed by the Spirit.

(2) The fact that he has seen the Lord Jesus after His resurrection, and has received a personal call from Him.

[1] 1 Cor. ix. 1, 2.   [2] 2 Cor. xii. 12.

(3) The power of effective preaching.

(4) A Divine authority to perform miracles.

(5) The power of conferring the Holy Spirit by the laying on of his hands, and that in such a manner that the gift shall be evident to all beholders.

In short, then, it seems that a true Apostle must have within himself all the gifts and powers which the Spirit confers upon man. And it was, doubtless, through their knowledge of the five signs mentioned above that the Ephesian Christians were enabled to detect, and expose as liars, those first pretenders to Apostleship of whom we read in the Lord's Epistle to the church in Ephesus.[1]

It will, perhaps, be as well to notice another function of the earlier Apostles, which would seem from the circumstances to have been only temporary. This was the founding and organization of churches. So Paul says to the Corinthians ;—" If to others I am not an Apostle, yet at least I am to you ; for the seal of mine Apostleship are ye in the Lord."[2] Similarly, he speaks of Epaphroditus as the Apostle of the Philippians ;[3] of his brethren as " Apostles of churches " ;[4] and of himself as " an Apostle of Gentiles."[5]

In each of these expressions the genitive is objective, conveying the idea of an Apostle sent to the Philippians, commissioned to found other churches, or directed to go to Gentiles. But the same case has a very different meaning in the title " An Apostle of Jesus Christ," which Paul usually gives to himself, and does not withhold from others.

Now, since Apostles, as well as the Lord's other gifts to men, are said to be given for the perfecting

---

[1] Rev. ii. 2.   [3] Phil. ii. 25.   [5] Rom. xi. 13.
[2] 1 Cor. ix. 2.   [4] 2 Cor. viii. 23.

of the saints, until we all come to the unity of the faith and the full knowledge of the Son of God, and since this purpose has not yet been accomplished ; therefore, it is evident that Apostles should be among us now. In the earliest days of the Dispensation, it seemed as if they would continue to appear ; for Barnabas was an Apostle,[1] and so, also, were Epaphroditus,[2] the four brothers of the Lord,[3] Silas,[4] Timothy, and others.[5] Moreover, since the church in Ephesus was praised, in A.D. 95, or 96, because she had applied the proper tests to men who claimed to be Apostles, it is clear that believers were still expecting these gifts of the Lord at a time when Paul had passed away, and John was the only survivor of the Twelve.

Again, the *Didache*, which may have been written before the Apocalypse, expresses the same expectation, and also contains rules for the reception and treatment of Apostles ; among which we find the ominous precept, that, if they should remain in a place more than two days, or if, not content with food, they should ask for money, they must be regarded as impostors.[6]

This passage, considered together with the result of the Ephesian inquiry,[7] shows that Satanic counterfeits were then rife, and that there was grave reason to remember the words of Paul ;—

"For such men are false Apostles, deceitful workers, fashioning themselves into Apostles of

---

[1] Acts xiv. 4, 14. Comp. 1 Cor. ix. 5, 6.
[2] Phil. ii. 25.
[3] 1 Cor. ix. 5 ; xv. 5–8 ; Gal. i. 19.
[4] Comp. 1 Thess. i. 1 with ii. 6.
[5] Rom. xvi. 7 ; 2 Cor. viii. 23, where the A.V. and R.V. have "the messengers of the churches," although the Greek is "Apostles of churches," without any definite article.
[6] *Didache* xi. 3–6.   [7] Rev. ii. 2.

Christ. And no marvel: for even Satan fashioneth himself into an angel of light. It is no great thing, therefore, if his ministers also fashion themselves as ministers of righteousness; whose end shall be according to their works." [1]

But, after the first century, Apostles altogether disappeared, and the churches were deprived of their greatest strength. This, as we have already seen, ought not to have been the case; and the only probable reason by which we can attempt to explain it is, that the very early apostasy from the faith, and introduction of the institutions and commandments of men into the churches, caused the Lord Jesus to withhold His most precious gifts, even as He did not many mighty works in His Own country "because of their unbelief."

It is, however, quite possible that He may once more send Apostles for the guidance of His people, amid the difficulties perplexities and dangers of these last days. Let us, therefore, keep well in mind the Scriptural tests which have been given to us; for by rigorously applying them, should the need arise, we should quickly discern whether those who claim to be Apostles of Jesus Christ are to be followed, or to be repudiated and avoided as ministers of Satan.

XXXV

PROPHETS

THE second order, that of prophets, consists of men who are caused to speak under the immediate inspiration of the Holy Spirit; so that, when the power is upon them, they do not necessarily know what they may be guided to say.

[1] 2 Cor. xi. 13–15.

The gift of prophecy has not, however, been confined to the present Dispensation: from the earliest times there were men through whom God chose to communicate His wishes and purposes to their fellows. Such were Enoch and Noah among the antediluvians, and Joseph and Moses in a subsequent period.

But, when the Israelitish polity was established, the spiritual instruction of the people was committed to the priests; for they were to "teach the children of Israel all the statutes which the Lord had spoken to them by the hand of Moses."[1] This they did for a while; but, during the times of the Judges, they became debased, and lost their spiritual power; so that they performed the ritual of the Sanctuary mechanically, and no longer instructed the people as to its real meaning. Hence the Lord began to transfer His work to prophets, whom from the time of Samuel He used, more systematically than before, as His mouthpieces to Israel. For the regularly appointed priests and Levites continued to fail in their duty, until they had made the oblations vain, the incense an abomination, the new moons and sabbaths, and the calling of assemblies, things that He could not away with.   He would, therefore, choose men after His Own heart, and, filling them with His Holy Spirit, send them forth, without any human ordination or permission, to preach His Word, to be instant in season and out of season, to reprove rebuke and exhort, with all longsuffering and teaching.[2]

And is He not carrying out His purposes in a somewhat analogous manner now, seeing that the churches are failing and apostatizing to Catholicism, free thought, or worldly vanities; and that so large a portion of His

---

[1] Lev. x. 11.   [2] 2 Tim. iv. 2.

real work is in the hands of those who look to Him Alone, and hold no commission from Ecclesiastical Hierarchies or from any human authority?

Prophets, however, as Paul declares, are an order that belongs to the present Dispensation, as well as to that which has passed by; and they are men who receive communications directly from God, just as Apostles do. But they are not, like the latter, endowed with all the gifts of the Spirit, and their inspired utterances are usually intended only for the edification of the churches, and are rarely addressed to those that are without. "Prophesying," says Paul, "is for a sign, not to the unbelieving, but to them that believe." [1]

And so, the Apostle regarded it as a power that should be commonly found in the churches, and ought to be earnestly desired and prayed for; both of which points are pressed in his Epistle to the Corinthians.

For, first, he speaks of prophecy as a Divine institution in the Church, that is, in the whole Body as its members succeed each other upon the earth during the times of the Church-period, or present Dispensation. For he says;—

"God set some in the Church, first Apostles, secondly, prophets, thirdly, teachers, then miracles, then gifts of healing, helps, governments, divers kinds of tongues." [2]

In this passage, evangelists are omitted from the list—perhaps, because they are regarded as a class of prophets; since the true evangelist speaks directly from the Holy Spirit, though his inspiration may be limited to one subject.

[1] I Cor. xiv. 22.   [2] I Cor. xii. 28.

Again, in another Epistle, he urges those who were
thus gifted to exercise their gifts ;—

"And having gifts differing according to the
grace that was given to us, whether prophecy,
let us prophesy according to the proportion of
faith." [1]

Yet again, he assumes a plurality of prophets in a
single assembly ; and so gives directions for regulating
their utterances, at the same time warning the prophets
themselves to exercise self-control ;—

"And let the prophets speak by two or three, and
let the others discern.   But, if a revelation be made to
another sitting by, let the first keep silence.   For ye
all can prophesy one by one, that all may learn, and
all may be comforted : and the spirits of the prophets
are subject to the prophets ; for God is not a God of
confusion, but of peace, as in all the churches of the
saints." [2]

The need of such rules as these testifies to the
frequency of the prophetic gift.   And we may find
examples of it in the prophets which came from
Jerusalem,[3] in those that were afterwards found in
the church at Antioch,[4] and in the four prophesying
daughters of Philip at Cæsarea.[5]

Indeed, it would seem that a church-assembly could
scarcely be complete, unless one prophet, at least, were
present.   For prophecy was the means of communication
by which the Spirit signified the will and purpose of
God, and conveyed the necessary instruction exhortation
or rebuke to His people.

Hence we find Agabus predicting the famine that

[1] Rom. xii. 6: comp. 1 Cor. xii. 10.   [4] Acts xiii. 1.
[2] 1 Cor. xiv. 29–33.   [5] Acts xxi. 9.
[3] Acts xi. 27.

was to come in the days of Claudius Cæsar,[1] and the bonds that awaited Paul at Rome.[2]

So, too, at Antioch, the Holy Spirit said, doubtless through one of the prophets ;—

"Separate Me Barnabas and Saul for the work whereunto I have called them."[3]

Again, to Timothy Paul says ;—

"Neglect not the gift that is in thee, which was given thee by prophecy, with the laying on of the hands of the presbytery."[4]

From which it appears, that the Holy Spirit signified, through a prophet, the call of Timothy to the ministry ; and that, when, in obedience to this intimation, the hands of the presbytery—among whom Paul included himself[5]—had been laid upon him, he received the necessary gift. In reference to the same event, Paul also says ;—

"This charge I commit unto thee, my child Timothy, according to the antecedent prophecies concerning thee, that, in conformity with them, thou mayest war the good warfare."[6]

A consideration of these three cases of Paul Barnabas and Timothy certainly suggests the thought, that there can be no real ordination, or, at least, no certainty of a real ordination, to an office requiring spiritual gifts, unless the Holy Spirit has previously intimated His choice. If so, we can well understand why the vast majority of recognized ministers exhibit no spiritual power whatever, either in promoting the

---

[1] Acts xi. 27, 28.
[2] Acts xxi. 10, 11.
[3] Acts xiii. 2. Compare v. 1, which mentions the presence of prophets in the assembly.
[4] 1 Tim. iv. 14.   [5] 2 Tim. i. 6.   [6] 1 Tim. i. 18.

sanctification of the saved, or in effecting the conversion of the unsaved.

In early times, before the Canon of Scripture had been completed, prophets were used to convey to believers those things which afterwards appeared in the written Word.   So Paul explains to the Ephesians ;—

" Ye can perceive my understanding in the mystery of Christ, which in other generations was not made known unto the sons of men, as it has now been revealed unto His holy Apostles and prophets in spirit ; " [1]

By "in spirit" he, of course, means in the spiritual sphere, in which Apostles and prophets, being what Paul calls πνευματικοί, or 'spiritual,'[2] could be made conscious.   And the fact that the mysteries of God were thus revealed to, and declared by, Apostles and prophets explains the meaning of those other words of Paul, in which he affirms, that believers are "built upon the foundation of the Apostles and prophets" ; [3] that is, upon the foundation which they laid, or, in plain terms, upon the revelations and doctrines which they taught.

Lastly, a true prophet, as one having access to the spiritual sphere, ought to have discernment in spiritual things ; and, on this ground, Paul puts forth the challenge ;—

" If any one thinketh himself to be a prophet or spiritual, let him recognize the things which I write unto you as being commandments of the Lord." [4]

The passage in the fourth chapter of the Ephesians tells us, that the prophetic gift, like the others there mentioned, was intended to remain in the churches

[1] Eph. iii. 4, 5.　　　[3] Eph. ii. 20.
[2] I Cor. iii. 1, xii. 1, xiv. 37.　　[4] I Cor. xiv. 37.

until the end of their period. And hence it is that Paul urges the Corinthians to " desire earnestly the greater gifts." [1] He does, indeed, add that he will point out a way still more excellent, and that love is to be desired even more earnestly than gifts. Nevertheless, his argument on that point is concluded with the words ;—

" Follow after love, yet desire earnestly spiritual gifts, but rather that ye may prophesy." [2]

For, as he explains, the prophet has a greater power of edifying the churches than all other spiritually gifted persons. And so, he sums up the whole subject with the commands ;—

" Wherefore, my brethren, desire earnestly to prophesy, and forbid not to speak with tongues. But let all things be done decently and in order." [3]

Yet, inestimably valuable as the prophetic gift is, it was not long before it passed out of recognition, and was supplanted by orders of human appointment. We do, however, find it mentioned in the *Didache*, where, as in Scripture, the prophet stands next in dignity to the Apostle ; but, unlike the latter, is acknowledged also as a local minister who might attach himself to a single church, and for whose maintenance provision must be made. The directions concerning him, in that most ancient of church-manuals, are so curious and interesting that we will quote them in full ;—

" And ye shall neither try nor judge any prophet who speaks in spirit ; for every sin shall be forgiven, but this sin shall not be forgiven.

" Yet not every one that speaks in spirit is a prophet, but only if he has the manners of the Lord. By their manners, then, shall the false prophet and the prophet be distinguished.

[1] 1 Cor. xii. 31.   [2] 1 Cor. xiv. 1.   [3] 1 Cor. xiv. 39, 40.

"And every prophet who, while in spirit, orders a table, shall not eat of it; or, if he does, he is a false prophet.

"And every prophet who teaches the truth, if he does not practise what he teaches, is a false prophet.

"And every approved genuine prophet who calls assemblies to exhibit a worldly mystery, provided he does not teach others to do what he himself does, shall not be judged by you, seeing his judgment is with God; for even so did also the prophets of olden time.

"But whosoever, being in spirit, says, Give me money or any other thing, ye shall not listen to him. But, if on behalf of others that lack he bid you to give, let no one judge him."[1]

This passage affords us some idea of the importance of the prophet in the early churches, and of the consequent prevalence of imposture. It indicates a desire, not merely to detect and expose fraud, but also to avoid the repeated testing of those who had been once proved and recognized as true prophets. Regarding such men as mediums of the Holy Spirit, it forbids their further trial or judgment, on the ground that such a course would be to doubt the Holy Spirit, and so to commit the unpardonable sin.[2] But the human element in the prophet seems to be ignored, and the precept is dangerous, restricting, as it does, the Scriptural command to try the spirits, whether they are of God.[3]

We should notice, that the prophet is not to be judged when he "speaks in spirit," that is, when he speaks in ecstasy, or from the sphere of spirit, which in his case is dominated by the Holy Spirit. We are, however, reminded, that false prophets, also, may speak

[1] *Didache* xi. 7-12. [2] Matt. xii. 31. [3] I John iv. I.

in spirit; and, therefore, that we must not accept a prophet simply for his supernatural power, but only if he adds to it the manners of the Lord Jesus, if he is constant in prayer, gentle, meek, loving, ready to forgive, self-sacrificing, long-suffering, and earnestly desirous of doing good to all men.

Two other tests for prophets follow. If a prophet, when in spirit, orders a table, he will not himself partake of it, unless he be a false prophet. The table referred to is a love-feast, which in early times preceded the Lord's Supper. For such a feast the rich members of the church brought the provisions; but, at the meal, both rich and poor sat down together, and fared alike.[1]

Now, a prophet, it seems, had the power of appointing one of these gatherings, but not for his own gratification. Therefore, whenever he was inspired to do so, he was to prove his freedom from selfish motives by declining to partake of the common meal. Otherwise, he must be regarded as an impostor.

Apparently, this curious precept is not without support in the New Testament; for it seems to throw light upon two obscure passages; in one of which Peter describes certain troublers of the churches as " men that count it pleasure to revel in the day-time, spots and blemishes, revelling in their love-feasts, while they feast with you." [2] Here " their love-feasts " may mean the feasts ordered by themselves; and, if so, Peter condemns them for breaking the law laid down in the *Didache* by joining with the brethren in the festive supper. Similarly, Jude says ;—

---

[1] As we have already seen, Paul had to deal with a gross abuse of this custom in the Corinthian church.

[2] 2 Peter ii. 13, where the context plainly shows that ἀγάπαις, and not ἀπάταις, is the true reading.

" These are (they who are) hidden rocks in your love-feasts, feasting together with you, fearlessly pasturing their own selves." [1]   The allusion is evidently to leaders in the churches, and their fault is that they join in the love-feasts, and, though professing to be shepherds of the flock, are really intent only upon feeding themselves.   It is, therefore, possible that they may have been the false prophets who had ordered the tables.[2]

The second test, also, is to be applied to the conduct of an inspired person.   If he teaches the truth, no matter how correctly, but does not practise it, he is a false prophet.   There can be little doubt as to this statement.   By causing his agents to teach the truth without living it, Satan contrives either to bring all teachers of the truth into contempt, or to soothe men with the stealthy suggestion, that profession is all that can be expected of them, and that no one can put righteous ideas into practice.   In this age of ever-increasing deception, it is well to remind ourselves of the characteristics of false prophets and teachers.   And this we may do very simply, by observing, that, at one extremity of their ranks, stand the men whose teaching is unexceptionable, but who infuse little or nothing of it into their lives ; while, at the other end, are those whose lives seem to be beautiful, self-sacrificing, and   saintly ;   but   whose   teaching   undermines,   or, perhaps, openly denies the revelations of the Almighty God.

Both of these types are what the Lord calls wolves

---

[1] Jude 12.

[2] Not without some relevancy, Dr. C. Taylor remarks ;—" A prophet who ordered a table and ate of it is, in modern parlance, a person who promotes schemes of public charity with an eye to his own profit or advancement."   This is a good application of the precept, but must not be allowed to obliterate its first meaning.

in sheep's clothing, and between them may be found every varying shade and blend of their errors.

The next verse has given great trouble to commentators, but seems to admit of a simple explanation. The rule which it contains is, probably, intended to prevent the too frequent testing of prophets. Accordingly, it directs that a prophet, who has been once proved and found to be genuine, is not to be judged if he should summon assemblies for the purpose of exhibiting to them a cosmic or worldly mystery, provided he does not teach others to imitate himself.

Here the difficulty lies in the expression "a worldly mystery," to which we may, perhaps, find a clue in the first verse of the ninth chapter of the Epistle to the Hebrews. There we are told, that the First Covenant had a cosmic or worldly sanctuary; that is, a sanctuary in this world. But the erection, though set up by men in the world, was a copy from a heavenly original. Hence "a cosmic mystery" may be the emblematic representation, in the world of sense, of some heavenly idea or decree. Such representations were often used by the prophets. So Isaiah was bidden to walk, as a captive would, naked and barefoot, for three years, in order to be "a sign and a wonder upon Egypt and upon Ethiopia."[1] He was thus to signify God's decree, that the inhabitants of both those countries should be led captive by the King of Assyria.[2] Similarly, Agabus bound his own feet and hands with Paul's girdle, and prophesied ;—

"Thus saith the Holy Ghost, So shall the Jews at Jerusalem bind the man that owneth this girdle, and shall deliver him into the hands of the Gentiles."[3]

[1] Isa. xx. 2, 3.   [2] Isa. xx. 4–6.   [3] Acts xxi. 11.

The words, " provided he does not teach others
to do what he himself does," seem to be a caution in
case the Spirit should, in special circumstances or for
a special reason, command something which would
not be right, or, at least, not expedient, in ordinary
times.   Perhaps, the framer of this canon had in mind
the instructions given to Hosea, " Go, take unto thee
a wife of whoredom and children of whoredom,"[1] which
the prophet was to do in order to bring forcibly before
the eyes of Israelites the fact, that God loved them
still, though they were turning unto other gods.   In
case, then, of a duly recognized prophet doing such
things as the Old Testament prophets had done, the
church was not to judge him, but to leave him in
the hands of God, provided that what he did was
represented as a sign or symbol only, and not proposed
as an example.

In the final verse, another safeguard is prescribed.
Should a prophet, when under inspiration, order money,
or anything else, to be given to himself, he was to
be dismissed at once as a false prophet : he was not,
however, to be so regarded if he bade his hearers give
help to others.

Such were the rules laid down in the *Didache* for the
testing of prophets, who, at that time, when Apostles
had, probably, become scarce, were reckoned as the
messengers of the Holy Spirit, and the first authority
in the churches.

Accordingly, as we have already seen, while a form
of prayer is prescribed in the *Didache* for ordinary use,
it is followed by an injunction to permit the prophets
to give thanks in whatever words they please.

In a subsequent chapter, we have an intimation, that

[1] Hos. i. 2.

prophets were sometimes expected to abide permanently with particular churches, and were not necessarily itinerants like Apostles and evangelists. So we read ;—

"But every true prophet who wishes to settle among you is worthy of his maintenance. . . . Therefore, thou shalt take and give all the firstfruit of the produce of winepress and threshing-floor, of oxen and sheep, to the prophets; for they are your chief priests."[1]

The last clause, of course, merely means that prophets are the heads of the churches, just as high priests were of the Israelitish Hierarchy ; and, therefore, that believers must give their first-fruits to the prophets, even as the Israelites brought theirs to the priest. For there is no hint, either here or in any other part of the *Didache*, that the prophets had sacerdotal functions.

If a church has no prophet, it is directed to give its firstfruits to the poor. From this we may infer that there were at the time some congregations which had no prophet. Already the prophetic gift was failing, and the guidance of the churches was being transferred from those who had special gifts of the Spirit, and were called of God Only, to the presbyters and deacons whom men elected for themselves.

Descending now to the times of Justin Martyr, we find, in the *Dialogue with Trypho*, a statement that the prophetic gift was still lingering in the churches ; and Justin thinks, that such a fact ought to convince the Jews of the transference of the grace of God from themselves to Christian believers.[2] Yet in his account of Baptism, the Lord's Supper, and the Christian mode of keeping the first day of the week, there is no mention

[1] Chap. xiii.　　[2] Dial. c. Tryph. lxxxii.

of either Apostles or prophets, but only of a president and deacons.[1]

What the compiler of the *Apostolical Constitutions* has to say on this subject does not give us a very exalted idea of the prophets in his period, if, indeed, there were then any true prophets at all. His chief anxiety, in the two chapters which treat of spiritual gifts,[2] seems to be to teach those who possess them not to think more highly of themselves than they ought to think. Evidently the gifts had been perverted and were dying out, at least in their purer and more powerful development. And, while they were failing, the unauthorised bishop had become the centre of power.

For our present purpose, it will not be necessary to trace the history of prophecy, real or false, through the centuries. We are only concerned to show what the Lord originally gave, and the fact that His gift gradually disappeared, or, at least, ceased to be recognized and seemed to disappear ; for it is possible, that, of the fervent and effective preachers, whose tongues of fire have from time to time awakened the slumbering churches, not a few may be found, on the Great Day, standing in the goodly fellowship of the prophets. There are certainly not many among us in these times who receive, and act upon, the command to covet earnestly the best gifts, and especially the spirit of prophecy ; but there may be some who have done so, and have obtained the reward of their obedience. The chief characteristic of such men would, of course, be the power of speaking weighty but yet altogether unpremeditated words, in which the closest scrutiny would fail to detect any divergence from the revealed Scripture

---

[1] See chaps. lxi., lxvi., and lxvii., in Justin's First Apology.
[2] Apost. Const. viii. 1, 2.

of Truth. And if a prophet be moved to foretell things to come, he has given his prediction as a credential, and upon its precise and clear fulfilment his reputation must depend. Should it fail, he has been convicted as a false prophet, inspired, not by the Spirit of the Living God, but by the spirit that now worketh in the children of disobedience.

XXXVI

EVANGELISTS

THE gift of the Evangelist seems to be similar in kind to that of prophecy, but it is far less comprehensive. The prophet is inspired mainly that he may teach, exhort, warn, rebuke, or encourage, the saved, though he may also be sent, like Jonah, to those that are without. But the peculiar work of the evangelist is to proclaim the glorious Gospel of the Blessed God to unsaved sinners. Of course, every believer must do this whenever, wherever, and in whatever circumstances, he has the opportunity ; but Paul is here speaking of those who are specially endowed for that office, who are made the mouthpieces of the Spirit, and through whom He speaks directly and with great power to the world, calling upon all men everywhere to repent, and to be reconciled to God through the Blood of the Lamb.

XXXVII

PASTORS AND TEACHERS

WE now come to the local officers of the churches, who ought to possess gifts of the Spirit fitting each of them to perform the twofold duty of " pastor and teacher." [1] It is evident that Paul is here referring to the presbyter or elder, of whose institution there is no mention in the New Testament. A possible reason for this fact is, that the office may have developed in a natural way, seeing that men of years gravity and experience are instinctively recognized as leaders of assemblies.

We must, however, also remember, that Christian congregations in Palestine were for some time called and regarded as synagogues. [2] Hence they would naturally imitate, more or less, the organization of the Jewish assemblies, each of which was governed by a college of elders with a Rabbi as president, or ruler of the synagogue. And so, we find elders recognized in the earliest churches, but no instance of a president occurs ; for believers, probably, decided that the last named officer was forbidden to them by the Lord's command ;—

" But be not ye called Rabbi ; for One is your Master, and all ye are brethren." [3]

If, then, the synagogue was, so far as might be, the model of the Palestinian churches, the latter would, probably, have adopted government by elders as a matter of course ; and such a supposition would readily account for the fact, that the institution of presbyters, being no new thing, is not noticed in Scripture. The question is, however, of slight importance ; for, whatever their origin may have been, presbyters were certainly recognized by the Apostles as lawful and necessary officers of the churches.

We first hear of them at a time of grave crisis. The persecution by Herod had commenced : James the son of Zebedee had been slain with the sword :

[1] See pp. 255-6.   [2] Jas. ii. 2.   [3] Matt. xxiii. 8.

Peter had been cast into prison, but had been liberated by an angel, and had departed from the city. The other Apostles had also dispersed ; and this fact seems to have been known at Antioch ; for, when the churches there had determined to send relief to the needy brethren at Jerusalem, they are said to have forwarded it, by the hands of Paul and Barnabas, not to the Apostles in that city, but to the presbyters. Hence some have suggested that the latter had been instituted by the Apostles to rule the churches which they themselves were about to leave ; for, at last, they had been made to see the necessity of carrying out the Lord's command to preach the Gospel unto the ends of the earth. But, of course, this is mere conjecture : we know nothing beyond the fact that presbyters were established in Jerusalem at the time, and that we soon find them in other churches also.

In the churches which they themselves had founded, the Apostles seem to have taken the appointment of elders into their own hands : but, subsequently, these officers were elected by the congregations. We must, however, again emphasize the fact, that there is as yet no recorded instance of a single presbyter presiding over a church. James himself evidently did not take the lead at Jerusalem as a presbyter, but only because, as we have already seen, he was an Apostle[1] and the brother of the Lord.

We now come to a point of great importance, and upon which we may elsewhere have more to say. When the system of government by elders was adopted in the churches of Greek-speaking Gentile believers, a name more in harmony with Greek ideas was given

[1] See 1 Cor. ix. 5, 6—verses which are concerned with Apostles only ; 1 Cor. xv. 5–8 ; Gal. i. 19.

to the presbyter, and he was called 'episcopus'—that is, 'overseer.' Now, this word is the Greek root of our term 'bishop'; but, in Apostolic times, it was used in a sense totally different from that which we attach to 'bishop.' Of this fact the translators both of our Authorised and of our Revised Version were well aware: we can, therefore, only repeat Dean Alford's indignant remark;—"It is merely laying a trap for misunderstanding, to render the word, at this time of the Church's history, 'the office of a Bishop.' The ἐπίσκοποι of the New Testament have officially nothing in common with our *Bishops*." [1]

Indeed, it is only too evident, that we may here detect one of those painful instances in which honesty in translation is waived, in order that prejudice and the ordinance of men may be supported against the Word of God. For our translators were not free from faults similar to those of the Jewish Targum-writers; but have deliberately obscured passages which throw light on the Apostolic form of church-government, lest the common people, who are ignorant of Greek, should discover that 'the office of a Bishop,' in our sense of the term, is entirely destitute of Divine authority.

Of course, to convey a right idea to English readers, ἐπίσκοπος should have been always rendered by its literal equivalent, 'overseer.' And, in the margin, the fact should have been pointed out, that 'overseer' and 'presbyter,' being synonymes, are sometimes interchanged.

For instance, Paul, when at Miletus, summoned to himself the "presbyters" of Ephesus, [2] and, in addressing them, said;—

---

[1] See the note to 1 Tim. iii. 1, in Alford's "Greek Testament."
[2] Acts xx. 17.

"Take heed unto yourselves, and unto all the flock in which the Holy Ghost hath made you overseers "[1]—R.V. 'bishops.'

So he bids Titus to ordain "presbyters" in every city ;—

"If any man is blameless . . . for an overseer"—A.V. and R.V. 'bishop'—"must be blameless."[2]

And Peter says ;—

"The presbyters, therefore, among you I exhort, who am a fellow-presbyter. . . . Tend the flock of God which is among you, exercising the oversight"—literally, acting as overseers or bishops—"not of constraint, but willingly."[3]

Thus only two orders of local ministers are mentioned in the New Testament, the presbyter or overseer, and, as we shall presently see, the deacon.

And so, we find Paul writing ;—

"To all the saints in Christ Jesus which are at Philippi, with the overseers"—A.V. and R.V. 'bishops'—"and deacons."[4]

These few words teach us, that there were several overseers—A.V. and R.V. "bishops"—in the small church at Philippi; that in addressing a Greek community Paul uses 'overseer' instead of 'presbyter'; and that he could not have considered the ministers to be above the congregation, since he mentions the latter first.

The necessary qualifications of a presbyter are enumerated in the third chapter of the First Epistle to Timothy. He must be blameless, must not have done anything which would furnish a just cause of complaint against him either from within or from

[1] Acts xx. 28.
[2] Titus i. 5–7.
[3] I Peter v. 2.
[4] Phil. i. 1.

without the pale of the church. He must be the husband of one wife ; that is, he must be a married man, but no polygamist. For, in dealing with members of the congregation, he would sometimes need to be acquainted with the details of married life ; and, moreover, could with greater propriety minister among women if he were himself married ; for he could then be no object of desire to the right-minded and law-abiding, such as all members of churches should be. Yet again, it was necessary that he should have proved his capacity for undertaking the care of a church by first showing that he could rule well his own house, and keep his children in subjection with all gravity. This is, of course, a requirement which only a married man could fulfil.

Furthermore, he must be sober, discreet in mind and orderly in conduct, hospitable, and apt in teaching : he must not be given to wine, must be no striker, must be forbearing and not contentious, and, above all, no lover of money. Nor must he be a recent convert, lest he should be blinded by pride, and so fall from his position as a church-overseer to that of an enemy of Christ, even as Satan fell from his first estate as an angel of light, and became the Power of Darkness.

And, finally ; instead of being a new convert, of whose life little could be known, he must have been some time before the world as a believer, and have maintained a character of the sort which men are forced to respect. For, should there be anything against him, he would not be able to escape the eager recriminations of those who love not the Lord ; and would thus become entangled in some snare of the Devil, perhaps through his own irritation and anger at the charges pressed upon him ; or, it may be, because his inability to clear himself might either drive him to take refuge in lies, or cast him into a hopeless depression.[1]

In another passage of the same Epistle, Paul gives the following directions ;—

" Let the elders that rule well be counted worthy of double honour, especially those who labour in word and in teaching. For the Scripture saith, ' Thou shalt not muzzle an ox when he treadeth out the corn.' And, ' The labourer is worthy of his hire.' Against an elder receive not an accusation, except before two or three witnesses. Them that are living in sin reprove in the presence of all, that the rest also may be in fear."[2]

Thus congregations were to honour their presbyters in proportion to the faithfulness shown by the latter in presiding over the particular work committed to their charge. The double honour, as we may infer from what follows, includes also double salary. The clause, "especially those who labour in word and in teaching," makes it clear that every presbyter was not expected to preach or teach in public. The duty of some was confined to ruling and maintaining order in the church.

Of the two expressions "in word and in teaching," the first seems to refer to preaching, the second to instruction communicated, perhaps, as in our modern Bible-readings, or by means of public catechizings. And, just as the Lord preferred the spirit of Mary to that of Martha, useful as the work of the latter undoubtedly was ; so here the elders, who, by diligent prayer and study of the Word, become in some degree acquainted with the mind of God, and able to expound

[1] See 1 Tim. iii. 1-7.   [2] 1 Tim. v. 17-20.

His mysteries to others, are, by His command, to be regarded as superior to those whose gifts and services are connected only with organization or the management of outward affairs. Nevertheless, a church will fare badly, unless it has elders that can rule as well as elders that can teach. Members of diverse kinds are necessary to the perfection of the body.

The rule, that an accusation against a presbyter was not to be listened to, except in the presence of two or three witnesses, would tend powerfully to diminish idle tales and false charges. The malicious accuser, or the mere scandal-monger, who would not hesitate to whisper an unfounded story into the ears of a single person, would be more careful of his evidence, if he knew that he could only be heard in the presence of two or three witnesses.

The R.V. reads, " at *the mouth of* two or three witnesses." But, to obtain this meaning, it has been necessary to depart from the simple rendering of the text, and to insert " the mouth of." Moreover, the precept then becomes superfluous ; for Timothy was well aware that the Law did not permit a man to be condemned upon less evidence than that of two or three witnesses : and he was not likely to have imagined that the case of presbyters formed an exception to this rule.

But, if any presbyter was living in sin, and so setting an open example of disobedience, he was to be rebuked before the whole congregation, in order that the warning might affect every member of it.

As representatives of a church, it seems to have been the duty of the presbyters to lay their hands on the head of any member of their congregation who was to be devoted to a particular work ; and this appears to have been done to signify the acquiescence of the congregation in the setting apart of the person for that sphere of labour into which the Spirit had called him. So Paul says to Timothy ;—

"Neglect not the gift that is in thee, which was given thee by prophecy, with the laying on of the hands of the presbytery." [1]

The Spirit had, it would appear, commanded, through the mouth of a prophet, that Timothy should be set apart for the work to which he was called ; and, upon his obedience to the call, which he signified by allowing the presbyters to lay their hands on him, he received the gift necessary for his office.

Referring, as most commentators think, to the same event in another passage, Paul says ;—

"For the which cause I put thee in remembrance, that thou stir into flame the gift of God which is in thee through the laying on of my hands." [2]

Paul, then, must have been one of the presbyters who laid hands upon Timothy. Or this second passage may refer to an earlier time, when, after having believed and been baptized, Timothy received the Holy Spirit through the imposition of Paul's hands. [3]

Yet another duty of elders, now altogether neglected, is set forth in the Epistle of James ;—

"Is any among you sick ? Let him call for the elders of the church ; [4] and let them pray over him, anointing him with oil in the Name of the Lord. And the prayer of faith shall save him that is sick, and the Lord shall raise him up ; and, if he have committed sins, it shall be forgiven him. [5]

[1] I Tim. iv. 14.   [2] 2 Tim. i. 6.   [3] Compare Acts xix. 6.
[4] That is, of course, for the presbyters of his own congregation or assembly.
[5] James v. 14, 15.

XXXVIII

DEACONS

THE lowest order of officers in Apostolic times were the deacons, who, as their name imports, were the servants of the churches. They do not seem to be referred to in the fourth chapter of the Epistle to the Ephesians, but are, probably, intended when Paul exhorts those who have the gift of ministry—διακονίαν—to give heed to their ministry.[1]

Again, when, in another passage, the same Apostle places "helps" and "governments"[2] among the gifts, it is not unlikely that he is thinking, in part at least, of deacons and presbyters.

Deacons were first appointed in response to the murmuring of the Hellenists, or Greek-speaking Jews, who had complained that their widows were neglected in the daily ministration of alms, and that undue favour was shown to the Hebrew-speaking widows. In response to this appeal, the Apostles directed that seven men of "good report, full of the Spirit and of wisdom," should be chosen by the people, and appointed to see to the distribution of alms, and so to relieve the Twelve of the whole burden of serving tables. These were called deacons, and their duties, as such, were confined to the supervision of the poor, and did not

---

[1] Rom. xii. 7. The word seems here to be used in its official and not in its general sense. For the latter would include teaching, which is, however, mentioned separately in the next clause. Moreover, Paul is speaking only of specific ministrations and functions, and exhorting every man to use his own particular gifts, and not to interfere with those of others.

[2] 1 Cor. xii. 28.

include preaching and teaching. Nevertheless, by an honest and conscientious discharge of those duties they could procure for themselves a good degree, or stepping-stone, to something higher.[1] And, accordingly, in the case of the first seven, we find that Stephen speedily became a teacher and prophet ; while Philip was, subsequently, promoted to be an evangelist.

In his directions to Timothy, Paul insists that the deacons must be grave, not double-tongued, not given to much wine, not greedy of filthy lucre, but men holding the mystery of the faith in a pure conscience. They must also, like the presbyters, be married men, husbands of one wife, known to be capable of managing their children and of ruling well their own houses. Moreover, they were not to be hurriedly elected, but were first to be put through a period of probation. Afterwards, if they were approved, they might be appointed to their office.[2]

The number of the deacons chosen for Jerusalem was seven. Hence the nominal Church—which has so often been superstitiously scrupulous in indifferent matters, while she was ignoring or distorting vital truth—insisted for some time in limiting the number of the deacons in a single city, however large it might be, to seven. And so, in a letter written, about the middle of the third century, by Cornelius Bishop of Rome to Fabius Bishop of Antioch, the former states that there were at the time forty-six presbyters in Rome, but only seven deacons and seven subdeacons. The subdeacons were intended to supplement the inadequate number of deacons ; but, apparently, of these also there could be but seven.

[1] I Tim. iii. 13.   [2] I Tim. iii. 8–13.

In 314 A.D., the fifteenth canon of the Synod of Neocæsarea in Pontus ordered as follows ;—

"According to the rule, there should be seven deacons only in a city, however great it may be. This may be proved from the Book of the Acts."

But, while the nominal Church persisted for some time in this silly adhesion to mere number, without regard to adequacy, she was, meanwhile, altogether changing the position and duties of the deacon, and making him, not the guardian of poor believers, but the supporter of the worldly Hierarchy which she had herself created. This may be seen in the following extracts from the so-called *Apostolical Constitutions* ;—

"For, as Christ does nothing without His Father, so neither does the deacon do anything without his bishop; and, as the Son without the Father is nothing, so is the deacon nothing without his bishop; and, as the Son is subject to His Father, so is every deacon subject to his bishop; and, as the Son is the Messenger and Prophet of His Father, so is the deacon the messenger and prophet of his bishop." [1]

"And let the deacon refer all things to the bishop, as Christ does to His Father. But let him order such things as he is able by himself, receiving power from the bishop, as the Lord did from His Father the power of creation and of providence. The weighty matters let the bishop judge; but let the deacon be the bishop's ear, and eye, and mouth, and heart, and soul, that the bishop may not be distracted with many cares, but with such only as are more considerable; as Jethro did appoint for Moses, and his counsel was received." [2]

[1] Apost. Const. ii. 30.   [2] Apost. Const. ii. 44.

When we have compared this description of the duties assigned to a deacon in the third century with those marked out for him by Paul in the first, we are able to form some idea of the rapid corruption of Christianity. For everything Divine was quickly laid aside, in order that a great Hierarchy, similar to, and presently identical with, the Pagan Kingdom of Satan, might be firmly built up ; that the mustard plant might be unnaturally forced into the dimensions of a tree ; that the nominal church might grasp and hold that power and dominion to which the true Church will lay no claim, until the Lord appears in glorious and irresistible power to vindicate it for her.

Of bishops, in the modern sense of the term, and still higher ecclesiastical dignitaries, we say nothing now ; since these are all of human, not of Divine, appointment ; and we are, at present, considering only those offices which have the direct sanction of the New Testament.

DIVERS GIFTS OF THE SPIRIT: THEIR
CONNECTION WITH THE BODY: AND
RULES FOR THEIR USE.

XXXIX

The Spiritual or Inspired.

I Cor. xii. xiii. and xiv.

WE have now considered what the Scripture says concerning the leaders and officers who were set over the churches by Divine command, both those who received their commission from God Alone, and those who were, also, elected by the particular church that needed their services.

But, apart from the latter, and in addition to Apostles prophets and evangelists, there were yet other spiritual[1] or inspired persons, endowed with divers gifts ministries and operations of the Spirit, by the exercise of which the spiritual vitality and power of the churches were maintained. Such gifted persons were not necessarily officers of the particular church to which they were attached, and might be chosen from any rank, or, in certain cases, from either sex. In kind, they did not differ from the more highly gifted Apostles, who, indeed, were reckoned among them ; for all the 'spiritual' alike derived their gifts and their power from "That One and the Self-same Spirit," although they were endowed in varying degrees and with very diverse gifts.

[1] πνευματικός is here used in the sense of 'under spiritual influence,' whether good or bad, and so 'inspired.'

Yet these gifts, essential as they were to the well being of the churches, were at the same time liable to be misunderstood, overestimated, exercised in a disorderly manner, displayed to gratify the vanity of the endowed, and generally abused.

Now, faults in this direction appear to have been conspicuous at Corinth, where the gift of tongues, especially, was exercised in the assembly to an unseemly extent, without any regard to the edification of the church, and, in part at least, by women.

Paul, therefore, devotes the twelfth thirteenth and fourteenth chapters of his first Epistle to the Corinthians to the subject of the spiritual or inspired; that is, of those who, after conversion and baptism in water, had received the promised baptism in the Holy Spirit, and with it some gift, which testified to the fact that they were members of Christ, and endowed them with power to serve Him. In this connection, we must not forget what has already been noticed, that Paul divides believers into two classes, the spiritual and the carnal, the latter of which, though saved by faith, are not yet endowed with the power of the Spirit.

But, before we enter into the details of the three chapters, it will be well to give a brief summary of their contents.

The Apostle begins the first of them by laying down rules whereby the Divine inspiration may be distinguished from the Satanic. Then, after enumerating some of the Divine gifts, and emphasizing the fact, that, diverse as they may be, they are all given by One and the Same Spirit, he proceeds to show, that their very diversity, when understood, points to a perfect unity. For it is exactly similar to the diversity which may be observed in the members of the human body, each of which is framed to meet some different need of the whole body, while all are guided by a single spirit of life and intelligence within them.

Now, in a sane person, these members do not act in a disorderly way, or so as to impede or neutralize one another ; but each of them performs its own proper function, and does this only when, at the bidding of the spirit within, it can profit the whole body.

So is it in the Body of Christ, the members of which, though variously gifted, should be all working in concert, each coming into action just when its peculiar function is required for the good of the Body. Hence every believer may reasonably covet the best gifts, in order that he may render the greater service. And, since it is only upon the spiritual that the gifts are bestowed, believers must strive persistently in prayer that they may receive baptism in the Holy Spirit, and so be moved from the carnal to the spiritual class.

And yet, Paul goes on to say, there is something which excels even gifts. This something is love, which he gloriously describes in the thirteenth chapter.

After this, in the fourteenth, he returns to the subject of the gifts, and proves that prophecy is a far greater endowment than speaking with tongues ; because the former always edifies those that hear it, while the latter does not do so, unless an interpreter be present. He then gives directions for the orderly exercise of these two gifts in the assembly ; but absolutely forbids the public use of them by women.

XL

THE SPIRITUAL GIFTS AND THE BODY

1 COR. xii

WE now return to the details of the twelfth chapter, which the Apostle begins with the remark, that he did not wish the Corinthians to be in ignorance respecting the case of the inspired.[1]

The words which follow may be thus paraphrased ;—You know, that, when you were Gentiles, you were forcibly led off by demoniacal inspiration to the voiceless idols which you once worshipped, just as from time to time you happened to be led. Thus you have already experienced what demoniacal inspiration is ; but a new influence, that of the Spirit of God, has now come upon you ; and you must learn to distinguish it from the power of Satan, lest the Wicked One should come to you fashioning himself as an angel of light. Therefore, I wish you to know, that, whatever may be the form of spiritual manifestation, every utterance which either plainly affirms, or points in the direction of an affirmation, that Jesus is accursed, does not come from the Spirit of God, but from that of Satan. On the other hand, every one who, in spiritual ecstasy, frankly acknowledges Jesus to be Lord, is doing what no inspired person can do, except he be influenced by the Holy Spirit.

[1] We prefer to understand 'spiritual'—that is, 'inspired'—'persons' rather than 'spiritual gifts'; because there is ample authority in the New Testament for the former meaning—see 1 Cor. ii. 15 ; xiv. 37—and it seems, perhaps, more suitable to the context, which immediately proceeds to distinguish between God-inspired and demon-inspired persons. The matter is, however, of little consequence, since the sense of the passage is much the same with either rendering.

Now, it is of the last importance that the full meaning of this declaration should be understood by the believers of our days. For again demoniacal manifestations are multiplying among us, and that with a subtlety sufficient to deceive any one who neglects to apply the prescribed test. Let the reader, therefore, carefully consider the directions of the Apostle.

In judging spiritual manifestations, everything must depend upon the tone of the utterance in regard, not to the Christ or the Son of God, but to the Man Jesus, Who is both. It is Jesus Who must be confessed as Lord. Not even demons will often, if ever, venture to deny that the Christ, or the Son of God, is Lord. But, if Jesus be confessed as such, He is thereby identified with the Christ and the Son of God, and this clearly amounts to a confession that Jesus Christ has come in the flesh.

Hence the test given by Paul is precisely the same as that which is prescribed by John in the memorable words ;—

"Beloved, believe not every spirit, but prove the spirits, whether they are of God ; because many false prophets are gone out into the world. Hereby know ye the Spirit of God : every spirit that confesses that Jesus Christ has come in the flesh is of God : and every spirit which confesseth not Jesus is not of God ; and this is the spirit of the Antichrist, whereof ye have heard that it cometh ; and now it is in the world already." [1]

Like Paul, then, John insists upon the confession of Jesus, because it involves the further confession that Jesus Christ has come in the flesh.

It must be remembered, that, at the time when Paul

[1] 1 John iv. 1-3.

wrote this Epistle, the Docetæ were already beginning to spread their deadly heresy. And the basis of their teaching was, that Jesus and the Christ were two distinct persons, the former being a pious Jew, and the latter a Divine emanation which came upon Him at His baptism, and deserted Him before His crucifixion.[1]

Virtually, then, in this verse we have set before us the two cases of the spiritual man—the one who speaks under the influence of the Spirit of God, and the one who is moved by the spirit of Satan. But, in the fourth verse, Paul proceeds to treat exclusively of the Divine inspiration.

" Now there are diversities of gifts, but the Same Spirit.

" And there are diversities of ministrations, but the Same Lord.

" And there are diversities of operations, but the Same God Who worketh all things in all persons."

Thus we have mention of gifts, ministries, and operations, connected respectively with the Holy Spirit, the Son, and the Father.

---

[1] Readers of the so-called "Gospel of Peter" will remember that it contains an excellent illustration of Docetic views. In his monograph on it, Mr. Rendell Harris remarks ;—

"We can verify that the writer did not believe in a suffering Saviour, for he tells us so expressly. 'They crucified Him between two malefactors : but He Himself was silent, as one who felt no pain.' Further we find, that, instead of the cry of Divine despair, which the Evangelists give from the Psalm in the words, 'My God, My God, why hast Thou forsaken Me ?' the writer has substituted the words, 'My Power, my Power, Thou hast forsaken me' (or, perhaps, as a question, 'Hast Thou forsaken me ?'). Now, here he has either reverted to some other translation of the Psalms than that of the Septuagint, or he has deliberately changed the language of the canonical Gospels to suit his own beliefs. But one thing is clear : he is a Docetist, and the Power which he represents as having left the Lord is the Christ which had descended upon Him at some earlier time, probably at His Baptism."

Of these, the gifts are various endowments of power, which enable their recipients to be effectual workers for God upon earth. They are bestowed by the Holy Spirit, according to His will, upon those who, after repentance and intelligent baptism in water, are then baptized in Him, according to the promise.[1] Each of them at that time receives one, at least, of the gifts, and, perhaps, more than one, and is thenceforth a spiritual or inspired person.

The ministries are the many offices and functions in the churches, which are appointed by the Lord Jesus with a view to the exercise of the gifts, and for the due discharge of which an account must be rendered to Him on the Day when we shall all be made manifest before his Judgment-seat.

The operations, or works done, are the effects resulting from the exercise of the gifts in the ministries; and such effects are brought about by God Alone. For a Paul, supremely gifted and appointed to the loftiest ministry, may plant, and an Apollos, almost his peer, may water; but it is only God Who can give the increase—God Who Himself directs and brings to their desired end all the energies of the Spirit, both in those who are gifted with them, and in those who are influenced by the gifted.

And so, everything connected with the gifts—whether it be their origin, their use, or their results—is derived from the Blessed Trinity, the Divine Three in One.

After this general statement, the Apostle enters into the subject of the distribution of the gifts, and enumerates several of them.

" But to each one is given the manifestation of the Spirit to profit withal.

[1] Acts i. 5; ii. 38; viii. 14–17.

"For to one is given, through the Spirit, the word of wisdom, and to another the word of knowledge, according to the Same Spirit:

"To a different sort of person faith, in the Same Spirit; and to another gifts of healings, in the Same Spirit:

"And to another workings of miracles; and to another prophecy; and to another discernings of spirits: to a different sort of person, again, divers kinds of tongues; and to another the interpretation of tongues:

"But all these worketh the One and the Same Spirit, dividing to each one severally even as He will."

To each one, then, of the inspired, since he has been baptized in the Spirit, there is given an outward manifestation of the Spirit's supernatural power that is working within him, in accord, of course, with the particular gift bestowed in his case. And these various manifestations are all intended to contribute to the general edification of the churches: they are never given for personal display, or for the private profit of him who exercises them.

By the two insertions of a stronger word, which we have rendered "a different kind of person," the gifts enumerated are divided into three distinct classes or groups.

The first of these includes the word of wisdom and the word of knowledge, in conferring which the Spirit acts upon the intellect.

The second comprehends faith, that is, extraordinary faith, such as can command supernatural power, together with some of its results—namely, gifts of healing, workings of miracles, prophecy, and discernments of spirits. In this group the Spirit acts upon the forces of the will.

The third class contains the ecstatic utterance of kinds of tongues, caused by the action of the Spirit upon the feelings and emotions; to which is added, as a necessary appendage, the interpretation of tongues.

To examine the first group in detail—"a word," or "utterance," "of wisdom," is the power of receiving and uttering the wisdom that comes down from above, which enables a man to apply what he knows of the things of God, revealing to him also, so far as is necessary, what he does not know; so that he may give inspired advice to others, or pronounce decisions in difficult matters. It is, probably, in reference to this gift that John says ;—

"And ye have an anointing from the Holy One, and ye know all things."[1]

Again ;—

"And as for you, the anointing which ye received of Him abideth in you, and ye need not that any one teach you: but as His anointing teacheth you concerning all things, and is true, and is no lie, and even as it taught you, ye abide in Him."[2]

Such a wisdom is ,therefore, near akin to revelation, with which it is joined when Paul prays, that God will give to the Ephesians "a spirit of wisdom and revelation in the knowledge of Him."[3] Indeed, if we may judge from its proximity to knowledge, revelation seems to be used for wisdom in the words ;—

"What shall I profit you, unless I speak to you either by way of revelation, or of knowledge, or of prophecy, or of teaching ?"[4]

[1] I John ii. 20.
[2] I John ii. 27.
[3] That is, of Christ ; Eph. i. 17.
[4] I Cor. xiv. 6.

In another place, it would seem as if "mysteries" were substituted for 'wisdom';—

"And if I have the gift of prophecy, and know all mysteries and all knowledge."[1]

As to the practical effects of the wisdom that is from above in the conduct of one who has received it, James tells us, that it is "first pure, then peaceable, gentle, easy to be intreated, full of mercy, and of good fruits, without variance, without hypocrisy."[2]

A man is said to have this wisdom "by means of," or "through," "the Spirit." Therefore, if he grieves That Spirit, his wisdom must fail.

"A word of knowledge" would also be an inspired utterance, but in a very different way; namely, by the Spirit acting upon humble and prayerful study of the Word. While, therefore, wisdom comes directly and altogether from above, that is, from the Spirit Alone, without any necessary exertion on the part of the recipient, knowledge, on the other hand, is produced by the action of the Spirit in conjunction with prayer over, and study of, what has been previously revealed. Hence wisdom would be found in the endowment of a prophet, knowledge in that of a teacher. Moreover, wisdom is indispensable to an elder, or pastor, who would rule well and give right decisions. Hence the connection of wisdom and knowledge is, perhaps, shown by the fact that pastors and teachers are joined together.[3] Of Christ Himself it is said, "In Whom are all the treasures of wisdom and knowledge hidden."[4]

In the second group, faith does not, of course, mean a mere saving faith, which is the possession of all true believers; but an extraordinary faith, that can move

[1] 1 Cor. xiii. 2.
[2] James iii. 17.
[3] Eph. iv. 11.
[4] Col. ii. 3.

mountains. Connected with such a faith, and, indeed, springing from it, are gifts of healings, workings of miracles, and prophecy. But as regards these, many demoniacal healers, miracle-mongers, and false prophets, are gone out into the world : therefore, a further gift is needed, that of discernment of spirits, in order that the Divinely endowed may be vindicated, and the Satanic counterfeits exposed.

Thus the nature and scope of the gifts in the second group are obvious from their very names ; but the third confronts us with difficulties. It is, however, obvious that the "kinds of tongues," of which we hear much in the fourteenth chapter, must be connected with the Lord's promise, that those who believed should speak with new tongues "[1]—an expression which at once forbids the idea of a power to speak barbarous or foreign languages already in use upon the earth.

And it is just as evident, that the Lord's promise was fulfilled in the "other," or "different kinds of," "tongues" with which the disciples spoke on the Day of Pentecost,[2] in the tongues in which Cornelius and his friends began to magnify God,[3] in the utterances of the twelve persons whom Paul baptized at Ephesus,[4] and in those of the inspired at Corinth.

But, while the multitude from many lands heard the Apostles speaking, each in his own dialect, the wonderful works of God, and so understood their words, Paul presently unfolds to us that the tongues spoken

[1] Mark xvi. 17. καιναῖς is omitted in some MSS., but is, without doubt, a genuine reading. If it were not so, we should have some difficulty in accounting for its insertion ; whereas we can readily understand its omission. For then the prediction could be explained of the Pentecostal tongues without damage to the traditional idea that they were utterances in foreign languages.

[2] Acts ii. 4–11.   [3] Acts x. 46.   [4] Acts xix. 6.

in his time were unintelligible to all, except those who were gifted with the power of interpretation.

In order to reconcile this apparent discrepancy, and, generally, to explain the strange phenomenon, we must, first, entirely set aside the theories and teachings which evolutionists have been so assiduously spreading. Language is not a convenience which the human race gradually evolved for itself, and which, after centuries of development, at last succeeded in displacing communication by gesture and symbol. Nay, it is an intuitive faculty, bestowed by God upon Adam when he was created, whereby men were enabled to express their thoughts in appropriate sounds, which were, it may be, something like what grammarians would call onomatopoetic words ; and which were understood naturally, somewhat in the same way, perhaps, as, when we are listening to the music of a great master, we can distinguish between the strains of exultation and of depression, of defiance and of pleading, of confidence and of despair.

And, consequently, until the fall had developed into the rebellion of Babel, all men spoke the same natural language, just as they will do again in the age to come. "For then," says the Lord, "will I turn to the peoples a pure language, that they may all call upon the Name of the Lord, to serve Him with one consent."[1]

Now it seems probable, that, when the Spirit descended at Pentecost, it was with such mighty power that the disciples, raised for the time far above the grossness of fallen flesh and into the spiritual sphere, saw, with a vividness inconceivable to us, the absolute pardon of their sins through Christ Jesus the Lord, their perfect peace with God, and the ineffable things

[1] Zeph. iii. 9.

which He had prepared for them. Thus, lifted above the thoughts or the languages of earth, and with the inspiration of the Spirit strongly within them, they spontaneously broke forth into praise ; and, bringing up from the deep recesses of their own spirit that pure tongue in which alone it is possible to speak perfectly of heavenly things, began to rejoice in hope of the glory of God.

And the same mighty influence of the Holy Ghost seems, also, to have so affected such of the hearers as were able to receive it that they, too, were raised to a spiritual ecstasy which enabled them to understand the spiritual language ; to be for the time as those gifted with the interpretation of tongues ; and to feel the naturalness and appropriateness of what they heard to such an extent that they thought they were listening each one to his own dialect.

But, in the subsequent times of the churches, the Spirit did not descend with such irresistible power as when He baptized the first members of Christ into one Body. Hence, although the rapturous ejaculations still occurred, only a few were gifted with the power of interpreting them: indeed—so strange are the present conditions of our being—the mind of the speaker himself did not always understand what his spirit was uttering. Nevertheless, even in this case he was edifying himself, and, if he were also an interpreter, could at the same time edify the church.

As to the meaning of the plural, "kinds of tongues," our present knowledge of spiritual things is far too limited to justify us even in hazarding a conjecture. Of course, it may be that there are dialects or tones in the spiritual language varying, in a manner which is altogether natural to spiritual beings, according to the kind of use which is from time to time required of it. And other suggestions might be made and elaborated; but, in all probability, with nought but wasted time as a result. Such things are too high for us in the present life, when we know but in part; and we do not—perhaps, could not—understand them.

Various, then, were the gifts; but they were all distributed by One and the Same Spirit, exercising His Own choice and discretion as to the particular gift to be bestowed upon each individual. For, while every one who was filled with the Spirit received some supernatural power, he did not choose it for himself, but was endowed with that which the Spirit deemed most suitable for him. And, although in primal times the gift was often communicated by the imposition of the Apostles' hands, yet the Apostles were merely the channels through which the grace was conveyed, and could not select the particular gift.

The gifts, then, are diverse; and, in the twelfth verse, Paul begins to give a reason for this fact, and to show that it was productive of order, and not of disorder. For He Who distributes to so many individuals is the One Spirit: it is the Self-same Spirit That bestows such diverse gifts. We may, therefore, reasonably expect the result to be unity, not confusion. And so it is; for, when we turn from the Spirit's action upon individuals to contemplate the effect of that action upon the churches, we find that the diversity of the members is the precise cause of the unity of the Body. For the Spirit does not apportion His gifts indiscriminately, but so arranges them that each endowed person may be useful to his brethren individually, and to his church as a whole.

This may be understood from natural things. For

just as the human body, though one, is made up of many diverse members; while all the members of the same body, though many in number, form but one body, which would be incomplete were a single member withdrawn; so is it with the Body of Christ.

"For in One Spirit were we all baptized into one Body, whether Jews or Greeks, whether bond or free; and were all made to drink of One Spirit."[1]

The reference is, doubtless, to the descent of the Spirit at Pentecost, and to His subsequent reception by converts, who had been previously baptized in water, at the laying on of the Apostles' hands. For, in speaking of the promise of the Father, the Lord had said;—

"John, indeed, baptized with water, but ye shall be baptized in the Holy Spirit not many days hence."[2]

Now it was this baptism of the Spirit which fused, as it were, the members of Christ into one Body. On the Day of Pentecost, as we read, there was a sudden sound from heaven, like the rushing of a mighty wind, which filled all the house wherein the disciples were sitting. And in this manner the Lord seems to have made the element of Spirit, in which they were being immersed, perceptible to their senses. Then there appeared unto them tongues parting asunder, like as of fire; and, when these apparitions had lighted on each one of them, they were all filled with the Holy Spirit. It is to this wondrous event, perhaps, that Paul specially alludes in the words;—

"And were all made to drink of One Spirit."

All were made to drink of One Spirit, and yet there are diversities of gifts. But is not this true, also, of the human body? It, too, is not made up of one

[1] I Cor. xii. 13. [2] Acts i. 5.

member, but of many, all equally belonging to it, and all needed by it.

The foot is not the hand ; nevertheless, it is a part of the body : the ear is not the eye, yet it also is one of the members.

And how could either of these be spared ? For, if the whole body were an eye, where were the hearing : if the whole were hearing, where were the smelling?

The foot and the ear are mentioned as being less prominent and less favoured than the hand and the eye. But, spite of their inferiority, they still belong, and are necessary, to the body. Let not, then, those members of Christ who are endowed with the less conspicuous gifts be discouraged : they, too, are equally organs of His Body, and indispensable to its well being.

Moreover, the members of the human body are arranged according to the good pleasure of God. It is He Who has placed the foot in the lowest part of the body, and set the ear back from the face. And well for us is it that He has made His wonderful arrangement of diversity in unity : for, otherwise, we might have found ourselves possessed but of a single sense, like certain creatures in the lowest grades of being. But now, many members go to make up one body, and yet they are so fitted and put together that all are required, if the result is to be perfection. The eye and the hand may, indeed, be the more prominent and brilliant members, but they would be of little practical use, unless they were assisted by the ears and the feet.

And we may go still further, continues the Apostle ; for those members of the body which seem to be weaker are even more absolutely necessary to it than the others. Perhaps, he is here alluding to the internal organs, which are covered by the body, and are indispensable to its very existence. And, in mentioning them, he may be referring to those quiet and unobtrusive believers, not seldom bedridden invalids, who support the active workers by their prayers and counsels; to the modest visitors and helps, ready to set their hands to anything for their Lord's sake, who never come to the front nor receive the public praises of men, and, for that very reason, are drawn into closer communion with God. Such saints, unnoticed and unthought of, frequently act the part of lungs and heart and stomach to their church, and are the real fosterers of its spiritual vitality.

"And those parts of the body which we think to be less honourable, upon these we bestow more abundant honour; and our uncomely parts have more abundant comeliness; whereas our comely parts have no need." [1]

That is, those parts of the body which seem to us less honourable, or which are uncomely, we decorate with clothes and ornament, so that we do not leave them uncovered as we do the face and hands. For the features, which are comely in themselves, have no need of artificial help from us.

So, in the case of believers who perform the humblest and most menial service in the churches, care should be taken to show them honour and marks of respect. There will, however, be no need to add honour to men whose gifts are sufficiently conspicuous and splendid in themselves to ensure consideration for their possessors.

"But God tempered the body together, giving more abundant honour to that part which lacked;

[1] 1 Cor. xii. 23, 24.

that there should be no schism in the body; but that the members should have the same care one for another."[1]

That is, God has so compacted the body that it is the true interest of all the parts to care for each particular one. He has so connected the members together, the feeble and the strong, the comely and the uncomely; so made the whole to depend upon each, and each upon the whole, that there is no danger of disunion among the parts, no fear that one member will be despised by another, seeing that each contributes indispensably to the well-being of all.

In such circumstances, the members cannot but sympathize with each other: for "whether one member suffereth, all the members suffer with it: or one member be honoured, all the members rejoice with it."[2] If the foot be thrilled with pain, the whole body is troubled: if the head be crowned with honour, every member instinctively assumes a corresponding dignity.

All this is, of course, to be applied to the churches— each of which is a microcosm of the great Church or complete Body of Christ—and especially to the dis- orderly assembly at Corinth. But Paul does not enter into details, which are sufficiently obvious: he merely points to the general application in the words;—" Now ye are a body of Christ, and individually members thereof."[3]

In this verse, it is strange that both the Authorised and the Revised version should have inserted a definite article where Paul did not place one; so that they read "Ye are the Body of Christ." Such an insertion involves a positive mistake; for the Corinthians were not the Body of Christ, but only a portion of it. And

[1] 1 Cor. xii. 24, 25.   [2] 1 Cor. xii. 26.   [3] 1 Cor. xii. 27.

hence it is easy to deduce Paul's meaning from analogous expressions in his writings. For instance, as we have already seen, he uses the word 'church' in two senses. Properly it signifies the complete Body of Christ, gathered during all the centuries of the present Dispensation: but he also applies the term to a single assembly upon earth, at some definite time, because the latter ought to be a microcosm or miniature of the whole Church. Thus the Corinthians were a church of Christ, and, upon the same principle, Paul called them "a body of Christ"; that is, a miniature of the complete Body into which they should ultimately be absorbed. In another passage of this Epistle, the words, "Ye are a temple of God,"[1] may be explained in the same way.

In the next three verses, we are reminded, that, since every individual is a member, no one can claim to be the whole body. Very mistaken, then, are those who would fain perform all the functions of a church.

The enumeration of gifts in the twenty-eighth verse exhibits them as corresponding to the organs and members of a human body. But He That endows men with them, and sets each endowed person in his place, is God Alone: for the Apostle knows nothing of Ecclesiastical Hierarchies and Successions. On the contrary, he says;—

"And some God set in the Church, first Apostles, secondly prophets, thirdly teachers, after that miracles, then gifts of healings, helps, governments, kinds of tongues."[2]

A peculiarity of expression is readily discovered in this verse, which may be accounted for as follows. Apparently, the Apostle was about to enumerate the

[1] 1 Cor. iii. 16.   [2] 1 Cor. xii. 28.

gifts as if all were on an equality. Then he seems suddenly to have remembered the insubordination of the Corinthians, and their folly in preferring the speaker in tongues to the Apostle, the prophet, and the teacher. Hence he introduces 'first,' 'secondly,' and 'thirdly,' which he had not originally intended to do, and so gives us an arrangement of the gifts in the order of their importance.

Apostles, prophets, and teachers, rank far above all other gifted persons; and this truth is emphasized by the fact, that their positions are precisely defined as first, second, and third. " Afterwards come miracles; then gifts of healings, helps "—or more correctly " helpings "—" governments, kinds of tongues." Thus " kinds of tongues," a gift which the Corinthians foolishly placed above all others, is found to be at the bottom of the list. They had made the last to be first.

Evangelists, which are mentioned in the parallel passage occurring in the Epistle to the Ephesians,[1] are here omitted. Probably the reason is, that a real evangelist is regarded as a prophet with limited power. For, if he possesses no further gift, he is inspired like other prophets for the preaching of the Gospel, but is not used by the Spirit as a medium for teaching the mysteries of God.

Of Apostles prophets and teachers we have spoken in the previous section; and miracles and gifts of healings are mentioned in the tenth verse of this chapter. " Helpings," perhaps, includes the love, the skill, and the tact, which the Spirit has bestowed upon some, and which enable them to act a subordinate part in government, to relieve the sick, the afflicted, and the distraught, to support the weak with unwearied

[1] Eph. iv. 11.

patience, and, generally, to render affectionate and effectual aid to others by helping them to bear their burdens. Such a gift would be specially useful to deacons ; while in "governments" the chief reference may be to presbyters or overseers, though the gift would, of course, furnish ability for any kind of rule or superintendence which might be needed in the churches. Of "kinds of tongues" we have already spoken.

All these gifts God has placed in the Church, just as He has arranged the organs and members that make up the human body. Surely, then, in a manner corresponding to that of the bodily organs, every man must exercise his own gifts. All cannot be Apostles, or prophets, or teachers, or miracle workers, or healers, or speakers in tongues, or interpreters of tongues. Nevertheless, every man should earnestly desire and strive after the better gifts, but must be careful not to assume possession of any until God has really bestowed it. For this mistake is common. The writer has known more than one case of a believer who, if he were about to speak to others, would have esteemed it a fault to think out beforehand what he should say, but supposed that he had a right to expect inspiration from God at the moment ; and the result has been miserable failure. The reason of this is obvious : the man had deemed himself a prophet, when, at the best, he was no more than a teacher.

The striving after the better gifts must, of course, be by prayer and supplication, combined with a diligent use of any gift which we may already possess. So may the two talents be made to gain other two. And, in agreement with—not in opposition to—his advice, the Apostle adds, " And a still more excellent way show I unto you." [1]   This more excellent way is love, without which the most splendid gifts would be accounted as nothing.

XLI

LOVE

1 Cor. xiii

THE wondrous Psalm of Love which follows is marred and rendered unnatural in the Authorised Version by the substitution of the word "charity" for "love"; for the former by no means represents the original.[2] Nor, indeed, could charity ever rise to the transcendent heights of these burning words.   Moreover, the modern idea of the noun 'charity,' which makes it signify a toleration of, and kindly feelings toward, any opinions or theories whatever, is as far removed from Divine teaching as the East is from the West.

The Bible urges love to all men, however deceived, deceiving, or depraved, they may be ; but it permits no such feeling, often misnamed charity, toward wrong doctrine or wrong doing.   These must be utterly discountenanced and abhorred ; while our love pity and prayers should flow forth abundantly for the misguided individuals who perpetrate them.

For love to all our fellow-creatures, and especially to those who are of the household of faith, is as the breath of the new creation, is that bond of peace which alone makes it possible to preserve the unity of the Spirit.

Therefore, Paul declares, that, even if he were a

[1] 1 Cor. xii. 31.   [2] ἀγάπη.

master of the tongues of both men and angels, and had not love, he would merely resemble a sounding brass or a clanging cymbal. The exercise of his power might, indeed, attract the attention of men, but there would be nothing of the Divine behind it, and, consequently, no possibility of good resulting from it. And, perhaps, he mentions "kinds of tongues" first, because, as we have already seen, that gift appears to have been regarded by the Corinthians as the most desirable ; although Paul, when mentioning the gifts in their order, assigns to it the lowest place of all.

Nevertheless, even the greater endowments were just as useless without love. For, even if he should have the gift of prophecy, and understand all the mysteries of God and all the knowledge connected with them, or should possess faith sufficient to remove mountains ; still, without love, he would be accounted as nothing in the sight of God. Or, to look in another direction, if he were to dole away all his property in mouthfuls to the starving, or, even if he were to go still further, and not merely give up his goods, but, like Shadrach Meshach and Abednego, surrender his very body to be burned for the truth's sake, and had not love, it would profit him nothing.

An objection has, however, been raised to this statement of Paul. How, it is asked, could a man possess such gifts as prophecy, the understanding of mysteries, or the working of miracles, unless the Divine love were in him ? That is a question which the Lord Himself has thus answered ;—

"Many will say to Me in That Day, Lord, Lord, did we not prophesy by Thy Name, and by Thy Name cast out demons, and by Thy Name do many mighty works ?

" And then will I profess unto them, I never knew you : depart from Me, ye that work lawlessness." [1]

Having, then, shown that no exercise of power or self-denial avails, unless it be prompted and carried out by love, Paul passes on to explain what love is. And this he does by setting forth fifteen of its characteristics. The first two indicate its nature generally, and are followed by eight negative signs, the mention of each one of which must have smitten the Corinthians with the conviction that they had fallen fearfully short of it. The description is then concluded by five positive characteristics.

" Love," begins the Apostle, " suffereth long, is kind." The first of these qualities is manifested in the meek and patient endurance of wrongs, even if they be oft repeated, without resentment : while the second is a gracious and benevolent feeling toward others, which moves us, whether they be friends or enemies, to relieve assist or cheer them, no matter at what sacrifice of selfishness, at how great inconvenience to ourselves. For Christians must beware of thinking themselves kind merely because they give out of their abundance. Nor does it profit them to give out of their poverty, to help others to their own inconvenience, or to suffer patiently, if the impelling motive be a desire, lurking, perhaps, at the bottom of their heart, to be well thought of by men. But he who suffers long, and is kind, from a purely unselfish motive, can do so only because the love of God is shed abroad in his heart.

Now follow the eight negative characteristics, all of which help to bring out the full meaning of long-suffering.

Love never envies the gifts or prosperity of others,

[1] Matt. vii. 22, 23.

Therefore, she is not tempted to boast of her own condition. Nor is she led on still further to inflation and pride. And, being free from vanity and pride, she does not exhibit that concentration on self, and consequent want of respect for others, which cause men to lose their sense of propriety, so that they say and do things that are unseemly and shameful.

Hence she avoids the most unseemly of all things, the eagerness to acquire and keep—by any possible means, and without a thought or care for others—whatever one's own soul may lust after.

Such an eagerness can scarcely escape observation : hence it is often challenged and sometimes thwarted by rivals, not without anger and strife on both sides.

But all this Love avoids, because she has no violent desire for self-gratification, and so is not provoked by those who, in seeking their own interests, are manifestly infringing her rights.

And, if any of them do her a wrong, she does not take account of the evil deed.

Nor does she feel a criminal joy when some adversary is detected in an unrighteous action, so as to bring advantage to herself; or when he is made to suffer by the iniquitous conduct of others. Over all such things she exults not, but mourns.

There is, however, one thing with which she can rejoice and sympathize, and that is the Truth, which seems here to be personified even as Love is. Love and Truth are very near of kin ; for real and unselfish Love comes, like Truth, from God Alone, and is, therefore, both pure and a purifier of those in whom she dwells. Hence she never fails to rejoice in sympathy with Truth, not even when the manifestation of the latter is contrary to her own interests. Yet, as we have seen above, when the detected unrighteousness of her foes brings advantage to herself, she finds no cause for joy, but only for grief.

It seems, however, possible, if not probable, that " the Truth " may here stand, mainly at least, for the truth of the Gospel. If this be the case, our attention is called to the fact, that, while Love cannot sympathize with unrighteousness, she does rejoice in the spread of the Divine message which checks it. Those who are influenced by her are thus set in sharp opposition to the men who hold down the truth—or check its development in themselves—in unrighteousness, that is, by living in an element of unrighteousness, and so breathing and practising it.

The mention of this quality introduces four other positive signs, which seem to illustrate the second general characteristic, or 'kindness.'

Love " covereth," or " concealeth," all things. This meaning of the Greek word gives a more suitable rendering than the " beareth " of the Authorised and Revised Versions ; since the latter is included in the presently mentioned quality of enduring all things. And we may understand the verb ' to cover ' in the sense of ' to excuse.' Love ever desires to throw a veil over the faults of others ; nor is she willing to exalt herself by exhibiting the crimes and sins either of her friends or of her adversaries.

From this it follows, that she is ready to believe all things, to accept any reasonable explanation which is offered to her—up to that point, at least, where sight gives the lie to trust.

But, even if she can believe no longer, she will, nevertheless, continue to hope.

Nor will she grow weary of her hope, but will hold

out, or endure, to the end ; if, perchance, her desires may at last be realized. For, indeed, she endures all things : neither slight, nor calumny, nor insult, nor even the infliction of death itself, can change her Divine nature. True to that nature, she will, even in her last agony, pray, "Lord, lay not this sin to their charge!" For the Greek word which is rendered " endureth " points to a brave patience, and may be illustrated by the fact that it is used, in Greek histories, of troops, which, though sharply charged by the enemy, yet maintain their ground, and will not give way. The same idea seems to be in Paul's mind when he says ;—

"Wherefore take up the whole armour of God, that ye may be able to withstand in the evil day, and, having done all, to stand."

That is, that ye may not only be able to resist the first, the second, and the third, shock of battle ; but, after it is all over, may still be found firmly maintaining your position.

There is, however, another point in which the supreme excellence of Love is demonstrated. For, being the great attribute of God Himself, which going forth from Him blends all His vast creation into one, from the footstool of His Throne to the farthest boundary of the Heavens, it is absolutely permanent, and can never fail. Varying Dispensations may veil or reveal, but cannot change it. It was not, like the previously mentioned gifts, prepared merely to meet special and temporary difficulties in the present world : nay, it is Heaven's greatest joy and blessing shed upon men below, and he who receives it will find, that, instead of leaving him when he shuffles off this mortal coil, it will only become purified and more intense as it again draws near to the Source from Which it sprang.

But this is by no means the case with other gifts. Even prophecy, the greatest and most to be coveted of them all, will presently lose its worth. For both it and the other gifts were bestowed as helps to the people of God during the present conflict with sin; and, when the ages of that conflict are past, and sin shall be no more, then the time for prophesyings will have gone by, and the perfected saints will have no further need of them.

So, too, tongues will cease, and such imperfect knowledge as we can now acquire will vanish away; for with our present powers we are incapable of more than partial knowledge, and, consequently, can only prophesy in part.

When, therefore, we shall be fully endued with the powers of the world to come, so that we have an absolute comprehension, and can distinguish all the facets of truth, then our present imperfect knowledge, together with the only partially intelligent worship in tongues which it prompts, and the incomplete prophesyings which are founded upon it, must disappear. All these things must be set aside, just as he who has come to man's estate will dismiss for ever the infantile thoughts and words which satisfied his earlier years.

"For now," Paul continues, "we see in a mirror,[1] in a dark saying;[2] but then face to face." The object

---

[1] δι᾽ ἐσόπτρου, literally, "through a mirror." This expression is apparently derived from the illusion by which the reflected object seems to appear on the other side of the surface of the mirror.

[2] Ellicott translates "in perplexing form," instead of "in a riddle" or "dark saying"; and paraphrases, "in a mirror, and in a form of baffling significance."

which we see is God in His purposes of grace and glory. But, in explaining the figure, we must remember that the mirrors of the ancients were made of metal—most commonly of a mixture of copper and tin—so that they could never present a perfectly distinct image. The mirror through which God is seen may, in the case of those who have no other, be the visible creation, in which they may behold His everlasting power and Godhead.

But the mirror of this passage is evidently revelation, especially that which comes by prophecy; wherein is seen, not merely the everlasting power and Godhead, but also the love and purposes of the Most High, though not with absolutely perfect distinctness. Hence the mirror is said to show the object which it reflects in an enigma, or riddle, that is, in a more or less dim and confused form ; so that the prophet, or student of prophecy, must concentrate his spiritually enlightened mind upon it, if he would understand what the Spirit wishes to communicate. " Concerning which salvation," says Peter, " the prophets sought and searched diligently, who prophesied of the grace that should come unto you : searching what time, or what manner of time, the Spirit of Christ which was in them did point unto, when He testified beforehand the sufferings of Christ and the glories that should follow them." [1]

As soon, then, as we are permitted to see face to face, we shall need the mirror no more. And the same may be said of the partial and fragmentary knowledge which is all that we are capable of receiving now. For this, too, will vanish away, when, by the power of the Lord, we are either raised from the dead or find our mortal bodies changed into the likeness of

[1] 1 Peter i. 10, 11.

His Body of Glory, so that the perfect intuitive knowledge of the emancipated spirit becomes ours. During
our present earth-life, God, indeed, knows us within
and without; but the faculties of our spirit are not
yet set free so that we can know Him. Nevertheless,
they will be freed hereafter; and then the imperfect
impressions, which are so useful to us now, will fade
and die in the rising light of a perfect knowledge,
by which we shall be able to understand the nature
and attributes of God, even as He now understands us.

Such a truth as this should remove all elation
and boasting from the minds of the gifted—for how
small a thing is it that they possess; and should make
them use whatever may have been entrusted to them
with fear and trembling. For they are no lords
wielding power among men, but poor probationers
in their time of trial, the result of which is at present
unknown—probationers of whom it is said, " Many shall
be last that are first, and first that are last." Yet, if,
being filled with the Spirit, they can humbly lovingly
and diligently spend and be spent in their Lord's
service, they shall presently hear Him saying, " Well
done, thou good servant: because thou hast been
faithful in a very little, have thou authority over ten
cities;" and the prize of their earth-life will have
been won.

But is there no sense in which we can carry the
gifts of the Spirit with us into the next world?
Certainly there is; for, when the Lord speaks of them
as talents, He represents the bond-servants who have
done well as taking them into the joy of their Lord.
For, by using each gift which we now possess, we are
not only enabled to do the Lord's will here below
but are also being fitted to hold, and trained to wield,

a power corresponding to it in the world to come. He that prophesies now will then, perhaps, receive greater communications, no longer in a dream or in a vision of the night, but directly from the Most High Himself: he who is gifted with the word of partial knowledge now, will then, as we have seen above, be filled with absolute knowledge; and so on.

Yet again, is there nothing that abides with us, intensified and purified, indeed, but essentially unchanged for ever? Without doubt there is; for the Apostle continues;—"But now abide faith, hope, love, these three; and the greatest of these is love."[1] In this somewhat unexpected introduction of faith and hope, two thoughts seem to be presented to our mind. First, of course, that faith and hope, also, as well as love, are permanent virtues, and will remain with us, unchanged for ever in themselves, though before long in very altered circumstances. And, secondly, that, although faith and hope abide for ever in the company of love, the latter is exalted far above both of them.

We must, however, remember, in regard to the first of these thoughts, that Paul is speaking, not only of faith as coming from hearing, of the faith in which we must walk now without the aid of sight;[2] but also of faith as nourished by sight, of that conscious dependence upon, and trust in, God which can never fail in His redeemed creatures, and is only increased by the vision of His glory.

And, although, in another passage, he tells us that "hope that is seen is not hope,"[3] yet must hope, too, always abide with us. For, even in the perfect state, we do not receive a full fruition of all the blessings of eternity in a moment, as though they were a sum

[1] 1 Cor. xiii. 13.   [2] 2 Cor. v. 7.   [3] Rom. viii. 24.

of money paid down at once.   No : they will be succeeding each other in an endless series of glories ; and so, the rejoicing hope of anticipation will never leave us.

While, however, faith and hope must abide for ever, equally with love, yet does the latter rise high above both of them.   For God can experience neither faith nor hope : these, from their very nature, are no more than creature-virtues.   But love is the very essence of His Being, and, therefore, the highest and most excellent of qualities.

The practical conclusion, to which all that has been said brings us, is now summarily stated.   Love, which is the most excellent way, must be the first and chief object of our pursuit ; neverthless, we must not neglect the spiritual gifts, but must earnestly desire them, and especially that of prophecy.

XLII

THE EXERCISE OF THE GIFTS IN THE ASSEMBLY

I COR. xiv

HAVING thus given general precepts in connection with the gifts, the Apostle proceeds to justify his preference for prophecy above all the rest, and then lays down laws for regulating the exercise of gifts in the assembly.

For the good of the assembly, then, prophecy is the talent most to be desired, and not the gift of tongues upon which the Corinthians seem to have set the greatest value.   For one who speaks with a tongue in the assembly speaks to God, and not to men, and no one understands what he says : he is uttering mysteries in spirit. Hence, unless an inter-preter be present, the public use of that gift is unprofitable, however strengthening and refreshing it may be to the gifted person himself. Let it, therefore, be exercised in private. For, in an assembly, the Lord would have us aim at the edification of all.

And this is just what the prophet is able to do ; for his words are intelligible, and are addressed to his fellow-believers to the end that they may be edified, whether by instruction, warning, rebuke, encouragement, or consolation.

Generally, then, we may say, that he who speaks in a tongue edifies himself ; while he that prophesies edifies the assembly.

But the Apostle had no wish to disparage the gift of speaking in tongues: on the contrary, he would rejoice if all the Lord's people could possess it ; yet would rather that they should prophesy. For, because of his power to affect others, he that prophesies is greater than the speaker in tongues ; unless, indeed, the latter be able also to interpret, so that the whole assembly may receive edification.

But now, continues the Apostle, seeing that tongues cannot be generally edifying to believers, unless they be accompanied by interpretation, what good could even I myself do you, if I came to you speaking in tongues, and did not address you either in the way of revelation, or of imparting knowledge, or of prophecy, or of teaching ? Why, even in the case of inanimate things which are made to produce a voice, whether pipe or harp, if they give no distinction to the sounds, how can we tell what is being piped, or what is being harped ?

It is just the same with the more powerful trumpet :

if its tones be indistinct, who shall prepare himself for the particular act of war which is to be commanded ? If it does not clearly sound the advance, when the general gives the order for it, or the retreat, when that is what is intended, of what use is it to the soldiers ?

Or, to take a third illustration, if your tongue does not utter words that can be easily understood, how shall what you are saying be known ? You are merely sending sounds into the air.

And, yet again, there are, it may chance, so many different kinds of voices in the world, and none of them is without meaning : all languages are made up of articulate words. If, then, I do not know the force, or meaning, of the voice that is speaking to me, I shall be a barbarian to the speaker ; and, in my judgment, he will be the same to me. It is impossible to deny this : take, then, a lesson from it ; and, since you are earnestly desirous of spiritual manifestations, let it be with a view to the edification of the church that you seek to abound in them. Covet them as those who have the Spirit of the Lord Jesus—not for your own good or vain-glory, but for the good of others.

And so, if any one speaks in a tongue, let him not do so merely to vaunt himself ; but let him, while in his ecstasy, pray that he may be enabled to interpret.

For, if I pray in a tongue, my spirit prays, but my mind is unfruitful, in that it cannot render what I am saying intelligible to the assembly, cannot lead on their thoughts with mine. Wherefore, so far as the assembly is concerned, my principle is, to pray, indeed, with my spirit, but to do so also with my mind, in order that I may at the same time interpret both to myself and to the brethren.

For, if thou bless only in spiritual ecstasy, in an

unknown tongue, how shall the brother who cannot interpret join in thy thanksgiving by saying the Amen? For thou, indeed, doest well in giving thanks, but the other understands nothing, and, therefore, is not edified.[1]

As to myself, continues the Apostle, I thank God that I speak with tongues more than you all. Nevertheless, when in the assembly, I had rather speak five words with my mind, so as also to instruct others, than ten thousand words in a tongue. Is not this the plainest common sense? Do not, then, brethren, be children in your understanding. As regards malice, be very babes indeed; but in your understanding be full-grown men.[2]

From such remarks as the above, it is easy to imagine what comments Paul would make, if he were on earth to-day, and were to hear the indistinct mutterings in a Ritualistic church, or the language, unknown to the common people, of a Roman Catholic service.

At this point in the argument, he draws an illustration—for it does not seem to be anything more —from the Law[3];—

"In the Law, it is written, 'By men of strange tongues, and by the lips of strangers, will I speak unto this people; and not even thus will they hear Me, saith the Lord.' Wherefore, tongues are for a sign, not to them that believe, but to the unbelieving; but prophesying is not for the unbelieving, but for them that believe."[4]

---

[1] I Cor. xiv. 16, 17.
[2] I Cor. xiv. 18–20.
[3] "The Law" is here used in a wider sense than is usual, being understood to include also the Prophets. For prophecy was sometimes viewed as a mere development of the Law and the promises in the Pentateuch.
[4] I Cor. xiv. 21, 22. See also Isa. xxviii. 11, 12.

In the passage quoted from the twenty-eighth chapter of Isaiah, the prophet is dealing with the debauched reprobates of Israel, and represents them as scoffing at him in the thick and stammering utterances of drunkenness. Whom, say they, does he seek to instruct? to whom is he ever explaining the Tidings? Does he take us to be infants just weaned, but lately removed from their mothers' breasts, that he keeps on irritating us with his precept upon precept, precept upon precept; line upon line, line upon line; here a little, and there a little?[1]

To which the prophet replies, You rail at me with the stammering and incoherent words of drunkards: the Lord will presently speak to you in a manner that will seem like what your own is, by the stammering lip and strange tongue of your foreign conquerors. Yes, He will do 'this, He Who once said to your nation, " This is the rest: give ye rest to him that is weary; and this is the refreshing." But they would not hear. And as to your complaints, that the Word of Jehovah is line upon line and precept upon precept, a monotonous repetition of petty rules and orders; since you reject that Word, it shall have the effect of ripening you for judgment: it shall prove a stone upon which you shall stumble and be broken, a net in which you shall be ensnared, a trap in which you shall be taken.[2]

In referring to this passage, Paul seems to be arguing merely from that analogy which may be detected in all God's manifold dealings with men. Just as He spoke to Israel, first in plain and loving words by the mouth of His own prophets, and, only after they had refused to listen to Him, in the

[1] Isa. xxviii. 9, 10.   [2] Isa. xxviii. 11–13.

partially or wholly unintelligible speech of their foreign oppressors ; so we may infer that tongues, which are also unintelligible, may, if rightly used, be a sign to hardened unbelievers, to those who have despised their opportunities ; while prophesying, on the contrary, edifies the true-hearted followers of the Lord.

Yet, although a proper exercise of the gift of tongues may be a sign to unbelievers, its abuse can only lead to disastrous consequences even in their case. For if—and this may have sometimes happened in Corinth—in the full assembly of a church, all those whose voices were raised, one after another, should break forth into ecstatic utterance, so that nothing but tongues should be heard, and there should be no interpretations, what would be the certain effect upon such novices or strangers as might have entered the room ?

They would exclaim that they must have strayed into the midst of madmen, not of persons inspired by God ; for that He could never have sanctioned an exhibition so meaningless, so devoid of edifying power and even of common sense.[1]

On the other hand, even if every speaker in succession were to prophesy before the assembly, nothing but blessing could follow. The intelligible clear and piercing messages, conveyed through the prophets by the Spirit of God, would not only affect believers, but would also produce an overwhelming conviction of sin in the mind of a novice, or a stranger ; would search his heart with the light of God, and lay bare all its hidden secrets. And overpowered by the awful revelation to himself of his real condition and imminent danger, the sinner would fall to the ground upon his

[1] 1 Cor. xiv. 23.

face, and confess that of a truth God was in that assembly.[1]

Such was the mighty and saving power of prophecy as Paul understood and had experienced it. Is it strange to find him wishing that all the Lord's people had this marvellous gift: strange that he bids us covet earnestly the best gifts, and above all that of prophecy?

But who heeds his inspired words? Who continues steadfastly in prayer that he may receive this great and most beneficent power? Who from the pulpit or the platform is ever urging believers to seek the gift, which, more than any other, would help in the work of accomplishing the number of the elect, and of bringing back the King? Is it wonderful that our ears are assailed on all sides with complaints of the apathy and deadness in churches, and of the want of power in individual believers, when no cry ascends from us for the restoration of that grace which would not only convict and save sinners, but would also rouse the slumbering saints, and set them before the world as a mighty power of God?

Now that the two gifts of prophecy and speaking in tongues have been fully discussed, Paul proceeds to lay down rules for their use in the assembly, and then forbids their public exercise by women ; on the ground that women are not permitted to speak in the assemblies, but must be silent, as a token of their acquiescence in that subjection in which it has pleased God to place them.

This part of the Epistle is of especial value to us, since it shows us how assemblies of the churches were wont to be conducted under the immediate supervision

[1] 1 Cor. xiv. 24, 25.

of Apostles, and how entirely their character was changed in subsequent times.

How, then, asks the Apostle, does the matter stand after what has been said? And his answer is, " When ye come together, each one "—that is, each one of the inspired or spiritually gifted—" hath a psalm, hath a teaching, hath a revelation, hath a tongue, hath an interpretation. Let all things be done unto edifying." [1]

From this it appears, that many spiritually gifted persons were expected to be in every assembly, and that all appropriate gifts were to be exercised, but only in such a way as to tend to the edification of all. And, finally, that every spiritually gifted member would be furnished by the Holy Spirit with something which would enable him to minister blessing to the whole assembly.

One might have a psalm or hymn of praise, such, perhaps, as those " psalms, hymns, and spiritual songs," of which Paul speaks elsewhere.[2] For it would seem that the reference is not to an Old Testament Psalm, or to a hymn previously composed, but to one inspired at the moment by the Spirit of God; [3] for we are here dealing exclusively with the exercise of spiritual gifts. Hence this power of extemporaneous praise will fall under the head of prophecy.

Hymns are, perhaps, mentioned first, because they would be appropriately used at the commencement of the meetings. So Pliny, in describing an assembly of Christians on the First Day of the Week, relates that they began by reciting, one after another, a hymn to Christ as God.[4]

---

[1] 1 Cor. xiv. 26.
[2] Col. iii. 16; Eph. v. 19.
[3] Such, perhaps, was the song of Hannah (1 Sam. ii. 1-10), and that of the Lord's mother (Luke i. 46-55).
[4] Plin. Epp. x. 97.

Another might have something to teach, impressed upon him by the Same Spirit—a word of wisdom, or a word of knowledge.

A third might be burning with a revelation from God, and be eager to proclaim it in prophetic utterance.

A fourth might be longing to give vent to an ecstatic thanksgiving; while a fifth might be ready to interpret the tongue in which the other would speak.

Such was the wealth, and such the diversity, of spiritual power by which the Apostolic churches were kept alive in the midst of adverse Judaism and Paganism. How different was their condition from anything that we see around us to-day! How countless the devices which Satan has introduced to check the influence of the Spirit, to set men under a human hierarchy in place of a Divine Power, and to substitute sensuous and mechanical worship for that which is spiritual and intelligent! How inefficient, and often worse than useless, is the ministry of a single and frequently un-converted cleric, as compared with that of the many Spirit-inspired members of a congregation in the first century!

But the power given by the Spirit might be abused by a believer's too eager desire to exercise it, and to push himself forward before others who were similarly or diversely gifted. Therefore, before proceeding to details, the Apostle lays down the general principle, that whatever is done in the assembly must be done with a view to the edification of all that are present, and not merely to gratify the vanity or the ambition of the gifted person.

Then he rules, that, should there be any speaking with tongues, not more than two, or at the most three, persons should be allowed to exhibit this gift at each meeting; and that they must do so in turns, that is, one at a time. Doubtless this rule was needed: impetuosity and forgetfulness of others were especially likely to characterize an outburst of ecstatic thanksgiving.

That confusion might be still further avoided, the same interpreter was to translate all the utterances. And, if no interpreter were present, then the speaker with tongues was to be silent in the congregation, and not to indulge in that which, profitable as it might be to himself, would, in its effect upon others, be nothing more than a personal display. Nevertheless, he was not to stifle the impulse of the Spirit which would bring him nearer to God, but must withdraw into privacy, and there relieve his spirit by speaking to himself only and to God.

As to the prophets, not more than two or three were to prophesy in each meeting; while the congregation—that is, those in it who had discernment of spirits, and so were capable—were to sift and judge what each prophet had said. For the spirits of the prophets required to be tried, in order that they might be detected and proved false, if false they were: or, otherwise, that, if they had exceeded their message, and added anything of their own to the Spirit's communication, it might be pointed out and rejected. So, in another place, Paul says;—" Quench not the Spirit; despise not prophesyings: prove all things; hold fast that which is good."[1]

But if, while a prophet was speaking, one of those who sat by should receive a sudden revelation, then the first speaker must cease, and give opportunity to the other. For the new communication would indicate

[1] 1 Thess. v. 19–21.

that something different needed to be uttered immediately : and the path of the Spirit must not be
obstructed.   Or, perhaps, the first speaker might be
unduly prolonging his utterance ; so that he was
beginning to mar the heavenly message by inter-
mingling it with his own thoughts.   Or he might have
uttered all that the Spirit had to say to those members
of the congregation with whom he was specially
commissioned to deal, in which case he would be
consuming the time that had been set apart for other
revelations.

Indeed, something of this kind seems to be intimated
in the thirty-first verse ;—" For ye can all prophesy
one by one, that all may learn, and all may be comforted." [1]   The meaning of which appears to be, that
all who were prophets must have an opportunity,
each of exercising his own gift, because the Spirit
does not light lamps to place them under bushels,
but to set them upon the lampstand —that is, in their
proper position in the church to which they are attached
—in order that they may give light unto every member
of the Lord's household.

Of course, the first ' all ' in this verse must refer
exclusively to prophets, and not to the whole congregation ; for all believers are not prophets,[2] yet none
but a prophet can prophesy.   And all the prophets
must speak, for the following special reason, as well as
the general one given above ; namely, because the Spirit
had chosen them as being suitable each for a different
class of mind and circumstances in the assembly.
Hence, unless they all spoke, every member of the
congregation would not learn, or be comforted, in the
special sense here intended.

[1] I Cor. xiv. 31.   [2] I Cor. xii. 28, 29.

Not, of course, that all the prophets could have an opportunity of speaking at every meeting; unless, indeed, there were but two or three of them. Yet it would not be difficult to arrange that every prophet should be heard in turn in the course of two meetings, if not in one; provided that the rule of the thirty-first verse were obeyed, and the intimations of the Spirit were suffered to check those who were too forward or too prolix.

It might, however, be objected, How could the prophets stay their ecstatic utterances? Borne onward, as they were, by an overpowering inspiration, they scarcely knew whether another was prophesying at the same time or not, and would be quite unable to restrain themselves if they did.

Now, this is doubtless true of demoniacal inspiration, or possession, by which men are carried away blindly, they know not whither. But it is not so in the case of the Divinely inspired. God delights only in free service, and, consequently, the Holy Spirit does not deprive the prophet of his self-control, or remove his responsibility. He can always restrain himself if he wills to do so, and is, therefore, able to obey the rule laid down for his guidance. Were this not the case, every fully endowed church would be liable to fall into a state of confusion and jangling disorder. But such a condition of things could not be permitted; for God is not a God of disorder, but of peace: in His churches the members will act in concert, the work of each one fitting in with that of the others; so that the result will be a perfect harmony of peace.[1]

[1] 1 Cor. xiv. 32, 33.

XLIII

Precepts regulating the Position and Behaviour of Women

1 Cor. xiv. 34–37 ; xi. 3–16 ; 1 Tim. ii. 11–15.

THERE was yet another matter in connection with the rules for the assemblies upon which it was necessary that Paul should comment. In Corinth, and, apparently, in Corinth alone, the women had been permitted to speak in the church-meetings, as though they were on an equality with the men. This was contrary to all Divine revelation, and to the custom of every other church : hence Paul gives very peremptory commands respecting it.

Probably, the mischief arose from the circumstance, that some of the women had received the gift of tongues or of prophecy, and so claimed their right to exercise it in the assembly. And this advance seems to have had a further development in the public challenging of male speakers by women, and the throwing out of pert or unseemly questions, which could only foster the vanity of those who put them, and would also destroy that dependence upon their husbands which God had been pleased to appoint as their special discipline.[1] For, evidently, it is only to the married women that Paul here refers : a merely decent Pagan modesty would be supposed sufficient to keep the unmarried from any thought of public acts. And, indeed, the customs of both Greeks and Romans would have forbidden the appearance of women as public orators.

[1] Gen. iii. 16.

It is not, however, unlikely that the circumstances of their previous life may have disposed some of the Corinthian converts to actions bolder than those of their sisters in other places. For they had lived in a city notorious for its impurity, and specially devoted to the Goddess of Lust, whose splendid temple, crowning the Acropolis and lifted high above the city, was disgraced by the continual attendance of a thousand consecrated harlots. It would scarcely have been possible to breathe such an atmosphere as this without suffering from its pestilential miasma. When women had to dwell among those who made the degradation of women a main feature of the national religion, they must certainly have been in danger of losing all the modesty and virtue of their sex.

But, to return to our immediate subject, it might be asked, Why, then, did God bestow the gifts upon women, if the latter were forbidden to exercise them?

They were not forbidden to use them in private for their own edification, or for that of their own family and circle of female friends, or, indeed, for that of any of their sex. They were only prohibited from speaking in public in the church-meetings. And it is clear, that believing women recognized and acted upon this prohibition; for, if we except the case of the Corinthians, there is no instance in the New Testament of a woman speaking in an assembly.

In the Old Testament, however, there are, apparently, two instances, occurring in a Dispensation in which the will of God was not so plainly revealed as it is now. Three prophetesses only, Miriam Deborah and Huldah, are mentioned—for Noadiah, who strove to injure Nehemiah, was obviously a false prophetess.[1]

[1] Neh. vi. 14.

And of these three, Miriam and Deborah may, possibly, have prophesied before the congregation.

But Miriam became so inflated with vanity that she even dared to censure Moses, and to put herself on an equality with him. Such audacity caused wrath to go forth from the Lord, and He smote her with a leprosy that made her white as snow. Her brother Aaron, whom she had persuaded to join in her mad rebellion, was compelled to supplicate the despised Moses for help ; and, at the entreaty of the latter, God consented to heal her ; but only after a terrible rebuke —a rebuke, too, administered in such a way as to inflict the deepest and most public humiliation upon the vain rebel. "If her father had but spit in her face," said the Lord, "should she not be ashamed seven days? Let her be shut up without the camp seven days, and after that she shall be brought in again."[1]

So the prophetess, who had essayed to take the place of Moses and lead Israel, was thrust out of the camp as unclean and unworthy to dwell even with the meanest of the people. Moreover, the attention of the whole congregation was fixed upon her by the fact, that the camp had to wait in the place where it was, until the time of her humiliation and her purification had been completed.

Deborah, too, seems to have been marred by a vanity very similar to that of Miriam. It would be difficult to find in any of the prophets a parallel to the conceit which prompted these verses ;—

" In the days of Shamgar the son of Anath,
   In the days of Jael, the highways were unoccupied,
   And the travellers walked through byways.

[1] Num. xii. 14.

> The villages were unoccupied in Israel, they were
> unoccupied,
> Until that I Deborah arose,
> That I arose a mother in Israel." [1]

And blinded by this conceit, she lost her spiritual insight, and praised the lying treachery of Jael which she should have condemned. And this, too, although she herself had been moved by the Spirit to predict that God would *sell* Sisera into the hands of a woman : in other words, that He would suffer Jael to accomplish the desire of her unscrupulously ambitious heart, but would afterwards exact the price, the full penalty of her guilt.

The third prophetess, Huldah, is the only one of whom no fault is recorded. She seems to have been held in great repute ; but there is no intimation that she ever prophesied in public.[2] When Josiah commanded the High Priest and others to inquire of the Lord, they at once recognized Huldah as the one through whom His Word might reach them. And it may be noted, that they went to her own house to commune with her in private.

Thus, of the three prophetesses of the Old Testament, there was but one who—so far as the Divine revelation informs us—preserved that modesty and self-abnegation which the presence of the Spirit ought to ensure. For the other two certainly endeavoured, to some extent at least, to use the power of God within them for the gratification of their vanity. And this fact may give us a hint as to one of the reasons that caused the

---

[1] Judges v. 6, 7. It will be noted, that the song is said to be that of Deborah and Barak: there is no, " Thus saith the Lord," in connection with it.

[2] 2 Kings xxii. 14–20; 2 Chron. xxxiv. 22–28.

prophetic gift to be so rarely bestowed upon women. In the female sex, the balance of the mind is more likely to be disturbed by that consciousness of Divine revelation which not even Paul had been able to bear with becoming meekness, unless God had given him a thorn in the flesh, a messenger of Satan to buffet him, that he might not be exalted overmuch.[1]

Prophetesses appear, also, in the New Testament, but are never mentioned as addressing assemblies, except at Corinth. Indeed, as Paul presently affirms, such a thing was contrary to the custom of all the churches.

We can, therefore, scarcely wonder at the somewhat indignant severity which characterizes his remarks upon the Corinthian innovation ;—

"Let the women keep silence in the assemblies : for it is not permitted unto them to speak ; but let them be in subjection, as also saith the Law. And if they would learn anything, let them ask their own husbands at home : for it is shameful for a woman to speak in the assembly. What? was it from you that the Word of God went forth? Or came it unto you alone?"[2]

The command which begins this paragraph could scarcely have been couched in stronger terms. Women are to be silent in the church-meetings ; because, in the general and natural order of things, it is not seemly for them to speak in such circumstances. Their duty is to remain in subjection, according to the words of the Law ;—

"And thy desire shall be to thy husband, and he shall rule over thee."[3]

[1] 2 Cor. xii. 7.   [2] 1 Cor. xiv. 34–6.   [3] Gen. iii. 16.

But to teach or preach in an assembly is, in Paul's judgment, the part of those that are in authority, and does not become subordinates.

Hence the present emergence of women from the position in which God has placed them signifies that His fundamental laws for human society are being set aside, and is ominous of coming judgment. When Isaiah enters into the details of his fearful statement—

"For Jerusalem is ruined, and Judah is fallen : because their tongue and their doings are against the Lord, to provoke the eyes of His glory [1] "—

he says ;—

"As for My people, children are their oppressors, and women rule over them. O My people, they which lead thee cause thee to err, and destroy the way of thy paths." [2]

Now the members of Christ must be scrupulous in their obedience to every Divine command. Therefore, a woman, even if her wish be no more than to gain a clearer comprehension of something which she has heard, must not be permitted to propose her question in the assembly, but must acknowledge her dependence on her husband by waiting until she can lay her difficulties before him at home. "For," adds the Apostle with forceful emphasis, "it is shameful for a woman to speak in an assembly."

The last thought seems to rouse his indignation against the Corinthians who had encouraged this kind of lawlessness ; to such a degree, indeed, that he ironically demands ;—"Or do you mean to claim that the Word of God proceeded first from you, or that you are its sole depositaries among the Gentiles, and,

[1] Isa. iii. 8.   [2] Isa. iii. 12.

on that ground, to defend your conduct in allowing practices unknown to other churches? That is, to put it in another form, Are you the original church, so that all others must take their pattern from you; or are you the only true church, so that we need not wonder at the difference between your customs and those of other communities which pretend to be churches? Since neither of these suppositions was really the case, the two questions set the conceit and impertinence of the Corinthian practices in strong relief.

In what follows, Paul stands upon his Apostolic authority. If any man, he says, has the reputation of being spiritual—that is, endowed with a spiritual 'gift,' or 'inspired'—let him prove that he is so by recognizing the things which I write to you as being a commandment of the Lord. But, if any one is ignorant of this fact, he must remain so, and suffer the consequences.

The last two verses of the chapter form a brief statement of the conclusion. "Wherefore, my brethren, desire earnestly to prophesy, and forbid not to speak with tongues. Let all things be done decently and in order." That is, as the Apostle has already urged, the gift to be chiefly desired is that of prophecy, because by its exercise the whole church is edified. But, although the speaking with tongues is an inferior endowment, do not forbid it, provided an interpreter be present. Quench not any manifestation of the Spirit, but above all things be careful not to despise prophesyings.

We must not, however, dismiss the subject of woman's position in the churches without some notice of a remarkable passage in the eleventh chapter of this Epistle, a passage, indeed, which seems to have been intended as a preparation for what is said in the fourteenth. For, in the former chapter, the woman is forbidden to pray or to prophesy with head unveiled ; in the latter, she is commanded to be absolutely silent in the assemblies.

In the eleventh chapter, Paul prefaces his argument by a general commendation of the Corinthians for remembering him, and holding fast the directions which they had received from him. Nevertheless, there were two serious disorders among them, the one touching the behaviour of their women, the other connected with the observance of the Lord's Supper.

And the very solemn way in which he proceeds to speak of the first of these defects, indicates the great importance which he attaches to it.

The Lord our God is a God of order : He has made and established things as He intended and wishes them to remain. And the series of ranks which is now in question begins from Himself ; so that the person who wilfully and deliberately violates the appointed order is assailing that of which the Almighty Creator is a part, and will in no wise escape judgment.

For the Divine order, which the Apostle here cites as the basis of what he is about to say, is no less than this ;—The man is the head of the woman, the Christ is the Head of the man, and God is the Head of the Christ ;[1] that is, The woman is subordinate to the man as the man is to the Christ, and as the Christ is to God.

Now, it is evident that the ranks of this series must be scrupulously recognized in the worship of the God

[1] 1 Cor. xi. 3.

Who not only arranged it, but also Himself stands at the head of the series as a Member of it. And, to this end, it was necessary to exhibit the relation of the human couple, that is the subordination of the woman to the man, by some outward token of subjection borne by the former. What this sign should be, nature itself seemed to indicate, namely, the wearing of a covering or veil upon the head. But, although this custom obtained in all other churches, it was not observed at Corinth. There the women not only prayed and prophesied in the assembly, but actually did so with unveiled heads; while some of the men—Jewish converts, perhaps, or others influenced by them—covered their heads when they prayed or prophesied.[1]

These irregularities, trivial as they might have seemed to carnal minds, were a great offence and insult to God. For in the assembly believers present themselves before Him : therefore, when they so appear, every one must openly acknowledge his or her proper order, as it was Divinely appointed.

Hence the veiled man dishonours his Head—not the head which he has veiled, but, as the third verse emphatically shows, his ruling Head, that is, the Christ. For he appears with the sign of subjection to other human beings upon his head, contrary to the institution of God, Who made him—so far as the sexes of his race are concerned—the ruler, and not the subject. And when the followers of the Lord Jesus break the laws of His Father, they disobey and dishonour their great Leader Himself.

In like manner, the unveiled woman dishonours her head, that is, the man, by refusing to wear the Divinely appointed badge of her subjection to him.

[1] 1 Cor. xi. 4, 5.

If, continues Paul, the woman presents herself to worship unveiled, it is as disgraceful as if she were shaven : for she has marked herself as shameless and disreputable.

Let her, then, be consistent, and, by also cutting off her hair, expose herself to the full. But, if it be a shame for a woman to be shorn or shaven, then let her show the modesty which nature itself has indicated, and veil her head.

So far Paul has based his argument upon the relation of the man to Christ his Divinely appointed Head, and upon that of the woman to the man as her rightful head. But now he adds three additional reasons, drawn from the relation of the man to God as his Creator, and from the purpose for which the woman was called into being.

(1) The man ought not to veil his head, because he is the image and glory of God, Who created him in His image and for His glory. But the woman is the glory of the man ; because, as the other reasons explain, she was made from him and for him. And the glory of the man must confess inferiority to the glory of God.

(2) The man was not made out of the woman, but the woman out of the man ; that is, she owes her origin to the man.

(3) The man was not created for the sake of the woman, but the woman for the sake of the man, that she might be a help meet for him.

" For this cause," the Apostle proceeds, " ought the woman to have authority upon her head, because of the angels." Now, " authority " is here, doubtless, used for ' a sign of authority.' " The wife," says Neander, " should have upon her head a symbol of the power which the man has over her." A very apposite illustration may be found in a passage cited by Barnes from Chardui, who, when speaking of the head-covering worn by Persian ladies, remarks, "Only married women wear it, and it is the sign by which it is known that they are under subjection." Paul does not, however, here confine his precepts to married women : he is enacting laws for the general relation of the female sex to the male.

The woman, then, should have the symbol of authority upon her head, and so acknowledge before God the subordination in which he has chosen to place her. And this she must do on account of the angels ; for they are continually around the servants of God, not only to protect, but also to correct and chastise them, according to His fixed laws, whenever His order and His rules are broken. So He warned the Israelites concerning the angel that was to go before them ;—

"Beware of him, and obey his voice : provoke him not ; for he will not pardon your transgression ; for My Name is in him." [1]

The angel would be inexorable, because, unless God chose to interfere, he must strictly carry out the laws laid down for him. The general subject of angel-government is, however, too important to be discussed here : we will, therefore, reserve it for another chapter.

But, some may object, why should beings so lofty as angels bestow a moment's care on so trivial a matter as a woman's veil ; or why, if she be not covered, should they exact punishment for so slight an offence ?

[1] Exod. xxiii. 21.

Such a question reveals an utter absence of God-consciousness, a self-absorption, which, so far as it may, regards the creation as its own, to be tampered with or altered at will. If, in this condition of mind, any one thinks to change Divine orders or times or seasons, he will at least feel his folly when he stands before the Great White Throne, under the eyes of the Almighty Creator Whose laws he, forsooth, has dared to disregard.

For to alter God's order in any way is a far greater offence than it is usually suspected to be. He has placed each of us in the sex, rank, and circumstances, most suitable for the discipline which He sees necessary in our several cases. What, then, must be the consequence of violating the laws attached to any appointed condition of life? For instance, if a woman, instead of giving heed to the command, " Unto him shall be thy desire, and he shall rule over thee," usurps authority over the man ; what will be the after-consequences? We will mention but one of them. For, to pass by any direct punishment that may follow, she has rendered useless the toils and sufferings of her earth-life. She has eluded, and so deprived herself of the benefit of, that discipline for which God brought her into the world, and how is the deficiency to be made good?

In no possible way that has been revealed to us. Since, then, the Divinely appointed, and, therefore, absolutely necessary, discipline has not been submitted to, the defaulter will, at least, be rejected by the Lord,[1] and so degraded to a lower estate than that to which she had been called. The First Resurrection, membership in the Body of Christ, and the Kingdom, will have

[1] I Cor, ix. 27.

been lost. For, certainly, God never will permit His arrangements to be altered or declined by foolish men or women without condign punishment.

The same remarks apply to the earliest discipline which He has ordained for us—obedience to parents. And let it be remembered, that, in this matter, the law of God recognizes no coming of age, no time when a man may cease to respect his father and his mother.

Under the same head comes the discipline of obedience to kings, magistrates, and those who are set over us. "For there is no power but of God; and the powers that be are ordained of God. Therefore, he that resisteth the power, withstandeth the ordinance of God: and they that withstand shall receive to themselves judgment." [1]

Under it, too, fall some cases that are rarely noticed. For instance, when God refused to receive Cain's sacrifice, and at the same time accepted that of Abel, He admonished the former, that, if he did well, he also should be accepted, and should be restored to the honour which properly belonged to him as the elder brother;—"And unto thee shall be his desire, and thou shalt rule over him." It appears, then, that God would have respect paid to elder brothers by the younger, in recognition of the order in which He has chosen to bring them into the world.

Other passages show, that He will not permit His creation in general to be tampered with, confused, or in any way altered; that, in all things, the physical and moral order of the world, which He has established, must be maintained;—

"A woman shall not wear that which pertaineth unto a man, neither shall a man put on a woman's

[1] Rom. xiii. 1, 2.

garment: for whosoever doeth these things is an abomination unto the Lord thy God."[1]

"Thou shalt not sow thy vineyard with two kinds of seed,[2] lest the whole fruit be forfeited, the seed which thou hast sown, and the increase of the vineyard. Thou shalt not plough with an ox and an ass together.[3] Thou shalt not wear a mingled stuff, wool and linen together."[4]

"Ye shall keep My statutes. Thou shalt not let thy cattle gender with a diverse kind:[5] thou shalt not sow thy field with two kinds of seed : neither shall there come upon thee a garment of two kinds of stuff mingled together."[6]

But to return to the passage which we are considering, Paul feared lest a perversion of what he had just said should produce disastrous consequences. His very decided words respecting the subjection of women might cause them to be despised by the other sex. Therefore, in the eleventh verse, he begins to add considerations which would check so wrong an inference. After all, the man and the woman, equally, are constituent parts of the Body of Christ:[7] they are

---

[1] Deut. xxii. 5. Not only the woman's veil, then, but every garment distinctive of sex comes under the notice of the Angelic courts.

[2] That is, so as to result in a mixed produce.

[3] "The ox and the ass take different steps, and they are supposed to dislike one another's odour."—R. B. Girdlestone.

[4] Deut. xxii. 9–11.

[5] There must be no attempt to improve God's creation: all creatures and things must be allowed to remain as He established them.

[6] Lev. xix. 19.

[7] So in Gal. iii. 27, 28 ;—"For as many of you as were baptized into Christ did put on Christ. There can be neither Jew nor Greek, there can be neither bond nor free, there can be no male and female : for ye are all one (man) in Christ Jesus." In the

dependent upon each other, and are blended together in Him. And He has not forgotten to exhibit this interdependence in the natural order which He has established. For, although the first woman was taken out of the man, and his headship was thereby unmistakably signified, yet every man who has subsequently appeared upon earth was born through the medium of a woman. And all things are of God, both man and woman and whatever else exists, together with all their relations and interdependencies. Therefore, the order which may be traced in creation, and in the conditions that were afterwards imposed upon the human race, is the order of the Supreme God, and must, accordingly, be respected and obeyed with the utmost diligence and conscientiousness.

The argument is concluded with an appeal to the inner consciousness of right-minded men, to the instinctive feeling which God has implanted in them, and from which they might know that it is unseemly for a woman to worship God with her head unveiled. For, in presenting herself before His Throne, she must wear the dress and insignia of the order in which He has been pleased to place her. So much is demanded even in royal courts upon earth.

The Apostle also cites nature, by which he means the creation-law, one of the " all things " which " are of God." If we study this, it will teach us, that long hair is a shame to the man, but a glory to the woman. For by bestowing it bountifully upon the latter, that

relations of the present life there are great differences between male and female ; but in Christ Jesus all are alike " sons of God "— v. 26 ; all without distinction are included in the one Man—comp. Eph. iv. 13—the mystical Body of Christ ; and so, as the Lord has told us, there will be no sex among the " sons "(*vioi*) of the Resurrection (Luke xx. 35, 36). *vioi* is also used in Gal. iii. 26.

it may form a mantle for her, nature itself indicates the lines which she must follow in her raiment, as well as in her mode of life.

But, if any one were inclined even now to dispute the matter, there was but one thing to be said to him. Neither the Apostles nor the churches of God had any such custom as that which he would defend. There remained, therefore, only these alternatives. He might prove, if he could, that Divine revelation had come solely to himself: otherwise, he must either conform to the custom of the churches, or withdraw himself from their communion.

But there is yet another passage on this subject which claims a brief notice. It runs as follows ;—

"Let a woman learn in quietness with all subjection.

"But I permit not a woman to teach, nor to have dominion over a man, but to be in quietness.

"For Adam was first formed, then Eve.

"And Adam was not beguiled, but the woman having been beguiled hath fallen into transgression.

"But she shall be saved through her child-bearing, if they continue in faith and love and sanctification with sobriety." [1]

These words were written to Timothy some years after the date of the Epistle to the Corinthians, and show that the Apostle's mind had not changed in regard to the subject before us, but was as decided as in the earlier times of his ministry.

The woman is to learn in quietness, and not to attract attention to herself by posing prominently in the assembly. Her part is to learn, not to teach. She must be in all subjection, and not usurp authority over

[1] 1 Tim. ii. 11–15.

any of the male sex.[1] The words, " I do not permit," are very decided.

For this subjection two reasons are given, neither of them being exactly the same as those which had been adduced in the Epistle to the Corinthians.

The first is Adam's priority in creation ; for since he and Eve were beings of the same kind, that priority indicated a priority of rank. And, indeed, as we are told in the parallel passage, the woman was created for the man's sake.

Then, again, Adam was not deceived into sin, but was persuaded, through love for his wife, to follow her into the darkness.

The woman, on the contrary, was deceived, and so became involved in transgression. She was more susceptible of flattery and guile, and, although she came last into being, was first in sin. Nevertheless, she should be saved through her child-bearing [2]—that is, in passing through it ; for, though a curse, it should not hinder her salvation—provided that she fulfilled the condition which applies to both sexes, namely, if she continued in faith and love and sanctification with sobriety of mind. The additional curse which was pronounced upon her, because she was the first in sin and the cause of sin to her husband, was that she should be subject to him, and should bring forth children in sorrow.

---

[1] I Cor. xi. 9.

[2] Alford remarks, that the construction is the same as in I Cor. iii. 15—" He himself shall be saved ; yet so as through fire." " Just as that man should be saved through, as passing through, fire, which is his trial, his hindrance in the way, in spite of which he escapes ; so the woman shall be saved through, as passing through, her child-bearing, which is her trial, her curse, her (not means of salvation, but) hindrance in the way of it." In other words, the pangs and dangers of child-bearing shall not be able to separate her from the love of Christ.

And the latter part of the sentence, of course, involved the care of the children when born, and the secluded home-life which such a care necessarily entails. If the woman willingly remained in this sphere—which the wisdom of God had prepared as, in present circumstances, the most efficient discipline for her—her trials, though in their origin a curse, should not obstruct but forward her salvation, if so be that she obeyed the Gospel of our Lord Jesus Christ.

But, it may be asked, if we are to receive the doctrine of these passages, what are we to say of the female preachers and teachers who now everywhere abound? We can only reply, If Paul's written words mean anything, he would certainly, were he now upon earth, forbid believing women to act such a part. And what he has written is confirmed by the whole of the New Testament, in which there is not a hint that women were to teach, or in any way to exercise authority over the church to which they belonged.

The Lord had two excellent opportunities for setting forth His wishes in regard to the matter. But, when He sent out the Twelve, they were all men, not six men and six women; and the same was the case with the Seventy. He never commissioned women to preach, but He by no means rejected their services. When He had healed Peter's wife's mother, "she arose and ministered unto them."[1] While He was preaching the good tidings of the Kingdom, there were "certain women which had been healed of evil spirits and infirmities, Mary that was called Magdalene, from whom seven demons had gone out, and Joanna, the wife of Chuza, Herod's steward, and Susanna, and many others,

[1] Matt. viii. 15.

which ministered unto Him of their substance."[1] He did not refuse the washing of His feet, nor the anointing with the precious ointment: He looked with love upon the weeping women who followed Him to the cross; and, after His resurrection, He showed Himself first to those women who had gone to His tomb, and turned their sorrow into joy.

From all this we see that Paul was filled with His Master's spirit when, in describing the good woman, he says;—

"If she hath brought up children, if she hath used hospitality to strangers, if she hath washed the saints' feet, if she hath relieved the afflicted, if she hath diligently followed every good work."[2]

For he does not add; If she hath preached the Gospel, or, if she hath edified the church.

And Peter, again, is in perfect accord with Paul; for he, too, enjoins upon women the duty of subjection and obedience, and bids them not to delight in plaited hair or jewelry or costly apparel, but to wear "the ornament of a meek and quiet spirit, which is in the sight of God of great price."[3]

The conclusion, then, to which we seem to be forced by the passages examined above is diametrically opposed to the opinions and practice of the present time. For women are now everywhere taking the place of preachers and teachers, whereas by the law of the New Testament they are positively forbidden to do this, except in the case of their children or their own sex. It has, indeed, been urged, from the eleventh chapter of the First Epistle to the Corinthians,[4] that a woman may pray or prophesy in public, provided

---

[1] Luke viii. 3.
[2] 1 Tim. v. 10.
[3] 1 Peter iii. 1–6.
[4] V. 5.

that her head be covered. But the fact, that, in the fourteenth chapter, Paul immediately follows up his directions for the public exercise of the prophetic gift with a peremptory order, that women should be silent in the assemblies, certainly gives the impression that his rule in the eleventh chapter was intended to refer exclusively to prophesyings in private.

Here, then, is a serious question for the consideration of those women whose only object in life is, by their obedience, to glorify Him That sitteth upon the Throne and the Lamb; and with them we must leave the matter.

Of course, it cannot for a moment be denied, that such teaching as we have just adduced from the New Testament is altogether at variance with the spirit of the age; but is the Bible ever in accord with that spirit?

Our Lord sets "the sons of this age" in sharp opposition to "the sons of light,"[1] to those which shall be "accounted worthy to attain to that age and the resurrection from the dead."[2]

Paul bids us not to be conformed to this age;[3] and tells us, that the wisdom which he speaks is not its wisdom, nor that of its rulers "which are coming to nought."[4] Hence he says;—

[1] Luke xvi. 8. In our versions αἰών is here rendered 'world,' as it is also in the subsequently quoted passages. Such a rendering is, however, inaccurate, and should have been applied only to κόσμος, which does mean the world. Of course, αἰών sometimes means an age in the sense of the people who live in it; and, in this case, it might be translated by 'world.' But, since our language will permit the more literal rendering, it is better to avoid confusion by retaining it.

[2] Luke xx. 34, 35.

[3] Rom. xii. 2.

[4] 1 Cor. ii. 6.

"Let no man deceive himself. If any one thinketh that he is wise among you in this age, let him become a fool[1] that he may become wise. For the wisdom of this world is foolishness with God."[2]

And too often the wisdom of God is foolishness with men ; who must, nevertheless, sooner or later discover that the foolishness of God is wiser than men.[3]

But Paul does not forget to render a competent reason for his aversion to this age ; for he warns us, that the great Adversary himself is the god of it.[4] And he reminds the Ephesians, that, when they were spiritually dead by reason of transgressions and sins, they walked "according to the age of this world, according to the Prince of the Power of the Air, of the spirit that now worketh in the sons of disobedience."[5] Thus, then, this age is directly con-

---

[1] That is, of course, Let him be willing to seem one to the world.

[2] 1 Cor. iii. 18, 19.   [3] 1 Cor. i. 25.   [4] 2 Cor. iv. 4.

[5] Eph. ii. 2. By "the age" we must understand the tendency of the age, to walk in accord with which is to walk in accord with Satan, who influences and controls it. For he rules the Power of the Air, or the aggregate of fallen angels and demons who are elsewhere called the Principalities, the Powers, the World-rulers of this Darkness, and the Spiritual Hosts of Wickedness in the supercelestial Places (Eph. vi. 12).

These supercelestial places—see p. 9, note 1—are, perhaps, their proper abode ; but they influence men by means of organizations in the air, or atmospheric heaven, which immediately surrounds our earth.

In the next clause, "the spirit that now worketh in the sons of disobedience," must be regarded grammatically as in apposition to the Power of the Air. It signifies the combined influence of the spirits of evil, whereby the various tendencies of thought and waves of opinion, which from time to time pass over our world, are set in motion. And there can be little doubt that this Satanic influence affects, not only the unregenerate, but also many believers, who, failing to watch and pray always and to maintain their communion

nected with Satan and the spirit that now works in the sons of disobedience, which latter is identical with the spirit of the age. We can, therefore, well understand the same Apostle when he says of the Lord Jesus ;—

"Who gave Himself for our sins, that He might deliver us out of this present evil age."[1]

Nor less so, when he laments the faithlessness of a fellow-labourer in the words ;—

"Demas forsook me, having loved the present age."[2]

Thus the present age is under the influence of Satan its god, and is hostile to the God That made the heavens and the earth, Whose commandments it is continually setting at nought. And all that it can do for believers is to indicate to them by its tendencies what they are *not* to follow.

with the Lord, are so deceived and misguided that they are made unawares to serve the purposes of Satan.

Perhaps, the collective expressions "Power of the Air" and "spirit that now worketh," are intended to remind us of the perfect and formidable unity among the spirits of evil. For, as the Lord Himself said, if they were divided against each other, Satan's Kingdom could not stand. With them, however, the bond of unity is not love, as it should be with us, but fear, self-interest, and hatred.

[1] Gal. i. 4.   [2] 2 Tim. iv. 10.

BECAUSE OF THE ANGELS,

OR

THE JUDICIAL COURTS OF HEAVEN

XLIV

The Judgment, the Council, and the Fiery Valley

Matt. v. 21, 22.

WHILE commenting upon the words, "For this cause ought the woman to have a sign of authority on her head, because of the angels," we could not confuse the main argument by entering into a digression upon angelic rule. Since, however, the subject is deeply interesting, and touches, not only the question of a woman's head-covering, but also the orderly obedience in all things of every believer, whether male or female, we will now endeavour to throw some light upon it from other Scriptures. And, as the basis of our theme, we will take two verses from the Sermon on the Mount;—

"Ye heard[1] that it was said to them of old time, Thou shalt not kill, and whosoever shall kill shall be in danger of the Judgment.

"But I say unto you, that every one who is angry with his brother shall be in danger of the Judgment; and whosoever shall say to his brother, Thou fool, shall be in danger of the Council; and whosoever shall say, Thou rebel against God, shall be in danger of the Fiery Valley of Hinnom."[2]

[1] Both the Authorised Version and the Revised incorrectly render "ye have heard."

[2] Matt. v. 21, 22.

359

Before we endeavour to penetrate to the meaning of these verses, it may be well to mention, that in saying, " Ye heard," and not, " Ye have read," the Lord points to a well known fact. For, when the Jews returned from the Babylonian captivity, the common people had forgotten their own language, and could no longer read or understand the Hebrew Scriptures. It was, therefore, the plain duty of the few learned among them to provide an accurate translation of the inspired books into the Aramaic dialect, which had then become the tongue of the masses.

But quite another thought was in their hearts : they preferred to seize their opportunity of retaining the source of Divine knowledge in their own custody, in order that they might get glory to themselves by doling it out at will to the people. And so, they made no translation which all men might peruse, but were wont to read off, from the sacred rolls in the synagogues, a paraphrastic rendering, supposed to be simpler than the original, and interspersed with their own explanatory remarks. Thus the people, unable to read the Law for themselves or to know anything of it, except through the loose renderings and biassed expositions of their teachers, too often failed to distinguish between the text and the human additions to it. And in this manner the Word of God was corrupted, and innumerable errors were received as Divine truths.

In the present time, also, we suffer in a somewhat similar way. For many traditional interpretations, which, if they be investigated, cannot be honestly maintained, and may often be traced to very unsatisfactory sources, pass current among us for Bible doctrine. How careful, then, should we be to prove all things, and to hold fast only that which is true ! For we have not the same excuse as the Jewish people. The Word of God, rendered plainly into our own tongue, is in our hands, and we can all read and study it for ourselves. Great, therefore, are our responsibilities.

Now, in the verses which we are considering, we have a specimen of the errors taught in the synagogues; for, in quoting the sixth commandment, the Lord does not confine Himself to pure Scripture, but gives it as the Scribes and Pharisees did, repeating what the people had heard from them.

"Thou shalt not kill" was, indeed, the law of God, suited to the immediate case of the Israelites in the condition in which they were brought out of Egypt, and capable of expansion into the widest spiritual meaning, as those to whom it was addressed advanced in experience and knowledge. For it did not deal with murder as a case for the judicial courts of men, but of its aspect before the Judgment-seat of the Living God. And, as men became more spiritually minded, they would perceive, that, if He Who desires truth in the inward parts condemns murder, He manifestly condemns, also, everything that might possibly lead to that crime. And hence they would sooner or later discover that "Thou shalt not kill" means, Thou shalt not hate.

But the Pharisees cut short the process, and did away with the possibility of arriving at the real meaning of the commandment, by confusing it with another of an altogether different character, which referred to the act of killing as an outward crime for the consideration of the judicial courts below.[1]

"And whosoever shall kill," was their gloss, "shall be in danger of the Judgment." Thus they gave the commandment a merely outward sense, and by the

[1] Exod. xxi. 12; Lev. xxiv. 17.

suggestion of earthly courts, removed the wholesome terrors of the great Judgment to Come, when the Omniscient God will search, not only into the outward actions of men, but also into their inmost thoughts, and will account the murderer in desire or intention equally guilty with the murderer in deed. For the sin of the former is in no way diminished because God has restrained him, by depriving him either of his courage or of his opportunity.

It is thus apparent, that by the words, " Ye heard," the Lord does not imply knowledge of the pure Word of God ; but refers to the distorted defective and powerless expositions of the Scribes and Pharisees. These did not disturb the slumbering consciences of men ; but, when He expounds the Word, how instantly does it flash through soul and spirit ! For He shows, that, although murder was the outward act condemned, amid the thunderings of Sinai, as the fearful culmination of the evil within, yet the law reaches to the very earliest feeling that might ultimately lead to murder, even to that of unexpressed resentment. And the same fact is also plainly declared by His beloved disciple in the words ; —" Whosoever hateth his brother is a murderer." [1]

The Lord now proceeds to mention three degrees of hatred which would render men liable to punishment under the sixth commandment : first, the hidden resentment ; then, the milder term of insult ; lastly, the stronger word of bitter wrath that will stop at nothing. Further than this He does not go ; for even the Pharisees would have admitted the justice of punishment for assault and violence.

It is probable that the word which the Authorised Version renders " without a cause " is spurious, since it

---

[1] 1 John iii. 15.

is omitted in several manuscripts. But, whether this be the case or not, the meaning of the passage remains much the same. For, even if " without a cause " be not expressed, it must, nevertheless, be understood ; since a comparison of other texts shows that anger is not absolutely evil.

There may, possibly, be times when a righteous indignation is permitted to the people of God ; only, however, in cases of wilful and malignant opposition, when, with the utmost exercise of love, it is impossible to say, " They know not what they do." " Be ye angry and sin not," says Paul ; but he quickly indicates how brief the feeling must be by adding, " Let not the sun go down upon your wrath : neither give place to the Devil."

If, therefore, we do essay to exercise this somewhat perilous feeling, we must be careful that the motive is really a zealous love of God, and not the mere selfish temper of an unregenerate man. We must judge ourselves severely in such a matter, and by no means allow a corrupt mind to justify its resentment for a real or supposed offence against itself by falsely calling it anger for God's sake.

The first word of insult, Raca, signifies 'empty,' ' vain,' or ' worthless,'—the English ' fool ' in its ordinary sense ; and is often used by Jewish writers as a term of contemptuous scorn.

The second, generally assumed to be Greek, is, in that case, correctly rendered by ' fool ' ; but must be understood in the peculiar sense of ' godless,' or ' reprobate,' which is a frequent meaning of ' fool ' in Scripture. Since, however, the Hebrew form Raca is retained in the first term of contempt, it seems natural to seek a Hebrew derivation for the second also. It will then be identical with מוֹרֶה a "rebel," the very word which Moses used ; when he spake unadvisedly with his lips, and said ;—" Hear now, ye rebels, must we fetch you water out of this rock ? " For the continual provocation of the Israelites had, at last, exhausted his patience ; and, forgetting how often he had previously deprecated the wrath of the Almighty, he was so carried away by his own indignation, that he dared to judge as only God may judge, and to condemn the people as rebels against heaven and against himself. But, because of the spirit of this hasty speech,[1] he was deprived of the Promised Land, and doomed to die in the wilderness.

Here, then, we may, perhaps, get a clue to the intensity of the sin of calling another ' rebel ' ; that is, ' rebel against God.' For whoever does this assumes, that, because he can bear no longer with his fellow, the patience of God is exhausted ; thinks that the will of the Most High must needs follow the leadings of his petty spite, and arrogates to himself the right of acting as God by adjudging his adversary to perdition.

And so, the Lord declares, that he who cherishes secret resentment is in danger of the Judgment ; and that he who would destroy another's character and influence among his fellows, so as to annihilate him out of his own way, is in danger of the Council ; while he who would consign his offending brother to the perdition of sinners, as an enemy of God, is himself in danger of the Fiery Valley.

Now, in the Judgment, the Council, and the Fiery Valley of Hinnom, there is a manifest reference to the Israelitish courts of law.

The Judgment points to the local courts which God commanded to be established in every city, and which

---

[1] Psa. cvi. 32–3.

sat in the gate.[1] No further particulars respecting them are given in Scripture; but Josephus tells us, that each of them consisted of seven judges, and had the power of inflicting death by the sword.

The Council is the Sanhedrim, the origin of which may be traced to the command to appoint a supreme Council, composed of priests Levites and the judge of those days, in the place which God would choose, that is, in Jerusalem.[2] This assembly had the power of inflicting death by stoning.

But it might also intensify the punishment by ordering the corpse of the malefactor to be thrown into the Valley of Hinnom, where it was either burnt or devoured by worms.

This valley of Hinnom, which is here called "the Gehenna of Fire, or "the Fiery Valley of Hinnom," [3] was on the south side of Jerusalem. On the brow of the hill that overlooked it—"the mount that is before Jerusalem"—Solomon built high places for Chemosh and for Moloch, and here the abominable rites were performed, and the children made to pass through the fire.[4] At the eastern extremity of the valley was Tophet, where in later times the custom of actually sacrificing children to Moloch was practised, having been, apparently, introduced in the reign of Ahaz,[5] and continued by Manasseh.

[1] Deut. xvi. 18.
[2] Deut. xvii. 8–13.
[3] Γέεννα for גֵּיא הִנֹּם‎.
[4] This rite was a sort of fire-baptism.
[5] Up to that time, Jewish children were only made to pass through the fire, apparently as a kind of purifying baptism (Lev. xviii. 21) in which they were neither burnt nor slain. But, in the days of Ahaz, they were actually sacrificed; for of that king we are told, in 2 Chron. xxviii. 3, that he "burnt his children in the fire, according to the abominations of the peoples whom

In order to put a stop to these abominations, Josiah
defiled the valley, and rendered it ceremonially
unclean, "that no man might make his son or his
daughter to pass through the fire to Moloch."[1]   From
that time it seems to have become the common cess-
pool of Jerusalem, into which the sewage of the city
flowed, and where it was customary to cast the dead
bodies of executed criminals, the carcases of animals,
and every kind of offal and corruption.   It is said,
moreover, that perpetual fires were kept burning there
for the purpose of consuming the filth.   And so, from
the accumulation of horrors that were connected with
it, Tophet became to the Jews a vivid type of the
place of the lost.

XLV

THE JUDICIAL COURTS OF ANGELS

SUCH, then, appears to be the literal meaning of the
Judgment, the Council, and the Fiery Valley of

the Lord cast out before the children of Israel."   In the corresponding passage, 2 Kings xvi. 3, the reading is different and
runs as follows ;—"Yea, and he made his son to pass through
the fire, according to the abominations of the peoples whom the
Lord cast out before the children of Israel."   But here the "Yea"
evidently points to something new, and a comparison with
2 Chron. xxviii. 3, shows that the milder term is not used, as
ordinarily, for the baptism of fire, but for the actual burning
of the children.   And, probably, we must interpret 2 Kings xxi. 6,
in the same way.

The prevalence of the horrid rite in later times is indicated
by Jeremiah's charges against the children of Judah, that they
had "built the high places of Tophet, which is in the valley
of the son of Hinnom, to burn their sons and their daughters
in the fire" (Jer. vii. 31).   And in Ezekiel, also, we read "Thou
hast slain My children, and delivered them up in causing them
to pass through the fire unto them"——that is, unto Moloch and
kindred deities (Ezek. xvi. 21).

[1] 2 Kings xxiii. 10.

Hinnom, to which the Lord here alludes. Evidently, however, He does not intend us to understand them in a literal sense, but rather as figures of something beyond them. For it is not possible that concealed anger should bring a man under the jurisdiction of any earthly courts. Doubtless, then, the Lord is speaking of heavenly judgments; for to them alone it belongs to search the heart and to try the reins.

This fact has been very generally recognized; and, accordingly, the Lord has been supposed to have pointed to the final punishments of the wicked under the figures of the Judgment, the Council, and the Fiery Valley.

But there is a strong objection to such a view; for, since His words are absolutely perfect, we must not imagine that we fully comprehend anything that He teaches us through the medium of earthly figures, unless our interpretation explains every particular in each figure. If, then, we adopt the common exposition in this case, how are we to account for the introduction of two courts, an inferior and local assize, as well as the high court in the metropolis? How, too, for the fact, that, whereas the punishments of the local courts ceased with death, the supreme authority might also commit the dead body to the flames? Is it possible to explain these particulars of the final Judgment, where there will be but one Judge, and but one sentence, in kind, at least, however it may vary in degree?

May not the Lord be alluding rather to the present spiritual government of the world, a mysterious subject concerning which many scattered hints may be found in Scripture, though they attract but little attention? For the minds of men are, almost universally, set upon things visible and material; and this is true also of many believers, who are wont to think more of their sects and organizations than of their Lord, and of the things which, though not seen, are far more real than those which are now visible. Few stay to reflect, that all the sights which feast their eyes in this short life are but as a painted curtain which must soon be withdrawn for ever, in order that the eternal existences may be revealed. They speak of that which happens as an accident, or a natural consequence, and seem to have little suspicion that every event is brought about and regulated by unseen spiritual powers.

Nevertheless, the Word of God plainly teaches us that such is the case, that there is such an Authority of the Air, and that even the operations of fire[1] and water,[2] and all the so called laws of nature, are kept in force by appointed angels.[3]

Satan, as we know, continues even now to be the Prince of the World and of the Authority of the Air, so that his angels still constitute the regular spiritual powers of the earth. But God, although He has not yet cast them down from their high places, interferes with and limits their influence by appointing loyal angels to protect His people, and to serve on behalf of those who shall inherit salvation.

These angels have each his appointed post: they are governed by princes of God;[4] and knowing well the general laws of His dealings with men, and, to a certain extent, it may be, His particular will in regard

---

[1] Rev. xiv. 18.   [2] Rev. xvi. 5.   [3] Rev. vii. 1.
[4] Apparently, the Thrones, Dominions, Principalities, and Powers, of Col. i. 16. "The Four and Twenty Elders" of Rev. iv. 4, would seem to be the Thrones.

to the individuals, families, churches, or nations, committed to their charge, they are, perhaps, for the rest, left to their own discretion in carrying out His purposes. And it is, probably, their deliberations respecting the course which they should pursue, and decisions as to the penalties to be inflicted, which are referred to by the Lord as "the Judgment." Indeed, it is not improbable that the local courts of Israel were established after the pattern of the angelic, even as the Tabernacle and its furniture were a copy from heavenly things.

Perhaps, the most instructive instance of an angelic court to be found in the Bible is that which is given in the fourth chapter of Daniel. When the great King of Babylon, as he drifted ever further and further from God, was ceasing to show mercy to the poor and beginning to ascribe to himself all the glory of his might, the angelic "watchers," into whose charge he had been delivered, seem to have held their court, and to have decided that he must receive a warning, which, if it should prove ineffectual, should be followed by a severe chastisement.

Accordingly, Nebuchadnezzar was made to see a dream which terrified him, and thoughts came to him upon his couch, and visions into his head, which troubled him. He beheld the lofty and wide-spreading tree which represented himself in all his majesty and power ; and, as he gazed upon it, "a watcher and an holy one" came down from heaven, and declared its doom. And what authority did the angel claim : what court had pronounced the judgment which he declared ? "This sentence," he said, "is by the decree of the watchers, and the demand by the word of the holy ones: to the intent that the living may know,

24

that the Most High ruleth in the kingdom of men, and giveth it to whomsoever He will, and setteth up over it the lowest of men."

These watchers, then, were appointed to vindicate the majesty of God, and to curb aud correct the sin of His servant Nebuchadnezzar. And in performing their duty, they seem to have acted upon the wisdom which He had given to them, and their knowledge of His will, without any immediate command from Himself.

How absolute the judicial powers sometimes entrusted to these watchers are, we may see in the case of the angel who was sent down to go before the Israelites in the wilderness. For God Himself gave the caution ;—" Beware of him, and obey his voice; provoke him not: for he will not pardon your transgression ; for My Name is in him." [1] He had received his instructions from God, and knew exactly where forbearance must cease and chastisement begin. He had no commission to pardon, but only to enforce the laws of God. Diligently, therefore, must the Israelites avoid sin, lest, perchance, they should step over the fatal line, and so render themselves liable to the inexorable punishments of their celestial leader.

Some will have it that the angel is Christ Himself, but that is a confusion. Whenever God is mentioned in the history of the wilderness-wanderings, the Second and not the First Person of the Glorious and Ever-blessed Trinity is indicated. And this fact is evident from, at least, three considerations.

First, it was impossible that the Father should approach the camp of Israel, because His Holy Presence could not have endured the proximity of sin,

[1] Exod. xxiii. 21.

but would instantly have become to it a consuming fire. Hence He is never mentioned as visiting our earth, until sin has been finally expelled from it, and Death, the last enemy, cast into the Lake of Fire and Brimstone. Then the Tabernacle of God will be with men, and He shall dwell with them.[1]

Secondly, Moses saw the Person of the Trinity Who was with Israel in the wilderness; but "no man hath seen God"—that is, as the context shows, the Father—"at any time: the Only Begotten Son, Which is in the bosom of the Father, He hath declared Him." [2]

Lastly, Paul tells us plainly, that it was Christ Who was tempted and provoked during the journeyings in the wilderness.[3]

Whenever, therefore, God is mentioned in immediate connection with the Israelites, we may be sure that Christ is the Person of the Blessed Trinity Who is particularly intended. Hence it is impossible to identify Christ with the angel whom He promised to send.[4] Indeed, a little farther on in the Book of Exodus, He declares that the angel would be substituted for Himself; for that He would not go up in the midst of so stiffnecked a people, lest he should consume them in the way.[5]

It is thus clear, that the angel was not Christ, but a created being: nor is it difficult to discover his name.

[1] Rev. xxi. 3. Comp. vv, 22, 23; also xxii. 3.
[2] John i. 18.
[3] I Cor. x. 9. There is good authority for the reading Χριστόν, though the R. V. has preferred Κύριον; and it seems more likely that the somewhat unexpected name " Christ " should have been changed into " the Lord," than that the text should have been corrupted in the other way.
[4] Exod. xxiii. 20, 23; xxxii. 34.
[5] Exod. xxxiii. 2, 3.

For, as we have elsewhere remarked,[1] the archangel Michael is described to Daniel as "your Prince,"[2] and as "the great Prince which standeth for the children of thy people."[3]   These phrases certainly imply that he is, by God's appointment, the spiritual ruler and protector of Israel.   And we are also told that their final deliverance will be effected by his agency.[4]   Even thus far, then, since Michael was the Prince of Israel in Daniel's time, and will be so until the great restoration, it would seem likely that he also went before them in the days of old, and led them into Canaan.   But the matter is put beyond a doubt by the well-known passage in Jude,[5] where Michael is found contending with Satan for the body of Moses, the Prince of God's people in collision with his inevitable foe, the Prince of this world.

Another probable instance of the judgment of angelic courts occurs in the twelfth chapter of "Acts."   For there the death of Herod Agrippa seems to be attributed to an angel, not specially instructed by God at the moment, but, apparently, acting upon fixed laws. Hence we are told, that, as soon as the vain king allowed himself to be saluted as a god, "immediately an angel of the Lord smote him, because he gave not God the glory."[6]   In the swelling of his pride, he strode recklessly over the limit which the Most High had set to His forbearance, and was instantly cut down by the sword of the angelic watcher.

Sometimes, however, God interferes, and holds men

[1] See *The Great Prophecies of the Centuries concerning Israel and the Gentiles*, p. 379 and note.
[2] Dan. x. 21.
[3] Dan. xii. 1.
[4] Dan. xii. 1. Comp. Rev. xii. 7–9.
[5] Jude 9.
[6] Acts xii. 20–23

back from the fatal boundary; and how striking an instance of this does the case of Balaam afford! For, as the disobedient prophet was hurrying to the king of Moab, intent upon gain and altogether forgetful of God, his ass suddenly turned aside from the road into a field. He smote her, and forced her back into the road; but she thrust herself in terror against a wall, and crushed his foot. He smote her again; but a third time she refused to go forward, and, finding that she could turn neither to the right nor to the left, she threw herself down beneath him. Then in anger he smote her with his staff; but God opened her mouth, and she rebuked his madness by asking whether she had been wont so to act in past time, and thereby suggesting the question, " Is there not now a cause?"

At that moment Balaam's eyes were opened, and, lo, so blinded had he been by greed, so impaired were his spiritual faculties by disobedience, that the very beast on which he rode had been the first to see a threatening form in the way, even the angel of the Lord with a drawn sword in his hand.

Balaam fell upon his face in abject fear; for in an instant he comprehended the situation, and realized his danger. He had gone to the very edge of the bounds which God had set for him, to the margin of the line which divided life from destruction: there was but a step between him and death.

Twice the angel had taken his stand so that there might be some possibility of turning aside, some hope of escaping his sword; but Balaam had not perceived him, nor felt the influence of his presence. Unconscious of spiritual things, and eager only for sordid gain, he had urged his reluctant beast to the very brink of death. But now the angel had placed himself in a

narrow part of the road, where there was no possibility of turning either to the right hand or to the
left. The end of forbearance had come : if Balaam
had again attempted to pass, his body would have
fallen lifeless to the ground. But the ass dropped
beneath him, and for the third time saved her master's
life.

Most instructive is the history. The way of Balaam
was perverse before the Lord ; and, therefore, while
he was journeying, the angel of the Lord came forth
to withstand him. The judgment had sat, the decision
had been given, and the limits laid down. If Balaam
passed a certain part of the road in the mind with
which he started—which, doubtless, was to speak the
word that Balak desired, and be promoted to great
honour—the inexorable sword of the angel should hew
him down. And this would have been the end, had
not God caused the ass to see the minister of vengeance,
and to turn aside ; so that a little longer space for
repentance might be given to the prophet.

Let us remember this when we are too eagerly pur-
suing some earthly gain or pleasure, busying ourselves
with the furtherance of our own will in forgetfulness of
God. The unseen angel of the Lord is in the way
with a drawn sword in his hand ; and, as we hasten
on our path, we cannot tell whether our next step
may not cross the fatal line.

Do we find obstructions in the way : are there
hindrances that retard our speed, or force us to turn
aside ? Let not our heart grow bitter with anger :
for these things, contemptible and troublesome as they
may seem, are, perhaps, intended in God's mercy to
act the part of Balaam's ass to us, to check our head-
long career before we reach the spot where the invisible

minister of chastisement, and, it may be, of death, has taken his final stand.

If we would but meditate on these judgments of the Lord, we should be constrained to pray more earnestly for the Spirit of Truth, Who Alone can guide us safely through the thickset perils of this dark world: and how humble and submissive would our hearts become! For, much as he may vaunt his liberty, man is subject to a government strong, irresistible, and, if defied, inexorable. Around every believer in the Lord Jesus two circles are drawn: if he overstep the first, he will find himself in the midst of perplexity and affliction: if he pass beyond the second, he is confronted with the Angel of Death.

Death, that is, of the body: for the redeemed cannot perish everlastingly, because their salvation depends, not upon themselves, but upon their Divine Substitute. Yet sometimes, perhaps we should say often, the penalty of temporal death is inflicted even upon the saved. If they abuse their privileges, and become unfruitful: if they fall into disobedience, and allow themselves to be blinded by the god of this age: if they be guilty of scandalous conduct, and so give occasion to the adversaries of the Lord to blaspheme, wrath may go forth from Him and consume them. He may cut them off from the earth; take away their hope of promotion; suffer them not to plant or to water in the vineyard; save them naked, as it were, like one who is just able to escape with his life from a burning house; bring them, indeed, at last, into life, but to find no treasure laid up for them, to feel that they have no works done in Christ to follow them, and to be their joy and crown of glory in the day of His appearing.

So, as we have already seen, did He deal with the

church at Corinth, when, because of their carnality, many among its members were weak and sickly, and many even slept. And, from the instances which we have been considering, these divers diseases and sundry kinds of death appear, sometimes at least, to be inflicted, in accordance with fixed laws, by the local courts of angelic watchers, to which our Lord would seem to be referring when He speaks of the Judgment, and to the cognizance of which His people become liable, if they even so much as allow a secret feeling of resentment to abide in their hearts.

Among the children of the world, the action of these courts is not so easy to trace. For the angels of God seem for the present to have but little concern with those who are under the jurisdiction of Satan ; except when their hatred to the people of the Lord Jesus is beginning to exceed its permitted bounds. Then the angelic watchers are well aware of the charge given to them to suffer no infringement of the Divinely inspired saying ;—

" Surely the wrath of man shall praise Thee :
    The remainder of wrath shalt Thou restrain." [1]

Therefore, whenever the wrath of man is rising higher than is necessary for the discipline of the people of God, the angelic watchers begin to interfere, and the power of the wicked is curtailed, or, perhaps, suddenly destroyed. For the people of God may be oppressed, but they must not be straitened ; thrown into perplexity, but they must not be driven into despair ; persecuted, but they shall never be forsaken ; smitten down, yet they may not be destroyed.

[1] Psa. lxxvi. 10.

XLVI

THE COURT OF GOD

WHILE, then, the local courts of Israel seem to be alluded to as a type of the judicial action of angels, it is not difficult to discover a higher spiritual authority corresponding to the supreme council at Jerusalem. From many examples, we know that God Himself comes down from time to time, to receive the reports of His angels, and to hold a great assize for the decision of cases which are too important, or too hard, for them.

Such a Court is described in the Book of Job, where we read, that, on a certain day, the sons of God came to present themselves before the Lord, and Satan came also among them. And then the wisdom of the great Judge was wonderfully shown forth. For, seeing in Job a fault of which the patriarch's own heart was unconscious, He delivered him to Satan to be sifted as wheat, that he might be brought to know himself, and to understand the righteousness of God. And, although the Adversary inflicted his reckless and cruel stripes in pure malignity, not waiting to try gentle measures at first, but at once going to the very extreme of the limit permitted to him; nevertheless, his malice was made to bring forth good. Job was purified: and his faith was so enlarged that he bewailed his hasty expressions of discontent, and resolved no more, by questioning God's wisdom and goodness, to utter that which he understood not, things too wonderful for him, which he knew not.

Another Court of God was seen by Micaiah, when he beheld the Lord sitting upon His Throne, and all the hosts of heaven standing by Him, on His right hand and on His left. It was a great assembly, in which the doom of the recreant and idolatrous king of Israel was determined and decreed.

That, again, was a Council of peculiar solemnity which the Lord and His angels held over the cities of the plain, when He came down to see if their wickedness was according to the cry of it. Little did the sensual Sodomites and the godless inhabitants of Gomorrah imagine, on that fatal day, that they were being weighed in the balances of God and found miserably wanting. They were thinking, as ever, of business pleasure or ease, and knew not that they had filled up the measure of their iniquities, that the decree had gone forth, and that, ere the morrow's sun had reached mid-heaven, they would have bidden a last farewell to his pleasant light, and have found themselves naked and shivering prisoners in the rayless dungeons of Hades.

But the Lord Himself reveals, even more plainly, the manner of these dread Councils, and their connection with events upon earth, in a memorable passage contained in the twelfth and thirteenth chapters of Luke's Gospel. He had been speaking solemn words to His Own disciples; and, meanwhile, a great multitude had gathered around the little group, a multitude irrepentant and self-satisfied; caring little for what He was saying, and comprehending it still less; ready enough to have their sick healed; eager even to follow Him, if He would but raise the standard of the Son of David, lead a revolt against the Romans, and restore the Kingdom to Israel; but utterly indifferent to His spiritual teaching, and to His mission to save His people from their sins.

As soon, then, as He had finished His discourse to

the disciples, He turned to this multitude, and addressed them with a stern sorrow. Why was it that they were so capable of interpreting appearances and movements in the sky, of deciding whether a storm or heat was to be expected, and yet could not discern the signs of that season of grace, that time of their visitation? Hypocrites that they were : it was because, much as they affected to venerate the things of God, they really cared for them not at all ; and, therefore, would not trouble to search into eternal realities even as diligently as they did into the tokens of the weather for one short day. Could they not understand, even of themselves and without any further teaching, the great problem of life which lay before every man, and what they ought to do in their gravest of circumstances? Certainly the power was with them ; but the desire to exercise it they had not. Then He would, at least, give them His advice upon the momentous subject ;—

"As thou art going with thine adversary before the magistrate, on the way give diligence to be quit of him ; lest haply he hale thee unto the judge, and the judge deliver thee unto the officer, and the officer shall cast thee into prison. I say unto thee, Thou shalt by no means come out thence, till thou hast paid the very last mite."

Here the Lord, apparently, alludes to Roman law, which He thus recognizes as supreme in Judæa—the time being that of the Fourth World-power. By it the creditor had the right of summoning his debtor to follow him to the magistrate's court. But, while they were on the way thither, it was still open to them to settle matters amicably between themselves, without the interference of the authorities. If, however, they once crossed the threshold of the court, the power of arrangement was taken out of the hands of both parties, and thenceforth the debt was regarded as a crime to be dealt with by the state, and which could neither be condoned nor compromised. Thus, when the summons had once been served, the only opportunity left to the debtor for obtaining a favourable settlement was during the short time occupied by the walk to the court.

Such was the striking figure which the Lord made use of to depict the real meaning of our present earth-life. For His advice presented at the same time a complete and simple view of the circumstances in which we all find ourselves, as soon as our eyes are opened to spiritual realities. We cannot, indeed, altogether comprehend these circumstances; since, at present, the Supreme God does not reveal the cause of His actions, nor give any account of His matters; for, if He should do so, there would be no room left for the saving exercise of faith.

Yet, although we do not know why or how, we are, nevertheless, well aware that each of us comes into this world conceived in sin and shapen in iniquity. And, consequently, the brand of death is at once set upon us by the violated Law of God, which thenceforth becomes our Adversary, and leads us along the road of life, our debt continually increasing as we go, until we arrive at the Judgment-court.

Yet, so long as we are still on the way, there is permission, at least, to settle the debt and avoid its terrible penalty, if we can find a means to do so. But, if we are once made to cross the threshold of the Court, which is death, there is then nothing for us but the inexorable Judge, the officer, and the hopeless prison. For "it is appointed unto men once to die, and after this comes judgment."

Such is our Lord's exposition of the present life, His revelation of its awful, though to most men concealed, meaning. Can we wonder that He urges upon us the supreme importance of procuring deliverance from our fearful Adversary, before the short, the uncertain, opportunity has gone by!

But many may be disposed to say, I do not at all feel that my life answers to this description: on the contrary, it is both pleasant and all-satisfying to me. Perhaps so: the question, however, is, not what easily deceived mortals may feel, but what the Lord declares to be the actual fact. For that *will* make itself felt some day, though Satan may surround us with illusions for a season.

Moreover, we could conceive, that a debtor, when following his adversary to the judgment-court, might occupy himself with gazing upon the attractive wares set out for sale, or with the varied incidents in the streets ; or he might fritter away in trifling conversation his last few minutes under the free light of heaven. But we should think poorly of his sanity, unless he were making the very utmost of his fast-vanishing opportunity by striving to negotiate a compromise, or to beg an extension of time ; or, if he could catch sight of one on the way, by intreating a friend to pay the debt for him.

We, however, cannot compromise with our Adversary : all that is due to God must be paid to the last mite.

An extension of time men have, indeed, often obtained. When they have now come to the Gates of Death, they have earnestly supplicated for a little longer space, and have promised to pay all, if the Lord would but have patience with them. And not seldom their prayer has been graciously heard, and they have been brought up again, from the very jaws of Hades, to the pleasant light of the sun. But the only result was a hopeless increase of the debt ; nor was there any deliverance.

No : there is but one way in which we can be quit of our inexorable Adversary ; and that the Lord could not as yet reveal, for He had not yet died. But we know well, that there is a Friend than Whom none has shown greater love ; for He has laid down His life for us. He stands ever in the highway of the world, through which every burdened sinner must pass on his way to judgment ; and He, if we will suffer Him, will pay the whole debt, and set us free for ever. For He has purchased the right to do so by shedding His Own most pure and precious Blood in place of our forfeited lives. Therefore, He can cry ;—" Verily, verily, I say unto you, He that heareth My word, and believeth Him That sent Me, hath eternal life, and cometh not into judgment, but hath passed out of death into life." And " blessed are all they that put their trust in Him."

Soon after the Lord had uttered the solemn words which we have been considering, some persons ran up, in great excitement, to tell Him of a terrible outrage that had just been perpetrated in the Temple, the murder by Pilate's command of a party of Galilæans.

There was enmity at that time between Herod and Pilate, between the ruler of Galilee and the ruler of Judæa ; and each of them was ready to injure the other, or his subjects, whenever an occasion presented itself. Now some unfortunate Galilæans had business in Jerusalem : it may be, of a secular kind, or, perhaps, they only desired to offer sacrifices in the Temple. They must, probably, have known something of the risk to which they would be exposed ; and we can well imagine their furtive side-glances and timid shrinkings as they threaded the streets with trembling steps. But no harm seems to have befallen them. And, at last, they took their sacrifices to the Temple, rendered, perhaps, a little bolder by their escape so far. Pilate might not after all be so bad as their fears had made him.

And so, they approached the Temple, probably by the Tyropæan Bridge, and passed under the Royal Porch into the Court of the Gentiles. Over its pavement of variegated marble they walked on, until they turned towards the Eastern entrance of the enclosure, and came into full view of the blazing plates of gold with which Herod had covered the façade of the building. Then they passed the notices that no Gentile might penetrate farther into the precincts on pain of death, and so ascended the white marble steps of the Gate Beautiful, which led into the Court of the Women. There they could breathe more freely ; they were now beyond the reach of their foes ; for, verily, not even Pilate himself would dare to violate that sacred enclosure. And, finally, with awed hearts and slower pace, they mounted the flight of fifteen white-glistening steps, passed through the Gate of Nicanor, and stood, in the double Court of Israel and the Priests, before the Great Porch of the Sanctuary with the Altar and the Laver in front of it. All their fears were now dismissed : there no harm could possibly befall them ; they were in the safest place in the whole world. And so, the priests received the animals for sacrifice, and turned them towards the West : the hands of the offerers were laid upon them, and the rite was proceeding in due course.

But, hark! what is that unwonted noise? Surely it cannot be the measured tramp of soldiers marching across the Court of the Women! Is the world turned upside down! Whether it be or not, there is no possibility of mistaking that tramp. It draws nearer: it is upon the steps of the Court of Israel! See the glittering spear-heads and the flash of brazen helmets, as the Gate of Nicanor is thrust open! A Roman cohort is rushing lawlessly upon the Galilæans, and their blood is soon flowing into the channels that are carrying off the blood of their sacrifices. They have fallen down slain in the safest place, and at the most unlikely time, that could be conceived.

Very possibly the persons who related this sad story to the Lord may have added their own comments. "How wicked," they may have said, "must these men have been, whom God abandoned to such a fate! How great must have been His abhorrence of them, seeing that He allowed them to meet with a violent and unexpected end even in that most secure of all places, His Own Sanctuary; and that, in His wrath, He permitted their blood to be mingled with that of their sacrifices!" But whether they openly expressed such a sentiment or not, we may, at least, infer from the Lord's reply, that something like it was in their hearts. The men of that age were just as ready as those of our own days to moralize upon the connection of sin and calamity in the case of others, without a thought of their own liability to the same awful law.

But the Lord sternly rebuked this foolish attempt to evade the true lesson of the catastrophe, which He pressed home with the words;—

"Think ye that these Galilæans were sinners

above all the Galilæans, because they have suffered these things? I tell you, Nay: but, except ye repent, ye shall all in like manner perish.

"Or those eighteen, upon whom the tower in Siloam fell and killed them, think ye that they were debtors"—that is, to God—"above all the men that dwell in Jerusalem? I tell you, Nay: but, except ye repent, ye shall all likewise perish."

The judgments of God are not intended to give us an opportunity of finding faults in others, but as a solemn warning to ourselves. The second calamity which the Lord mentions was, doubtless, a recent event that had been much talked of in Jerusalem. Contemporary writers give us no information respecting it; but, from our knowledge of Eastern customs, we may suppose that it, probably, took place in the evening; that the eighteen may have wended their various ways from different parts of the city, and arrived one after another, or in twos and threes, at the base of the tower. There they, perhaps, reclined beneath the frowning wall to enjoy the cool of the day, and, it may be, began such trifling conversation as usually arises in a fortuitous gathering. But suddenly they were startled by an awful sound from above, and, looking up, saw the vast wall descending upon them. A wild shriek rent the air, but was quickly stifled in the crash of the falling masonry, and in a moment the eighteen were crushed out of life.

But neither were those unfortunates necessarily worse than other men. No: they had had their opportunity of understanding, and profiting by, the present life: their allotted time of visitation had passed by, hour by hour, day by day, year by year, until, at last, it was gone: the decree had been issued; and they

25

had, accordingly, been gathered by the Angel of Death to the appointed place of slaughter. For such frightful catastrophes are no mere accident; but the execution of the deliberate judgment of the Almighty.

The Lord has now disclosed the inner and real meaning of our unregenerate life upon earth—in its whole extent from birth to death—that it is simply a hurried progress to judgment. And He has also warned us, by two examples, that death, which ends our opportunities and delivers us to the Judge, may take place suddenly, in most unlikely places and times, and by most unexpected means. But to those who have ears to hear He will reveal yet more, though only in a parable; and will explain to them still more clearly the connection between the Council in the Heavens and catastrophes on earth.

"A certain man had a fig-tree planted in his vineyard; and he came seeking fruit thereon, and found none. And he said unto the vinedresser, Behold, these three years I come seeking fruit on this fig-tree, and find none: cut it down; why doth it, also, cumber the ground? And he answering saith unto him, Lord, let it alone this year also, till I shall dig about it, and dung it. And if it bear fruit, well: but if not, after that thou shalt cut it down."

There should be little difficulty in interpreting these simple words, if we remember what has preceded them.

Every one who has been made to hear the truth is as a fig-tree planted in the vineyard of the Most High, and planted, too, for one purpose only—that he may bring forth fruit unto God. Now, at all times, indeed, do His eyes behold, His eyelids try, the children of men. But there are also stated seasons, though we know them not, when He passes by to test the condition of those in whom He has placed the potentiality of bearing fruit to Himself. So we are told that He tried, or proved, Abraham on a special occasion;[1] and also, that, when the princes of Babylon came to Hezekiah, "God left him, to try him, that He might know all that was in his heart."[2]

The earthly husbandman will look upon that which he has planted, in the first year and in the second, and will feel no disappointment at his failure to find fruit, because he knows that the tree has not yet had time to mature. But, in the third year, he deems it fair to form his judgment; for if the tree be still without fruit, there is then little chance that it will ever bear: it is barren, and must be removed.

So does God patiently wait during the period of our immaturity: but, at the time which corresponds to the third year in the case of the tree, that is, when it is now due season for the grace that has been given to exhibit itself in works, He comes again. And, if He still finds nothing but leaves, then the Council is held.

He speaks with the Vinedresser, the Head of the Church—for to Him all judgment is committed—and bids Him fell the tree, cut short the wasted, and, therefore, also corrupting, life.

But He, Who ever liveth to make intercession for us, pleads for a little longer trial, for yet one year more. Ordinary means have, indeed, failed: but He will dig about the tree with the spade of affliction, and loosen, and, where necessary, sever, the too spreading roots which bind it to earth, and are wasting underground that strength which ought to be sending forth sweet fruit toward the light of heaven. He will also supply

[1] Gen. xxii. 1.   [2] 2 Chron. xxxii. 31.

it with more nourishment; so that, if it should be induced by its altered circumstances to make fresh efforts, it may not lack anything that can help it. In plain terms, the man who is represented by the tree shall be disturbed and troubled; his heart shall be thrilled with pain, or anguished by bereavements or by loss of that upon which he has fixed his desires. The brightness of his life shall become overcast and dark: he shall be minished and brought low through oppression, affliction, and sorrow. But, at the same time, his spiritual aids shall be increased. The Spirit of God will plead more powerfully with him; and, perhaps, will also send to him a messenger, an interpreter, one among a thousand, to show unto him the righteousness and the love of God.

If these means produce the desired effect, then is it well with the man; but, if not, the sentence goes forth. There is some sudden catastrophe, an attack of some fatal malady, some occurrence which men, who see not the sword of the Destroyer, call an accident; and the decree of the Council has been executed: the barren tree no longer cumbers the ground.

XLVII

The Final Sentence. Conclusion

Such, then, seems to be the spiritual signification of the Judgment and the Council. As regards the extreme penalty inflicted by the latter, namely, the consignment of the body after death to the Fiery Valley of Hinnom, that also will readily find its antitype.

For the Great God, the Almighty Creator, can not

only kill the body, but has also power to cast both body and soul into Hell. His Own people He chastises in life, and sometimes even punishes them with temporal death. But to those rebels who will not accept the conditions of pardon, who trample under foot the Blood of the Son of God——to them trouble will not cease with the execution of the sentence, "Dust thou art, and unto dust shalt thou return"; nor even with the setting of the Great White Throne. For, having refused to learn submission in the acceptable time, having despised the days of their visitation, they will, at the close of those days, be consigned, first, to the prison of Hades, and then, after the final Judgment, to the "Lake of Fire and Brimstone."

Terrible, then, are the warnings conveyed by the Lord under the figures of the Judgment, the Council, and the Fiery Valley of Hinnom. Primarily, indeed, He is speaking of but one kind of sin ; but His words manifestly apply to every transgression disobedience and iniquity, whether in thought, in word, or in deed. And they disclose the awful fact, that we are under the continual surveillance of watchers, who, though unseen, behold our every action, by night as well as by day, penetrate even to the inmost thoughts of our bosom, and, in accordance with the fixed laws of God, inflict punishment that may involve the death of the body.

Nor is this all ; for, at certain unknown times, the Lord Himself passes by, to see, and to judge.

Let us never suffer this awful truth to fall out of our remembrance ; for, at any moment, He may be deciding our fate. There is no stir in the air when

He comes by : neither the swift strong wind goes
before Him, nor the earthquake, nor the devouring
fire : He veils the dazzling light of His Presence.   But,
if ever we are deferring something which the love of
Christ should constrain us to do at once ; if ever we
are disposed to careless ease, saying in our hearts, My
Lord delayeth His coming ; if ever we are about to
indulge in some secretly cherished sin ; if ever we feel
that we have a lie upon our lips ; if ever we are being
carried away by the gaiety and frivolity of those with
whom we dwell—in these and all similar temptations,
let us violently check ourselves with the thought, It
may be that this is the very moment of the Lord's
visitation : it may be that He is even now standing
above to judge !

THE MYSTERIES AND CATHOLICISM

XLVIII

THE GREAT RELIGIOUS FEATURE OF ANTIQUITY

WHOEVER with unbiassed mind can compare the injunctions and practices of the Apostles, as recorded in the New Testament, with what has been aptly termed "secondary Christianity," must feel moved to cry out with the prophet of tears, "How is the gold become dim! How is the most pure gold changed! The stones of the Sanctuary are poured out at the top of every street."[1] For how soon did the living faith of believers, and the all-powerful operations of the Spirit, subside into a dead formalism, a system of ceremonies and doctrines unknown to the writers of the New Testament: how speedily were the churches welded into a worldly community directed by an unspiritual and unfruitful Hierarchy!

But, in order to understand the influences by which this transformation was effected, we must not only admit the general tendency of men to corrupt what is delivered to them, but must, also, have some conception of the prominent religious feature of the world at the time when the Gospel began to be preached in it. For religious teaching was then carried on mainly, indeed almost exclusively, by means of vast and wide-spreading institutions known as the Mysteries, the rites

[1] Lam. iv. 1.

393

of which were celebrated in profound secrecy, and to which admission could be obtained only by a solemn initiation.[1]

These institutions might be found, at least, in every civilized nation, and, probably, also among uncultured tribes. And, although they varied much in outward observances, as well as in non-essential teaching—according to the temper of the country to which each belonged, and the particular deity in whose honour it was celebrated—they, nevertheless, seem to have been intimately connected with each other, and to have all taught the same fundamental doctrines.

They were a kind of established international religion, and, unless a man connected himself with them, his progress in the public service was barred, and he had little chance of succeeding in the world. For, whatever might be his piety, and however unexceptionable his conduct, he became an object of suspicion if he had not been initiated. Indeed, it was the neglect of this supposed duty which formed the basis of the charge of impiety and atheism against Socrates, and cost the philosopher his life. Of course, if at any time the secrets were divulged by an initiated person, or if in any circumstances, no matter how accidental, one not initiated caught a glimpse of the Mysteries, death without mercy was the immediate penalty.

Persons of all ranks and ages, and of both sexes, were admitted as initiates. And so Apuleius, in his

[1] There was, indeed, a public worship of the gods, as well as the secret services of the Mysteries, and this was open to all, even to the uninitiated. But it was regarded by the initiated merely as a means of keeping the lower classes in order; and in it the gross stories of the gods were understood literally; whereas in the Mysteries they were said to be philosophically explained.

description of the great procession in honour of Isis, says ;—" Then came a multitude of those who had been initiated into the sacred rites of the goddess, consisting of men and women, of all classes and ages, resplendent with the pure whiteness of their linen garments." [1]

Here the expression "of all ages" includes children, but not infants. Hence the latter, in case of their premature decease, were placed in the gloomy parts of Hades, and could not enter the sunlit myrtle-groves of the initiated. [2]

Among the Greeks, the Mysteries of the Dii Cabiri at Samothrace had the reputation of being the most ancient ; but the Eleusinian connected with Ceres, and the Dionysiac, or Bacchic, were the most popular, and were intimately associated with each other.

In Egypt, the Mysteries of Isis were supreme ; and in Persia, those of Mithras. But, about the time of the Lord's appearance upon earth, the former had been recognized in Greece, and had become popular at Rome ; while the latter were introduced into Rome in A.D. 101. These two societies had the most manifest and powerful influence upon Christianity, which they corrupted in the direction of what is now called Catholicism.

There is little doubt that the Eleusinian Mysteries were near akin to the Egyptian, which, again, are said to have been introduced from India. But the Aryans who migrated from Babylon, through Bactria, to India would certainly have carried the Chaldean system and Mysteries with them. This consideration accounts for the fact, that some ancient authors speak of the Mysteries as having been brought from Chaldea to

[1] Apul. *Metam.* xi.　　　　[2] Virg. *Æn.* vi. 426-9.

Egypt;[1] since they did originally, at least, come from that quarter, even if their route was so circuitous as to pass through India.

It is probable, then, that the earliest form of religion among the Aryans of India was substantially the same as that of the Chaldeans, from whose country they had originally migrated. This religion was, indeed, corrupted by the Brahmans; but Buddha claimed to have recovered it; for he did not profess to be the revealer of a new faith, but only a restorer of old paths. Hence the Buddhist religion, in its purest form, is, perhaps, essentially the same as the Chaldean. That its foundation-doctrine, at least, is identical with that of the Mysteries, we shall presently see.

Thus the great ancient religion, distributed over the whole world, seems to have originated in Chaldea, where it was probably revealed and established by those fallen angels, who, after the Deluge, consorted with the daughters of men.[2] In it we recognize the system of Satan, framed to counteract the revelation of God, and to turn men away from faith in Him to a vain search after holiness and eternal life by means of sacerdotal ceremonies, by the aid of demons, and by the teachings of demon-inspired hierophants.

---

[1] For instance, Zonaras, in speaking of Egyptian science, remarks;—"For it is said to have come from the Chaldeans to Egypt, and to have been carried from thence to Greece." But, to understand this statement, we must remember, that none but the initiated were permitted to study science. Pausanias, on the other hand, while ignoring Egypt, regards the Chaldeans and Indians as having originated the doctrines of the Mysteries. "I know," he says, "that the Chaldeans and the Magi of the Indians were the first who pronounced the soul to be immortal: from them the Greeks learned their doctrine, and, above all, Plato the son of Aristo."—Paus. Messen. xxxii.

[2] Gen. vi. 4. See *Earth's Earliest Ages*, pp. 211-12.

XLIX

THE PROBABLE MEANING OF INITIATION

FROM Babylon, then, the religion of the Mysteries was disseminated over the broad earth by the tribes which migrated thence, in various directions, after the confusion of tongues. And so, it happens that there is neither race nor nation which does not show traces of the ancient Chaldean legends in its religion, its folk lore, and its fairy tales. Hence, too, we may explain the remarkable fact, that savage and even cannibal tribes are to this day found to be cultivating Mysteries, into which their youth are regularly initiated as soon as they are deemed to be of fitting age. Nor is it unlikely that by a study of their strange customs as they are now, or were lately, practised, we may obtain some clue to the real meaning and intention of Chaldean, Indian, Egyptian, and Greek initiations. For, although the method and form of procedure have been very diverse among different peoples, its object has, probably, always remained the same.

The writer has recently learnt some curious facts respecting initiation as practised by the Fangs of Western Africa from the experiences of the late Rev. A. W. Marling, who laboured for seventeen years among those cannibal tribes. Mr. Marling was a scholar of some ability, who gave up his prospects in life for the arduous duties of the mission field, and, soon after he had settled in the country of the Fangs, discovered among them a kind of secret association which they called *Beetee*.[1] He observed that those of

---

[1] Having no acquaintance with the language of the Fangs, we have spelt this word phonetically, according to the pronunciation which we heard.

them who had been initiated into it were, apparently, united by a strong feeling of brotherhood ; while non-initiates were regarded with scant esteem. But his endeavours to elicit some particulars respecting the ceremony and meaning of initiation met with no success.

At last, however, when he had gained the confidence of the natives, they did permit him to see their preparation for the rite. A young man who was to be initiated was laid upon the ground, and was bidden to chew the root of a certain plant which was given to him. This root had the property of inducing unconsciousness ; and the lad, as he kept chewing it, became more and more drowsy. He was watched by the natives with some anxiety, and tested from time to time, until he appeared to be altogether insensible to any outward impression. Then four men, having raised him upon their shoulders, carried him away ; and Mr. Marling was allowed to see no more.

But there was also present a young American missionary, in whom curiosity overcame every other feeling ; so that he determined, if it were by any means possible, to know the end. Accordingly, he crept cautiously under the bush, and so, contriving to escape observation, followed the procession until it halted. The place was unfrequented, weird, and partly enclosed by a gloomy forest, near to which stood a small shrine with a kind of altar, rendered horrible with skulls and luridly burning lights, in front of it. The men who were bearing the unconscious lad stood before this altar, and then deliberately, and with violence, threw their burden upon the ground. The shock of the fall aroused the lad, who started up in horror at the scene before him, and with a wild howl fled into the forest.

It was afterwards ascertained from converts, that this was the usual manner of initiation ; that the novices always fled into the forest, where they were supposed to commune with the spirits which thenceforth took charge of them, and where, also, they not seldom perished, and were seen no more ; but that, in most cases, they returned to their tribe in the course of two or three days, and were from that time regarded as capable men.

What, then, could be the object of so strange a proceeding ? We can imagine but one, which is also suggested by what is said to take place in the forest. Probably, the effects of the drug, combined with the shock of the violent awakening and the terrors of the wild scene and of the fiery skulls with which he was confronted, so loosened the hold of the man's spirit upon his body, that the demon, who was waiting for that purpose, was able to take possession of it. And so, the initiate would be thenceforth under spirit-control, reduced, possibly, to the condition described to the writer by a lady whom the Lord had delivered from English Spiritualism, and who said ;—" When I was under the control of the spirits, my condition became so abject that, at last, I did not dare to do anything without their guidance, not even to cross the street." But it is likely that the conscience of the savage does not resist the demons as that of a perverted Christian would ; so that, in the former case, the relations between the controlled and the controllers are not so strained. Indeed, the savage regards the demons as his gods, and, therefore, obeys them more or less willingly. Moreover, he believes that they give him skill and good luck in hunting, and help him against his foes : he knows, too, that he would be of little account among his people, unless he had by initiation obtained this supernatural aid.

Kohl, in his interesting account of the Ojibbeway Indians, informs us that those tribes were accustomed to effect the same purpose by a different method. The candidate for initiation was led into the forest, in the deepest part of which a sort of hammock was constructed for him on the branches of a tree. He was then directed to recline upon it, and remain alone, neither eating nor drinking, plucking no berries, nor even swallowing the rain-water that might fall. So he must lie, perfectly still, through day and night, until the spirit came to tell him of his fate and to bestow blessing upon him.

Here the solitude and fasting, which lasted a week or ten days, seems to have made an opportunity for the demons, just as the opiate and violent awakening does in the case of the Fangs.

A chieftain, named "The Cloud," gave Kohl an interesting narrative of his own initiation. In the spring of the year in which he was considered to be of proper age, he was led into the forest by his grandfather, who helped him to arrange his couch, gave him directions, and then left him alone. He strove to obey the injunctions laid upon him, and controlled himself for three days; but, on the fourth, his patience broke down. He plucked and ate the acid leaves of a little plant which grew near his tree; and then the cravings of hunger overcame every other feeling, so that he walked up and down in the forest devouring everything edible that he could find.

His fast was broken, and he was obliged to return home without having accomplished his purpose. His account of his reception is suggestive;—"They reproved me, and told me that I had done wrong, at which I felt ashamed. They said, that, since I had broken my fast, it was all over with my dream, and that I could not try again until the next spring: I might by this time have been a man; but must now remain a useless fellow for another year, which, at my age, was a disgrace."

This admonition shows how entirely the Indians depended upon the spirit, or spirits, into union with which they were brought by initiation; how unreservedly they placed themselves under the sway of these denizens of the air, looking to them alone for help and blessing.

In the spring of the following year, " The Cloud " was successful: he completed his term of fasting, and the spirit appeared. His response to the questions put to him leaves us in no doubt as to his aspirations. " What," said the spirit, " doest thou there? " " I am fasting," was his reply. " Wherefore, then, dost thou fast? " rejoined the spirit. " Because," he answered, " I desire to obtain power, and to know what my life shall be."

Then, in obedience to the command of his supernatural visitant, his spirit left his body, and floated through the air, following its guide in an eastward direction, until they had reached the spirit-land. There he was conducted into the presence of four white-haired men, sitting beneath a splendid canopy, who approved of him, and, because of his high spiritual tendencies, conferred power upon him to become a mighty hunter, and to live to a great and honourable old age. And so, his spirit journeyed back to the body, and he found himself in an exhausted and dying condition; for he had fasted ten days. But he was saved by

26

his grandfather, who had been awaiting his return to earthly consciousness, and had brought with him food and restoratives.

Now, it seems more than probable that the ancient initiations, however diverse they may have been in procedure, or in the means used to prepare the candidate for the spirit's entrance, were, nevertheless, intended to effect the same purpose as those of modern savages. For, in descriptions of the former, we hear of the signs and tokens by which the goddess was accustomed to make her presence felt, and sometimes of her actual appearance. And the same phenomena occurred when the rites were those of a male deity. We see, therefore, no reason to doubt the truth of Wilder's remark on the Eleusinian Mysteries ;—

"These observances once represented the spiritual life of Greece, and were considered, for two thousand years and more, the appointed means for regeneration through an interior union with the Divine Essence."

But, of course, what Wilder calls, "an interior union with the Divine Essence," we understand to be the entrance into the initiated person of a demon or spirit of the air.

Further into this subject we cannot go : but ample corroboration of what has been said might be drawn from Indian and Chinese sources, and also from the records of that so-called Spiritualism which, for the last fifty or sixty years, has been Paganising America, England, and the Continent. Enough, however, has been laid before the reader to enable him to form a judgment upon our inference, which is this ;—

Man cannot stand alone without spiritual support.

God knows this, and, therefore, offers us "the Spirit of Life in Christ Jesus," which will give strength for whatever lies before us here below, and ultimately bring us into His Presence where there is fulness of joy, and to His Right Hand where there are pleasures for evermore.

Satan, also, knows it; and he, too, is ready, for his own purposes, to supply our deficiency by means of the demons of the air.

And initiations, whether ancient or as practised among modern Pagans, are one mode of introducing these demons to their post.

The action of the spirits of evil would thus be precisely analogous to the entrance of the Spirit of God, by which he that is joined to the Lord becomes one spirit.[1]   So, if the demons take possession of a man, he is joined to, and becomes one spirit with, Satan : he is thenceforth guided by the spirit that now worketh in the children of disobedience.

We can, then, readily feel the force of Paul's words to the Corinthians ;—

" I would not that ye should have communion with demons. Ye cannot drink the cup of the Lord and the cup of demons ; ye cannot partake of the table of the Lord and of the table of demons." [2]

Here the Bible assumes that it is possible to establish a communion with demons ; and, if such a fellowship be confirmed, the result must be analogous to that of communion with the Lord, not merely in the present age, but also in that which is to come. For those who have entered into it must share the fate of the demons to whom they are joined ; just as those who are one with the Lord must follow Him into the Heavenly Kingdom, that they may be with Him where He is, and may behold His glory.

[1] 1 Cor. vi. 17.   [2] 1 Cor. x. 20, 21.

In the mention of the cup and the table, we may discern a reference to the actual ceremonies of demon-initiation. For a cup of drugged wine was given to the candidate—probably for the same reason as that for which the Fang is made to chew the root which renders him unconscious—and he also ate a wafer in honour of the goddess, and to signify his communion with her.

From all this, we may see why it is that Scripture sets the demons and the Lord Jesus in direct opposition to each other, as in the passage quoted above. There is a similar antithesis in the eighteenth chapter of Deuteronomy. For there Moses, in the Name of the Lord, sternly forbids the Israelites to have dealings of any kind with familiar spirits. The Canaanites had hearkened to the mediums who were possessed by such spirits, and had, consequently, become abominations to the Lord, Who was about to destroy them out of their land.[1] But Israel was not suffered so to do: a better Guide should be given to them ;—" The Lord, thy God, will raise up unto thee a Prophet from the midst of thee, of thy brethren, like unto me ; unto Him ye shall hearken."[2] This Prophet was the Lord Jesus,[3] Who is thus promised to those that should have no communion with demons.

Again, in the First Epistle to Timothy, Paul speaks of the greatness of the mystery that leads us to godliness, that is, the mystery of the incarnation, of the Word made Flesh.[4] But, in the immediately following verses,[5] he predicts, that, in later times, many will lose their faith in this mystery, and in all the blessings

[1] Deut. xviii. 9–14.
[2] Deut. xviii. 15–19.
[3] John i. 45, vi. 14 ; Acts iii. 22, 23.
[4] 1 Tim. iii. 16.
[5] 1 Tim. iv. 1–5.

that flow therefrom, because they will listen to seducing spirits and teachings of demons. Again, then, the demons are the antagonists of the Lord Jesus; and once more, as the Spirit expressly declares, will men return to the very wickedness that brought ruin upon the Canaanites of old. Nor will they escape the just punishment of such a revolt; for then the Lord Jesus will be revealed from heaven, "with the angels of His power, in flaming fire, rendering vengeance to them that know not God, and to them that obey not the Gospel of our Lord Jesus."[1]

L

THE LESSER AND THE GREATER MYSTERIES

THE general plan of the Mysteries was a masterly organization, admirably adapted for the carrying out of one obvious aim, namely, to bring the whole world into bondage to the powers which directed the higher rites and teaching. They were divided into the Lesser and the Greater, and these appear to have been absolutely distinct—the one affording no more than the exoteric teaching, but the other the esoteric, or the real secrets of the Mysteries, called the Aporrheta.[2] Initiates of the Lesser were termed *Mystæ*, those of the Greater *Ephori* or *Epoptæ*.[3]

"Undoubtedly," says Ouvaroff, "he who was initiated in the Greater knew all that the Lesser

---

[1] 2 Thes. i. 7, 8.
[2] That is, "the things that must not be uttered," or "divulged."
[3] There were two grades in the Greater Mysteries, as we shall presently see. Hence it has been supposed that the term *ephori* was applied to initiates of the lower grade, while those of the higher were called *epoptæ*. This, however, is uncertain.

Mysteries contained, but there is nothing to prove that every Mysta might become an Epopt, or, in other words, that those who were adepts in the Lesser Mysteries might, on that account, claim initiation into the Greater. Every Greek, without distinction of age or of origin, might be admitted to the Lesser Mysteries : barbarians, in process of time, enjoyed the same privilege. If to obtain admission to the Greater Mysteries had been a matter of equal facility, could they have exercised the same influence, would they never have been divulged ?[1]

"This double doctrine, which raised a wall of partition between the philosopher and the people, is a distinguishing feature of antiquity, inherent in all its institutions, in all its systems, and in all its civilization. Christianity, in destroying the double doctrine, became a grand epoch, even in the history of philosophy. The division of the Mysteries into the Greater and the Lesser belonged to the very nature of the institution : the Greater Mysteries were reserved for an inconsiderable number of initiated persons, because they contained revelations which would have given a mortal blow to the religion of the state : the Lesser Mysteries were within the reach of all men."[2]

[1] Plato appears to refer to the fact that only a few of the initiated were really in possession of the secrets, when he remarks ;— "For, as those who attend the Mysteries say, there are many wand-bearers, but few inspired persons."—*Phæd.* 37.

[2] Ouvaroff's *Mysteries of Eleusis,*" pp. 36–8.

LI

PREPARATION FOR THE LESSER MYSTERIES: FASTING, CONFESSION, BAPTISMAL EXPIATION AND REGENERATION, HOLY WATER, SIGN OF THE CROSS

THE initiation into the Lesser Mysteries was preceded by fasting, and the aspirant was severely interrogated by the Hierophant as to his past life, and adjured to conceal nothing, under pain of the displeasure of the gods. The avowed object of this confession was to exclude from participation in the Mysteries any one whose character should not prove to be blameless: but the real design was to get the postulant under the power of the priest, by putting the latter in possession of his secrets. And, from the story of Hercules in Apollodorus, it appears, that, even if the postulant had incurred blood-guilt, the difficulty could be easily surmounted ; for, after a full confession, the priest was empowered to absolve and purify him.

This confession was of course secret, and the only revelation of it with which we remember to have met is contained in the story of a *bon mot* ascribed by Plutarch to the brutal and unscrupulous Lysander, by whom it was uttered to the Hierophant who was examining him with a view to his initiation into the Samothracian Mysteries ;—

"When he was being questioned at Samothrace, the priest bade him mention the most lawless deed that had been perpetrated by him in his lifetime. To which he replied, ' Is it at your bidding, or at that of the gods, that I am required to do this?

Being told that it was at the bidding of the gods, he said, 'Well, then, stand aside, and I will tell them, if they are inquiring.'"

It is scarcely necessary to remark, that, in this practice, we have the origin of confession to a priest in the Catholic Churches. No hint of such a thing is to be found either in the Old or the New Testament: it was, however, well known in Paganism.

But other preliminaries, also, were necessary before initiation could take place. The postulant was baptized, and fasted several days.

"In the Mysteries which obtain among the Greeks," says Clement of Alexandria, "cleansings hold the first place, as also does the bath among the Barbarians. After these are the Lesser Mysteries, which have some foundation of instruction and preliminary preparation for what is to follow them." [1]

Allusions to the Pagan baptism are frequent in the "Fathers."

"In many sacrilegious rites of idols," says Augustine, "persons are reported to be baptized." [2]

Justin Martyr's First Apology contains the following curious passage;—

"And the demons, having heard this washing published by the prophet, cause those who enter their temples, and are about to approach them with the view of offering libations and burnt sacrifices, also to sprinkle themselves with water. They cause them, moreover, to bathe themselves entirely as they depart *from the sacrifice*, before they go into the sacred enclosures where their images"—that is, the images of the demons—"are placed." [3]

[1] Clem. *Alex. Strom.* v. 11.   [3] Just. Mart. *Apolog.* i. 62.
[2] August. *Contr. Donat.* vi. 25.

Here the sprinkling at the entrance to the Temple reveals the origin of the Catholic use of 'holy water,' to which no parallel can be discovered in either the Old or the New Testament.

If we inquire what benefit was supposed to result from the Pagan baptism, we have already seen that it was regarded as a cleansing, or purification from sins ; but Tertullian tells us something more. "Certainly," he says, "persons are baptized at the games of Apollo and those of Eleusis ; and this they think that they do unto regeneration and impunity in their perjuries." "For they are admitted," he has previously said, "by bathing to certain sacred rites of some Isis or Mithras."[1]

Yet, again, in another treatise, he affirms, that the Devil "in the Mysteries of idols emulates even the very things of the Divine sacraments. He, too, baptizes some, to wit, his believing and faithful people : he promises them an expiation of sins from the bath, and so to this day initiates them into the Mysteries of Mithras. There he seals his soldiers in their foreheads" —that is, makes the sign of the mystic Tau, or the cross, upon their foreheads : "he celebrates, also, the oblation of bread, and brings in an imitation of resurrection, and purchases a crown under the sword."[2]

In these rites of the Mysteries, which were practised centuries before the Christian era, we may discern the source from which the Catholics drew the unscriptural doctrine of Baptismal Regeneration ; who it was that taught them to make the sign of the cross on the forehead at baptism ; and how they came to substitute the wafer—always used in the Mithraic ceremony— for the broken bread, and to turn the Memorial Supper

[1] Tert. *De Bapt.* v.   [2] Tert. *De Prescript. Her.* xl.

into an oblation or sacrifice. The patterns of all these things were found in Paganism, not in anything that had been commanded or practised by the Lord or His Apostles.

LII

THE ORPHIC HYMNS. SEX IN DEITY. THE GREGORIAN MUSIC.

AT certain stages in the initiatory and other rites, hymns of invocation were sung to the particular deities whose aid was required, and some of these compositions, known as the Orphic Hymns, have come down to us. Those of them which end in prayer for a blessing on the mystic rites were, probably, chanted either at the beginning or at the end of the ceremonies. Others entreat the favour of the gods for one newly initiated, and must, apparently, have been sung at the conclusion of the ordeal. Two hymns are addressed to deities who might exercise a malignant influence—the Titans and Corybas—and to these the petition is, that they will avert their cruel wrath. Other frequently repeated prayers are for " royal health," or " health with soothing hand," for " riches that confer much happiness," for " an easy ending to a happy life," and so on.

In the hymn to Misa, which is another name for Iacchus or Bacchus, that deity is described as being of twofold nature, both male and female : on which Taylor remarks ;—"This mixture of the male and female in one and the same Divinity is no unusual thing in the Orphic theology." And, indeed, the introduction, in some way or other, of sex among the deities is common to almost all Pagan religions, and became very popular, evidently because it lowered the gods to the level of men, and so enabled the latter to do as they would with less compunction and fear. Of course, the idea found its way into nominal Christianity and the communities which affect relationship with it, and developed among them in two forms.

First, the Blessed Trinity has been blasphemously affirmed to consist, like the Pagan trinities, of Father Mother and Son. In this case, the Spirit is represented as feminine, and, in the Catholic Churches, is usually identified with the Lord's human mother. But such impious and idolatrous teaching is directly contradicted by Scripture. For πνεῦμα, which is the Greek for spirit, is a neuter noun; but, whenever it is used for the Holy Spirit, any pronoun connected with it is placed in the masculine gender. So we read, " Howbeit, when He,[1] the Spirit of Truth, is come, He shall guide you into all the truth." [2]

But, still further, the Bible gives a plain indication that sex is an institution belonging exclusively to such a condition of things as now prevails in our world; that is, to a reign of sin and death. For, to quote our Lord's Own words,

"They which shall be accounted worthy to obtain that age, and the resurrection from the dead, neither marry nor are given in marriage; for neither can they die any more: for they are equal unto the angels, and are the sons of God, being the sons of the resurrection." [3]

Those, then, who obtain the resurrection from the dead neither marry nor are given in marriage, because they do not die, but are like the angels.

Hence it appears, that, because there is no death in

[1] ἐκεῖνος.   [2] John xvi. 13.   [3] Luke xx. 35, 36.

heaven, therefore neither marriage relations nor sex [1] are found there : such conditions are merely temporary, having been arranged by God to meet the exigencies of this present world, which, through sin, has fallen under the law of decay and death, and so is continually needing that the gaps in its ranks should be filled up.

But, although the Bible makes this point very clear, its teaching has been obscured to English readers by the Authorised Version, which, from some unaccountable cause, has omitted the conjunction 'for,' or 'because,' in the clause, " for neither can they die any more." Yet the word is found in all the best manuscripts, and is, moreover, of the greatest importance to the sense of the passage, showing, as it does, that the clause which begins with it explains that which precedes it.

The second way of corrupting the truth is to speak of God as both Father and Mother, like Bacchus and some of the Hindu gods. In recent times there has been a frightful recrudescence of this blasphemy among Spiritualists, Theosophists, Christian Scientists, and others ; but what has been said above is sufficient to demonstrate the falsity and abominable wickedness of such a doctrine, in regard to which we would not utter a word more than is necessary. For there cannot be a greater profanity than to connect the nature of

---

[1] That there is no sex in heaven might have been inferred from the fact that there is no marriage there : but the Lord's words seem to indicate it, also, in another way. For, in speaking of those who will obtain the First Resurrection, He, of course, included persons of both earthly sexes. It would, therefore, at first sight, have seemed more appropriate if He had used a term common to both sexes, and spoken of " children of God," and " children of the resurrection." But, in each case, He has preferred the word "sons "—*viol*—in order, probably, to show that there will be no difference of sex in the Heavenly Kingdom.

the Great God with such purely human matters ; and we have no wish to be one of those to whom He will presently say ;—

"Thou thoughtest that I was altogether such a one as thyself!"[1]

Nevertheless, one note of warning is necessary. In order to corroborate the doctrine just mentioned, certain Theosophists have invented a new derivation for the Hebrew *Shaddai*, which in our versions is correctly rendered "Almighty."[2] They suppose it to be connected with a word, *shad*, which signifies a woman's breast. But such a derivation is impossible, and, so far as we are aware, has never been proposed by an unbiassed scholar. It is, however, given in Gerald Massey's *Book of Beginnings*, in such terms as we would not transcribe ; the inference, of course, being that the title *El Shaddai* proves the motherhood of God.

This perversion would in itself be of little importance ; for we expect such things from those who are preparing the world for its last rebellion. But, when the Powers of Evil begin to propagate some new error, they are wont to obtain help from very unlikely quarters, and sometimes induce those who would naturally oppose their scheme to become its unconscious supporters. And this they too often effect by means of that restless and self-seeking spirit which will at times impel even

---

[1] Psa. l. 21.

[2] It is formed from the root שָׁדַד to be strong, mighty ; and, sometimes, to act as a mighty one, to destroy. Twice we find a play on these two meanings in the phrase, "like a *shod* from the *Shaddai*," that is, "like a mighty destruction from the Almighty." See Isa. xiii. 6, Joel i. 15. There is also a word שֵׁד derived from the same root, and which is, indeed, a singular of *Shaddai*, and means 'mighty one,' 'lord,' being usually applied to fallen angels. *Shaddai* itself is the well known plural of majesty, signifying Great or Supreme Lord, Almighty.

believers to catch at any chance of putting forth something new. Hence it has happened that more than one Christian writer has taken up the Theosophical derivation of *Shaddai*, and explained the word as meaning first 'full-breasted,' and then 'bountiful.' The irreverent incongruity of such a derivation for one of the grandest titles of the Most High should have checked them ; and not less so the use to which Satan was likely to apply it. For, if it could be once established, it would, doubtless, be adduced as a Scriptural proof of the motherhood of God.

But, to return to our immediate subject, the Orphic hymns, and, perhaps, one or two of those which have come down to us as "Homeric," were chanted by a chorus, or choir, to music which, in all probability, was subsequently transferred to the Catholic Church. Some interesting remarks bearing upon this subject are made by the Roman Catholic priest Eustace in his *Classical Tour*. Speaking of the music used at St. Peter's in Rome, he says ;—

"The chaunt or music used by the Papal choir, and, indeed, in most Catholic cathedrals and abbey churches, is, excepting in some instances, ancient. Gregory the Great, though not the author of it, collected it into a body, and gave it the form in which it now appears. The chaunt of the Psalms is simple and affecting, composed of Lydian, Phrygian, and other Greek and Roman tunes, without many notes, but with a sufficient inflection to render them soft and plaintive or bold and animating. St. Augustine, who was a good judge of music, represents himself as melted into tears by the Psalms as then sung in the Church of Milan under the direction of St. Ambrose, and seems to apprehend that the emotions produced by such harmonious airs might be too tender for the vigorous and manly spirit of Christian devotion." [1]

Now, in the early centuries of the Christian era, Lydia and Phrygia were greatly addicted to the Chaldean Mysteries, and, being both of them countries famed for song, were likely to have contributed largely to the music of the rites. But the same Mysteries were celebrated, also, at Rome; and thus the Lydian and Phrygian airs would have become known in that city, and so might have been passed on to Milan and other places. It is, therefore, probable that Gregory was much indebted to them, and to the Roman and Greek Mystery-music, for his collection, though he may have found the greater part of it already in use for Christian services.

And this supposition becomes the more reasonable because, to say nothing of the universal influence of the Mysteries upon the Catholic Church, the early Christians do not seem to have had much original music of their own; while that which was used for the chanting of the Orphic and Homeric hymns would no doubt furnish the most suitable of all the Pagan tunes for adaptation to the Psalms. And, perhaps, the adapted strains may give us a hint of their origin by their effect; for any one who is acquainted with the Gregorian music will have noticed its peculiarly mesmeric influence.

Eustace's remark on these airs, and Augustine's experience of them, remind us of the verses of Milton;—

> " And ever, against eating cares,
> Lap me in soft Lydian airs."

[1] *Classical Tour*, vol. i. pp. 368–9.

For delicious music will often enfold those who yield themselves to it in a certain mist of sensuousness, so thick that, for the moment, no restless cares can penetrate it; but, alas! how quickly does the aerial protection vanish, leaving us once more exposed to every shaft of sorrow!

And what permanent good can anything that is merely sensuous procure for us, even if it should include all the meretricious attractions of the false Church? For splendid buildings, gorgeous vestments, and picturesque rites, for the eye, with sweet odours for the scent, and ravishing music for the ear, although they may bewitch our consciousness with the most agreeable sensations, can penetrate only as far as the soul. But this latter, according to the Bible, is no more than the animal life, the intellect and the emotions—that part of us, in brief, by which we are enabled to enjoy God's creation, but not God Himself. For He is Spirit, and they that worship Him must do so in spirit and in truth.

Now our spirit can neither see the sights nor hear the sounds of this world: it does not receive its impressions from the senses, but only from spirit; that is, if we are Christ's, from the Spirit of God. Hence prayer, to be really successful, must be uttered in the Holy Ghost;[1] nor can we preach the Word of God effectually without the same help.[2]

But, when we are in spirit, our consciousness is transferred more or less to another sphere: we see its sights and hear its sounds, which are all unknown to our earth-life.

"Immediately I was in spirit," says John, "and,

---

[1] Rom. viii. 26, 27; Jude 20.   [2] 1 Cor. ii. 4, 13.

behold, a Throne."[1] The scenery of Patmos had suddenly receded and disappeared, and he was gazing upon the Judgment-throne of God. So, in another place, we read, " I was in spirit in the Day of the Lord, and I heard behind me a great voice, as of a trumpet "[2]—a voice which would have been inaudible to the ears of his body.

Thus a knowledge of Biblical psychology dissipates the idea that any holy spiritual influence can be set in motion by appeals to the senses.

And it is worthy of notice, that, when the three component parts of our being are enumerated from God's point of view, the order is spirit, soul, and body ;[3] because God's influence commences in the spirit, then lays hold of the emotions and the intellect, and, lastly, begins to curb the body.

But, from the standpoint of the Evil One, we have "earthly," "soulish" (ψυχική), and "demoniacal" (δαιμονιώδης)[4] ; because Satan's influence enters by the clay-made body, then seizes upon the soul ; and, if it can also gain possession of the spirit, causes the man to become as a demon, or evil spirit, even while yet in the flesh ; and so drives him beyond the reach of salvation.[5]

---

[1] Rev. iv. 2.   In the original, there is no definite article with ' spirit '; so that we should not render, "the Spirit." Our translators did not understand the meaning of the words, and so introduced the article as a gloss; but what John wishes to tell us is, that his consciousness was suddenly transferred to the spirit-sphere, so that he saw with the eyes of his spirit, and no longer with those of his body.   These remarks apply also to Rev. i. 10.

[2] Rev. i. 10.

[3] 1 Thess. v. 23.

[4] James iii. 15.

[5] Because when his spirit has been developed on the side of the Evil One, he will then rebel against God with spiritually intelligent malignity, and so commit the unpardonable sin against the Holy Ghost. For a fuller discussion of the threefold nature of man, see the author's *Earth's Earliest Ages*, pp. 103–110.

27

LIII

ANCIENT AND MODERN USE OF INCENSE—DR. ROCK'S DEFENCE OF THE PRACTICE EXAMINED.

DURING the chanting of the Orphic hymns, incense was burned, but not indiscriminately : for the kind that must be used in each case is prescribed beneath the title of the hymn. The different kinds selected are storax, frankincense, saffron, myrrh, manna, and poppy. Occasionally some of these are combined : sometimes aromatics generally are prescribed : a fumigation with torches was to accompany the invocation of Night : various odours should be used for Pan and Rhea ; any seeds, except beans and aromatics, for Earth ; and any perfume but frankincense for Bacchus Amphietus.

There is no doubt that we have here the source from which the Catholic Church draws its custom of incensing. Whether it is as discriminating in the use of aromatics as were the Hierophants of old, we know not ; but the subjoined extract will show that it is, generally, quite as minute in its directions ;—

"A quarter of an hour before the celebration the Thurifer should present himself at the sacristy, put on his cassock and cotta, and, in default of the acolytes, assist the Sacred Ministers to vest.

"The Priest, Deacon, and Sub-deacon, being vested, the blessing of the Incense to be used in the procession takes place, immediately before leaving the sacristy. The Celebrant receives the spoon from the Deacon, who says, 'Be pleased, reverend father, to give a blessing' ; he then takes incense from the *Navicula,* or incense-boat (held by the Deacon, who receives it from the Thurifer), and puts it on the burning charcoal in three several portions, each time sprinkling it in the form of a cross. Then, in accordance with the Deacon's prayer, he blesses the incense with his right hand, saying, ' Be thou blessed by Him in Whose honour thou art to be burned.' The thurible is held by the Thurifer whilst the incense is put in. . . The Celebrant, standing before the midst of the Altar, turns round by his right, and then, with his side to the Altar, puts incense into the thurible, the Deacon ministering the spoon and holding the boat as before. The Priest then blesses (*secreto*) the incense with the words already mentioned. He then receives the thurible from the Deacon, and incenses the midst of the Altar and the two corners. The Celebrant himself is then incensed by the Deacon. After the Introit, the Priest again incenses the Altar. The next incensing takes place before the Gospel— the midst of the Altar is alone incensed by the Deacon—the lectern from which the Gospel is read is *never* incensed.

"When the oblations are placed upon the Altar they are incensed by the Celebrant, who is afterwards incensed by the Deacon. An acolyte then incenses the choir. The next and last incensing takes place (in the West) after the consecration. When the consecration and adoration of the Sacred Body are over, the Deacon rises and removes the pall from the chalice ; and after the consecration and adoration of the Precious Blood he replaces it—the chief assistant having incensed the Body and Blood of our Lord.

"N.B. When a Bishop assists *pontifically*, he blesses the incense." [1]

[1] *Directorium Anglicanum*, pp. 92-4.

These directions are followed by instructions to the Thurifer to make certain genuflections; to hold the thurible in his left hand if the incense be not blessed, in his right if it be; and to grasp the utensil with his little finger and thumb in appointed positions during the ceremonial part of the function and in processions, and in a different manner upon other occasions.

Whence, then, comes all this useless mummery: so unlike anything that we read of our Lord and His immediate disciples?

"The primitive Church imitated the example of the Jews, and adopted the use of incense at the celebration of the Liturgy," replies Dr. Rock.[1] And he defends his position by quotations from the Apostolical Canons, Hippolytus, Ambrose, and Ephrem Syrus.

But, if the primitive churches imitated the Jews in the matter of incense, why is there no mention of, or allusion to, this fact in the New Testament; or, at least, in the *Didache*—a manifest product of Jewish Christians, written towards the end of the first century? Why do we find no hint of such a practice in Justin Martyr's account of the manner of holding the Lord's Supper in his days? For Justin, too, was well acquainted with the ways of Jewish Christians, through whom the imitation of Jewish customs, had there been any, would, we presume, have come.

As to Dr. Rock's citations, they are all drawn from writers, not of the primitive churches, but of the Catholic Church, in whose works we expect to find traces of Paganism.

The *Apostolical Canons*—dating, perhaps from the middle, but more probably from the end, of the second

[1] *Hierurg.* vol. ii. pp. 335–6.

century—are characterized by Harnack as "the last step but one" in the development by which the Apostolic government of the churches, as described in the New Testament and in the *Didache*, was changed into the Catholic Hierarchy. They, therefore, contain much that was unknown to the primitive churches ; for Catholicism is a blend of Paganism and Christianity.

The extract said to have been taken from Hippolytus belongs to the *De Consummatione Mundi*,[1] which is classed among the spurious works attributed to that author. Most probably it was forged, like many similar productions, with the view of propagating Catholicism ; for the mention of incense in the churches is not its only error. It also styles our Lord's human mother Theotocos, or mother of God, thus implying that He derived His Divine, as well as His human, nature from her. But nothing is to be found respecting either of these two points in the genuine works of Hippolytus.

Finally, the works of Ambrose and Ephrem the Syrian contain gross superstition : these men were pronounced Catholics, and neither of them can be regarded, even in the very least degree, as an authority by those who are investigating the usages of the primitive churches.

So much, then, for Dr. Rock's quotations. He has not adduced a tittle of evidence that the primitive churches used incense. And, in addition to what has been said above, there is yet another reason which forbids the theory that the Catholic Church followed the practices of Jews in this matter. For, in the Hebrew ritual, there is no incensing of human beings, or of inanimate objects : no, the sweet odours were

[1] *De Consumm. Mundi* xxxiv.

burned only before the Living God. And, indeed, the Old Testament itself points out, that such usages as we have quoted from the *Directorium Anglicanum* are Babylonian and Pagan. For what was the first impulse of the Chaldean Nebuchadnezzar, when his mind was overwhelmed with the Divine revelation that flowed from the mouth of Daniel? It was to fall upon his face and worship the prophet, and to command that they should offer an oblation and sweet odours to him.[1] It must, then, have been Paganism that the Catholic Church imitated, not the Mosaic ritual; and this fact fastens upon her members "the blasphemy of them that say they are Jews, and they are not, but are a synagogue of Satan."[2]

LIV

THE INCENSE AND PURE OFFERING OF THE GENTILES

MAL. i. 11.

THERE is yet another argument which is sometimes adduced in favour of the Catholic practice of incensing. It is founded upon the perversion of a prophecy in Malachi, which runs thus;—

"For, from the rising of the sun even unto the going down of the same, My Name *shall be* great among the Gentiles; and in every place incense *shall be* offered unto My Name, and a pure offering; for My Name *shall be* great among the Gentiles, saith the Lord of Hosts."[3]

[1] Dan. ii. 46.   [2] Rev. ii. 9, iii. 9.   [3] Mal. i. 11.

This verse, it is urged, must refer to the present age, in which the Gospel is being preached among the Gentiles ; and, in that case, the pure offering can only be the Eucharist, with which, therefore, incense is plainly associated.

Such is the plea: but, before we proceed to examine it, we may notice, that, even if the proposed interpretation were correct, there would still be no warrant for such incensing of persons and things as is now carried on in Catholic churches. For, in one particular, at least, the prophecy is in perfect accord with the Mosaic ritual : the incense is to be offered only to the Name of the Lord. But we believe the interpretation itself to be altogether untenable, and will now endeavour to prove our conviction by examining the prophecy.

In the first place, then, a careful consideration of the context will leave us without doubt as to this point — There is nothing figurative in the verse : its contents must be accepted as a literal prophecy. In the previous portion of the chapter, God has been entering into judgment with the Jews ; for He had chosen them as His people, but they had dishonoured Him in every way, had even offered polluted bread upon His altar, and had deemed the blind and the lame and the sick of their cattle to be sufficiently good for a sacrifice to Him!

Therefore, He tells them, that He had no pleasure in them, neither would He accept any offering at their hands.

And then follows our verse, in which He says, that, because of the wickedness of His people Israel, He will abolish a law which He gave through Moses. He had, indeed, commanded that no incense should be used in worship, save in His Temple at Jerusalem; and, also, that no sacrifice should be offered, except in the precincts of the same place. But He would some time change all this, and permit, not only Israelitish priests, but Gentiles also, to offer incense to His Name and a pure offering; and to do so, not only in Jerusalem, but in any place, wherever they might chance to be.

Now, from the nature of this declaration, as well as from the context, it is evident that we are to understand literal incense and literal offerings, such as the Levitical priests were wont to offer.

But there is another important point to be settled. At what time do these words find their fulfilment among the Gentiles—at the time when they were uttered, or in the future?

To this it might be replied, Well, in your version of the text you have rendered, " My Name shall be great," and so on; and that at once decides the question as to the time.

Yes: but we have put each " shall be " in italics, to show that it is not found in the original. The fact is, that, in accordance with a common Hebrew idiom, the verb 'to be' is altogether omitted; and, whenever such an omission occurs, we are at liberty to supply either the present or the future tense, according to the requirements of the sense or the context.

Now, in the case before us, we believe that the sense absolutely demands the future, and that for a very simple reason. In the time of Malachi the Gentiles certainly did *not* offer incense and a pure offering to the Name of Jehovah; for all the Gentile nations, without a single exception, were worshippers of false gods.

We are thus compelled to supply the future, and not the present tense ; and to regard the words as a prophecy, and not as a statement of what was then taking place.

We have not, however, yet arrived at the end of our difficulties. For, if the words were prophetic, at what precise time may we look for their fulfilment ?

Many would persuade us that they are being fulfilled now by the use of incense in certain apostate churches. One almost despairs of ever helping such people to an understanding of the Bible.

Malachi was a Hebrew prophet ; and, therefore, all that he says is exclusively connected with Hebrews, or with Gentiles in some relation to Hebrews, and with times in which God is dealing with Hebrews. Of the Church he neither knew, nor was commissioned to speak, anything. For, in the New Testament, we are repeatedly told, that the Church was a mystery hidden from the ages, and never revealed until the days of the Lord Jesus and His Apostles.[1]

While, then, we may find in the Old Testament much instruction in regard to the nature of God and His ways with man, many glorious prophecies disclosing His purposes respecting the earth and its inhabitants, and, above all, wondrous unfoldings of the mind of Christ and of His loving work on our behalf, we shall, nevertheless, search in vain for information concerning the doctrines and acts of worship that are peculiar to the Church. For this is contained only in the New Testament.

Again, the incense and pure offering are to be presented by Gentiles ; and, in our Dispensation,

---

[1] See Rom. xvi. 25, 26 ; 1 Cor. ii. 7 ; Eph. iii. 5, 9 ; Col. i. 26. Compare also Matt. xiii. 35.

Gentiles are distinguished from the Church as sharply as they are from the Jews. For Paul divides the world of the present age into three classes—the Jews, the Gentiles, and the Church of God.[1] The Gentiles, then, are without the pale of the Church ; so that, if anything be revealed concerning them, we know at once that it does not concern the Church—directly, at least—but those only who have no part or lot with her.

It is, then, sufficiently evident, that the prophecy refers to the Gentiles in their connection with Israel ; and but one more point remains to be settled—When precisely does it find its fulfilment ?

Now, so far as its words are concerned, it might have done so in the period which extends from the days of Malachi to the rejection of the Lord and the expulsion of the Jews from Palestine. But it did not ; for, during that period, the Gentiles served other gods.

Again, since Malachi was a Hebrew prophet, we must, of course, pass by the Church-period that followed, during which the whole Twelve Tribes are Lo-ammi, 'Not-My-People.' Even, however, if such an omission were not necessary, there has never yet, in the present Dispensation, been a time when the Gentiles everywhere, from the rising of the sun even unto the going down of the same, have in any sense offered incense and a pure offering to Jehovah. Nay, indifference, apostasy, and an idolatry at best scarcely veiled, have polluted the spiritual life of every century ; and, according to our Lord's own declaration, but few have

---

[1] 1 Cor. x. 32. In the original text, we find " Greeks," and not " Gentiles." But, at that time, all civilized nations were included under the denomination of Greeks, because Greek civilization was then prevailing throughout the Roman Empire. Hence, in Rom. i. 14–16, Paul regards the Romans themselves as Greeks.

found the strait gate and the narrow way. Indeed, we may go yet further : for there are vast Gentile countries towards the rising of the sun that have never yet even acknowledged the Name of Jehovah.

But this age will soon be ended, and the last Seven Years of the Jewish period be setting in : will the Gentiles at that time fulfil the prophecy? Most certainly not ; for the Scripture tells us, that they will then be in open and defiant rebellion against God, and will be worshipping Satan and the Antichrist.

We are thus driven upon our last refuge, the Millennial Age : is that the Dispensation in which the Gentiles, throughout the broad earth, will do what the Lord has predicted by the mouth of Malachi ? From the first we might have known that it must be then, and could be at no previous time. For the prophet speaks of an age when the Name of the Lord will be be great everywhere, when the whole world will give glory to God, and the knowledge of the Lord will cover the earth as the waters cover the sea. But, as many a prophecy tells us, this happy consummation can never be brought about, until He Himself comes in Person, to judge the world with righteousness and the peoples with equity, until His glorious Millennial reign. Then, when Israel stands, revealed, delivered, and redeemed from all iniquity, the jubilant command will go forth ;—" Rejoice, O ye nations, with His people ! " For what shall the receiving again of Israel be, but life from the dead ?

But, when His people is redeemed, the Messiah Himself will build the Temple of the Lord ;[1] and, as we read in the last chapters of Ezekiel, the services and the sacrifices will be restored as of old ; and rejoicing

[1] Zech. vi. 12, 13.

Israel will once more say;—"Look upon Zion, the city of our solemnities!"

Yet, although the glorious Temple, whose boundary walls are to be some four miles in circumference, will be the grand centre of worship, to which all the nations will go up once a year, it will no longer be the only spot where incense and sacrifice may be offered. In that point, the law of Moses will be changed; and the Gentiles, when they have rejoiced in the Lord and magnified His Name throughout the earth, will be permitted to offer their incense and their sacrifices in whatever place they may chance to be abiding.

Many, however, are offended at the suggestion of literal sacrifices in the next age. It is altogether opposed to their ideas of what is seemly and right: therefore, it cannot be true. But, when we are searching into the revelations of the Most High God, what have our opinions and notions of propriety to do with the matter? It is our part simply to believe what is revealed, and, if we do not understand it, to be confident that the Judge of all the earth will do right, and will presently show that the foolishness of God is wiser than men. In the passage before us, in the closing chapters of Ezekiel, and in other places, it is declared that sacrifices will be renewed in the next age; and the Scripture cannot be broken. But, as regards the reason for their renewal, of that we seem to have no revelation, and must, therefore, wait until the Lord be pleased to unfold to us the perfect wisdom of His plans.

One thing, however, is worthy of notice. Sacrifices were commanded from the fall of Adam to the death of the Lord Jesus, and incense from the time of Moses; and both will again be offered when Israel is restored.

This makes it seem probable that they are forms of worship proper for the inhabitants of earth. But, in the present age, in which God recognizes no earthly people, they are forbidden: we are to concentrate our thoughts upon the Great Sacrifice once offered for sin; and, instead of approaching God with the blood of bulls and of goats, are to make our requests known in the Name of Him Who poured out His Blood for us, nearly nineteen centuries ago, and Whose intercession is better than the most precious incense.

For God is not now preparing inhabitants for the earth, but a people which He may remove from its confines to dwell in the heavenly places with Christ. And it would seem, that, unless we can learn to worship Him in spirit and in truth, without any sensuous aids, we cannot be made meet for that glorious destiny.

LV

THE SPIRITUAL MEANING OF INCENSE

WE must not leave this interesting subject without a word on the spiritual significance of incense. There are many who think that it points to prayer; and they turn for corroboration to the second verse of the hundred and forty-first Psalm, a literal rendering of which is, " Let my prayer be accounted incense before Thee, and the lifting up of my hands (be accounted) the evening oblation." Our versions have, " as incense," and " as the evening sacrifice "; but the particle which would justify that rendering is significantly omitted. For the sense seems to be as follows. When David wrote the Psalm, he was far away from the Temple, where alone incense could be burned before the Lord, and the evening oblation offered. Therefore, he intreats that his prayer may be accepted in the place of incense, and the lifting up of his hands in that of the evening oblation. Thus his words by no means intimate that incense signifies prayer, nor the evening oblation the lifting up of hands.

And, indeed, there are other passages from which we can prove indisputably that incense does not represent prayer, but something added to prayer, by which the latter is rendered acceptable to God. What, then, could that something be but the merits and intercessions of the Lord Jesus?

So, in the eighth chapter of the Apocalypse, we are told respecting the angel with the golden censer, "And there was given unto him much incense, that he should add it unto the prayers of all the saints upon the golden altar before the Throne. And the smoke of the incense, with the prayers of the saints, went up before God out of the angel's hand."[1] And again, in the fifth chapter, we read that the elders had "golden bowls full of incense, which are the prayers of the saints;"[2] where the Greek of the original makes it clear, that the bowls, and not the incense, are the prayers of the saints.

Incense, then, represents the merits and death of the Lord Jesus and His intercession for us. Hence we can understand why it was to be burned before the Lord, every morning when the lamps were dressed, and every evening when they were lighted;[3] and why strange incense was forbidden.[4] Hence, too, we readily perceive why, on the great Day of Atonement, the High Priest dared not, on pain of death, enter the Holy

[1] Rev. viii. 3, 4.
[2] Rev. v. 8.
[3] Exod. xxx. 7, 8.
[4] Exod. xxx. 9.

of Holies, unless his censer was sending forth a cloud
of incense to cover the mercy-seat.[1]   And well can we
comprehend that awful scene, when wrath had gone
forth from the Lord, and Aaron was bidden to take
his censer, and run quickly to stand between the dead
and the living, and to make atonement for the
people.[2]

But how saddening, that these grand lessons, setting
forth the power of our Lord's intercession for us,
should be obscured and lost amid the trifling with
strange incense that is now being carried on in many
of our churches !

LVI

DOCTRINE OF THE LESSER MYSTERIES

OF the general idea among the Greeks, that salvation
could be obtained only by initiation into the Lesser
Mysteries, we may find abundant proof.

For example, in explaining the Greek words for
initiation, the Scholiast on the " Frogs " of Aristophanes
remarks ;—

"An opinion used to prevail among the Athenians,
that whoever had been taught the Mysteries was
accounted worthy of Divine honour after his death
in the present world.   And this is the reason why
all men were so eager for initiation."

We are thus enabled to understand a passage in the
"Peace," another comedy of Aristophanes, which at
first sight seems enigmatical.   For when Hermes finds
Trygæus beginning to dig up Peace, whom War has

---

[1] Lev. xvi. 12, 13.   [2] Num. xvi. 46-48.

thrown into a well, and covered with stones, the following conversation ensues ;—

> "*Herm.* Do you know that Zeus pronounced sentence of death upon any one who should be found digging her out?
>
> *Tryg.* Is it, then, now absolutely necessary for me to die?
>
> *Herm.* Be well assured that it is.
>
> *Tryg.* Then lend me three drachmas to buy a bit of a pig; for I must get myself initiated before I die."[1]

This request of Trygæus is explained by the Scholiast from the fact that all candidates for initiation were required to sacrifice a young pig. Hence, in the "Acharnians," the starving Megarean, who in despair has disguised his daughters as little pigs, offers them for sale to Dicæopolis as "pigs fit for the Mysteries."[2]

The effect of initiation when the initiated have passed into Hades is frequently alluded to. Thus, in the *Phaedo* of Plato, we read, that those who instituted the Mysteries for mankind intimated, that "whoever should arrive in Hades unexpiated and uninitiated should lie in mud; but that he who should arrive there purified and initiated should dwell with the gods."[3]

And so the deceased initiates were represented as rejoicing in the Elysian fields : and hence Dionysius and Xanthus, in their passage through the underworld, met with them, not in the murky regions of Hades, but in a place of myrtle groves, encircled by a most beautiful light; and heard them singing ;—"For to us alone who have been initiated are the sun and the light joyous."[4]

---

[1] Aristoph. *Pax* 364–8.
[2] Aristoph. *Acharn.* 719.
[3] Plato *Phaed.* 38.
[4] Aristoph. *Ranae* 422–3.

So, too, Apollodorus, in describing the twelfth labour of Hercules, relates, that, before the hero ventured to descend into the infernal regions,[1] he went to Eleusis to get himself initiated by Eumolpus. But an obstacle stood in the way ; for it was not lawful to initiate foreigners into these Mysteries. The hindrance was, however, removed from his path by Pylias, who consented to adopt him as his son, and so to naturalize him. Then he presented himself for initiation ; but, in his preliminary confession, it was discovered that he was debarred from the Mysteries on account of blood-guilt, because he had not been purified since the slaughter of the Centaurs. Eumolpus, however, purified and absolved him : then the initiation was effected, and Hercules was enabled to make his successful descent into Hades through the entrance on Mount Tænarus.

On his return, Euripides makes him tell Amphitryon, that he had been so fortunate as to be admitted to a sight of the Mysteries below, his initiation on the earth having entitled him to share the privileges of the initiated among the dead.[2]

But initiation into the Mysteries was supposed to confer great advantages upon the living, as well as upon the dead. For instance, the Scholiast on Apollonius of Rhodes [3] informs us, that the initiates of the Samothracian Mysteries could always obtain an answer when they prayed to the gods.

Again, Cicero praises the Eleusinian Mysteries in these terms ;—

"For, of all the many excellent and Divine things that your Athens seems to have produced and

---

[1] That is, to fetch up Cerberus. See Apollod. *Bibl.* ii. 5, 12.
[2] Eurip. *Herc. Fur.* 613.
[3] See Scholiast on Apollon., Arg. i. 918.

diffused among men, nothing is, in my opinion, superior to those Mysteries by which we have been raised from a rude and savage condition to that cultivation which befits men, and have been endowed with gentler manners. And so, we have recognized what are called the initiations as expressing the true principles of life; for we have learnt from them, not only how to live joyously, but also how to die with a better hope." [1]

If we examine the teaching of the Lesser Mysteries, which, in part at least, seems to have leaked out, we shall at once perceive its affinity with the Buddhistic, Egyptian, Platonic, and other ancient philosophies, as well as with modern Spiritualism and Theosophy. It sets forth matter and the material world as the cause and concomitant of all evil. The human soul existed from everlasting, and was originally Divine; but it fell from its heavenly sphere, became involved in matter, and was, consequently, subjected to passion, emotions, lusts, and every kind of evil: and the condition into which it had thus lapsed was termed 'generation.'

Hence the all-important task before it was to discover and acknowledge its real state: to perceive that what men call life is really death, that what presents itself to the eyes of the body, and seems to be solid and firm, in the material world, is but a phantasmal illusion that veils the eternal realities. As soon as the soul apprehended this truth, it began to yearn for freedom from matter and all its ills, and for a return to its original and purely spiritual condition, which it could obtain only "by an interior reunion with the Divine Essence." And this reunion could be effected by the ceremonies and teachings of the Mysteries,

[1] Cic. *De Legg*. ii. 14.

but in no other way. He who was duly initiated, and could assimilate the teachings of the Hierophants, would at death be freed for ever from the prison of a material body, and would dwell as a happy spirit with the gods. But he who had not been initiated would be cast into gloom, and, perhaps, subjected to torments, in Hades. At intervals he would return to the world in divers kinds of body, either ascending or descending in the scale of being, according to the deserts of each previous life. And these changes would continue, until by suffering he had become purged from his gross and evil proclivities, and was fitted to partake of the sacred Mysteries, and to receive and obey the teaching of the Hierophants, which would at last open to him the Elysian gates.

In the temporary punishments of Hades, we see the origin of the Catholic Purgatory, though the Catholic churches have not hitherto ventured to add the doctrine of re-incarnation which is necessary for the completion of the scheme.

LVII

THE MYSTERY-PLAYS

IN order to enforce the teaching which we have just described, dramatic scenes in the lives of the gods were exhibited to the wondering eyes of the initiates, by what means, or in what precise manner, we do not know. Possibly, the Hierophant may have used an apparatus something like that by which our dissolving views are produced; or, for ought we know, he may have been aided by demoniacal power. And here, apparently, we may see the origin of the Mystery-plays of the Dark Ages, which certain clergymen have been recently striving to revive, and of that awful profanation of our Lord's sufferings and death which is acted every ten years in the village of Ober-Ammergau.

These dramas varied in the different Mysteries, because each was usually taken from the life of the god in whose honour the particular Mysteries were celebrated. But their motive was invariably the same: they were always divided into three acts—the loss or disappearance,[1] the search,[2] and the finding;[3] which corresponded respectively to the fall of the soul from the empyreal heights, its sojourn in the material world, and its restoration.

In the Eleusinian Mysteries, the symbolical representations were taken from the myth of Ceres and her daughter Proserpina—the carrying off of the latter by Pluto while she was gathering flowers in the Sicilian plains of Enna; the wanderings of the disconsolate mother, through the length and breadth of the earth, in search of her; the discovery of Proserpina in Hades, and her partial restoration. For she could not be wholly restored, because she had eaten the food of the dead, and, therefore, could never be entirely freed from the power of Hades.

In the Dionysiac Mysteries, the story of Bacchus Zagreus was the subject of the scenes that passed before the eyes of the initiates—his cruel dismemberment by the Titans, and the boiling and roasting of his limbs; the destruction of his murderers by the thunders of Zeus, before they could devour their horrid banquet; the preservation of the heart of Bacchus by Pallas, and of his limbs by Apollo; and his final restoration to integrity, to life, and to divinity.

---

[1] ἀφανισμός.   [2] ζήτησις.   [3] εὕρεσις.

Lastly, the initiates of Isis gazed upon the strange murder of Osiris, enclosed and stifled by the conspirators in the coffer of Typho ; upon the journeyings of Isis in quest of the coffer, and her subsequent search for the scattered limbs of her husband ; and upon the final elevation of the latter to the ranks of the gods.

From these examples it will be seen that the several Mysteries, though apparently diverse, yet communicated, so far as the origin and destiny of man is concerned, precisely the same fundamental dogma. And a multiplicity of incidents in the great dramas seem to have supplied a basis for other doctrines, especially that of metempsychosis, or the passing of spirits, which at death were found unfit for deliverance from the bondage of matter, into body after body, until they were purified by suffering.

Such teachings are briefly summed up by Pindar in the fragment, which has come down to us, from his dirge for an Athenian initiate ;—

" Happy is the man who has seen those Mysteries before he goes down beneath the hollow earth. He knows what must come after life, and he knows, also, its divine origin." [1]

LVIII

INITIATION INTO THE LESSER MYSTERIES

DOUBTLESS many other things, also, which have never been divulged, were taught in the Lesser Mysteries ; and occult knowledge and supernatural experiences were among the privileges of the initiate. Of these we can, of course, say nothing ; but will quote what Apuleius chooses to tell us of his initiation. After

[1] Pind. Fragm. cii.

speaking of his baptism, or cleansing with water, by
the priests for the expiation of his sins, and of the ten
days during which he abstained from flesh and wine,
he proceeds as follows ;—

"When these days had been fully observed by me
with reverential fasting, the day appointed for the
divine pledge had now arrived, and the sun in his
downward course was ushering in the evening.   Then,
lo, crowds flock together from all sides, each person
honouring me with divers presents, according to the
ancient custom of the sacred rites.   Afterwards, when
all the profane had been removed far away, the
priest takes me by the hand, and brings me, clothed
in a new garment, into the inner chambers of the
sanctuary itself.

"Perhaps, curious reader, you may be eagerly
inquiring what was then said, and what was done.
I would tell you, if it were lawful to tell: you should
know, if it were lawful for you to hear.   But the
ears that heard these Mysteries, and the tongues that
divulged them, would incur an equal penalty for such
rash curiosity.   I will not, however, torment you with
protracted anguish, held in suspense as you, perhaps,
are by a religious longing.

"Hear, then, but believe only what things are true.
I approached the confines of death, and, after treading
the threshold of Proserpina, returned therefrom, being
borne through all the elements.   At midnight, I
saw the sun glittering with his brilliant light.   I drew
near to the gods infernal and the gods celestial, and
worshipped in their immediate presence.   Lo, I have
recounted to you things of which, though you have
heard them, you must still of necessity be ignorant."[1]

[1] Apul. *Metam.* xi. 23.

LIX

THE MORALITY OF THE MYSTERIES
CATHOLIC "ECONOMY"

As to the general tone of the morality that was inculcated at the Mysteries, our limits will permit us to quote but one example, which we take from Augustine's exposure of the principles of Varro. That " most acute and most learned "[1] writer, in speaking of religious obligations, says ;—

"There are many truths which it is not merely useless for common folk to know, but expedient that people should believe the precise contrary to them, even though in doing this they believe what is not true ; and it was for this reason that the Greeks were wont to conceal their initiatory rites and Mysteries by silence and within walls."[2]

Hence the initiates of the Mysteries were compelled to live a lie. They were taught to regard the instructions of the Hierophants as absolute truth, and the widely differing superstitions of the populace as false ; nevertheless, they were directed to profess their belief in the latter, and to conform to them outwardly ; for that it was necessary to frighten and keep down the mob by religious fictions and phantom-horrors.

Here we have a very high and ancient precedent for that diplomatic suppression of truth which the Alexandrian "Fathers" adopted under the name of 'economy,' in which the Jesuits have the credit of being consummate masters, which Newman carefully instilled

---

[1] Aug. *De Civ, Dei,* vi, 6.　　　　[2] Ibid. iv. 31.

into the leaders of the Tractarian Movement,[1] and which appears to have been largely used by the Society of the Holy Cross, the Confraternity of the Blessed Sacrament, the Order of Corporate Reunion, and similar organizations, which were carried on in secret, so long as this was possible.

Thus were the initiates demoralized from the first; and when they had once consented to set expediency above truth, there would be little difficulty in persuading them to abandon other honest scruples. In their very initiation, they were stamped with the brand of him of whom it is said, that, " when he speaketh a lie, he speaketh of his own ; for he is a liar, and the father thereof." [2] And far, indeed, were they removed from

[1] In a letter from the Rev. R. F. Wilson to J. H. Newman, dated August 9th, 1836, the following significant paragraph occurs ;—

" By-the-bye, why will you economise so unnecessarily at times ? as if to keep your hand in. You sent Major B. away with a conviction that you looked on D. as a very fine noble character. As he had received this information fresh from you, I did not venture to say anything subversive of your judgment; so now he will, probably, publish the high admiration and respect with which D. is looked up to by his late comrades—more especially by Mr. Newman." —Mozley's *Letters and Correspondence of J. H. Newman*, Vol. ii., p. 207.

We extract one other instance of " economy " from Walsh's *Secret History of the Oxford Movement*, p. 59 ;—

" The first clergyman placed by the Society of the Holy Cross in charge of the (St. George's) Mission was the late Rev. Charles Lowder, and to him, on May 31st, 1856, the Rev. Bryan King wrote as follows ;—' Upon the principles of your scheme for the Mission, of course, I quite agree ; as to the time for carrying some of them out and the Christian *Economy and Reserve to be observed (respecting some of them)*, of course that must be left to the members of the Mission.' This Reserve and Economy was particularly shown in the earliest Reports of the ' St. George's Mission,' in which its Ritualistic character was studiously kept out of sight, and thus, no doubt, many were induced to aid it who would otherwise have withheld their subscriptions and donations on conscientious grounds."

[2] John viii. 44.

Him Who has declared, that "all liars shall have their part in the lake that burneth with fire and brimstone."[1]

We will mention one other incentive to a particular kind of immorality, which characterized the Mysteries. The didactic dramas exhibited to the initiates were horribly obscene, and, which was still worse, represented the gods as delighting in every kind of abomination. As a mild example of this feature, we may cite an incident from the Eleusinian shows. When Ceres, as she wanders in quest of her lost daughter, cannot be allured from her sadness, a peasant woman, named Baubo, makes a disgustingly indecent exposure of herself before the goddess (!), who is thereby moved to merriment and forgetfulness of her trouble.[2]

And, such being the nature of the deities, we cannot wonder that it was customary to raise obscene symbols before them, and to address them in corresponding terms: nor is it strange that the dramatic scenes which represented their acts should be impure and defiling.

But these abominable practices appear to have heavily oppressed the conscience of the more pure-minded of the initiates; and Porphyry, in his epistle

[1] Rev. xxi. 8.

[2] "Isocrates speaks of 'good offices' rendered to Demeter by 'our ancestors,' which 'can only be told to the initiate' (*Panegyr.* 28). Now these cannot be the kindly deeds reported in the Hymn; for they were publicly proclaimed. What then were the *secret* good offices? . . .

"Can Isocrates have referred to *this* good office?—the amusing of Demeter by an obscene gesture? If he did, such gestures as Baubo's are as widely diffused as any other pieces of folk-lore. In the centre of the Australian desert, Mr. Carnegie saw a native make a derisive gesture which he thought had only been known to English schoolboys. Again, indecent pantomimic dances, said to be intended to act as 'object-lessons' in things *not* to be done, are common in Australian Mysteries."—Lang's *Homeric Hymns*, pp. 86-8.

to Anebo the Egyptian, asks for an explanation of them. The attempted solution of the difficulty by " Abammon the Preceptor,"[1] in response to Porphyry's question, is worth consideration as an example of the corrupting influences of Mystery-teaching.

"But yet another reason may be assigned for these practices. The energies of the human passions that are in us, if altogether restrained, become more violent, but if allowed to have their play for a brief season, and only to a proper limit, they take their pleasure with moderation, and are satiated ; and so, becoming purified, they yield to persuasion even without force. And for this reason, when we gaze upon the emotional passions of others in comedy or tragedy, we instinctively check our own, and moderate them, and purge them away. Just so, in the sacred ceremonies, by the help of certain disgraceful sights which we see and utterances which we hear, we free ourselves from the harm that, in case of actual deeds, results therefrom.

"Such practices, then, as these, are introduced for the healing of the soul that is in us, for the mitigation of those evils that adhere to it through generation, and for the purpose of freeing and releasing it from its bonds. And, on this account, Heraclitus appropriately termed such things 'remedies,' as being intended to heal dread disorders, and as freeing our souls from the calamities that are involved in generation."[2]

The fearful perversion, by which the presentation of impure and lewd scenes before the eyes of the initiates was regarded as a remedy for their easily

---

[1] Probably a *nom de plume* of the well-known Iamblicus.
[2] Iambl. *De Myst.* i. 11.

excited passions, is incomprehensible to minds that have not been carefully trained for its reception : it supplies a vivid illustration of the first chapter of the Epistle to the Romans, and of the deadly corruption with which the earth was overspread by the religion of Satan.[1]

"This," remarks Gale in his comments on Iamblicus, "is as true as if he had said, You will put out a fire if you pour a little oil into the furnace." On such a principle, one should be able to save the young tiger from becoming a man-eater by suffering him to taste human blood.

Yet his constant study of, and entire devotion to, Paganism has caused "the English Platonist," Thomas Taylor, to regard this doctrine as "so rational that it can never be objected to by any but quacks in philosophy and religion"; and he strives to persuade us, that "the purity and excellence" of the Mysteries "are perpetually acknowledged." His own book on the Eleusinian and Bacchic Mysteries, and especially the illustrated American edition of it, is the best refutation of his plea.

But Augustine, who wrote when the Mysteries were still a living influence in the world, came to a very different conclusion respecting them. The demons, he says, who directed them were, indeed, supposed, in the secrecy of their shrines and inner chambers, to give some good moral precepts to certain persons who, as being initiates, might be called their elect : why, then, was everything which they placed before the eyes of the public full of the most horrid impurity?

---

[1] Let it be remembered, that not merely natural, but also unnatural, lusts were exhibited in these Mystery-plays, and that the latter were freely attributed to the gods.

But his strong feelings on this subject will be best expressed by a free rendering of his own words ;—

"In what place, or at what time, the initiates of the Heavenly Virgin were wont to hear the precepts of chastity, we know not. But this, at least, we know. In front of her very shrine, where we used to contemplate her celebrated image, there, amid the general crowd that flocked together from all quarters and took its stand just where each man could, we were accustomed to gaze with the keenest interest on the shows that were going on, beholding, as we turned from one side to the other, here a solemn procession of harlots, there the Virgin Goddess. She was adored with supplications, while disgraceful ceremonies were being performed before her. There we saw no shamefaced mimes, no too modest actress : all the requirements of the abominable rites were supplied to the minutest particular. One was soon made to know what was pleasing to the Virgin Deity ; and the show was such that even the matron had learned something new when she returned home from the temple. Some of the more discreet women did, indeed, turn away their face from the lascivious motions of the actors, and learnt the art of wickedness by means of side glances. For a feeling of shame in the presence of men restrained them from daring to look boldly on the lewd gestures : yet still more powerfully were they restrained from daring to condemn with chaste mind the rites of the goddess whom they were adoring. Meanwhile, they were being taught publicly, in the temple, actions for which one would, at least, require secrecy, if they had to be done at home ; and human modesty, if there were such a thing in the place, must have been greatly wondering why men could not freely indulge in those crimes which, in the presence of the gods, they were actually learning as a matter of religious teaching, and in the belief that they would incur divine anger if they omitted to have them set forth.

" For what spirit can that be, which, with an unseen spur, incites the utterly corrupt minds of men, goads them on to adulteries, and gloats over the success of their efforts, unless it be the same as that which revels in filthy religious rites, setting images of demons in the temples, and loving to see representations of vices in the shows ;—the same as that which whispers words of justice in secret, to deceive even the few that are virtuous ; while, in public, it is ever repeating its allurements to wickedness, that it may secure its hold upon the countless crowds of evil doers ? " [1]

Such is the picture of Paganism as directed by the demons of the Mysteries, which has been drawn for us by the hand of Augustine. It would seem almost impossible to conceive a more corrupting influence. And yet, so deadly a system as this was allowed to infuse its principles into Christianity, until, in many points, it had transformed the latter into its own image, and the community called the Church had become worldly, sensuous, and demoniac ; even as Jerusalem was spiritually called Sodom and Egypt.

LX

THE GREATER MYSTERIES. THE NUMBER OF THE BEAST

As regards the Greater Mysteries, we know but little beyond that which was exhibited in public. At least

[1] Aug. *De Civ. Dei*, ii. 26.

a year must have elapsed since the candidate had been initiated into the Lesser at Agrae; but it by no means followed that he would necessarily be admitted to the Greater. Should he, however, be deemed worthy, he would then be privileged to hear the Aporrheta, the secrets which it was not lawful to divulge, and would become an ephor, and, possibly, afterwards an epopt.

The secret teachings of the Aporrheta seem never to have been divulged : they were, probably, a revelation, more or less, of the real doctrines and aims of the vast community, or rather of those few who were leading it whither it knew not. It would seem that they were much the same in all the various Mysteries, just as it is said, that, diverse as are the Brahmanic and Buddhist religions, yet the *yogis*, or higher initiates, of both of them seem to fraternize and believe the same things.

But it is worthy of note, that Apuleius represents his second initiation as being connected with Osiris, a male deity and the supreme god. These are his words ;—

"And whilst I was discussing my religious doubt in my own mind, and was pondering it, aided by the counsels of the initiated, I discovered a thing that was quite new and marvellous to me ; that is to say, that I had been initiated only into the Mysteries of the goddess, and had not yet been enlightened by the Mysteries of the great god and parent of the gods, the invincible Osiris. For, although the essence of their divinity and their religion is connected, or rather is united, nevertheless, there is a very great difference in their initiatory rites. Hence, I was to understand that I was also called to be a servant even of the great god."[1]

[1] Apul. *Metam.* xi. 27.

From other authors, too, it seems that a male deity appeared to the higher initiates, who were probably taught that he alone was supreme. His countenance was described as being of a highly intellectual but pensive and severe cast; and it is likely that he was none other than the great Adversary himself, whom the Pagans believed to have been driven out of heaven by the ruling god, but regarded as a lover of men, and as showing himself more indulgent to them than his vanquisher. Moreover, they thought that he was soon to return in triumph, and to restore the golden age: but that, meanwhile, he was concealed in that part of Italy which was, consequently, called Latium, or the 'hiding-place,'[1] the adjective from which, Latinus would signify 'the Hidden One.'

Hence we may infer the true meaning of the famous passage in Irenæus, which has been mis-interpreted by "Historicists." For they affirm that Irenæus, in calling our attention to the fact that the number 666 is contained in Latinus,[2] signified no more than that the Beast was to be a Latin man, that is, the Pope, or rather, according to their explanation, a long series of Popes. But there would be little mystery in the enigma, and no need whatever of "the mind that hath wisdom" to solve it, if it merely expressed the fact that the Antichrist is to be connected with the Fourth Empire: that, indeed, had been already revealed in other prophecies. The meaning seems, however, to be quite different: the writer, who had, probably, himself been an initiate before his conversion,

---

[1] They derived it from *lateo*, to be hid, whence comes our English word '*latent*.'
[2] In Greek, the language in which the computation is made, Λατεῖνος.

informs us of the belief of some, that the Antichrist would prove to be the concealed deliverer whom the Pagans were expecting, and who, in the language of the Mysteries, was sometimes called Latinus, or the 'Hidden One.' And, to this very day, Brahmans, Buddhists, and Theosophists, are looking for the *avatâr* of a mighty one, who is to change the aspect of the world, and to restore the times of joy; while even Mahometans are talking of their coming Mahdi, and many Jews hope for the appearing of an earthly leader, whom they will hail as their long-expected Messiah.

LXI

THE APPEARANCE OF DEITIES OR SAINTS: HIOUEN-THSANG AND THE SHADOW OF BUDDHA

THE appearance of a deity, or a supernatural being, to initiates, to devout worshippers, or to specially favoured mortals, is an idea which is by no means confined to the Mysteries, but has been widely spread over the earth, from the most ancient times down to the date of the apparitions at La Salette, Lourdes, Knock, and Llantony Abbey, in our own days. And a very curious instance of it is to be found in the Chinese book, *The Travels of Hiouen-thsang*, translated into French, some years ago, by M. Stanislas Julien.

The subject of the narrative was a devout and learned Buddhist priest, who lived towards the middle of the seventh century, and, being unable to procure further help for his religious studies in China, resolved to make his way to India, the country of Buddha. His adventures on the journey were marvellous, and his description of the populous flourishing and civilized cities of Central Asia at the time surprises us—almost as much as did the recovered library of Telel-Armana by its disclosure of the condition of Palestine and the surrounding countries a century and a half before Moses.

When the adventurous traveller had reached Peshawur, he was told of a wondrous cavern in which the shadow of Buddha sometimes appeared to those that were worthy. Thither he assayed to go, undeterred by the warning of dangers by the way; and, not without peril, arrived at the mouth of the cave. What followed we will quote from Max Müller's review of the narrative.

" He passed a stream rushing down between two precipitous walls of rock. In the rock itself there was a door which opened. All was dark. But Hiouen-thsang entered, advanced towards the East, then moved fifty steps backwards, and began his devotions. He made one hundred salutations; but he saw nothing. He reproached himself bitterly with his former sins—he cried, and abandoned himself to utter despair, because the shadow of Buddha would not appear before him. At last, after many prayers and invocations, he saw on the eastern wall a dim light, of the size of a saucepan such as the Buddhist monks carry in their hands. But it disappeared. He continued praying, full of joy and pain, and again he saw a light, which vanished like lightning. Then he vowed, full of devotion and love, that he would never leave the place until he had seen the shadow of the ' Venerable of the Age.' After two hundred prayers, the cave was suddenly bathed in light, and the shadow of Buddha, of a brilliant white colour, rose majestically on the wall,

29

as when the clouds suddenly open and display, all at once, the marvellous image of the 'Mountain of Light.' A dazzling splendour lighted up the features of the divine countenance. Hiouen-thsang was lost in contemplation and wonder, and would not turn his eyes away from the sublime and incomparable object."

By the "shadow" of Buddha, we are to understand his spirit, which was said, also, to appear to the faithful on his high altar between the lights placed on either side, as in a Catholic church. In his *Buddhism in Christendom*, Mr. Arthur Lillie has two plates representing this apparition, the one from a Chinese source, the other from Amarâvati, on which he remarks ;—

"I give the Buddhist high altar with its lower altar in front, like that of the Catholics ; with its lamp perpetually burning, like theirs, its artificial flowers, thurifers, and tall candlesticks with wax candles made out of a vegetable wax. Votive tablets, like dolls' tombstones, crowd it with offerings to the dead. In the Middle Ages, Catholic churches were similarly choked. In front of Buddha is the Sambo or three-sided box, hollow behind. Always in front of it is represented the cross made up of four circles, the four stages of spiritual growth. 'I regard the sacred altar as a royal gem, on which the shadow of S'akya-Tathâgata '—that is, the spirit of Buddha—'appears.' [2] See Plate xiii. p. 210. This —Plate xii—is from the Chinese ritual, and the accompanying bas-relief from Amarâvati reminds

[1] Max Müller's *Buddhism and Buddhist Pilgims*, p. 38.
[2] Beal's *Catena of Buddhist Scriptures*, p. 243.

one of the Armenian collect[1] which describes Christ
with His saints as also descending in the chariot
of the four fiery faces."[2]

LXII

"THE REAL PRESENCE"

THE altar, then, is that on which the shadow, or spirit,
of Buddha is revealed between the lights placed on
either side of it ; and the reader who has seen pictures
of the Roman Mass—such as the one from Le Brun
which is given in Dr. C. H. H. Wright's useful pamphlet,
" The Service of the Mass "—will scarcely fail to observe
the exact correspondence between the Pagan and the
Catholic doctrine. And the close connection between
nature-worship and Catholicism may be further illustrated
by the following extract :—

"The two sentinel or standard candles, with their
spiry flames, are the mystic tremendous pillars, or
uprights, known in the Temple of Solomon by the
names of Jachin to the right hand of the altar, and of
Boaz to the left hand of the altar.[3] They are twin
candles, though separate ; and they witness to the

[1] It runs as follows ;—"Thou who, seated in Majesty on the
fiery chariot of four faces, ineffable Word of God, hast come down
from heaven for Thy creatures, and deigned to-day to sit at table
with Thy disciples. Surprised with admiration, the seraphim and
cherubim and principalities of the celestial cohorts gathered round,
crying in their astonishment, Holy, Holy, Holy, is the Lord of
Hosts." It is a chariot with four faces that brings down Buddha,
in the form of a little white elephant, to be born on earth.

[2] *Buddhism in Christendom*, pp. 207–8.

[3] Since this extract is taken from a mystic writer, we need not
notice the alleged connection of the candles with the two pillars in
the front of Solomon's Temple. That is, probably, no more than an
exoteric explanation intended for the uninitiated, and does not point
to the real meaning of the lights.

presence of the Divinity disclosed in his aspect of fire ; and, therefore, in all true living effective celebrations they are absolutely necessary to be LIGHTED, if the Holy Eucharist is to be construed as a Divine sacrifice. If accepted only as a commemorative Communion Supper—partaken of at a Table—they need not be lighted. Indeed, at a mere Communion Service, implying the possibility of no Real Presence, they have no meaning. . . . They are masculine to the right hand, which is the place of the Sun of the macrocosm ; feminine to the left hand, which is the place of the Moon, or mother of the macrocosm. They are the double, the great cleft—to speak in mystic figure ; or the division from between which the Sun of Righteousness displays splendid. From the centre-line they are supposed to file to the right hand and to the left, borne by unseen archangelic hands ; and to part from before it to disclose the Cross or the sun where the Ideal, or the Divine Man, is possible as crucified.

But we cannot go on with this mystical rhapsody. What has been already quoted, together with the subjoined words,[2] will suffice to show whither the writer is leading us, so far as our present subject is concerned ;—

"It is sought in this book particularly to see if, when we turn our eyes in all adoring faith to that mystic East, we may not spiritually find the Lord Jesus, He Whom we have come out to find, turning eastwards, or to the altar, really to discover Him personally and bodily. For in that way only can we know Him. We look for HIM upon that Altar,

[1] Jennings' *Live Lights or Dead Lights*, pp. 177–8.
[2] Ibid., pp. 197–8.

awful and awing. . . . In short, we seek Him as the visible, although Glorified, Man, in order that we may know Him as a Man-at-All, or as anything like ourselves—as a thing to know, or to have an idea about in any way."

So far as we can make out the meaning of these words, they signify, that the great hope of the faithful in the "Holy Eucharist" is to catch a glimpse of the shadow or Spirit of the Lord Jesus—or rather of the being, whoever he may be, that is indicated under cover of His Name—appearing between the lighted candles. And such an idea, as we have shown, is common to the Mysteries and to Buddhism, but is unknown to the New Testament. Such appears to be what is truly meant by the Real Presence.

LXIII

THE HIEROPHANT, OR PETER, WAS THE FIRST POPE
THE PONTIFEX MAXIMUS

To return now to our immediate subject, the Greater Mysteries, we find that there were four principal ministers who performed the ceremony of initiation.

First, the Hierophant,[1] a celibate priest, who took the leading part, and interpreted or explained the mystic dramas and doctrines to the ephors or epopts. It was his duty to communicate to them certain sacred writings, the contents of which might be heard by none but the higher initiates. These writings were preserved within two great stones, aptly joined together, and called Petroma, which were never separated save in the dead of night.[2]

---

[1] ὁ ἱεροφάντης. [2] Paus. viii. 15, 1.

The oriental name of the Hierophant was Pether or Peter, that is, 'Interpreter'; and it is from this Peter, and not from the Apostle, that the Pope really derives his succession. For when Damasus received the ring of the Pontifex Maximus[1] from the Emperor Gratian, he became the Peter, or Interpreter, of the established religion of the Roman Empire. But that religion was then a blend of Paganism and Christianity; so that those who were inclined to the latter were told that Peter was the Apostle, while the Pagans were well aware that Peter the Hierophant was the Pope's real predecessor.

It was this strange coincidence in names that induced Western Catholics to claim as their first Pope the particular Apostle who, of all the Twelve, was the most unfit to support the traditions of the Papacy. For Peter, after he had once opened the Kingdom of the Heavens to Gentiles by preaching to Cornelius, was thenceforth reckoned among the three Apostles who were to go to the Jews, leaving the Gentiles to Paul.[2] Secondly, there is no reliable evidence that Peter ever was at Rome: indeed, as an Apostle of the circumcision, he had no special business there. Thirdly, Peter was married,[3] which is contrary to the law of the Roman Church; and, not only so, but he actually took his wife with him on his missionary journeys.[4] Fourthly, he denied his Lord; and, lastly, he was neither infallible nor supreme; for, on one occasion, Paul had to resist him to the face, because he stood condemned.[5]

[1] In Dion. Hal., ii. 73, the Pontifex Maximus is called the Hierophant. See also iii. 36, and Plutarch. Num. Pompil. ix.
[2] Gal. ii. 9.   [3] Matt. viii. 14.   [4] 1 Cor. ix. 5.
[5] Gal. ii. 11. That Peter did not resent this interference, we may learn from the very touching reference to Paul in his Second Epistle to the dispersed Jews;—"And account that the long-

Probably the title of Pontifex Maximus, which is still borne by the Popes as it was by the Pagan Chief Pontiffs before them, has a meaning similar to that of Hierophant or Peter. Literally, Pontifex signifies a 'Bridge-maker'; but we may pass by, as absurd and intended only for the uninitiated, the explanation given by the Halicarnassian Dionysius,[1] and other writers, who would have us believe that the priests in Rome were called Pontifices, because they had the care of the Sublician Bridge. Upon which Plutarch remarks, that, whereas the Pontifices were instituted by Numa Pompilius, certain historians state that the Sublician Bridge was not opened until the later reign of Ancus Marcius.[2] It is, then, more likely that the priests were styled Bridge-makers in a figurative sense, as being those who alone could bridge the chasm between the seen and the unseen worlds, which they were supposed to do by instruction and ceremony, as being the revealers of, and the leaders on, the way to the abodes of the blest. Hence their head was called Pontifex Maximus, or the Chief Bridge-maker.

suffering of our Lord is salvation; even as our beloved brother Paul, also, according to the wisdom given unto him, wrote unto you; as also in all his Epistles, speaking in them of these things" (2 Peter iii. 15, 16). This passage is valuable as a proof that Paul did write an Epistle to the Hebrews, besides his other Epistles. And there is no reason to doubt that it was the one which has come down to us under that name. The objections which have been raised by opponents of the Bible, and by literary dilettanti, vanish before intelligent and unbiassed investigation. In no kind of literary work does a man's style vary so much as in epistolary composition, which must always be accommodated to the circumstances in which, and the people to which, one is writing.

[1] Dion. Hal. ii. 73.   [2] Plutarch. Num. Pompil. ix.

LXIV

INITIATION INTO THE HIGHER MYSTERIES

FOR the ceremony and instructions connected with initiation, the Hierophant had three assistants. These were the Torch-bearer,[1] the Attendant at the Altar,[2] and the Herald.[3]

Of the initiation itself Mr. Wilder quotes the following description, in his introduction to Taylor's *Eleusinian and Bacchic Mysteries* ;—

" Let us enter the mystic temple, and be initiated —though it must be supposed that, a year ago, we were initiated into the Lesser Mysteries at Agrae. We must have been *mystæ* (vailed) before we can become *epoptæ* (seers) ; in plain English, we must shut our eyes to all else before we can behold the Mysteries. Crowned with myrtle, we enter with the other initiates into the vestibule of the temple— blind as yet, but the Hierophant will soon open our eyes.

" But first—for here we must do nothing rashly— first we must wash in this holy water ; for it is with pure hands and a pure heart that we are bidden to enter the most sacred enclosure.[4] Then, when we have been led into the presence of the Hierophant, he reads to us, from a book of stone,[5] things which we must not divulge on pain of death. Let it suffice that they fit the place and the occasion ; and, though you might laugh at them if they were spoken outside, still you seem very far from that

---

[1] δᾳδοῦχος.   [2] ὁ ἐπὶ βωμῷ.   [3] ἱεροκῆρυξ.   [4] σηκὸς μυστικός.
[5] πέτρωμα.   Explained exoterically as being a reminiscence of Moses' two tables of stone : but it may be connected with the oriental root *pathar*, "to interpret." See p. 454.

mood now, as you hear the words of the old man (for old he always was), and look upon the revealed symbols. And very far, indeed, are you from ridicule, when Demeter seals, by her own peculiar utterance and signals, by vivid coruscations of light and cloud piled upon cloud, all that we have seen and heard from her sacred priest ; and then, finally, the light of a serene wonder fills the temple, and we see the pure fields of Elysium, and hear the chorus of the Blessed. Then, not merely by external seeming or philosophic interpretation, but in real fact, does the Hierophant become the Creator [1] and revealer of all things ; the Sun is but his torch-bearer, the Moon his attendant at the altar, and Hermes his mystic herald. But the final word has been uttered, "Conx Om Pax." The rite is consummated, and we are *epoptæ* for ever." [2]

LXV

THE HIEROPHANT, OR PRIEST, AS GOD

ONE point in the foregoing description we must notice, especially since it is confirmed by Porphyry : we mean the transformation of the Hierophant into the Creator. There is something analogous to this in the Tibetan ceremony, which has been called "the Eucharist of Lamaism," and the bread and wine of which are supposed to confer "the deepest life-power," or "undying life." The preparation of the magic food and

---

[1] δημιουργός.

[2] We must not for a moment suppose that, in this sketch, we have a full description of the ceremony of initiation. The sketch is made up of a few particulars which are thought to have been divulged ; but it certainly does not include the significant and essential part of the proceedings.

wine, together with other matters, occupies two or three days ; and what then happens we will quote from Waddell's *Buddhism of Tibet*.[1]

"Everything being ready, and the congregation assembled, the priest, ceremonially pure by the ascetic rites above noted, and dressed as in the frontispiece, abstracts from the great image of Buddha *Amitayus*[2] part of the divine essence of that deity, by placing the *vajra* of his *rdor-jehi gzun-t'ag* upon the nectar vase which the image of *Amitayus* holds in his lap, and applying the other end to his own bosom, over his heart. Thus, through the string, as by a telegraph wire, passes the divine spirit, and the Lama must mentally conceive that his heart is in actual union with that of the god *Amitayus*, and that, for the time being, he is himself that god. Then he invokes his tutelary-fiend, and through him the fearful horse-necked Hayagriva (Tamdin), the king of the demons. The Lama with this divine triad—namely, the Buddha and the two demon-kings —incorporate in him, and exhibiting the forms of all three to spiritual eyes, now dispenses his divine favours."

The favours are, of course "the wine of life" and "the pills of life," the latter being made of flour sugar and butter.

From this prevalent idea of Paganism, that the Hierophant, or priest presiding over the Mysteries, became God, and from this alone, are we able to explain the position taken by the Roman priest in the Mass. For, from one point of view, the Mass is regarded as a Mystery-play, representing the facts connected with the sufferings and death of our Lord. And its

[1] P. 446.   [2] That is, Lord of Infinite Life.

avowed object is to excite feelings of devotion in the minds of the people for what are plainly called "the Sacred Mysteries."

Thus, according to the popular interpretation, sanctioned by the Roman Church, the intention of the priest's vestments is to make him a living representation of Christ. The biretta points to the crown of thorns ; the amice to the cloth with which the Jews covered our Lord's face [1] in the hall of Caiaphas, when they smote Him, and cried in mockery, " Prophesy unto us, Thou Christ, who is he that smote Thee ? " [2] The alb, also, is said to represent the robe with which Herod clothed the Lord, when he and his men of war set Him at nought, and mocked Him ; [3] the girdle, the cord with which He was secured in the Garden of Gethsemane ; the maniple on the left hand, the thongs wherewith He was bound to the pillar to be scourged ; the stole, the rope by which he was led to crucifixion ; and the chasuble, His seamless robe. And so, as a mystical writer has expressed it ;—

" The theory of the ' Sacrament,' of the sacrifice of a Victim on the altar of the World, is that the priest, as the representative expiant . . . is *himself* the emblemmed ' Christ,' undergoing, in the processes of this inexpressible grandly acute celebration, all the typical accumulated agonies resultant from, and atoning for, the first ' Fall,' and reconciling to God

---

[1] Mark xiv. 65.

[2] Matth. xxvi. 68.

[3] Luke xxiii. 11. The alb is a white robe, and this, at first sight, does not seem to agree with the " gorgeous " of the A.V. and R.V., since the word which they use is usually associated with the brighter and richer colours. But their rendering is inappropriate ; for the Greek word λαμπρός properly means white, but points to a glistering as opposed to a lustreless white. So λαμπρὸς ἐσθής is used for *toga candida* in Polyb. x. 5, 1.

from them, as the paid penalty, and so the elected expiation ! For Man himself, in life, is the Martyr."[1]

Where such representations and such statements are prevalent, it is not wonderful that even the educated regard the priest as standing in the stead of God, and as having power to exercise the exclusive prerogative of God, that is, the forgiveness of sins ; while the uneducated receive him for all practical purposes as God Himself. But it is important to know that the precedent for this comes from Paganism, and not from Christianity.

And this fact, again, proves that the popular and authorised Roman Catholic exposition, as given above, does not divulge the true meaning of the priest's dress ; but is merely an exoteric comment intended to convey the idea that what takes place in the Mass is Christianity. Hence the frequent inappropriateness of the dress to the proffered explanation : the biretta, to cite one instance, does not at all remind us of the crown of thorns.

LXVI

A THIRD ORDER OF INITIATES CORRESPONDING TO BISHOPS. APOSTOLICAL SUCCESSION. THE TONSURE.

IN discussing the entrance-initiation into the Greater Mysteries, we hinted that the Aporrheta which were revealed in connection with it would not include all the aims and secrets of the society ; for there was yet a third initiation,[2] accessible only to a few who were

[1] Jennings' *Live Lights or Dead Lights*, pp. 176-7.
[2] As we have already remarked, it is held by some scholars that the initiates of the second initiation were called ephors, and that only those who had obtained the third privilege were epopts.

thought worthy of the honour, and capable of the responsiblity which it involved. It was the consummation of all that had gone before ; and the initiates were crowned, and authorised thenceforth to teach others what they had learned themselves. They were eligible for any office connected with the Mysteries, from that of Hierophant downwards : through them alone could candidates be admitted to the privileges of the great society : they were its real rulers and directors, and, probably, the only members who were fully acquainted with its aims and secrets.

From this it will be evident, that the doctrine of Apostolical Succession, which cannot be found in the New Testament, is also derived from the Mysteries. For, in connection with the latter, no one had authority to teach the secret doctrines or to initiate others, save those who had received the third initiation at the hands of duly qualified Hierophants. And this third initiation seems to correspond to the third order of clergy in the Catholic Churches, that of bishops ; whose office, as we have already seen, has no Scriptural warrant.

But, although the Lord never appointed bishops, and they seem to have been introduced merely for the purpose of assimilating the churches to the Mysteries, and of uniting and organizing them as an earthly power, yet there are very many who accept as an article of faith the doctrine, that spiritual grace descends solely through this third order ; and that, if there be no bishops, there can be no church ! Just so, if there had been no Hierophants, there could have been no Mysteries.

An illustration of the working of this idea in the Catholic Churches may be found in Scarth's *Story of the Old Catholic and Kindred Movements*. The writer is dealing with the Church of Utrecht, which had but.

three bishops, and, since she was out of communion with Rome, could get no others should she chance to lose all three at one time : because bishops can only be made by bishops. Now, in 1810, two of these bishops had died, and so, says the writer, the Church of Holland "hung on a single life, that of Gisbert de Jong, Bishop of Deventer." He afterwards adds ;—

> "We have watched the struggling little church through many dangers and vicissitudes, but her narrowest escape was yet to come. One dark night the Bishop of Deventer missed his footing and fell into a canal, being only just saved after some minutes of terrible peril, during which minutes the existence of the Church of Utrecht hung trembling in the balance. She seems to have been preserved on purpose to do a great work." [1]

Is not this doctrine, that the very existence of a church depends upon its bishops—an order which the Lord neither appointed nor sanctioned—a frank avowal that the Catholic Church derived her orders and laws from other sources, and not from Him ?

Apuleius seems to intimate that the third initiation was specially concerned with Osiris, whom he styles "the god better than the great gods, and the highest of the greater, and the greatest of the highest, and the ruler of the greatest." [2] Since his reference is confined to the deified fallen angels and demons, we can readily understand to whom this grand title is given. In connection with his final initiation, Apuleius remarks ;—

> "And that I should not have to mingle with the rest of the crowd when ministering to his sacred rites, he chose me to be a member of the college

---

[1] Pp. 98–9.   [2] Apul. *Metam.* xi. 30.

of his own *pastophori*,[1] nay, even to be one of the quinquennial decurions. Finally, then, after my head had been shaved,[2] I joyfully entered upon the duties of the college—most ancient as it was, and founded near the famous times of Sulla—without attempting to shade or cover my baldness, but exposing it to view whithersoever I turned."

This baldness was, of course, the priestly or monkish tonsure, which was essentially Pagan,[3] and was found wherever the Chaldean religion had penetrated. The custom, which, if it were the round tonsure, signified dedication to the many named sun-god, is so ancient that, after God had brought Israel out of Egypt, He forbade the Aaronic priests to follow what was then the practice of Egypt. " They shall not," He said, "make baldness upon their head."[4] Indeed, the tonsure was so decided a mark of Paganism that it was some time before it could be established in the Western Church.

This seems to be proved by the following remarkable words from Jerome's commentary on Ezekiel ;[5]—

" As to what follows, 'Their heads they shall not shave, nor suffer their locks to grow long, but polling they shall poll their heads'; by this it is clearly shown, that we ought not to have shaven heads, like the priests and worshippers of Isis and Serapis."

This is the opinion of a prominent ecclesiastic towards the close of the fourth century, one, also, who

---

[1] Priests who carried the image of the god in a sort of shrine, just as images are now carried in Roman Catholic processions.

[2] This seems to show that all initiates of the third or highest degree were priests.

[3] What Apuleius says is sufficient to prove that; but see also Juven. vi. 523, and Mart. xii. xxix. 19.

[4] Lev. xxi. 5.　　　　[5] xliv. 20.

was a rabid supporter of monasticism, and of other
Catholic practices and doctrines.

Among Roman Catholics, the tonsure is sometimes
called the tonsure of Peter, which it undoubtedly was
—not, however, of Peter the Apostle, but of Peter the
Hierophant, who was a celibate and tonsured priest,
and of whom we have spoken above.[1]

LXVII

The Working of the Leaven

Such, then, was the great institution which was
covering the earth with its various branches at the
time of the Lord's First Advent, and was influencing
human legislature, education, social life, politics, religion,
and history in general, far more than is usually conceived ; which, moreover, as we may see from the many
allusions to it by contemporary writers, had entwined
itself in the heart of the people. Of the last mentioned
fact a proof may be found in the indignation expressed
by the populace of Athens when they thought that
Alcibiades had divulged certain secrets of the Mysteries.
Also in an incident related by Zosimus, who tells us
that Pretextatus pleaded with Valentinian not to abolish
the Mysteries—though their immorality could not be
denied—on the ground that "the Greeks would regard
life as unsupportable, if they were not permitted to
celebrate those most sacred Mysteries which bind
together the human race." Valentinian yielded to the
plea, and, consequently, did not enforce his very salutary
law, which forbade nocturnal sacrifices as being the main
cause of the scandals that he wished to avoid.

[1] See p. 454.

It is, then, easy to conceive how formidable an obstacle was presented to Christianity by the organizations of the Mysteries. For the countless clubs of initiates had their lodges in every city and large village; included among their members almost all citizens of rank, wealth, or weight in counsel; and exercised a vast influence by means of their specious teaching, supernatural shows, art-culture, and, with those who inclined to such things, by their brilliant festivals, and by the frequent opportunities which they afforded for the indulgence of lust.

But their leaders were not slow to perceive that in Christianity they had a dangerous rival, and they observed its steady and rapid progress with dismay. The result of their jealousy and apprehension was a desperate attempt to stamp out the new faith by what are usually called the Ten Persecutions. Soon, however, it became manifest that this means had little chance of success: therefore, another plan, also, was adopted, and carried out during the period of intermittent persecution.

Every species of Paganism, Polytheistic Monotheistic and Pantheistic, seems at that time to have combined against Christianity. A sort of eclectic religion was put together, in which all might join: it was composed of scraps from many quarters, faced with a considerable amount of Christian terminology, but with very little Christian doctrine, and that little carefully neutralized in some way or another. For its main constituents were drawn from the Mysteries: it was a digest of Pagan philosophy and mysticism, presented in their most intellectual form; albeit some other features of the Mysteries, more likely to impress the uneducated multitude, were also retained. Moreover,

30

the supernatural was called in, apparently from the same source, and in much the same manner, as in modern Spiritualism.

The movement, which began with Neo-Platonism, was, possibly, inaugurated by the remarkable set of dialogues after the manner of Plato, known as the " Poemandres," which dates from about the beginning of the second century. This work is attributed to Hermes Trismegistus, which is, probably, a *nom de plume*; but the real authorship and origin of the book are involved in impenetrable mystery.

In form and nomenclature, Neo-Platonism was assimilated more and more to Christianity, though its essence was altogether diverse from the latter ; and it was soon presented as the true Christian faith. But care was taken to retain in it just enough of what it pretended to be to stifle the qualms of those who, while conscious that Christianity was a Divine revelation, were also anxious to retain their respectability among their fellows by remaining attached to the fashionable religion, and so to make the best of both worlds.

Its final form seems to have been fixed by a writer as unknown, and as much enveloped in profound mystery, as Hermes Trismegistus ; but who, despite the fact that the appellation involved him in several anachronisms, was said to have been Dionysius the Areopagite. And the dismal result of his books, which influenced Christendom for more than a thousand years, was that compound of idolatry superstition and priestly domination, the Harlot Church of the Dark Ages, which thenceforth obscured the gracious offers of God to man, and persecuted and killed, whenever it could, those who sincerely desired to obey His commandments.

With these facts of history in view, we may well understand why the leaders of the Oxford Movement persisted in regarding the Christians of the fourth century, and not those of the first, as the primæval Church, which ought to be accepted as a model by all succeeding ages. From their own standpoint, they were right; for it was not until that time that *their* Church had become firmly established, and was able to displace and treat as heretics the servants of the Lord Jesus. And, strangely enough, the means by which the ancient Catholics effected their purpose were precisely the same as those which the Oxford conspirators have used so successfully to transform the once Evangelical Church of England into a Catholic community, actively engaged in destroying the pure doctrines of Christ, and in preaching salvation by the aid of sacraments and human priests. For these Neo-Platonists worked by means of secret societies; foisted themselves among the simple believers as if they, too, were brethren in the Lord, though their object was to draw away His disciples into their own corrupt society; and surreptitiously and gradually introduced Pagan ceremonies, images, and false doctrines, one by one, into the churches. And so, the leaven worked, until it had penetrated the whole lump.

LXVIII

THE TRANSFER OF PAGAN TERMS TO NOMINAL CHRISTIANITY

BUT, while the ceremonies and doctrines of the Mysteries were being transferred to the churches, their terminology, also, was adopted by Christians.

One of these terms is our word 'Sacrament,' which

is neither itself Scriptural nor conveys a Scriptural idea ; but is merely the Anglicized form of *sacramentum*, a Latin expression for the Greek μυστήριον, a mystery. Hence, even in the Prayer-book of the Church of England, the Lord's Supper is called "these holy Mysteries." But such a term for it is unknown in the New Testament, and was subsequently introduced merely because the initiates fixed upon the Memorial Supper as the one thing in Christianity which they could most easily metamorphose into a Mystery or Sacrament. Then associating Baptism with the bath which preceded initiation, they called it, also, a Mystery or Sacrament, though they often dropped all disguise, and spoke of it plainly as initiation.

Now there can be no doubt that they would have used the term Sacrament in the same sense as at the Pagan Mysteries, from which, in this signification, the word was derived ; that is to say, it would have meant some mechanical ceremony carried out by a duly qualified priest, which, when accompanied with certain spells incantations or invocations, was believed to produce a magical result. Thus, as we have already noticed, the Hierophants taught that initiation made a man sure of happiness in the next world. And, similarly, the act of Baptism would have been understood to purge away sin, and to cause regeneration, like the Pagan cleansings ; while the Lord's Supper would have been regarded as effecting, or perpetuating, "an interior union with the Divine Essence."

But, as we have already pointed out, both the Baptism and the Lord's Supper of Scripture are merely symbolical actions intended to express confession and remembrance of what has previously taken place, and not to ceremonialize people into life.

In this way, then, the meaning and intention of the Christian ordinances were changed, and they were assimilated to the Pagan Mysteries; so that the technical terms connected with the latter, such as 'Mysteries,' 'sacrament,' 'initiation,' 'mystagogue,' and so on, began to be heard in the nominally Christian churches. And a specimen of the way in which the semi-Pagan church-men of early times were wont to talk may be seen in the response of "the priests of Christ" to Constantine, when he was inquiring of them the way of salvation. As usual in those days, they seem to have known nothing of the Blood of Jesus Christ that cleanseth from all sin. They did, indeed, state that He had died and returned to life on the third day; but, according to Sozomen, they saw no expiation in this; their only inference from the great event was as follows;—

"On this account, they said, there was hope that, at the close of the present dispensation, there would be a general resurrection of the dead, and entrance upon immortality; when those who had led a good life would receive accordingly, and those who had done evil would be punished. Yet, they continued, the means of salvation and purification from sin are provided—namely, for the uninitiated, initiation according to the canons of the Church, and for the initiated, abstinence from renewed sin. But as few, even among holy men, are capable of complying with this latter condition, another method of purification is set forth, namely, repentance; for God, in His love towards man, bestows forgiveness on those who have fallen into sin on their repentance and the confirmation of their repentance by good works."[1]

[1] Sozom. *Hist. Eccle.* i. 3.

Here the "uninitiated" are the unbaptized, whether Pagans or catechumens. If they were initiated, that is, baptized according to the canons of the Church, they might be saved. In other words, the ecclesiastical authorities could ceremonialize sinners into salvation —a doctrine which obtained in the Mysteries, from whence the terms used are derived; but is nowhere to be found in the New Testament.

LXIX

APOSTOLICAL TRADITION

BUT the Mysteries and the so-called Christianity of early times had also another feature in common, to which we have already alluded. Both of them taught a double theology, the exoteric and the esoteric. In the Mysteries, the former might be divulged to initiates of the Lesser Mysteries, or even to outsiders; but the latter was strictly reserved for the higher initiates. And the two teachings were often contradictory; for the exoteric was not regarded as necessarily true: it was merely what the leaders of the initiates wished the common people to believe, and was invariably in accord, more or less, with popular ideas. But the secret doctrines termed the Aporrheta, or 'the unutterable,' contained the real faith of the leaders, and, doubtless, unfolded their fundamental principle of action and its ultimate source.

Just in the same way, we find that the teachings of the nominal Church were classified as τὰ ἔκφορα, or the things that might be freely set forth before all men, and τὰ ἀπόρρητα, or the secret things that were not to be divulged either in familiar conversation, or in catechizings, or in assemblies which were open to catechumens, Pagans, or other uninitiated persons.

Hence a preacher, when he had come to the edge of an ἀπόρρητον, would abruptly check himself with the words, "But the initiated know what I mean." [1] Many examples of this might be cited, especially from Chrysostom.

A knowledge of this unscriptural division of doctrines into secret and open, which so manifestly points to the influence of the Mysteries, will help us to understand an important passage in Basil's treatise "On the Holy Spirit," which runs thus :—

"Now of the secret doctrines—δόγματα [2]—and public definitions—κηρύγματα—which are preserved in the Church, there are some which we hold from Scriptural teaching, but others we received, handed down to us in Mystery-teaching, from the tradition of the Apostles. And both of these sources have the same authoritative force in regard to religion." [3]

Thus, according to Basil, the truths of Christianity are derived from two sources—the Scriptures and Apostolical tradition ; and he would have us believe, that the authority of the latter is equal to that of the former. What, then, is this Apostolical tradition which we are bidden to revere and obey as we do the Bible? He explains that it was handed down in Mystery-teaching ; and, if we examine the context of the

---

[1] ἴσασι δὲ οἱ μεμυημένοι.

[2] It is well known to scholars that Basil's use of the word δόγματα is peculiar to himself ; for by it he expresses what other writers would call ἀπόρρητα, or secrets that must not be divulged. "Secret doctrines," he presently says, "are observed in silence ; but public definitions are proclaimed to the people." Consequently, with him κηρύγματα is equivalent to ἔκφορα. See Casaub. *Exerc. ad Baron.* xvi. 43.

[3] *De Spiritu Sancto*, xxvii.

passage, which we propose presently to do, it will be evident that μυστήριον is here used, in its proper meaning, of a secret revealed to initiates. And by such revelations, if we are to believe Basil, the tradition was passed down from one generation to another.

But how could the Apostles have been connected with the Mysteries? They certainly never were so; and the tradition falsely ascribed to them probably originated in the following manner. It is well known, that, in the séances of modern Spiritualism, demons are wont to appear, representing themselves to be spirits of the dead, and often of the illustrious dead, and delivering communications and commands falsely affirmed to come from those whom they personify. Now, there is nothing new under the sun, and it is a fact beyond doubt, that the spirits of the air were accustomed to practise the same deceits in earlier ages, both in connection with the Mysteries and Pagan religions generally, and also among the Gnostics and the Neo-Platonists of Alexandria.

It is probable, then, that some of these ministers of Satan feigned to be the spirits of Apostles, and uttered authoritative messages, or commands, as if from those whose personality they affected. And, this being so, their communications would have a place among the instructions given by the Hierophants to novices, and would be specially useful for the work of corrupting Christianity.

But who, it may be asked, would pass on such communications to the churches, and gradually induce belief in them? For work of this kind there would, alas! have been no lack of agents. Just as in our own days there are many professing Christians who will not give up the world and its enjoyments, and some who do not scruple even to attend Spiritualistic séances ; so, in those times, there were reputed followers of the Lord Jesus who would not altogether abandon their Heathen practices, who went sometimes to the Amphitheatre, sometimes to Pagan festivals, or, if they were initiates, to the Mystery-shows. Such men would soon begin to think of uniting the churches and the Mysteries, that they might retain the advantages of both, and would do their best to utilize anything that might possibly forward so desirable an end. Besides which, there were, also, not a few who appeared to be zealous believers, and had, perhaps, obtained much influence through their seeming piety ; who, however, were not really Christians at all, but had hypocritically joined themselves to the churches with the deliberate purpose of corrupting them. Nor was it long before the success of their efforts became manifest.

If this explanation be accepted, we are at once able to understand the otherwise strange fact, that Apostolical tradition bears no resemblance whatever to Apostolical teaching as recorded in the New Testament. For the latter is the testimony of God, Who caused holy men to speak as they were moved by His Spirit ; but the former is the counteracting testimony of Satan, delivered by demons of the air to the children of disobedience. Such, then, is the probable origin of Apostolical tradition —a device so useful to the crafty initiates, when they were restoring the Polytheism of the Pagans by changing the names of its gods [1] and some of its terminology, and then declaring it to be the only true Christianity.

[1] Emanuel Deutsch refers to this transformation as the time " when the gods of Greece and Rome went into exile—either degraded into evil spirits or promoted into Christian saints."— *Literary Remains*, p. 182.

LXX

Jewish Tradition

BUT, in regard to this point of Apostolical tradition, we must not forget the instructive historic parallel which the previous dispensation supplies. For, in depriving the Scriptures of their virtue and power by means of tradition falsely ascribed to a Divine origin, Satan was merely repeating tactics that had already proved eminently successful.

The Jews, too, had a tradition, through which, as the Lord Himself tells us, they transgressed and made void the commandment of God. They taught that it had been given to Moses at Sinai, and was afterwards transmitted orally through the centuries. As Lightfoot says ;—

"The deliverers of the Cabala, or unwritten law, they will name you as directly from generation to generation as the Papists will name you Popes successively from Peter. 'Moses'—say they—'received this traditional law from Sinai, and delivered it to Joshua, Joshua to the elders, the elders to the prophets, and the prophets to Ezra's great synagogue.'"[1]

They also professed to know the particular individuals who were its successive recipients, both before and after the Babylonian captivity. Lightfoot's remarks on the change which they experienced after their return from Babylon are worth quoting ;—

"Before their captivity into Babylon, they were all for idolatry ; but after their return out of captivity,

[1] Lightfoot's Works, vol. v. pp. 204-5.

they abhorred idolatry, but were all for traditions : they changed naught for naught, or rather naught for worse. For, indeed, their traditions, one may justly say, were more destructive than their idolatry."[1]

LXXI

BASIL ON TRADITION AND INDISPENSABLE PAGAN PRACTICES

THUS, then, to return to our subject, the passage quoted from Basil, together with many others, seems to show that there was a conspiracy of pretended Christians, who while they professed to be an inner and better instructed circle, were really following the practices and propagating the doctrines of the Pagan Mysteries.

Possibly the reader would know what some of these practices were—practices which Basil admits to be non-Scriptural, while he seems to confess that they owed their origin to the Mysteries.[2] But to the uninitiated, at least, he would, probably, have been willing to class them under the heading of " Apostolical tradition." We will, however, leave him to speak for himself. After the words quoted above from his treatise " On the Holy Spirit," in which he affirms that the authority of Apostolical tradition is equal to that of Scripture, he proceeds as follows ;—

" And this no one will gainsay—no one, at least, who is even moderately versed in the institutions of the Church. For should we attempt to reject such customs as have no Scriptural authority,[3] on the

---

[1] Lightfoot's Works, vol. vi. p. 374.   [2] See pp. 271–2.
[3] Literally, " the customs that are unwritten "; but, as the context indicates, Basil means those that are not found in the sacred writings which we call the Scriptures.

ground that they are of little weight, we should be unconsciously injuring the Gospel in its vital parts, or, rather, should be reducing our public definition to a bare phrase and nothing more.[1]

"For instance, to take the first and most general example, Who was it that by means of Scripture taught us to sign with the form of the cross those who have put their trust in the Name of our Lord Jesus Christ? What Scripture taught us to turn to the East at the prayer? Which of the saints has left us in Scripture the words of the invocation at the displaying of the bread of the Eucharist, and of the cup of blessing? For we are not, in truth, content with those things whereof the Apostle or the Gospel made mention, but add, both in preface and conclusion, words of a different kind,[2] which we received from non-Scriptural teaching, believing them to be of great importance in regard to the validity of the sacrament. And we bless both the water of baptism and the oil of anointing, and, still further, the person himself who is being baptized. On the authority of what Scriptures do we do this? Do we not rest upon tradition preserved in silence and mystic? Nay, what written word taught us the very rite of anointing with oil? And the custom of triple immersion, whence came it? And, as regards the

[1] That is, What we proclaimed to the people would be all that there was to say, as if the matter were an ordinary one. Men would not be impressed with the idea that there was some profound mystery involved in the simple words, which was known only to their priests; and we should lose the authority and influence, with which the possession of secret knowledge endows us. Basil, however, presently gives as a reason for the unwritten tradition, that it prevents the people from despising the secret doctrines through their familiarity with them.

[2] ἕτερα.

other customs pertaining to Baptism, from what
Scripture do we derive the renunciation of Satan and
his angels? Do we not get it from that undivulged
and secret teaching which our fathers guarded in a
silence that has baffled meddling curiosity and inquisitive searchings? For well had they learnt the
lesson, that the awful solemnity of the Mysteries
must be preserved in silence. For how could it
be reasonable to parade in written documents the
exposition of things upon which the uninitiated are
not even permitted to look?"

At this point, Basil endeavours to strengthen his
argument by affirming, that Moses acted upon the
principle of the Mysteries, because he kept the ' profane '
without the pale of the Tabernacle, suffered only the
more pure to enter the hypethral Court, reserved the
attendance upon the services for the Levites and
the offering of sacrifices and other priestly duties for the
priests, and suffered only one man chosen out of the latter
to enter the Holy of Holies, and that but once a year,
on an appointed day, and at a fixed hour. And these
arrangements, he declares, were made by Moses, because
he knew that what is trite and can be at once comprehended is quickly contemned ; whereas a keen interest
is naturally associated with the recondite and the
unfamiliar.

"In the same manner, then," he continues, "the
Apostles and Fathers, who laid down laws for the
Church from the beginning, preserved the awful
solemnity of the Mysteries in concealment and silence.
For that is absolutely no mystery at all which is
bruited abroad at random among the common people.
This is the reason for our tradition of unwritten
things, that the knowledge of our secret doctrines

may not become neglected and contemned by the many because of their familiarity with them. For a secret doctrine is one thing, a public definition quite another : for the former are observed in silence, but the public definitions are proclaimed to the people. One form of silence, also, is the obscurity which Scripture has employed, and which makes the meaning of the secret doctrines difficult to be understood with a view to the profit of the readers."

In this remarkable passage, Basil maintains that the authority of tradition is as great as that of Scripture; because, if we reject tradition, we shall, though we may not know it, be injuring the Gospel in its very vitals. What, then, are these traditional practices which, while he acknowledges them to be unscriptural, he yet declares necessary to the vitality of the Gospel ? The specimens which he presents to us are as follows ;—

The signing catechumens, that is to say, applicants for admission into the Church, with the form of the cross.

Turning to the East in prayer, that is, to the quarter which, as the Old Testament tells us, belongs to Satan, not to God.

Adding to the Lord's institution of His Supper words avowedly of quite a different character and meaning from any which He spoke or commanded.

Changing the simple form of Baptism, as delivered, explained, and practised, by the Lord's Apostles, into an elaborate rite that cannot be performed without the aid of so-called 'priests,' to bless the water in order to render it efficacious, to bless the oil of the anointing—the anointing itself being another of their own inventions, and to bless the person who is being baptized. These additions, as we have before remarked, are manifestly intended to render human priests indispensable to the ordinance, and to withdraw the Lord Jesus, the True and Only Sanctifier, further and further from sight.

The anointing of the whole body with oil before Baptism, which is superfluous, and cannot be intelligently explained by anything that Scripture reveals in regard to the rite.

The triple immersion, which hopelessly confuses the scriptural meaning of Baptism. For by Baptism we are, in a figure, buried with Christ, while we, typically, rise with Him to newness of life as we emerge from the water. But Christ was buried and rose again once, not three times.

The renunciation of Satan and his angels—a silly pantomime,[1] followed by a vow which no man can perform. We should rather send up the petition, "Lead us not into temptation, but deliver us from the Evil One!"

Such are the superstitious practices on which, according to Basil, the very existence of the Gospel depends. But their real effect is to hide Christianity with a covering of Paganism, while its root is being stealthily cut away. And, to prove this, we need go no further than the copious writings of Basil himself. For, though we search through the three great volumes of the Benedictine edition, we shall not be able to find a single plain announcement of justification by faith in the redeeming Blood of the Lord Jesus.[2] And of what use is Christianity without that fundamental doctrine?

[1] See p. 158.
[2] Two passages have, indeed, been cited by Faber as teaching justification by faith: and one of them—which had been previously quoted in the *First Book of Homilies*—if it be isolated, may, perhaps, seem satisfactory. But if the context and the general

Yet Basil, like most of the Fathers, has little or nothing to say of the expiating Blood, and, therefore, could never have felt its cleansing power. Nevertheless, he will talk fluently, and sometimes well, upon doctrines of Scriptures which are not vital ; but he also introduces, as if they were of the greatest importance, strange things, which are not merely non-Scriptural, but are also manifestly inspired by a spirit antagonistic to the teaching of the Holy Spirit in the Word of God. And the result is, that, while he may occasionally give us interesting disquisitions, he has no spiritual power : his writings could never save a soul from death, nor draw those who are saved nearer to their God. We are thus compelled to agree with Isaac Taylor's estimate of him ;—

"In a word, this Father was an intellectualist of a high order : he found in Christianity a sublime philosophy, and a world of splendours among which his lofty imagination took its ecstatic flight. His asceticism was an intellectual and imaginative abstraction from the vulgarities of animal life ; his morality, a softened Stoicism ; his orthodoxy was Trinitarian Platonism."

Let us then, consider for a moment the practice which he has placed at the head of his list of indispensable things, the signing catechumens with the form of the cross, which is exoterically explained to signify the cross of Christ. Now, if we can contemplate it without bias, the first thought which strikes us is the extreme unnaturalness of such an act, as well as of all the adoration and veneration which is paid to the cross.

teaching of Basil be taken into consideration, we shall scarcely be able to retain our first impressions. As regards the other passage, Faber himself is evidently somewhat dubious.

Why should the wooden implement with which Satan destroyed the human life of the Lord Jesus be venerated, worshipped, and marked as a sign upon His people? If a dear friend of ours, or a greatly beloved relative, chances to be assassinated, do we carefully preserve the dagger, or the pistol, which was used to effect the vile deed? Do we venerate it, want to impress its form upon ourselves and upon all those who loved the lamented victim? Do we proceed to work ourselves into so morbid a condition as to affirm that we cannot think of him, unless we place the wretched instrument of his death before our eyes? And do we, at last, begin to forget him in it, to substitute it for him in our affection, and almost, or perhaps altogether, to worship it?

Surely, if any one should so act, he would be regarded as a fit subject for a commission of lunacy. Why, then, do men commit this very folly in the case of the cross of Christ? If, indeed, their object were to celebrate Satan's temporary victory, such conduct might be rational; but on what other ground could it be justified?

It would seem, then, that some motive other than the love of Christ must have originally prompted this cross-veneration, and that it could only have been explained in the Catholic manner after men had become superstitiously addicted to it.

Was it, then, ever known in Pagan worship? Most certainly it was. You may find it among Babylonian and Assyrian remains: you may see it in the hand of all the greater Egyptian gods:[1] you will find that it

---

[1] In the form of the *crux ansata,* on which C. W. King has the following remarks;—" It is astonishing how much of the Egyptian and the second-hand Indian symbolism passed over into the usages

has ever been an object of veneration among the Buddhists : the Druids trimmed and bound their sacred oak into its shape : and the Spaniards were amazed as they beheld it set up and worshipped among the Pagan natives of Mexico.

And everywhere the meaning of the symbol was the same : it signified life and fecundity. For it represented the conjunction of the sexes, and was the great symbol of Nature-worship. And this fact enables us to understand why sometimes, as among the Buddhists and Manichæans, it appears as a sprouting and flowering cross.   Here, too, we may perceive the origin of the address to it in the Roman Office of the Cross ;—" Hail, O cross, triumphal wood, true salvation of the world, among trees there is none like thee in leaf, flower, and bud." This rhapsody was actually versified by the Oxford conspirators, for members of the Church of England, in the subjoined words ;—

> " O faithful cross, thou peerless tree,
>   No forest yields the like of thee,
>   Leaf, flower, and bud.
>   Sweet is the wood, and sweet the weight,
>   And sweet the nails that penetrate
>   Thee, thou sweet wood."

But, still worse, it appears, in another form, in *Hymns*

of following times.   Thus, the high cap and hooked staff of the god became the bishop's mitre and crosier: the term *nun* is pure Egyptian, and bore its present meaning: the erect oval, symbol of the Female Principle of Nature, became the Vesica Piscis, and a frame for Divine things: the Crux ansata, testifying the union of the Male and Female Principle in the most obvious manner, and denoting fecundity and abundance, as borne in the god's hand, is transformed by a simple inversion, into the Orb surmounted with the Cross, and the ensign of royalty."—*The Gnostics and their Remains*, p. 72.

Ancient and Modern, the most popular Hymnal of the Established Church ;—

> " Faithful Cross, above all other
>   One and only noble Tree,
> None in foliage, none in blossom,
>   None in fruit thy peer may be ;
> Sweetest wood, and sweetest iron ;
>   Sweetest weight is hung on thee."

Can it be possible that England accepts this Pagan and sentimental nonsense as Christianity, and that, too, in the dawn of the twentieth century ! The time has surely come for the fulfilment of the prophecy, " Darkness shall cover the earth, and gross darkness the peoples."

But, if the veneration of the cross by Christians seems to be unnatural, and we know that the symbol was an object of universal worship in the Pagan world, can we find any historical instance of its transference from Paganism to Christianity ? Upon this point the following quotation from Wilkinson's *Ancient Egyptians* may throw some light, and will, at least, show that eminent authorities have caught glimpses of the phenomenon to which the reader's attention is being directed.

" Another ceremony represented in the temples was the blessing bestowed by the gods on the king at the moment of his assuming the reins of government. They laid their hands upon him ; and presenting him with the symbol of life" (that is, the *crux ansata,* of which Wilkinson gives two woodcuts), " they promised that his reign should be long and glorious, and that he should enjoy tranquillity, with certain victory over his enemies. . . . He (the King) was welcomed (by the gods) with suitable expressions of approbation ; and on this, as on other occasions, the sacred *tau*, or sign of life, was presented to him— a symbol which, with the sceptre of purity, was usually placed in the hands of the gods. These two were deemed the greatest gifts bestowed by the deity on man. . . . A remarkable fact may be mentioned respecting this hieroglyphic character "—that is, the *tau*, or *crux ansata*—" that the early Christians of Egypt adopted it in lieu of the cross, which was afterwards substituted for it, prefixing it to inscriptions in the same manner as the cross in later times." [1]

That is, they continued to venerate the *tau*, or *crux ansata*, after they had assumed the name of Christians, just as they had done when they were avowed Pagans. But, in course of time, when it became necessary to conceal their too obvious Paganism beneath a thicker veil, they changed the *crux ansata* into the more ordinary form of the cross, which, however, had precisely the same meaning, though it did not express it quite so broadly.

Putting together, then, all the facts that have been adduced, we would explain the origin of veneration for the cross, as follows ;—

The symbol was an object of adoration in Pagan Nature-worship as the sign of life.

Its form resembled generally that of the cross on which slaves, and those who were not Roman citizens, were executed.

Satan took advantage of this coincidence, and brought about the death of the Lord Jesus by means of the cross,[2] his purpose being to thrust into

---

[1] Wilkinson's *Ancient Egyptians* (1878), vol. iii. pp. 363-4.

[2] At the dread time of His death, the Lord appears to have submitted Himself to the power of Satan, according to the foredetermined counsel of God. Such is evidently the meaning of His words to those who arrested Him ;—" This is your hour and the

Christianity a most corrupting symbol and idol of Paganism.

He was thus enabled to furnish Pagan converts with an excuse for continuing a favourite cult, the previous veneration which they had felt for the symbol of life causing them to overlook the incongruity of its appearance as a cross among Christians. The tendency of such an introduction to corrupt the faith, and to materialize that which should have been exclusively spiritual, is obvious. Moreover, it proved a powerful aid to those treacherous initiates who had outwardly joined the churches with the deliberate purpose of doing them what mischief they could.

Thus, to venerate the cross is pure Paganism: it is He Who suffered upon it for our sakes That we must venerate, worship, adore, and serve with all our heart and soul and strength. Should we, however, be taunted with the ignominious circumstances of His death, then must we be willing to share His shame, to become, like Him, as the filth of the world and the offscouring of all things, and to cry with His Apostle, We glory in the cross of our Lord Jesus Christ. But if the form of the wooden cross be presented to us, we can but answer as Paul would have done, It is the accursed tree, and the symbol of superstition.

Power of Darkness" (Luke xxii. 53): that is, This is the hour destined by God's decree for the carrying out of your work; for the multitude which I see before Me is directed by the Power of Darkness that must now have its short-lived triumph.

And it would seem that Satan's resolve to use the power put into his hands to the utmost, just as he did in the case of Job, was that which finally sealed his doom. For, when the Lord intimated that the hour for His sufferings and death had come, He added, "Now is the judgment of this world. Now shall the prince of this world be cast out." See John xii. 27–33.

The second of Basil's indispensable practices is the turning to the East in prayer, and the reason which he gives for it is, again, thoroughly unsatisfactory. "We all look towards the East at our prayers," he says; "but few know that we are seeking our old country, the Paradise which God planted in Eden towards the East." [1]

Now we have already commented on this turning to the East, and have shown that it is incompatible with the New Testament, which teaches that God is Spirit, and must be worshipped in spirit and in truth without any regard to locality; and also that it directly contradicts the Old Testament, which records, that, when God did prescribe locality to His earthly people, the West, and not the East, was chosen as His quarter; for the Sun of Righteousness can rise only where the sun of this world sets. [2]

Basil's tradition is, therefore, opposed to the Word of God; and his exposition of it is no less so. For believers in the Lord Jesus do not seek the terrestrial Paradise, which the Lord God planted eastward in Eden: on the contrary, they are commanded to seek the things that are above, where Christ is, seated on the right hand of God; to set their affections on the things that are above, not on the things that are upon the earth.

The additional words added, "at the displaying of the bread," to the Lord's institution of His Supper

---

[1] *De Spiritu Sancto*, xxvii.

[2] The reader will now see, that they who admit these first two indispensable practices of Basil make the subjoined extract as true of *their* Christianity as it undoubtedly is of all other religions;—

"The sun and, as I have already indicated, the organs of sex, are the fundamental symbols of every religious worship known to us, each alike Catholic in their acceptance, their necessity, and their functions."—*Keys of the Creeds*, p. 60.

are, according to Casaubon and the Benedictines, the invocation in the Liturgy by which the priest entreats for the presence of the Holy Spirit, to so bless and sanctify the elements that they may no longer be mere bread and wine, but be changed into the mystical Body and Blood of Christ. This, it is scarcely necessary to say, effects a complete transformation in the Lord's ordinance, so that it no longer resembles the simple thanksgiving-memorial which He has appointed. And the only possible object of the addition was to establish the priest as indispensable to the validity of what was now called the Mystery or Sacrament. For Basil and his friends had their eyes fixed upon Pagan precedents: it mattered nothing to them that such things as priests —ἱερεῖς—were unknown to the churches of the New Testament.

Of the many rites added to Baptism, amid which the simple Scriptural form, together with its meaning, was lost, we have already spoken. Even when they were not absolutely wrong in themselves, these rites were a sore encumbrance to the ordinance, and none of them in any way elucidated its Scriptural interpretation. Their only possible object was to magnify above measure the unauthorised priest, and, by the multitude of his acts, to obscure the great expiatory work of the Lord Jesus.

We may thus perceive that Basil was no Christian minister: he was a teacher of strange things, skilfully arranged, by means of catch-words and surface-arguments, to pass for Scripture, or for an alleged oral tradition handed down from the Apostles; and so to deceive the ignorant or the unwary. But a slight investigation suffices to expose their Pagan origin and decided antagonism to the Word of God.

According to Basil himself, these practices and doctrines were derived " from that undivulged and secret teaching which our fathers guarded in a silence that has baffled meddling curiosity and inquisitive searchings," because they knew that they ought so to preserve the " awful solemnity of the Mysteries." Now it is very clear, that, as he wrote these words, he must have had the Pagan Mysteries in his mind, though, when dealing with the uninitiated, he may have taught otherwise. For the practices and doctrines which he derives from these Mysteries, as well as the very idea of secrets reserved exclusively for the higher initiates, are altogether Pagan. Hence, although the Mysteries may have been exoterically explained to mean nothing more than the " Eucharist," and although this delusion was kept up by the practice of excluding all but initiates from the place where it was celebrated ; yet those who were thought worthy of esoteric teaching must have been aware that such was not the case, and that the process of infusing Pagan practices and doctrines into Christianity was being stealthily but rapidly carried on.

They must have smiled grimly when they saw that Christians were being cajoled into worshipping the Pagan symbol of life, into turning with supplication to the quarter of the sun-god, and into submitting to a useless ritual, whereby the Great God, His Son Jesus Christ, and the powerful operations of His Spirit, were being gradually withdrawn from their sight by the impotent juggleries of human priests.[1]

---

[1] Some such feeling as we have here attributed to the higher initiates seems, also, to find a place in the breasts of modern Pagans. So, in reference to the Eastward position and the fact that all the Church festivals are arranged astronomically, that is, are based upon the worship of the hosts of heaven, E. Maitland remarks ;—
" So little is there strange and recondite in these facts, that

And, if they wished to entice lax, but influential, Christians into their own inner circle, they were by no means wanting in plausible explanations and arguments. They would, perhaps, point out that the Mystery-teaching was the older revelation ; that the Gospel was subsequently vouchsafed for the sake of the common people, whose intellect could not receive the deeper disclosures ; and, moreover, that much of the Gospel was communicated through the Mysteries ; for was it not in their secret meetings that they had received those supernatural disclosures, collectively known as Apostolical tradition, which were quite as authoritative as the Scriptures ? And was it not left to them to reserve the most important revelations as secrets intended only for themselves, while they gave out what they deemed suitable to the people ?

There are other points which it would be interesting to notice in this passage from Basil ; as, for instance, the fact that he attributes the Tabernacle arrangements to Moses, as though they had been the result of the lawgiver's own will and wisdom, and not a revelation from Jehovah. After such a mistake, we do not wonder that the reasons which Basil assigns for these arrangements are false, low, and unworthy. It is evident that he had never caught the spirit of the Pentateuch, nor

it is a perpetual marvel among the initiated, how even the least incredulous of the laity contrive to ignore them—a marvel not unmixed with apprehension as to the result that would follow from their becoming enlightened. The blind impetuosity, on the other hand, with which Protestant sects indignantly denounce idolatry Pagan or Catholic, while themselves offering palpable homage to the sun under the name of Christ, is to us a never-failing source of amusement."

"To no less a person than Sir Isaac Newton the world owes both the first suggestion that the Christian festivals were determined upon an astronomical basis, and a detailed list of instances of correspondence."—*Keys to the Creeds*, pp. 61 and 65.

realized the awful majesty of Jehovah, Whose glory dwelt in the Holy of Holies.

But we must close this already too protracted chapter with a few remarks on one other point only— his idea, that what he would, probably, have called religion is chiefly made up of Mysteries to be known only by priests and initiates. Such a view was in fullest accord with Pagan conceptions, and was, indeed, a fundamental doctrine of the Mysteries. But it is nowhere to be found in the Bible, which, although it certainly does mention " secret things," is careful to teach that they " belong " exclusively " to the Lord our God." [1] Such secrets, then, must not be pried into by us, lest He be compelled to deal with us as He did with Job, until we confess, " I have uttered that which I understood not, things too wonderful for me, that I knew not." [2]

" But," continues the same Scripture, " the things that are revealed belong unto us and to our children for ever, that we may do all the words of this law." [3] Whatever, then, God may have been pleased to communicate is open and free to all men : none may dare to keep for himself, or for a chosen few, utterances that are Divine. It is true, that some men, owing to their spiritual condition, are unable to receive many of God's revelations : that fact, however, opens a question altogether different to the one before us, and does not affect the truth, that men may not reserve God's gifts to themselves and those of their own standing or party. On the contrary, they must be ready and eager to share them with all ; and that so much the more, because whatever God reveals during these ages of sin is given solely for one purpose. Not to gratify our

[1] Deut. xxix. 29.   [2] Job xlii. 3.   [3] Deut. xxix. 29.

curiosity or pride : not to make us seem wise in our
own eyes : but only to aid our return to the path of
obedience.

LXXII

The Origin of the Word "Mass"

To the influence of the party, which was endeavouring to corrupt Christianity, and which soon became
dominant, we must, doubtless, attribute another imitation
of Paganism to which we have referred in a previous
chapter. Whenever initiations or any secret rite of
the Mysteries were about to commence, a solemn pro-
clamation was made, that all the profane or uninitiated
should depart ; and, if any one contrived to escape
notice and remained, death was the penalty.

Just in the same way, about the third century,
or, it may be, a little earlier, the Christians began
to exclude all unbaptized, or, as they termed them,
uninitiated, persons from their assembly-room during
the Eucharist, which they then celebrated with closed
and guarded doors.

So in the *Apostolical Constitutions*, a direction is
given, that at the conclusion of the first service, and
before the Lord's Supper begins, a deacon shall proclaim ;—

"Let none of the catechumens, let none of the
hearers, let none of the unbelievers, let none of the
heterodox, remain here." [1]

This was said to be the command of James, the
brother of John the son of Zebedee : it is, therefore,

[1] Apost. Const. viii. 12.

a specimen of the so-called "tradition of the Apostles." Yet, as we have already shown, the churches knew nothing of it in the time of Justin Martyr, that is, about A.D. 150.

The *Apostolical Constitutions* also direct as follows ;—

"Let the deacons stand at the doors of the men, and the sub-deacons at those of the women, that no one go out, nor the door be opened, even for a believer, at the time of the oblation."[1]

From this custom Catholics have attempted to find a derivation for the word *missa*, the Mass, in order to conceal its real origin. They make it to be another form for *missio* or *dimissio*, the dismissal of an assembly ; and so affirm, that, because the Mass was celebrated after the dismissal from the ante-communion service, therefore the communion service took its name from the dismissal which immediately preceded it.

Thus Pelliccia, after noticing the somewhat hopeless attempt to connect the word with the Hebrew מִסָּה,[2] remarks ;—

"But, if we are not prepared to accept this ingenious attempt at solving a knotty point of interpretation, the explanation which Isidore offers of the word is the only other one worthy of our attention. 'Missa,' he says, 'is derived from the word *dismissing*. For at the time when the priest is beginning to consecrate the Lord's Body, the deacon is to say, after the Gospel, 'If any catechumen is present, let him go forth'; and because catechumens are then dismissed from the church, the service is, therefore, called 'Missa' from their dismissal.' . . . And thus the name of *Missa* was given to the Sacri-

---

[1] Apost. Const. viii. 11.   [2] Deut. xvi. 10.

fice from the circumstance that it, properly speaking, began with the dismissal of the catechumens."[1]

It is, however, far from likely that the name of what was considered to be the most important of all services would be derived in so strange a way as this ; and the dubious manner in which Pelliccia and other writers suggest it is an evidence of their uncertainty. So marked a rite would almost surely be named from one of its own most prominent features. Hence, as it seems to us, C. W. King points to the true origin of the disputed word in the following passage ;—

"In the particulars that have come down to us of the celebration of these Mithraic sacraments, certain singular analogies arrest our attention. The 'bread' used was a round cake, emblem of the solar disk, and termed the *Mizd*, in which word Seel detects the etymology of the name *Missa* applied to the Bloodless Sacrifice ; for this *Mizd* was certainly the prototype of the Host, which is circular and of the same dimensions."[2]

We have already referred to the fact, that, in the early years of Christianity, the initiates of Mithras and Isis were the most fashionable and influential Pagan communities, and, consequently, the chief agents in corrupting the churches. In the introduction of the Mithraic *mizd* we have a conspicuous instance of this corruption, and an easy explanation of the way in which the Lord's Supper came to be called "Holy Mysteries" through the influence of false Christians, and was turned into a Mass. Thenceforth a round wafer of Mithras was given to each communicant in

---

[1] *Polity of the Christian Church*, translated by J. C. Bellett, pp. 215-16.
[2] King's *Gnostics and their Remains*, p. 53.

place of a piece from the one broken loaf, which alone can signify the One Body of Christ that was broken for us, and the fact, that "we, who are many, are one loaf, one body; for we all partake of the one loaf."[1]

Of the Virgin-goddess Isis, from whose Mysteries virgin-worship appears to have been first introduced into the churches, we have spoken elsewhere;[2] and have also shown, that the Catholic Madonna and Child are merely a perpetuation of Isis and Horus; and that a similar goddess and child may be found in connection with every Pagan religion. Moreover, we have given proof that Isis was declared to be immaculate and ever-virgin, in spite of the birth of her son Horus; and that this is the origin of the Catholic doctrine of the Immaculate Conception. For the Scriptures do not permit perpetual virginity to be attributed to the human mother of the Lord Jesus; since they never speak of her as a virgin after the birth of her Firstborn Son, and, moreover, inform us that she subsequently bore several sons and daughters.[3]

LXXIII

Summary and Inference

FURTHER investigation into the deeply interesting but painful subject before us is forbidden by our limits. We can only add a summary of what we have proved, and a very brief but inevitable and most important inference therefrom.

It will, then, be readily admitted that the following

[1] 1 Cor. x. 17.
[2] See *The Great Prophecies of the Centuries concerning Israel and the Gentiles*, pp. 428-36.
[3] See Appendix.

list includes most of the distinctive institutions doctrines and practices of Catholicism, as opposed to primitive or Evangelical Christianity ;—

1. The appointment of human priests as mediators between God and man.
2. A belief in Sacraments, or the priest's power to ceremonialize into life.
3. Confession to a priest.
4. Signing with the form of the cross, and adoration of the same symbol.
5. Turning to the East.
6. Baptismal Regeneration.
7. The use of round wafers, instead of the broken bread, in the Mystery which is substituted for the Lord's Supper.
8. The placing of lights on either side of the altar, but not in its centre.
9. The Real Presence.
10. The use of incense.
11. The priest taking the place of Christ in the Mystery of the Eucharist, as he does that of God when he absolves after confession.
12. Celibacy of the theurgic priest.
13. A third order of clergy, that of bishops, who correspond to Hierophants.
14. Apostolical Succession.
15. A Peter as the first Pope.
16. Retention of the title of Pontifex Maximus by the Popes.
17. The tonsure.
18. The doctrine of Purgatory.
19. And, generally, that of salvation by one's own works and sufferings.
20. The use of holy water.

21. Apparitions of deities or saints.
22. The worship of saints or minor gods.
23. Virgin-worship.
24. Worship of the Madonna and Child.
25. The doctrine of the Immaculate Conception.
26. Doctrines and symbols with a double interpretation, the one being designed to conceal the true meaning from outsiders, the other to reveal it to the initiated, or to the members of a secret society.
27. " Economy," and, generally, action based upon the principle, that the end justifies the means.
28. The exhibition of Mystery-plays.
29. The carrying of images in processions.

Now, we have proved, that these twenty-nine institutions doctrines and practices were established taught or practised in connection with the Pagan Mysteries, centuries before the Christian era. And not one of them is either commanded or allowed to the churches in the New Testament. Nay, we may go still further, and say that every one of them is more or less directly opposed to the Divine teachings vouchsafed to the people of the Lord in the present age.

What, then, is the only possible inference from these facts ? This, that Catholicism is simply Paganism with a Christian nomenclature, and is not Christianity at all.

LXXIV

Historical Developments

WHEN, with the help of the Alexandrian School, nominal Christianity had taken the shape which Newman, and others like-minded with him, would have us regard as the Primitive Church, the Mysteries began to disappear from the avowedly Heathen world; but the simultaneous appearance of their rites and doctrines within the pale of the Church indicated, that they had merely changed their name, their quarters, and, to some extent, their dress. It was the Church now that began to preach salvation by means of priests and ceremonies.

Whether the Mysteries in their absolutely Pagan form, and with their purely Pagan object, were still carried on in private, cannot be determined by those who are unconnected with them. Yet certain Spiritualistic and Theosophic books affirm that they have descended even to the present day. " I have witnessed," says one writer, " many of these degrees being worked, and they surpass anything that can be written for the public. Not only in sublimity and devotion are these rites wonderful, but in the knowledge the students obtain of the dominion of Gods and Saviours over mortals, and of the different heavenly divisions of Jehovih's [1] judgments. Only by witnessing these things can any one realize the ground on which the members know their power."

But, whether the avowedly Pagan Mysteries are still carried on or not, their influence is sufficiently apparent in the churches, as, indeed, it has been through all the centuries of the Christian era.

To this fact the Mediæval Church testified in its propagation of the doctrines and practices which we have just enumerated. Ecclesiastical architecture, both in the form and in the decoration of its splendid cathedrals and churches, exhibited everywhere the signs and symbols of the old Nature-worship—signs and symbols

---

[1] This is the writer's invariable spelling of the Great Name.

with which the morals of the priests, the monks, and the nuns, were by no means always inconsistent.

Full of images, too, were these churches : nor were they now known only as the houses of the One Almighty God, but were dedicated to various saints, both male and female, corresponding to the gods and goddesses of the Lesser Mysteries. And raised high above all other idols was the statue of the Virgin-Goddess, still, as she was in Pagan times, the most popular of all deities. For a deity she was, and is to-day, to the Harlot Church, even as the countless saints are deities also. The populace have never been skilled in hair-splitting with such words as *latria, hyperdulia*, and *dulia* : nor, indeed, have the educated troubled themselves about such matters, save when they have had to defend their church against charges of Paganism. But, say what they would, their religion was Polytheistic, their "Christianity" nothing but Paganism attempting concealment behind a very insufficient mask. And sometimes, as in the case of the Knights Templar, even this mask was partially withdrawn.

There was, however, a weak point in the Ecclesiastical Hierarchy : it was by no means satisfied with moral and spiritual power : its creed could be contented only if it might act as Satan's viceroy, and rule over the material world now while he is still the prince of it. But, to do this, it found that it must suppress the intellectual faculties of the people, and teach them to bear the yoke of subjection by imposing an authority that in process of time became irksome. And so, at last, the minds of men began to turn from the Harlot to the Beast : the undisguised spirit of Hellenism was evoked, and the period of the Renaissance set in.

Its greatest triumph was in Italy, the seat of the

false Church: its culmination, the reign of Lorenzo de Medici at Florence, where, revelling in Hellenic literature and art and a gorgeous sensuousness, the citizens discussed the propriety of discarding the very name of Christianity, and of calling their new religion what it really was, that is, pure Hellenism. This movement, of course, withdrew men still further from God: for, in the Mediæval Church, corrupt and wicked as it was, there were yet some honest souls that strove to worship Him, and trusted in the expiation effected by His Son, the Lord Jesus Christ. But, in the Hellenic revival, there was no place for such as these.

A fearful state of things followed in Italy France and Spain, out of which Popery emerged, victorious, indeed, but no longer all-powerful as before. For, in England Germany and Switzerland, the breaking down of its barriers had opened the way for a purer Christianity, for the preaching once more of the good tidings of great joy—a free salvation through the Blood of the Lamb, and the Water of Life for any one who is willing to take it.

Two centuries later, the revived power of the Papacy received another disastrous blow through the French Revolution; the authors of which openly professed infidelity and Hellenism, and shook the foundation of faith, not only among Roman, but even among Greek Catholics.

And, although Rome has again, to some extent, recovered herself, yet the government is no longer in her hands, and she has a hard conflict to maintain with the infidels and anarchists of the Continent. Of the avowed worship of Satan in France and Italy, we have spoken in another volume.

Meanwhile, as soon as the tension of the struggle

with Rome ceased, there passed over the Protestant countries a spirit of worldliness, indifference, and unbelief. And, although this was somewhat tempered by Evangelical revivals in the eighteenth and nineteenth centuries, yet the Oxford Movement in England, the triumph of the Catholic party in Germany, and the unprecedented spread of Romanism in the United States of America, have renewed the hopes of the Papacy, and improved the prospects of Christianized Paganism. At the same time, the prophets of the " Higher Criticism " are, to a considerable extent, neutralizing the counteracting influence of the Bible ; while the teachings of Spiritualists, Theosophists, and Free-thinkers generally, are casting up a highway for the return of undisguised Nature-worship. Already the Classical gods are regarded by certain Theosophists as real existences ; and books have appeared treating Christianity as no better than other religions, and even comparing it unfavourably with Classical Paganism and Buddhism.

LXXV

Dr. Mivart's Apology for Polytheism

It would be scarcely possible to select a more striking instance of unmistakable, though disguised, leaning towards Polytheistic Paganism than that which may be found in Dr. St. George Mivart's article on " The Continuity of Catholicism," which appeared in the *Nineteenth Century* for January, 1900. One portion of this startling pronouncement is so vivid a revelation of the thoughts which are now rising in the hearts of many that we must quote it at some length ;—

" I have heard a man devoted to the cause of

Catholicity express himself as follows, when seeking the advice of a learned and austere priest ;—

"'Monotheism, in the highest sense of that term, is, of course, an indisputable truth, but can it be entirely defended as popularly understood? Newman has thrown some doubts on this matter. He seems to doubt whether that Infinite Energy which pervades the universe—God—"falls, or can be brought, under the idea of earthly number?" The idea "number" most certainly implies "comparison," "distinctness," and "similarity," and we cannot predicate "unity" of God without the idea of "number." Can God be *thus* spoken of as being absolutely One? He has many attributes, some of which our reason reveals to us, while there may be many more which are altogether beyond our powers of conception. There is no doubt a certain "analogy" between the "attributes" and "modes of being" of man and of God, but there is also an infinite and most mysterious difference. A man is not always actually "loving" or actually "angry," he is for the most part but potentially one or the other. But with God nothing is potential ; His every energy is an actual, eternal, act of His Essence. Thus it cannot be denied that the nature of God's attributes, like the nature of God Himself, is incomprehensible to us. Moreover, God's attributes, while distinct, are each of them equally "God," and therefore substantial. We can hardly, then, venture to affirm or deny that they are "substantially distinct" and "distinctly substantial." At the least it seems that reason must admit that they may be much more so than is commonly supposed. But does not this really amount to Polytheism? And, indeed, we may well ask why may we not, in this way, attribute "plurality" to God? There are certainly some attributes and aspects of the Deity which may not be unfitly represented by such Pagan Gods—by Zeus, Athene, Ares, Aphrodite, Nemesis, Eros, Demeter, and Pan. In a sense, the Paganism of Greece and Rome was "true" and "righteous," and the worship of the Heathen, as Cardinal Newman has said, "an acceptable service."

"'Among the attributes of God, revealed by reason, are some as to which the Christian revelation is silent; and the study of nature manifests to us Divine activities which do not seem to harmonise with that idea of His Being which is set before us by ecclesiastical authority.

"'The student of biology finds the living world replete on every side with phenomena, which, while they clothe the earth with beauty, minister, not merely to sexual reproduction, but often to mere pleasure. Certainly the devotee of biological science might well find himself moved by his studies to adore two divinities to which they specially point, namely Eros and Aphrodite.

"'There are, to my knowledge, good Catholics who feel drawn to worship God directly, but are repelled by the symbols often set before them; such as by the figure of an old man clad in a cope and wearing a papal tiara, or some representations of the 'sacred heart,' or of that bird distinguished by no intellectual or moral ornithological pre-eminence—the dove. Among such devout persons are some who would prefer to worship God under one of His attributes, symbolised by representations more resembling Athene or Apollo, and who have specially felt the want in Christianity of a female symbol of

Divinity ; for, of course, God is as much female as
He is male. I have heard there are persons who
go to the Brompton Oratory to there worship the
Madonna, as the only available representative of
Venus ; and we have lately read of the recent worship
(in Paris) of Isis, by persons who regarded the goddess,
whose veil no man has drawn aside, as no inapt
symbol of the inscrutable power that everywhere
meets, yet everywhere escapes, our gaze as we seek
to probe the mysteries of Nature.

"'In conclusion, I would ask whether it would be
lawful for me, as a Catholic, to worship God as Zeus
or Athene if I am in truth devoutly moved so to
adore Him.'

"The answer," says Dr. Mivart ; "given, in my
hearing, by the learned and devout priest in question
was as follows ;—

"'Most certainly it is lawful for you to do so,
provided you find it helps you to advance in virtue
and religion. But you must only do it privately : it
would not at present be right for you to carry on a
public worship of that kind.'

"I myself subsequently asked the same question
of three other learned and experienced priests, and
received a similar reply from them all."

In the first part of this remarkable extract, the
reader will note the skill with which the logical hair-
splitting is devised to lead up to the proposition, that
the worship of Heathen deities is lawful, provided we
allow that they are all attributes of the One God, each
of which attributes is itself a god. This theory, however, seems to be merely a different way of stating the
Pagan doctrine, that Zeus was the father of the gods,
so as to render the acceptance of the same possible by

the many who have some intellectual knowledge of Christianity, but have never felt its power. Indeed, the nameless author of the proposition is frank enough to admit, that its conclusion does not differ from Pagan Polytheism, the educated votaries of which would, probably, have given a somewhat similar explanation of their creed, had they been pressed. But, just as all history shows us, that the worship of a god through the medium of an image quickly passes into the worship of the image itself in the case of the uneducated and thoughtless multitude, and induces some tint of superstition even upon the minds of the more philosophic; so the worship of an attribute of God soon causes that attribute to be regarded as a distinct and independent deity.

Of course, we must not omit to observe, that the premises for the conclusion which Dr. Mivart quotes are not drawn from the Scriptures of God, but from the doubts and speculations of Cardinal Newman, which have already led so many souls astray from the paths of truth. And for those who can put their trust in such illusions, the purely speculative argument may, perhaps, suffice—suffice, that is, during the present age, in which it is permitted to every man to think as he pleases, until the arrival of the Day of Death; after which judgment and retribution must come.

But those who are well aware, that no man can penetrate the secrets of the Divine Nature, and that there is no knowledge of them upon earth, save that which is revealed in the Bible, must form a very different conclusion.

For they are influenced by the words of Moses, which Christ Himself has quoted;—" Hear, O Israel, the Lord our God is One Lord."[1] With the Scribe

[1] Deut. vi. 4; Mark xii. 29.

they respond ;—"Of a truth, Master, Thou hast well said that He is One ; and there is none other but He."[1] And they have read with awe His Own declaration ;— "I am the First, and I am the Last ; and beside Me there is no God. . . . Is there a God beside Me ? Yea, there is no Rock; I know not any."[2]

But the world will never believe such a declaration while the present age continues ; and of this fact the Church of Rome affords a remarkable proof, in spite of all her protestations, and all her deceptive distinctions between *latria*, *hyperdulia*, and *dulia*. She is Polytheistic, and her principal deity, in practice if not in theory, is the great goddess of the Pagan world, whom, as a concession to Christianity, she now calls "the Blessed Virgin Mary."

There is, also, another conclusion which we cannot avoid. The argument that the attributes of God can never be merely potential, like those of men, but must be always actual, and that, being distinct, they are each of them equally God, and, therefore, substantial, is a line of thought which could scarcely have entered a man's mind, unless he had been previously biassed in favour of Polytheism. Hence its appearance in the midst of us to-day can only be referred to those "teachings of demons" which, as Scripture warns us, must bring about the great and final "falling away."

For, that such "teachings" must tend to Polytheism, we may learn from what is continually going on in Heathen lands, where demon-possession of the most afflicting kind is, as it ever has been, a frequent calamity. Attempts are made to deliver the victims of this oppression by various methods, one of which is sometimes successful. But, when all have failed, the last resource

[1] Mark xii. 32.   [2] Isa. xliv. 6 and 8.

among the Chinese is thus described in Dr. Nevius'
interesting work on *Demon Possession and Allied
Themes*;—

"Now we proceed to those who, though involun-
tarily possessed, yield to and worship the demon. The
demon says it will cease tormenting the demoniac,
if he worships it, and will reward him by increasing
his riches. But if not, it will punish the victim, make
heavier his torments, and rob him of his prosperity.
So people find that their food is cursed. They
cannot prepare any, but filth and dirt come down
from the air to render it uneatable. Their wells are
likewise cursed : their wardrobe is set on fire: and
their money very mysteriously disappears. . . . When
all efforts to rid themselves of the demon fail, they
yield to it, and say ;—' Hold! Cease tormenting, and
we will worship thee !' A picture is pasted upon
the wall, sometimes of a woman, and sometimes of
a man, and incense is burned and prostrations are
made to it twice a month. The demon being thus
reverenced, money now comes in mysteriously instead
of going out.

"Even mill-stones are made to move at the demon's
orders, and the family become rich at once. But it
is said that no luck attends such families, and that
they will be eventually reduced to poverty. Officials
believe these things, and palaces are known to have
been built by them for the demons, who are, however,
obliged to be satisfied with a humbler shrine from
the poor.

"A further stage is reached when the demon says ;—
' It is not enough that you worship me privately
at your own house : you must go about to declare
my power, and influence your neighbours.' By this

time the demoniac's will is almost powerless : he, therefore, goes forth immediately.   Hitherto, if he had worshipped a demon, he would scarcely have owned it except with shame.   Now he boasts of his power, and professes to heal diseases by the demon's aid."[1]

Similar testimony could be drawn from the annals of every Pagan race, ancient or modern.   And, taken together, it seems to prove that the vanity and self-seeking of fallen angels and the demons of the air have been and still are the cause of Polytheism.   Moreover, we cannot but think that the Classical distinction of the gods as greater and less—*Dii majores et minores*—may be accounted for by the fact, that the former were angels of Satan, while the latter were but demons. On this supposition, it is quite natural that Dr. Mivart's friend, in his desire to revive Polytheism, should suggest a return to the famous names of ancient gods and goddesses.   For the very same angels and demons who were formerly worshipped under those names are, perhaps, eager to resume that dominion over men of which Christianity has more or less deprived them.

As to Newman's assertion, that Paganism, " in a sense, was true and righteous," and Pagan worship " an acceptable service," such a statement is a direct contradiction of Scripture, which calls the Heathen gods ' abominations,' and in which we find the command ; —" Ye shall break down their altars, and dash in pieces their obelisks, and hew down their Asherim, and burn their graven images with fire."[2]

[1] *Demon Possession and Allied Themes*, pp. 65–6.   Dr. Nevius was for many years a well-known and able missionary in China. The evidence which he has collected has been corroborated, and amplified, by many Chinese and Indian missionaries with whom the present writer has conversed on the subject.

[2] Deut. vii. 5.

The next paragraph assigns to God attributes which, it affirms, are discovered by reason, though revelation is silent in regard to them. The allusion is to the sexual relations, which are most impiously connected with the Creator, though, as we have already shown from Scripture, such relations are not merely confined to the creature, but are also, apparently, restricted still further to those races which are subject to death.

But they absorb much of the thoughts and attention of fallen man, and, in most cases, his strongest desires are toward them: therefore, forsooth, they must be blasphemously, and in defiance of Scripture, attributed to the Supreme God, in order that an excuse may be found for personifying and deifying them. This is the true spirit of Paganism: and surely it is a religion after fallen man's own heart, that what he loves, and would enjoy unlawfully, should become his deity.

The biologist, we are told, from the nature of his studies would be especially moved to adore Eros and Aphrodite, Cupid and Venus. No doubt: and he would have many followers, who would soon feel the need of believing the flagitious legends of their deities, in order that, with such examples before them, they might take their own fill of pleasure without fear and without remorse.

That good Catholics are often repelled by the images and symbols set before them for worship, we can well understand: that they should wish to exchange those objectionable objects for the images of Athene and Apollo, emphasizes the fact, that Catholicism, the religion of the senses, is the road that leads back to Paganism. O that they would rather, like the Thessalonians, turn " to God from idols, to serve the Living and True God, and to wait for His Son from the heavens ! "

To feel the want in Christianity of a female symbol of Divinity is to repudiate Christianity altogether, for the reason that it does not pander to the lusts and desires of the flesh; for he who cherishes such a craving stands on the other side of the line which divides the Christian from the Pagan. He remains a fallen and unredeemed man, and a slave to fleshly lusts, which, if he does not repent and cry to God for help, will finally submerge him in the Lake of Fire and Brimstone.

We have already proved, that Scripture forbids any such carnal idea as that of a female element in the Deity.

That many Catholics worship the Madonna as the only available representative of Venus has long been known to those who are interested in such matters. In that way the ancient nature-worship is still carried on, and, indeed, is the chief worship in the Roman Church, at least in places that are far removed from Protestantism.

"At Rome," says the Rev. Mourant Brock, "the worship of Christ—I speak with reverence and sorrow —has gone out of fashion, and a goddess has taken the place of God. It is Mary, and not Jesus, who reigns there.

"If you doubt this, sit for a while, as I have done, before the statue just mentioned, or any other statue of the 'Man of Sorrows,' and observe how many worshippers you have to record. Then go to the Augustine, and stay awhile before the famous image of Mary in that church. Write the sum of the multitude of her adorers, and you will see that, if He has units, she has hundreds for each of them."[1]

[1] *Rome Pagan and Papal*, p. 127.

The Egyptian Isis, whose worship is said to have been resumed in Paris, is, as we have seen, the actual goddess through whom what we now call Mariolatry was first introduced into the Church. And in the Roman community she has been, and is, distinctively represented by the numerous and sometimes famous Black Virgins.

The question with which Dr. Mivart's friend concludes his oration—Whether he may as a good Catholic, worship God as Zeus or Athene, if he be so disposed—is sufficiently startling. Yet the answer of the "learned and devout priest," and the similar reply of "three other learned and experienced priests" to Dr. Mivart himself, surprise us even more. For it appears that a good Catholic may lawfully personify God's attributes, or what he chooses to regard as God's attributes, and worship them, severally, under the names of Pagan deities, provided only he does so in private; for "at present" he must not recklessly cast off the veil in public.

But why this qualification, 'at present'? Is a time coming when it will be right to resume the worship of Zeus and Athene in public? and are there even now Pagan "Marranos" in the Catholic Churches? Is it to such a goal that Romanism is leading us with its goddesses and saints, which, indeed, are all Pagan deities under false names?

The ex-priest Edward Maitland seems to have held doctrines identical with those of Dr. Mivart and his friend. For he discerns one great key to the Creeds of Christendom in the theory, that, since God made man in His Own image, therefore, to understand God, man must learn "more and more to see in his Maker the original and counterpart of himself; and, recognizing

one point of family likeness after another, to ascribe
to Him every organ faculty and quality that he finds
in himself, only divested of limitation."[1]   Now it was,
of course, by this very process that the Pagan gods
were created.   And no notice whatever is taken of the
fact, that by the fall man's nature was altogether
changed from what it had been when he came fresh
from his Creator's hands ; and that Adam, consequently,
begat a son in his own likeness, not in God's, and after
his own fallen image.[2]

Hence the chasm between Monotheism and Polytheism is easily bridged ;—

"A favourite practice in all non-monotheistic
religions was to cut up humanity, as it were, and
distribute its various qualities, moral and other,
among several deities, making one the impersonation
of power, another of wisdom, another of love ; and
in having also separate gods to represent, not merely
separate nationalities, but separate human pursuits,
as war, peace, music, agriculture.   All these mytho-
logic systems, Pagan though they were, and sectarian
in respect of their failing to ascribe perfection in all
respects whatever to one and the same supreme
Being, were yet essentially Catholic in so far as
they proceeded on the principle of making God in
man's image, the image of man's best, divested of
limitations."[3]

Thus four learned and experienced Roman Catholic
priests and two intelligent laymen of the same Church,
one of whom is said to be "devoted to the cause of
Catholicity," agree in the conclusion ;—That virtual
Polytheism is not merely permissible, but, in certain

[1] *Keys of the Creeds*, p. 22.   [3] *Keys of the Creeds*, pp. 22–3.
[2] Gen. v. 3.

cases, even advisable. And an ex-priest brings us to the logical ultimate of purely human teaching by declaring, that God can be discovered and understood only in one way ; that is, if we assign to Him all the attributes of man at his best, but without limitations.

Such is the outcome of a false and demon-inspired Christianity : the Pagan form of the Harlot is, at length, becoming plainly visible, as she throws aside the veil which has never more than partially concealed it. Nor can we doubt, that many followers of the Beast, who is destined to destroy her,[1] will come forth from her own bosom. For teachings similar to those which we have been considering are by no means rare in the Roman Church. And, although they are usually propagated in secret, their results are now being made manifest to all men in the recent and numerous defections of Rationalistic priests and laymen, especially in France and Austria. For they are rapidly preparing the world for its climax of rebellion in the universal worship of the Antichrist, and even of Satan, who will give to the Beast his own power, and his throne, and great authority.[2]

But it is not only in the Catholic Church that such sentiments are heard : they may be detected, also, in many other quarters ; for, whenever Satan is permitted to advance his schemes, men of all shades of opinion fall, one after another, into his ranks, until the whole world is arrayed against those who keep firmly to the Word of God and the testimony of Jesus Christ. We must, however, for the present, forbear to illustrate this point, save by a single instance which caught our eye while we were writing these pages ;—

"' All the attributes that the human mind has

[1] Rev. xvii. 16-18.   [2] Rev. xiii. 2.

ascribed to God are the attributes of the human mind itself; but only one man has ever had the sense to claim them, and he was Jesus of Nazareth!' said the Rev. Francis Edgar Mason, of Brooklyn, at a Metaphysical Convention in New York.

"Mr. Mason further declared, that man, when at his best, was equal to God; that nature exists but to assist man; and that disease is ignorance, resulting from the conception that man amounts to something less than God."

When such blasphemies as these are not uncommon, surely the most obtuse among us can, at last, perceive how manifest is the fulfilment of the prediction, that upon those who would not receive the love of the truth God would send a working of error, so that they should believe "the lie."[1] And "the lie" is, of course, the revelation of the Lawless One, in all the power of Satan, as the king and god of this world; while the working of error must be sought in that Mystery of Lawlessness which, from the days of Paul, has been ceaselessly preparing the minds of men for the final outburst of rebellion.

LXXVI

A Parallel and a Warning

OUR unpleasing task is now accomplished. We might, indeed, go on to trace the influence of the Mysteries upon the churches in many other points; but what has

---

[1] It is difficult to understand why both the A. V. and the R. V. have omitted the definite article which appears in the Greek Text before "lie." "The lie" is, of course, contrasted with "the truth," the love of which men would not receive—the latter being what God has declared concerning the Christ; while the former is Satan's testimony to the Antichrist.

33

been already set before the reader is amply sufficient to convince him, that the many doctrines usages and rites of Catholicism which cannot be found in the New Testament are drawn directly from Pagan sources. And, still further, that the Pagan leaven in this Eccle-siastical Christianity has corrupted, and in many cases altogether destroyed, the meaning and power of such Divine revelation as it still retains.

In what other light, indeed, could we view the cloud of mediators which it has interposed between God and man, thus depriving the latter of direct appeal to, and communion with, His Maker? For he is told that he cannot approach the Great God in his own person; but must do so through priests, through tribes of minor deities called saints, and through the Virgin Goddess, Queen of Heaven, who is represented as being more merciful than the Lord, Who loosed us from our sins by His Own Blood. Thus the Scripture is ignored which says;—

" There is One God, One Mediator, also, between
    God and man, Himself a Man, Christ Jesus;"[1]
and so the deceived one is lured on, until he has unawares become priest-ridden and a worshipper of many gods.

The principle of this doctrine of countless mediators is naturally grateful to sin-conscious men, and was conspicuous in the various Gnostic systems; but it seems to have been finally established in the Catholic Church by the Pseudo-Dionysius. According to his theory, there are nine descending orders in the Celestial Hierarchy, through all of which, in succession, every communication from God must pass, and then be delivered by the lowest of them to the highest order of

---

[1] 1 Tim. ii. 5.

the ascending Ecclesiastical Hierarchy upon earth, that is, to the bishops. Thus Dionysius sets the Lord Jesus aside, and knows not that a man who is clothed in His righteousness may pass boldly through the sundered veil to the Throne of Grace, to the very Mercy-seat itself. In opposition to Paul, he affirms that God is very far from every one of us ; nor does he respect the marvellously condescending and tender words of the Almighty Himself, as declared by His Prophet ;—

" For thus saith the High and Lofty One That inhabiteth eternity, Whose Name is Holy : I dwell in the High and Holy Place, with him also that is of a contrite and humble spirit, to revive the spirit of the humble, and to revive the heart of the contrite ones." [1]

Again, we have found that the Catholic Church insists upon forms, ceremonies, sacrifices, and superstitions, the like to which were well known in the Pagan world, but which cannot be discovered in the New Testament ; and, indeed, are altogether antagonistic to Divine teaching. For their tendency is ever to exalt, not the Lord Jesus, Who often occupies no more than the background of such services, but the Church, and, especially, the priests and the Hierarchy.

And yet, in the whole of the New Testament, there is not a single mention either of a priest,[2] or of a bishop in the Catholic sense of the term, among the authorized rulers teachers and spiritually endowed persons in the churches. What, we may well ask, is the only reasonable inference to be drawn from such a fact ? Or does God vouchsafe revelations simply that men may criticize and improve them ?

But, still further, according to the whole system of

---

[1] Isa. lvii. 15.   [2] ἱερεύς.

the New Testament, there is no |longer any room for sacrificial priests, as we may learn plainly enough from the tenth chapter of the Epistle to the Hebrews. For those grand and convincing verses show, that, since the sacrifices of the Law had to be continually repeated, it was evident that they could not perfect those who drew nigh by means of them. Had they done so, they would have ceased to be offered ; because the worshippers, cleansed once for all, would have had no further consciousness of sin. But the Israelitish worshippers were not found to be in such a case ; for the blood of bulls and goats could never take away sins ; nor did the sacrifice of such victims meet the will of God. Therefore, the Mosaic arrangement, which could not satisfy the claims of justice, and was instituted only for the instruction of men, had to be abolished, and a new order of things established.[1]

For the Lord Jesus Alone was able to do the will of His Father, and He stood ready to receive the Body that had been prepared for Him, and to appear in the world, that He might put away sin by the sacrifice of Himself. The mighty deed was accomplished, and then could there be a fulfilment of the prediction ;—

"It is too light a thing that Thou shouldest be My Servant to raise up the Tribes of Jacob, and to restore the preserved of Israel : I will also give Thee for a light to the Gentiles, that Thou mayest be My salvation unto the end of the earth."[2]

Thus, by the death of the Lord Jesus, the will and righteousness of His Father were completely satisfied, and a ransom was found sufficient to deliver every penitent sinner from going down into the pit. And

[1] Heb. x. 9.   [2] Isa. xlix. 6.

all men are now invited to exult in the glowing words of the Apostle ;[1]—

"By which will we have been sanctified through the offering of the Body of Jesus Christ once for all.

"And every priest indeed standeth day by day ministering and offering oftentimes the same sacrifices, the which can never take away sins; but He, when He had offered one sacrifice for sins for ever, sat down on the right hand of God, from henceforth expecting till His enemies be made the footstool of His feet.

"For by one offering He hath perfected for ever them that are being sanctified."[2]

There is no mistaking the force of these verses. They emphatically declare, that sacrifices which have to be offered continually are of no avail; and that the One and Only Sacrifice, which can both take away sins and perfect for ever them that draw nigh unto God by means of it, has been offered once for all; so that there can now be no possible supplement or addition to it.

The occupation of the sacrificial priest has, therefore, passed away: there is no further need of him. And, indeed, if any man now pretends to such an office, he has sinned more grievously than Korah; for, in defiance of this Divine declaration, he has usurped the prerogative, not of Aaron, but of the

---

[1] Heb. x. 10–14.

[2] τοὺς ἁγιαζομένους, the present participle. It indicates those who, having been foreknown predestinated called and justified, are now going through the process of sanctification. In v. 10, the perfect passive tense is used—"we have been sanctified." But there the reference is, not to intrinsic holiness, but to that which is imputed to us in Christ Jesus (1 Cor. i. 30).

Almighty Son of God Himself; and has insulted Him in denying that, by His one offering of Himself, He has for ever perfected them that are being sanctified.

Alas! it is a rebellion of this kind that is now spreading throughout the length and breadth of our own land, and acquiring strength day by day. Beginning with the Oxford Movement, it has now prevailed to such an extent that few, indeed, are the bishops in the whole Anglican Church who do not more or less openly favour it. And the influence of so rapid a transformation is producing disastrous effects upon many of those who did run well. For, even with a great number of the Evangelicals, compromise has become the order of the day—although, as a matter of fact, they have given up point after point without the slightest reciprocal concession on the other side, until they seem to be in danger of losing all their distinctive marks. And how in such circumstances can the power of the Holy Spirit remain with them? Because of the abounding of lawlessness, the love of the many has grown cold; so that, in their hearts, the Lord Jesus is superseded by Churchism. And, unless it should please Him to interfere in some unexpected manner, it is evident that the National Church will soon have rejoined the Roman apostasy and resumed her place among the doomed daughters of Babylon.

For, notwithstanding the efforts of the Protestant press and platform to reassure their party, there can be no doubt that, during the last fifty years, the spirit of the English people has undergone a radical change: the majority of the nation is now either favourable to the Romeward movement or profoundly indifferent to any ecclesiastical revolution which may be going on around them.

The history of Israel is repeating itself in the annals of our beloved country, which for the last century, at least, has been manifestly holding a position more or less analogous to that of the people of God in the previous Dispensation. For Great Britain, whose special preparation for her mission seems to have commenced with the powerful revivals of the eighteenth century, was afterwards endowed with a mighty extension of territory and an exceptional power and influence. And the object of these gifts was, that the pure Word of God might be borne by her missionaries to the ends of the earth. She became the great centre and chief motive power of God's work in the world ; and even now, spite of her apostasy and growing indifference, she still remains the Headquarters of Christianity among men.

In such circumstances, then, what warning does the favoured nation of old press upon us? A solemn one, indeed. For, like our own people, Israel did not long sustain the pure worship of God. Even Solomon was induced by his foreign wives to turn aside after other gods. Then Jeroboam set up the calves at Bethel and Dan, giving out that they represented the God Who brought Israel up out of Egypt, and Who must be adored through them. Hence "the sins of Jeroboam wherewith he made Israel to sin" became a proverb ; until another arose even more wicked than he, and Ahab suffered his wife Jezebel to make all Israel bow the knee to Baal and Astarte. Jeroboam, so far as his profession went, had broken only the second commandment ; but Ahab violated, also, the first.

And so, altars to other gods began to be raised in Israel, and a little later in Judah ; and strange incense was offered to them. Then all the abominations of the Heathen spread like a flood over the two lands.

The Baalim were everywhere adored : the obscene Asherah, inciting to lust, was set up near their altars : altars to the Host of Heaven were erected even in the Courts of the Temple, and a graven image was placed in the very House of God itself. An unlawful intercourse was carried on with the demons of the air and the fallen angels, just as among the Pagans : mesmerisers, sorcerers, soothsayers, and mediums with familiar spirits, were consulted in every perplexity, for every craving of curiosity : and Israelitish babes, while their mothers stood by, were cast into the white-hot arms of Moloch, and miserably burned amid the din of drums and cymbals.

But these abominations brought ruin in their wake : the prosperity of Israel waned, flickered, and was gone. Against Solomon God raised up bitter and implacable enemies : the good land was rent asunder into two Kingdoms, often bitterly hostile to each other : and their inhabitants were punished and worn down by famines, foreign invasions and oppressions, and manifold calamities, until, at length, they were driven from their homes, and dispersed into every region under heaven.

So was it with the children of Abraham ; and does not England seem to be moving in the same direction as that in which Israel went to his doom ?   Do not the crosses and crucifixes that are ever multiplying in the land, and the now frequent elevation of the host, bear testimony to the prevalence of the sins of Jeroboam ; while the numerous statues and pictures of the Madonna cause a cry to go up to God, that the sin of Ahab is being revived, and the worship of the Queen of Heaven restored ?   Moreover, intercourse with the foul spirits of the air, ever the concomitant of Paganism, has fearfully increased ; so that the land is filled with mediums and those who have familiar spirits; while divination, astrology, necromancy, palmistry, and even onacho-mancy,[1] with every kind of fortune-telling, are, as they always have been, largely resorted to by a people that are forsaking their God.

For, whenever the true doctrines of Scripture are taught and received, whenever men worship the Father in spirit and in truth, and believe on His Son Jesus Christ, then the demons are abashed and driven away by the Presence of the Holy Spirit of God. But, where Paganism prevails, or Catholicism is enticing men toward it, thither the legions of darkness gather, and bring into play all those devices stratagems and systems by which they have ever enslaved the nations of God-deserted men to superstition, to licentiousness, and to themselves.

But, if England has thus turned into the apostate path of Israel, how can she, except she repent, hope to escape the fate of Israel?

"By their unbelief they were broken off, and thou standest by thy faith. Be not highminded, but fear: for, if God spared not the natural branches, neither will He spare thee."[2]

If England turns again to mediæval idols; if her heart is no longer faithful and obedient to her God;

---

[1] That is, divination by means of the nails. It is thus explained in the *St. James's Gazette* of Jan. 24th, 1901;—

"A new occult science known as onachomancy, at present creating quite a craze in New York, has been introduced to the West-end of London by two professors who have crossed the Atlantic on a special mission. It is claimed that the future can be predicted by means of the nails. An unguent of wax and oil is rubbed on the nails, which are then exposed to the sun, and the light penetrating the surface makes certain lines visible that enable the seer to prophesy."

[2] Rom. xi. 20, 21.

if she ceases to send messages of His pure Word to the ends of the earth, and for Gospel-truth begins to substitute a propagation of Churchism, Sacerdotalism, and Catholic error—will not her power and influence, also, be cut short; her fair possessions be reft from her, and given to others? For God hates hypocritical compromise more than direct opposition, the lukewarm more than the absolutely cold; nor will He accept worship, which He has not ordained, merely because its terms and language are partially drawn from the New Testament.

May we not even now perceive the premonitions of coming wrath? Do we not already hear the distant moaning of the storm that may presently be beating fiercely upon our heads?

What will be the outcome of this bitter and implacable hatred of our country, which so largely prevails on the Continent and in other parts of the world? Are our conflicts with comparatively insignificant foes usually so protracted, costly, and full of mistakes and reverses, as the Boer War has proved to be? Was there no Divine punishment in the accession to power of the statesman whose folly in the past rendered such a war inevitable; who, moreover, Romanized the Anglican Church, and deprived our nation of its last claim to be called Christian by procuring the admission into Parliament of those who openly vaunted their disbelief in God? Is there no curse of God in the presence among us of fellow-citizens who, with demoniac tenacity, do what they can to embarrass any Government that displays ability and firmness; who intrigue with our foes, and spread false and malignant reports of our officers and soldiers in the front; while they see nothing but good in any that are opposed to us, no matter how treacherous and brutal they may be? Can we be indifferent to the rivalry that is springing up on all sides against the foreign trade which is our great source of wealth and power, and to the increasing difficulties of the labour-question which is hampering us at home? Do we refuse to see the finger of God in the new disease, influenza, which seems to have settled among us, and is slaying its thousands; in the alarming recrudescence of small-pox during the last few years; and in the repeated threatenings of that terrible scourge, the plague, of which we had begun to think that this part of the world was for ever rid?

But we need not extend the list: there are ominous signs, both in the Empire and in the rest of the world, that the clouds of woe may be gathering above us. And, if we inquire why this should be so, the answer is ready. There is in the midst of us a wide-spreading apostasy, and departure from God, which—to omit other national sins that cannot now be discussed—may well make us apprehensive of coming judgments.

In such circumstances and amid so many warning-signs, let us, if we be true believers, consider our own ways, and see if there be in them any direct dis-obedience to, or neglect of, the commandments of God —not as they are set forth by any church or sect, but as they are written in His Own Word. And earnestly should we pray for the pardon of such sins, and for the aid of the Spirit, that we may overcome them, and henceforth walk obediently in all things, and not merely in those to which our fallen nature feels no repugnance. For it is not meet that the beloved of the Lord should add to the sins of their nation and strengthen the cry of wickedness which goes up to God, and causes the destroyers to issue forth from before His Throne.

This is emphatically a time in which all they who fear the Lord should speak often one to another, exhorting one another, and that so much the more as they see the Day so evidently approaching. And yet, when we look around us, we find but little disposition to think or talk of this momentous subject. Some years ago there seemed to be much expectation of the Lord's return : now we hear of it but rarely. The Bridegroom has tarried, and many sons of the bridechamber have become weary of waiting for Him. A deathlike slumber has stolen over the great body of professed believers ; that is, over their spiritual faculties : for they are often active enough in the spheres of sense and humanity, and will talk all the day of divers philanthropies, of temperance-work and anti-opium crusades, and of the humanizing effects of education, of music, and of the fine arts. But of Him Who loved them and gave Himself up for them, they know not what to say. If it is from the fulness of the heart that the mouth speaks, there is very little of Him in their hearts : if they do love Him, they must love Him best at a distance ; for they never express a desire for His return, nor evince any joy or interest when others speak of it.

Indeed, most of those who call themselves Christians seem to be passing, in close company with the world, through some "enchanted ground," where the mists and miasmas of earth so affect them that they cannot compose and concentrate their minds upon heavenly subjects—no, not even upon the Lord Jesus Himself: nor can they keep distracting thoughts of things below from breaking in upon their feeble and ineffective attempts to pray. And they never seem to hear, above all the mingled din of earth, that Voice, which is as the sound of many waters, saying ;—

"If, therefore, thou shalt not watch, I will come upon thee as a thief, and thou shalt not know what hour I will come upon thee!"[1]

The Lord be merciful to all those of us who believe on Him in our land and throughout the Empire, and startle us out of our slumber, that we may arise from the dead, and receive light from Him ;[2] and that so we may be found of Him, when He comes, shining as lights in the world, holding forth the Word of Life.[3]

And may He grant that a great and irresistible wave of God-consciousness may pass over our nation and its colonies and dependencies in the five divisions of the globe ; so that the people may awaken to a sense of their apostasy, and repent, and turn again to their God, before the days of our visitation are ended, and the despairing cry resounds from disillusioned and panic-stricken multitudes—"There is wrath gone forth from the Lord!"

[1] Rev. iii. 3.   [2] Eph. v. 14.   [3] Phil. ii. 15, 16,

APPENDIX

THE BRETHREN OF THE LORD

THE actual blood-relationship of our Lord to those persons who in the New Testament are called "His brethren," and are usually mentioned in connection with His mother, is a truth of the greatest importance in the present crisis. For, when once admitted, it bars the way against that doctrine of Paganism which has ever corrupted the nominal Church more powerfully, perhaps, but, at least, more persistently, than any other, namely, the worship of the great goddess, or Queen of Heaven, under the disguise of the "Virgin Mary."

And just as the fact, that the Lord's brethren were the real sons of the mother of His flesh, was vigorously assailed in the early centuries of our era, so now it is either ignored or openly denied by many, because the reasons which formerly rendered it distasteful are once more working actively among us.

For there is a great revival of Mariolatry, which is now gaining ground in countries hitherto regarded as Protestant. We have ourselves seen a table, intended to serve as an altar, and crowned with lights, placed under a painting of the Madonna in an English church. And this is no solitary case; for the worship of Mary is taught by many of our Ritualistic clergy, and, within the last few years, conspicuous images of her have been set up even in the two great national churches, St. Paul's Cathedral and Westminster Abbey. We note, too, that in the *Churchman's Pocket Book* for 1897 published by the Society for the Propagation of Christian Knowledge, she is boldly called Theotokos, that is to say, the Mother of Christ's Divine Nature, a title which implies that she is herself a goddess.

But, while Mariolatry is thus progressing in the religious world, that which it represents, namely, the worship of the female principle in nature, has of late found favour with many Secularists—such as Strauss, Comte, and John Stuart Mill—and prevails extensively among Spiritualists and Theosophists.

Now this widespread error, which may ultimately prove a bond of union to men of very diverse opinions, is at once deprived of all the support which it affects to draw from Christianity, if the Lord's brethren can be shown to be the veritable sons of His mother. For the Heathen goddess of many names, with which men have ever been seeking to identify her, was declared to be the mother of a divine son and yet at the same time a virgin. "Immaculate is Our Lady Isis," is the inscription upon an Egyptian sard ; and in what does it differ from the dogma of the Immaculate Conception as promulgated at Rome in 1854? Hence the importance of the question—Were the brethren of the Lord the actual sons of Mary?

But to an unprejudiced mind there could be no question at all. Were we without interest in the controversy, we should, upon reading of the Lord's "mother and His brethren," instinctively understand the "brethren" to be related to Him, in the flesh, in the same literal sense in which His mother was. And if any feeling within us forbids so obvious a conclusion, that feeling certainly does not spring from the Scriptures, which contain nothing that could possibly suggest it.

On the contrary, the simple command to Joseph, " Fear not to take unto thee Mary *thy wife*,"[1] is sufficient to show that the usual conjugal relations subsisted between the pair after our Lord's birth. And the plain narrative, that Joseph " took unto him *his wife*, and knew her not till she had brought forth her Firstborn Son,"[2] affords conclusive evidence, that Matthew, at least, had no wish to guard us against the

---

[1] Matth. i. 20.   [2] Matth. i. 24, 25.

legitimate meaning of his words. For had he so desired,
why did he repeat the phrase "took unto him *his wife*"; and
why did he not prefer the word "only-born"[1] to firstborn[2]?
For the latter certainly implies other children, or others
standing in a similar relation, as when the Lord Himself is
designated "the Firstborn of many brethren";[3] or "the Firstborn from the dead."[4] But "only-born" rigorously excludes
other children, as when we are told that the widow of Nain's
son was "the only-born son of his mother."[5]

Again; the significant, but much neglected, fact, that, in
Scripture, Mary is never called a virgin after the birth of her
Firstborn Son, is in itself fatal to the purely Heathen doctrine
of her perpetual virginity.

And lastly; it cannot have been without design that, in
a Psalm repeatedly applied to Christ in the New Testament,
and immediately preceding a verse both the clauses of which
are cited by inspired writers as referring to Him,[6] we should
find the words ;—

"I am become a stranger unto My brethren,
And an alien *unto My mother's children*."[7]

It is unnecessary to say more ; the Bible certainly assumes
the brethren of the Lord to be the actual sons of His mother,
upon whom—with two memorable exceptions, of which we
shall speak presently—it always represents them as being in
attendance. So carefully did He Who knows the end from
the beginning anticipate the attempt to identify the Saviour's
earthly parent with Isis the ever-virgin mother of Horus—just
as also, in the plans of the Tabernacle and the Temple, He
directed that the Holy of Holies should be set in the West,

[1] μονογενής.
[2] πρωτότοκος. One or two MSS. read "until she had brought forth
a Son," omitting "her Firstborn." But this, as Alford remarks, is "an
omission evidently made from superstitious veneration for Mary."
[3] Rom. viii. 29.
[4] Col. i. 18 ; Rev. i. 5.
[5] Luke vii. 12. So also ix. 38.
[6] Psa. lxix. 8 ; compare John ii. 17, and Rom. xv. 3.
[7] Psa. lxix. 8.

and so at once distinguished His worshippers from the multitudinous votaries of nature and the sun, who turned towards the East.

But in this case, as in many others, human corruption quickly made the Word of God of none effect. In very early times, the wish to assimilate Christianity to Paganism by furnishing it with a virgin-goddess, together with the prevailing tendency to asceticism, resulted in a theory, that Joseph was a widower when he espoused Mary, and that the " brethren " were his sons by his first wife.

The origin of this theory is betrayed by the sentiments of its supporters. Not a particle of evidence can be adduced in its favour; for there is no historical mention of a previous marriage of Joseph; nor do the fictitious elder half-brothers appear in the few incidents of the Lord's birth and childhood which are revealed to us. Even Jerome taunts those who believe in it with "following the Apocryphal writings, and inventing a wretched little woman, Melcha, or Escha."

But, in order to Paganize Christianity, it was not enough to dispose of these brethren: it was also necessary to show that Mary *could* have had no other children besides her First-born. Accordingly, about the middle of the second century, the " Protevangelium Jacobi " represented Joseph as being, at the time of his second marriage, a very old man with adult children. Unfortunately, however, for the reputation of that work, it allowed him no daughters, although the New Testament mentions the Lord's sisters,[1] as well as His brothers. But the idea of Joseph's extreme age became very popular in Apocryphal writings, and is worked out from them, with grotesque extravagance, in the Coventry Mystery-plays which are preserved in the British Museum.[2] And, while the

---

[1] Matth. xiii. 56.

[2] According to these "Mysteries," which were performed in the streets upon a stage with wheels, Mary's birth was miraculous: she was brought up in the Temple, and waited upon by angels: she devoted herself to chastity, and hence is often painted in a nun's dress. But, since it was necessary for her to marry, Joseph was miraculously selected as her

doctrine of Mary's virginity was being thus disseminated, the name of Theotokos, or Mother of God, was also assigned to her, with the intention of conveying the natural inference, that the Godhead of Christ, as well as His human Body, proceeded from her ; and, therefore, that she must herself have been a goddess.

Towards the close of the fourth century, a number of female devotees, who had migrated from Thrace to Arabia, gave out that they were priestesses of Mary, and commenced an idolatrous worship which, by the form it assumed, seems to indicate an identification of her with Ceres. On appointed festival days, they conveyed about in chariots—such as the Pagans used in their religious processions—certain cakes, or wafers, consecrated to her, and called *collyrides*,[1] from which they derived their own name of Collyridians. After presenting these cakes as offerings, they then ate them. The ceremony was, perhaps, an adaptation of the harvest festival of Ceres, known as the Thesmophoria ; or, more probably, of the *mizd*, or round wafer used in the worship of Mithras.[2] This last is the prototype of the *host*, and the origin of the Roman Catholic term *missa*, the Mass.

Of course, so open a deification of the Lord's human mother was not carried on without considerable opposition.

husband—a man so enfeebled by age that he could scarcely walk or even lift up his hands. Ludicrous and repeated efforts are made to impress his senility upon the audience : it would be difficult to imagine anything more degrading than the treatment of the subject. Yet, in Catholic times, the English people were taught that this abominable profanity was Scriptural history : and the extreme rarity of the Word of God in the national tongue enabled the Roman Hierarchy to maintain the lie with impunity.

[1] From the Paganized Christian point of view, this would, of course, be a transfer of the Lord's Supper to the worship of Mary.

[2] "In the particulars which have come down to us of the celebration of these Mithraic sacraments, certain singular analogies arrest our attention. The 'bread' used was a round cake, emblem of the solar disk, and termed the mizd, in which word Seel detects the etymology of the name *missa* applied to the 'bloodless sacrifice' : for the mizd was certainly the prototype of the Host, which is circular and of the same dimensions."—King's *Gnostics and their Remains*, p. 53.

In a note, King expresses an opinion which cannot but be shared by every unprejudiced scholar, that "the popular derivation of *missa* from the

It was, however, defended with fanatical violence by Epiphanius, Bishop of the Cyprian Salamis, who invented a name for the opponents of his idolatry, calling them Antidicomarianites, or " Adversaries of Mary."

Among those who objected to the new goddess was one Helvidius, a lawyer of Rome. This man, shocked by Jerome's extravagant praises of celibacy, undertook to confute the obnoxious views, and, in the course of his argument, maintained, that, after the birth of the Lord, Mary had become a wife, and the mother of children.

To this statement Jerome, who was greatly the superior of Helvidius in learning and dialectics, and who either disliked or distrusted the theory of Joseph's previous marriage, replied, that the brethren of the Lord were not the sons of His mother, but merely His cousins. The spirit in which he put forth this opinion may be gathered from his boast, that he thus claimed virginity, not for Mary only, but also for Joseph. The argument by which he supported it is a worthless tissue of errors, and may be stated as follows ;—

In the list of the Twelve, there are two Apostles bearing the name of James. And we also read of James the Lord's brother.

This last must, however, have been one of the Twelve ; or, otherwise, there would have been three persons of the same name.

And, in such a case, how could one of them have been called " James the less," a term which implies that there was but one other ?

concluding words of the service, ' Ite, missa est,' is absurd in the extreme." It is always the object sacrificed that gives its name to the rite, and in this case the object is the wafer. Even the Rabbins affirm that the circular form of the wafer is a symbol of the sun, and that it is offered to the genius of that luminary as a victim.

Hence the reason why the Church of Rome insists so strongly upon the roundness of the host. " If," said John Knox, " in making the roundness, the ring be broken, then must another of his fellow-cakes receive that honour to be made a god, and the crazed or cracked miserable cake, that once was in hope to be made a god, must be given to a baby to play withal."

Moreover, in writing to the Galatians, Paul narrates, "But other of the Apostles saw I none, save James the Lord's brother,"[1] thus classing the latter with the Twelve.

This argument, the basis of Jerome's whole theory, may be disposed of without much trouble.

For such an expression as "James the less" is not to be found in the original of the New Testament : the Apostle is called "James the little."[2]

And the words of Paul should be rendered, "I saw no other of the Apostles"—that is, no other save Peter who has just been mentioned—"but only James, the Lord's brother."

Such then, was the false foundation upon which Jerome was content to build the subjoined theory ;—

Since James the Lord's brother is mentioned after the death of James the son of Zebedee, he must be identified with James the son of Alphæus.

Now the latter had a brother named Joses, and, in the Gospels of Matthew and Mark,[3] there is record of a Mary the mother of James and Joses being present at the crucifixion. She must, therefore, have been the wife of Alphæus.

But, in the fourth Gospel, in place of the mother of James and Joses we read of a Mary of Clopas, the sister of the Lord's mother, standing by the cross.[4] This must, therefore, be the same as the wife of Alphæus,[5] who is thus proved to be the sister of the Lord's mother.

Hence her children were His cousins, and they are called His brethren merely because that term is often applied to any near relations.

This elaborate superstructure is as worthless as its founda-

---

[1] Gal. i. 19.
[2] Ἰακώβου τοῦ μικροῦ, Mark xv. 40.   [3] Matth. xxvii. 56 ; Mark xv. 40.
[4] John xix. 25.
[5] The two names Clopas and Alphæus might be identified, since both forms could be derived from the same Aramæan original. Jerome was not, however, aware of this fact.

tion, and a single fact will suffice to prove our assertion. James the Lord's brother *could* not have been the son of Alphæus, for the latter was one of the Twelve; whereas, of the Lord's brethren we are told, without reserve, that they did not believe on Him.[1] How, then, could any one of them have been an Apostle while they were all unbelievers? But, [although there is no necessity for further discussion, we will, nevertheless, add one or two remarks which will help the reader to a still clearer view of the standing of Jerome as a teacher.

And, first, Mary the wife of Clopas is not to be identified with the sister of the Lord's mother. For the passage in John should be read as follows;—

"Now there stood by the cross of Jesus His mother and His mother's sister, Mary the wife of Clopas and Mary Magdalene."

Not three only, but four women are mentioned, and they are arranged in couples, just as the Apostles are in the list of the Twelve.[2] And, by so understanding the passage, we avoid an absurdity; for, according to Jerome, both the Lord's mother and her sister must have borne the same name of Mary! Indeed, some supporters of his theory are bold enough to affirm that the Jews frequently gave the same name to sisters; but, so far as we are aware, they offer no evidence of the prevalency of so irrational a custom.

The argument from the names James and Joses is also valueless; since there were but a very few names in common use among the Jews at that time, as, indeed, we might gather from the frequent recurrence of certain appellations in the New Testament. Hence it is probable that many women in Judæa might have been called mothers of James and Joses.

Lastly, the assertion that "cousins" may be styled "brothers" is scarcely true, in an absolute sense at least.

[1] John vii. 5.　　　　[2] Matth. x. 2-4; Luke vi. 14-16.

The instances adduced by Jerome [1] occur in affectionate or rhetorical appeals : he is unable to cite any from plain matter-of-fact history, such as that of the Gospels. His theory is rendered still more improbable by the mention of the Lord's sisters ; and there is yet another difficulty. If the " brethren " were the cousins of the Lord, why were they found in continual atttendance upon His mother while their own parent was still alive ? It could not have been from any feeling of veneration on account of her Son ; for in Him they did not believe.

Such, then, is Jerome's attempted explanation, the most remarkable fact in connection with which is, that learned men should ever have admitted so faulty and preposterous a theory within the range of their theology. Its author was less tenacious of it than some of his disciples ; and, in the Epistle to Hedibia, which belongs to his later years, he evinces a complete change of mind by disowning the identification of the mother of James and Joses with the sister of Mary. Since this is the citadel of his position, it is clear that he must have discovered its untenableness, and so have deliberately abandoned it.

Bishop Lightfoot, in the essay appended to his Commentary on the Epistle to the Galatians, decides peremptorily against Jerome ; but, after wavering between the literal theory and that of the half-brothers, finally inclines, like Hilary of Poitiers, to the latter, for the subjoined reason. He conceives it to be impossible that our Lord, when on the cross, " would have snapped asunder the most sacred ties of natural affection " by commending His mother to the care of John, if she had had four sons of her own living at the time.

But, while it is always dangerous to substitute our own theories for the plain and literal sense of Scripture, there is, in this case, no excuse whatever for such a course. For, provided that we be content to waive tradition and hold to revelation, the alleged difficulty may be very easily removed.

[1] Gen. xiii. 8, xxix. 15.

In the single passage of the Gospels in which our Lord's brethren appear without their mother,[1] they display a strong spirit of opposition, and we are told that they did not believe on Him. Hence the reason why the mother is no longer with them: she had kept the sayings of Jesus in her heart, and, therefore, had faith to follow Him even to the cross: she had once attempted to interfere with His actions, and had learnt her lesson from the rebuke [2] which she then received.[3]

But, if the brethren were unbelievers, and were even then angry with the Lord because He refused to seek popularity, what must have been their feelings as they saw His ministry becoming more and more opposed to the prejudices of their nation, and perceived that the consequent hatred to His person was increasing every day? Is it not more than probable that their growing dislike to Him, now heightened by the fear of family disgrace, would alienate them from His mother who persisted in her faith? And thus, neglected by her own sons in her time of deepest trouble, she would be in sore need of temporary protection, which the Lord graciously provided.

So far there is surely no difficulty; but, at this point, tradition steps in and adds a story, opposed to all reasonable inference from Scripture, that Mary remained under the protection of the Apostle John for the rest of her life. There can be no doubt that this is a pure fiction, devised to support the theory of her virginity; for the Bible plainly indicates that she returned to her sons after their conversion.[4]

The tender heart of the Lord yearned for His brethren in the flesh; and, accordingly, after He had appeared in His risen Body to Peter, to the Twelve, and to the five

---

[1] John vii. 3-9.   [2] John ii. 4.

[3] Thus our latest glimpse of the brethren, before the crucifixion, reveals them separated for the first time from their mother, and casting reproaches upon the Lord; whereas, at the cross, the mother is seen deserted by her sons. It is impossible to deny the significance of such a fact.

[4] Acts i. 14.

hundred brethren, He presented Himself to His brother James. Who can doubt the effect of the glorious sight ? The eyes of James were opened, and he beheld no longer the carpenter's son of Nazareth, the executed malefactor, but the Conqueror of Death, the Lord of All Power, the Only Begotten Son of the Father. By his testimony, or, it may be, by special revelation to each of them, the other brethren were also converted before the Lord left the confines of earth.

We can readily understand how such a change of mind would affect them in regard to their neglected mother, who seems to have been at once removed from the temporary protection of John to the loving care of her own family. And so it happens, that, in the list of those who continued in prayer in the upper room, waiting for the promised power from on high, we find the mother of Jesus and His now believing brethren again united.[1]

So utterly, then, does every attempt to prove the perpetual virginity of the Lord's mother break down. She is never described as a virgin after His birth ; for she then became the wife of Joseph, to whom she bore four sons and, at least, two daughters.[2] And, indeed, had she been different from other women, and of a spotless and Divine nature, the whole plan of salvation would have failed. For to redeem the ruined race of man, it was necessary that the Lord should take upon Himself human nature ; and whence could He have received that nature, save from the mother of His flesh ? She was, therefore, a woman of like passions with other women, and leading a life similar to theirs. And, although, as the angel declared, she was certainly blessed among them, she is never said to have been blessed above them. Equally with all her sisters, she needed the Atoning Blood of Him Who was born into the world through her, and would have been lost without it. Nor will the honour that was done to her, in itself, secure her future pre-eminence. During the

---

[1] Acts i. 14.
[2] At least, two, because the Pharisees speak of them as our Lord's " sisters." (Matth. xiii. 56.)

Lord's ministry upon earth she was ever kept in the background, and He plainly signified to her that she must not interfere with His work. Nay, when an enthusiastic woman cried out, "Blessed is the womb that bare Thee and the breasts which Thou didst suck," He instantly replied, "Yea rather, blessed are they that hear the Word of God, and keep it."

To this we may add, that Mary is not once mentioned in the twenty-one Epistles and the Apocalypse, and only once, and that merely in a list of names, in the Acts.

In regard to this matter, then, the mind of God is revealed so plainly in His Word that none but those who despise that Word, and bow to another authority, can possibly be misled. The worship of the Virgin Mary is a return to an idolatry as marked as that of Baal and Astarte. And the latter was, doubtless, defended by arguments as specious and as fallacious as those which are now used in favour of the former. What is Baal, an Israelite might have said, but another name for Jehovah, the form under which the Phœnicians are accustomed to worship the same God as Israel? And as for Astarte, she might have been explained, in a too prevalent modern fashion, as merely the feminine expression of the Deity, corresponding to the feminine element in the human race, a wondrous unfolding of the Great "Two in One."

But we know what God thought of the introduction of Baal-worship, and of the wretched Ahab who caused Israel to sin by it, and speedily brought down ruin upon himself and his kingdom. Nor will He be more lenient to those who are now introducing the worship of the Virgin and of saints and angels. For He is still a jealous God, and will brook no rival.

To the Almighty Triune Jehovah Alone must we offer adoration and worship.

To the Father, Who so loved the world that He gave His Only Begotten Son for it.

To the Son, Who said, " Lo, I am come to do Thy will, O God "; and, in obedience to that will, suffered Himself to be wounded for our transgressions, and to be bruised for our iniquities; submitted to have laid upon Himself the chastisement that would bring us peace, and bore the stripes by which we are healed.

And to the Holy Spirit, the Comforter, who takes of the things of Christ and shews them unto us, and by Whom we were sealed unto the day of redemption.

For all other beings, save the ineffable Three in One, are but fellow-creatures and fellow-servants with ourselves, though they may, indeed, be gifted with a far higher degree of rank and power.

INDEX

ACTS, the three, which manifest the Lord's power to quicken and authority to judge, 28.

Adversary, the, of whom we must give diligence to be quit, 379; figure of, taken from Roman law, 379–80; lessons from, 380–2.

Age, the spirit of the, always at variance with the Bible, 353; proofs of this, 353–4; the reason of it, 354–5.

Angel, the, who went before the Israelites in the wilderness, 370; commission of, 370; was not the Lord Jesus, 371, but the Archangel Michael, 372.

Angels, local government of, 368–76; their judgment of Nebuchadnezzar, 369–70; of Herod Agrippa, 372; of Balaam, 373–4; action of among the children of the world, 376.

Anger, sometimes lawful, but must be brief, 363.

Antidicomarianites, 534.

Apostasy, the present, in England, 518.

Apostle, the, meaning of the term, 256; could not be a bishop, 257; must have seen the Lord Jesus, 257; the signs of, 257–8; had power to confer the Holy Spirit, 258; five characteristic marks of, 258–9; apparently endowed with all the spiritual gifts, 259; founded and organized churches, 259; should be with us in the churches now, 259–60; disappeared after the first century, 260–1; may reappear, 261; Satanic counterfeits of, 261.

Apostolical Succession, origin of the doctrine of, 461; illustration of the effects of, 461–2.

Apparitions of deities or supernatural beings, 448; on Buddhist altars and between the lights, 450–1; similarity of this to the "Real Presence" in the Mass, 451.

Apuleius, his account of initiation into the Lesser Mysteries, 437–8; his remarks on his final initiation, 462–3.

Assembly, the, in Apostolic times, described, 329–30.

Attributes of God, the, deification of is the revival of an old Pagan doctrine, 502–4; certain of alleged to be discovered by reason, 508.

Augustine, believed baptism to be necessary for the salvation of infants, 151; theory of in regard to the dying thief, 151.

BAPTISM, seldom mentioned in the Epistles, 106; meaning of the word, 106–7; the Lord's command respecting, 109–11;

543

Printed by Hazell, Watson, & Viney, Ld., London and Aylesbury.

CPSIA information can be obtained
at www.ICGtesting.com
Printed in the USA
LVHW061346311221
707634LV00007B/129

9 781162 589374